Personal Rule in Black Africa

Africa, 1981

Personal Rule in Black Africa

Prince, Autocrat, Prophet, Tyrant

ROBERT H. JACKSON
AND
CARL G. ROSBERG

UNIVERSITY OF CALIFORNIA PRESS
BERKELEY / LOS ANGELES / LONDON

UNIVERSITY OF CALIFORNIA PRESS
BERKELEY AND LOS ANGELES, CALIFORNIA

UNIVERSITY OF CALIFORNIA PRESS, LTD.
LONDON, ENGLAND

PRINTED IN THE UNITED STATES OF AMERICA

FIRST PAPERBACK PRINTING 1982
ISBN 0-520-04209-3

2 3 4 5 6 7 8 9

Library of Congress Cataloging in Publication Data

Jackson, Robert H.
  Personal Rule in Black Africa.

  Includes index.
  1. Africa—Politics and government—1960-
2. Authoritarianism—Case studies. 3. Despotism—
Case Studies. 4. Oligarchy—Case studies.
I. Rosberg, Carl Gustav, joint author. II. Title
DT30.5.J32   320.96   80-25439

Governments set up overnight, like everything in nature whose growth is forced, lack strong roots and ramifications. So they are destroyed in the first bad spell. This is inevitable unless those who have suddenly become princes are of such prowess that overnight they can learn how to preserve what fortune has suddenly tossed in their laps, and unless they can then lay foundations such as other princes would have already been building on.

NICCOLO MACHIAVELLI

The presidential regime expresses the spirit of Negro-African philosophy which is based not on the individual but on the person. The president personifies the Nation as did the Monarch of former times his people. The masses are not mistaken who speak of the "reign" of Modibo Keita, Sekou Touré or Houphouet-Boigny, in whom they see, above all, the elected of God through the people.

LEOPOLD SEDAR SENGHOR

Contents

Preface

WE have written this book out of two convictions. The first is that political science is primarily about politics and politicians—not about society, culture, psychology, or economics. Although these factors can play an important role in political life, politics and the actions of politicians are not reducible to them; the political realm is autonomous, and political actors are free to make their own choices. Politics can, of course, take place in many different contexts, but the most important context remains the state. And within the modern state the most important politics is national politics. In the national political theater the key players to watch—the dramatis personae—are the national politicians who make the play—the "game" of politics—what it is; and the stars in all national political dramas are the ruler and his associates and rivals.

Our second conviction is that the most settled kind of national politics takes place within a framework of institutions. Institutional offices and rules by definition restrain and moderate the acts of powerful men and are the tools of civil government. This is not to say that governments cannot be civil without them, but if they are, it is due entirely to the civic virtues—the civility—of the men who rule. Politics and government without the benefit of institutions, it follows, are at best uncertain and problematic and at worst dangerous; for this reason one of the historic tasks of political men has been to build and develop political institutions so that political life need not depend upon civic virtue alone. A primary focus of political science is the actions of political men, which are studied in order to better understand how political institutions are developed, maintained, or destroyed.

But this is a study of politics and politicians operating largely without the aid of effective institutions and in a manner that discredits the institutions that exist and renders them of limited or little value. It is not a study, therefore, of the most settled kind of politics, but it is a kind of politics which has been common both in many historical settings and in the contemporary world —especially the Third World, and specifically Black Africa. And it is a fascinating kind of politics, perhaps the most fascinating— as Machiavelli showed in *The Prince*—for it is largely contingent upon men, upon their interests and ambitions, their desires and aversions, their hopes and fears, and all the other predispositions that the political animal is capable of exhibiting and projecting upon political life. This is a study of the African Prince and other types of African rulers who have conducted the affairs of their states largely through "personal politics," and it is a study of a distinctive kind of political system that these rulers have fashioned, for the most part unintentionally: the system of personal rule.

In writing this study we have benefited from the help and advice of many individuals and institutions. Our colleagues and students have contributed to our thinking on a wide variety of issues and have saved us from a number of conceptual and factual errors. We would particularly like to thank Virginia Adloff, Charles Andrain, Patricia Anglim, Reinhard Bendix, Alan Cairns, Thomas Callaghy, David Cantor, Michael Chege, Elizabeth Colson, Andrew M. L. Deng, George Feaver, Judith Geist, Joel Gerston, Ernst Haas, Elbaki Hermassi, Chalmers Johnson, Kenneth Jowitt, David Laitin, Michael Lofchie, Milos Martic, Stephen Milne, Humphrey Nwosu, Fidelis Okoli, Robert Price, John Ravenhill, Donald Rothchild, Paul Sack, Russell Stout, Richard Stren, and Luise White. A special thanks is owed to James Coleman, who stimulated and assisted us in our initial thinking about governance in the post-independence Black African states. Both the Social Sciences and Humanities Research Council of Canada and the Institute of International Studies of the University of California, Berkeley, have supported parts of this study. The creative and meticulous editorial work of Paul Gilchrist and Bojana Ristich greatly enhanced the manuscript. Cleo Stoker of the Institute provided invaluable assistance and encouragement. Peggy Phillips carefully prepared parts of the typescript. Our appreciation extends to Consuelo Bennett, Susan Chisolm, Ann Mine, and Nadine Zelinski for their efficient and accurate typing of numerous drafts, and to Bodine Brown for her many kindnesses.

Our major acknowledgment is to the Carnegie Corporation of New York. The generous support and encouragement of the officers of the Corporation over a number of years have enabled us to carry out the extensive background studies without which this book could not have been written. Finally, we both owe much to the patience and understanding of our families, who have been abandoned for lengthy periods of time during the writing of this book.

RHJ
CGR

1

Introduction

POLITICS in most Black African states do not conform to an institutionalized system. They are not an activity in which individuals and organizations engage publicly to win the right to govern or to influence a government's policies within an overall and legitimate framework of agreed-upon rules. Rather like international politics, the political "game" in most African states is not yet governed by regulations that effectively prevent the unsanctioned use of coercion and violence.[1] Consequently, politics are more personalized and less restrained, resulting in higher stakes but also in greater risks for those who actively engage in the political game and greater uncertainty for the general public.

African politics are most often a personal or factional struggle to control the national government or to influence it: a struggle that is restrained by private and tacit agreements, prudential concerns, and personal ties and dependencies rather than by public rules and institutions. The consequences of such politics have usually been increased political instability and occasionally the deterioration of the game of politics into a "fight" among personal and factional contenders for power. But, speaking generally, the result has not been the political disorder that Hobbes and some other theorists would lead us to expect.[2] The contemporary African political experience suggests, rather, that a relatively stable public life is attainable in large-scale territorial states that are neither institutionalized "civil societies" nor anti-political totalitarian regimes. In many African countries that presently lack effective political institutions, a measure of political order has been attained without

1. Our use of the political metaphor "game" is influenced by F. G. Bailey, *Stratagems and Spoils: A Social Anthropology of Politics* (Toronto: Copp Clark Publishing Co., 1969), ch. 1.
2. See Thomas Hobbes, *Leviathan*, ed. Michael Oakeshott (New York: Collier Books, 1962); see also Samuel P. Huntington, *Political Order in Changing Societies* (New Haven and London: Yale University Press, 1968). Stable systems of personal rule can be located conceptually between civil society and Hobbes's "state of nature," or, in Huntington's terms, between institutionalized politics and praetorianism.

the complete suspension of politics. But it is usually an order resting on personal-political arrangements, which are more subject to repudiation and therefore to disruption than are legitimate institutions.

The public political realm in Black Africa, especially the realm of competitive party and electoral activity, has been greatly reduced in scope and significance since the high-water mark of open politics achieved during the terminal colonial era of African nationalism.[3] In their quest to monopolize the control of state power following independence, most of Africa's rulers—soldiers and civilians alike—adopted practices of authoritarianism, with the consequence that national public politics withered and a world of largely private power and influence emerged. Politics became a kind of "palace politics" engaged in by privileged members of a ruling oligarchy and sometimes by a wider circle of elites who at most could only tenuously and unofficially represent the broader interests of social groups and classes. In seeking to understand the character of African political systems, we must therefore set aside the preconceptions and categories of institutionalized public politics and consider the older and historically pervasive practices of palace politics that were common in societies prior to the modern democratic revolution.

By most informed accounts personal rulership plays a very important role in the political life of the new states of Black Africa.[4] One cannot explain the sources of political order and disorder in Africa by considering solely the effects of the underlying social and economic environment upon rulers and their actions.

3. Nelson Kasfir, *The Shrinking Political Arena: Participation and Ethnicity in African Politics, with a Case Study of Uganda* (Berkeley, Los Angeles, London: University of California Press, 1976). Also see Ali A. Mazrui, "Political Science and the Decline of African Nationalism," in *Expanding Horizons in African Studies*, eds. Gwendolen M. Carter and Ann Paden (Evanston: Northwestern University Press, 1969), pp. 147–56.

4. While there are a number of valuable political biographies and political histories which provide insights into particular cases of rulership, only a few political science studies have centered upon rulership or leadership as such. (These must be distinguished from anthropological studies of traditional African rulership, of which there have been many. For a recent compendium, see William A. Shack and Percy S. Cohen, eds., *Politics in Leadership: A Comparative Perspective* [Oxford: Clarendon Press, 1979].) Among the political science studies are Henry Bretton, *The Rise and Fall of Kwame Nkrumah: A Study of Personal Rule in Africa* (New York: Praeger, 1966); John R. Cartwright, *Political Leadership in Sierra Leone* (Toronto and Buffalo: University of Toronto Press, 1978); Christopher Clapham, "Imperial Leadership in Ethiopia," *African Affairs* 68, 271 (April 1969); René Lemarchand, ed., *African Kingships in Perspective: Political Change and Modernization in Monarchical Settings* (London: Frank Cass & Co., 1977); Ali A. Mazrui, "Leadership in Africa: Obote of Uganda," *International Journal* 25, 3 (Summer 1970): 538–64; and

Why is it that some countries that have changed little economically and socially, if at all, have experienced dramatic changes of rulership? Why have some countries with markedly different underlying socioeconomic characteristics had similar kinds of rulership? While some problems that confront contemporary African countries, such as economic underdevelopment, are basic material ones which are very likely beyond the reach of rulers and governments—certainly in the short and medium runs—there are others (sometimes overlooked) having to do with the quality and general conditions of public life which can be decisively affected by the actions of rulers and other leaders. It is apparent from the historical evidence that African rulers and other leaders are not captives of their environments: they have intervened, sometimes decisively, in the public life of African states, making some economically and socially unpromising countries orderly and some otherwise promising countries disorderly and insecure. In the provision or the destruction of such "political goods" as peace, order, stability, and non-material security, the actions of Africa's rulers and other leaders have been more important than anything else.[5]

An historical *raison d'être* of large-scale, national government has been to provide political goods, which are the conditions that make social and economic life beyond the confines and security of the small group possible. It is often difficult for individuals who have lived all of their lives under effectively institutionalized governments, which seem to provide political goods more or less automatically, to realize the importance of such goods for individual or collective action. But it requires only a moment's reflection for us to see how crucially important these goods are, and why Hobbes and most other political theorists before and since have concentrated their attention on the requirements for their realization.

This book will study the ways in which Africa's rulers and other leaders have provided or failed to provide political goods without

---

Philip Short, *Banda* (London and Boston: Routledge & Kegan Paul, 1974). Two general statements on rulership are Dankwart A. Rustow, ed., *Philosophers and Kings: Studies in Leadership* (New York: George Braziller, 1970), and W. Howard Wriggins, *The Ruler's Imperative: Strategies for Political Survival in Asia and Africa* (New York and London: Columbia University Press, 1969).

5. Our use of the concept "political goods" owes much to Pennock, who conceives of the state as a provider of such collective goods as order, security, welfare, justice, and liberty (see J. Roland Pennock, "Political Development, Political Systems, and Political Goods," *World Politics* 18, 3 [April 1966]: 420–27). While Pennock's definition remains somewhat implicit, we define a "political good" as a favorable general condition—rather like fair weather—enjoyed by a state's population, both as individuals and as a collectivity, that may be seen to derive, directly or indirectly, from the activities of governments and other political actors in a state.

the aid of effective political institutions. We have tried to discover and make explicit the common features of regimes of personal rule, without losing sight of the fact that there are different types of personal rulers in contemporary Africa. In addition to providing a general account of the theory and practice of personal rule, we provide a typology to serve as a middle ground between general statements about personal rule that might be too abstract and too far removed from the stuff of politics and history, on the one hand, and narrow-focused country or single-leader studies that might succumb under a welter of particular facts and events, on the other. The typology enables us not only to categorize Africa's more important rulers and their regimes, but also to draw distinctions among rulers in the same analytic category. We can thereby gain further insight into both the characteristic *modus operandi* of a specific type of rule and reasons for the relative success of rulers of the same general type, as well as the characteristics of more and less successful rulers across the typology. In other words, we are trying to make explicit both the general characteristics and dynamics as well as the variations to be found among African systems of personal rule. It is important to emphasize that by "personal rule" we do not mean merely a focus on rulers and other leaders—nor are we interested in the rulers' "personalities."[6] We do not mean merely one aspect or dimension of a polity or government. We mean, rather, a distinctive type of political *system* with operative principles and practices that can be apprehended by the political scientist.

Thinking in systemic terms about personal rule reveals that it is less the ruler as a person—for instance, his personal authority or "charisma" (or lack of it)—that determines the relative stability of a polity than his political skills and acumen: his experience and understanding of the opportunities and constraints that govern his actions and those of other leaders, and of the best methods for influencing and controlling other leaders and the country. Great political leaders may indeed be born and not made, but it is difficult not to conclude that Africa's most successful and enduring rulers have been politically sophisticated men who have learned from experience about the resources and limitations of their own political systems.

6. The theory of personal rule has nothing in common with recent psychoanalytical studies of rulers and other leaders, or studies of political personalities or political psychology; its emphasis is on the socio-political, not the psychological. For a recent and outstanding study of leadership emphasizing psychological factors, see James MacGregor Burns, *Leadership* (New York: Harper & Row, 1978).

Personal rule is a type of political system that is by no means confined to contemporary Black Africa. On the contrary, it is among the most common forms of political life to be found both in the contemporary world and in history. It may thus be worthwhile to comment briefly on the historical presence of personal rule. In the history of the modern state there have been many periods when men have governed countries unassisted and unrestrained by institutional rules. Indeed, the political institutions that we associate with the modern state often did not take hold until powerful rulers had first established effective governments and associated their personal authority with state structures. In most European states, strong personal rule preceded the successful establishment of impersonal, constitutional government. In general, personal regimes may be thought of as typical of transitional periods, when one institutionalized order has broken down and another has not yet replaced it. In early modern European history, good examples of such a transition are the states which emerged out of the late medieval period; during the Renaissance and the civil and religious warfare which followed, the boundaries, structures, and institutions of these states were not yet settled in the minds of people; as a result, absolutism became a widespread system of rule.

African states appear to us to be a species of early modern states emerging out of the collapse of European colonialism. Most indigenous African political institutions were either undermined or subordinated by the introduction of the colonial state and its aftermath of African nationalism, while the structures of the successor African states, based on various democratic designs, have so far failed to take root. There also seems to be emerging in contemporary Africa a pattern of personal-bureaucratic rule bearing some similarities to European absolutism and despotism. Many African rulers are trying to build up the bureaucratic apparatus of the central state as an instrument of the ruler's will to dominate. This seems to be in character with rulers in many other parts of the Third World, as indeed with the rulers of the Communist world. In this regard, many non-Western states and a growing number of African ones may be thought of as still highly personal and arbitrary at the top but increasingly bureaucratized at lower levels, like the Soviet Union or China. Some writers may be inclined to view the Soviet political system, and perhaps the Chinese, as fully institutionalized.[7] But to the extent that these regimes remain vulnerable at the highest levels to succession uncertainties and even to

7. Huntington, p. 1.

plots and conspiracies (with or without bloodshed), as rivals contend for supreme political power and the boldest, strongest, and most astute among them is the winner, they remain personal regimes at the apex of power. Indeed, both the Soviet Union and China, like many Third World states, continue to face problems of succession which cannot be handled by the application of institutional rules intended to prevent succession struggles. In the case of contemporary African countries, personalism is likely to extend much further down the power hierarchy, but we can discern a tendency toward increasing bureaucratization, often because of the continuing influences of the colonial bureaucratic legacy and contemporary predispositions toward state managerialism and neomercantilism. These tendencies have been most pronounced in Houphouët-Boigny's Ivory Coast and Banda's Malawi, where autocracy has been a marked feature of personal rule.

Of course, personal rule is only one dimension of African political life, and the study of personal rule is only one approach to an understanding of contemporary African states. But the study of personal rule is an approach that highlights important features of African politics that other approaches play down or neglect altogether: clientelism and patronage, factionalism, coups, purges, plots, succession crises, and similar characteristics and dynamics of institutionless government. In this study we have attempted to place such phenomena into a framework of theoretical explanation. We have tried to provide such an explanation by seeking answers to questions which are seldom asked in comparative and African political studies: What is the logic and character of systems of personal rule? How are they different from other systems of rule, particularly institutional rule? What circumstances are favorable to the development of systems of personal rule? What are the *modi operandi* of different types of personal rule? What are some of the important effects of personal rule generally and its sub-categories specifically upon the modern African state, and what is its ability to provide political goods? What have been the achievements and limitations of personal rule in Africa? Finally, what are the prospects for the achievement of more impersonal and enduring systems of institutionalized government in this world region?

One way to clarify the distinctive characteristics of personal rule is by placing the theory of personal rule within the analytic traditions of social and political science. However, before we consider the relevant traditions from which we can develop our concept of personal rule, it may be worth inquiring briefly into the reasons for political scientists' relative neglect of rulership as a subject. We suggest that there have been at least two basic reasons for this neglect: (1) the dominance of a social science-oriented methodology in contemporary political analysis and a decline of interest in the study of political institutions; (2) the concern that the study of rulers will become bogged down in particulars and produce little more than the idiographic studies associated with narrowly conceived political history or political biography.

The social science approach to political science manifests itself in methodological orientations that have the effect (among other things) of playing down rulers as independent agents in political life and therefore as important subjects of political analysis.[8] Among these orientations are the quantitative and the structural, which have inclined political scientists to seek explanations of politics in impersonal phenomena that lie beyond the personal intentions, wills, abilities, idiosyncracies, or fortunes of political actors. Typically, political actions are seen to be the results either of unconscious psychological factors specific to an actor or of impersonal social forces external to him. To understand such actions, the study of political socialization or of class structures is often regarded as of primary importance. The effect of such social science reductionism is to view political actors not as free agents operating in a contingent world who are responsible for their actions, but as products of their class position, their political socialization, and other social and psychological forces over which they have little control. It therefore plays down the capacity of such actors to influence historical events—whether for good or ill, intentionally or unintentionally—and to organize and control systems of political behavior or fail to do so. In our reading of contemporary African history we consider it impossible to ignore the crucial role played by rulers and other politicians and misleading to play down the profound effects of their actions and omissions on the public

8. Rustow has commented: "In the growing body of systematic social science, there remained less and less room for explicit attention to leadership. . . . As the older institutional-legal approach to the study of government came to be considered less and less adequate, [political scientists] began to adopt a new vocabulary of structure and function from cultural anthropology and a new technique of survey research from social psychology. Amid the verbal abstractions of the one and the quantitative correlations of the other, the political animal—be he citizen or ruler—was in danger of disappearing from the political scientist's view" (Dankwart A. Rustow, "The Study of Leadership," in *Philosophers and Kings*, ed. Rustow, pp. 3–4).

life of the new African states. Nor have we been able to consider such actions merely as secondary effects (i.e., dependent variables) of psychological or sociological factors (i.e., independent variables).

A related reason for the neglect of rulership as a subject for political scientists very likely is the concern that it must assume the character of descriptive, non-comparative historical or biographical studies. On this view political *science* cannot include idiographic studies—the reporting, chronicling, and describing of unique events. However, classical studies of rulership have not necessarily been merely descriptive, and we have not found it necessary to study rulership in a purely descriptive fashion (although we recognize the possibility of such an approach). For example, Machiavelli provided maxims and precepts that were intended to serve as a basis for "a new science of statecraft."[9] We might not wish to call his account of rulership scientific, but it is certainly one that is rich in theories and generalizations. In this study we have been interested in particular African rulers in order to discern in their conduct patterns of behavior that are susceptible to generalization. We have found evidence in contemporary Black Africa of a common pattern of personal rule and of several distinctive types of personal ruler. In addition, we have developed a view of personal rule as a distinctive kind of institutionless polity. In other words, our intention has been to write a theoretical account of the political system of personal rule in Black Africa, not descriptive or biographical accounts of particular African rulers; we hope that the result is consistent with the intent.

We have found that rulers and other critical leaders, like political structures when they are effectively institutionalized, can create and maintain the expectations that come to govern a system of political conduct. The key political actors or offices can become (so to speak) the center of gravity around which lesser actors and the broader strata beyond them revolve. Our account of personal rule has been influenced by three distinctive traditions of analysis that hold such an authority-centered view of political and social systems: (1) classical political theory, especially of the early modern state, (2) Weber's sociology of authority and the sociology of clientelism, and (3) comparative government theory. The political theories of Machiavelli and Hobbes are often in the background (and sometimes the foreground) of our analysis: not in the literal

9. Herbert Butterfield, *The Statecraft of Machiavelli* (New York: Collier Books, 1962), p. 16.

sense that we are applying their analyses directly to African ruler-ship (if that were possible), but in the sense that many of their insights about rulers and personal power render more intelligible the actions of African politicians. In their statecraft, particularly in their awareness of the uncertainties and contingencies of per-sonal power in the political worlds they inhabit, many of Africa's most successful rulers resemble Machiavelli's "Prince." Undoubt-edly, many also would like to enjoy the power, control, and se-curity—the Sword—of Hobbes's "Leviathan." We have learned much from Weber's sociology of leadership, especially his account of charismatic and patrimonial domination,[10] which has influ-enced our thinking primarily by suggesting points of departure. The work of Guenther Roth has been particularly helpful in this area.[11] We have also been influenced by the literature on political clientelism,[12] but we have sought to combine theories of patronage and clientelism with more traditional accounts of rulership found in political theory.

The analytic tradition which has had the greatest influence on our thinking about personal rule is the study of comparative gov-ernment that focuses upon political institutions: their nature, the historical conditions that give rise to them, and their importance for political life. We are not referring here to the microscopic and highly legalistic studies sometimes associated with the term "com-parative government" (which have done much to discredit it in the eyes of contemporary political scientists),[13] but to the more wide-ranging tradition of theoretical-institutional analysis associated with a long line of distinguished writers from Montesquieu and Tocqueville to Carl Friedrich and John Rawls. Regrettably, the theoretical categories and insights of this tradition of political analysis seem to have largely disappeared from the contemporary study of comparative politics; insofar as "institutions" are still of interest to political scientists, the meaning of the term is quite dif-ferent from what it once was. Thus the classical concept of a politi-

10. See Max Weber, *Economy and Society: An Outline of Interpretive Sociology*, ed. Guenther A. Roth and Clause Wittich (New York: Bedminster Press, 1968), esp. vol. 3, pp. 1102–19. See also Reinhard Bendix, *Max Weber: An Intellectual Portrait* (Berkeley, Los Angeles, London: University of California Press, 1977), pt. 3.

11. See his "Personal Rulership, Patrimonialism, and Empire-Building in the New States," *World Politics* 20, 2 (January 1968): 194–206.

12. See, for example, Steffan W. Schmidt, James C. Scott, Carl Landé, and Laura Guasti, eds., *Friends, Followers and Factions: A Reader in Political Clientelism* (Berkeley, Los Angeles, London: University of California Press, 1977).

13. For a penetrating critique of such studies, see Harry Eckstein, "On the 'Sci-ence' of the State," *Daedalus* (Special Issue on "The State") 108, 4 (Fall 1979): 1–20.

cal institution as an impersonal system of rules and offices that effectively binds the conduct of individuals involved in them has been supplanted, under the influence of modern sociology, by the concept of an institution as a system not of *rules* and *offices*, but of *roles* and *relations*. The two concepts are substantially different: a rule is a standard of conduct, whereas a role is an expectation of conduct which may be in violation of the rules, as with corruption. An example of a sociological concept of "institutions" is Huntington's definition: "stable, valued, recurring patterns of behavior."[14] What is required for an adequate definition of "political institution" is the union of rules and behavior. Institutions are not only rules nor only behavior (or patterns of behavior); they are conduct in respect of rules—that is, the rights and duties of individuals *and* their effective performance of these duties.

As a form of analysis, role theory gives inadequate attention to a basic feature of an institutionalized state: its use of rules to govern conduct. Rules are the tools of a civil society. In an institution the rule and its authority always stand above the person and his power or ability. In an effectively institutionalized state, the rules are respected by all persons no matter how important they may be; indeed the rules in a well-established state with a strong institutional tradition appear entirely natural. In a state without effective institutions, rules are defied or ignored; they appear artificial and without value and meaning. The tradition of comparative institutional analysis explores, among other things, not only the form and substance of such rules in a political system, but also the degree of respect for them and the conditions underlying public attitudes toward them.

The opposite of institutional rule—obviously—is non-institutionalized government, where persons take precedence over rules, where the officeholder is not effectively bound by his office and is able to change its authority and powers to suit his own personal or political needs. In such a system of personal rule, the rulers and other leaders take precedence over the formal rules of the political game: the rules do not effectively regulate political behavior, and we therefore cannot predict or anticipate conduct from a knowledge of the rules. To put this in old-fashioned, comparative government terms, the state is a government of men and not of laws.[15] We believe that this definition is generally applicable to African states. In defining "institutions" we have followed Rawls:

14. Huntington, p. 12.
15. In classical definitions of constitutionalism, personal rule is the standard contrast: "By constitutional government is meant, in the first place, a form of government

> By an institution I shall understand a public system of rules which de-
> fines offices and positions with their rights and duties, powers and im-
> munities, and the like. These rules specify certain forms of action as
> permissible, others as forbidden. . . . An institution may be thought of in
> two ways: first as an abstract . . . system of rules; and second, as the . . .
> [realized] actions specified by these rules. . . . A parliamentary institu-
> tion exists at a certain time and place when certain people perform the
> appropriate actions, engage in these activities in the required way, with a
> reciprocal recognition of one another's understanding that their conduct
> accords with the rules they are to comply with. . . . A person taking part
> in an institution knows what the rules demand of him and of the others.
> He also knows that the others know this and that they know that he
> knows this, and so on.[16]

Most African states have *abstract* constitutions and institutions
in the Rawlsian sense, but very few have them in fact: the formal
rules of the political game do not effectively govern the conduct of
rulers and other political leaders in most places most of the time.
Insofar as rules are followed by African rulers, it is only after they
have been changed by the ruler or oligarchy in question to suit his
or their personal-political convenience. But rules of expediency
are not, patently, rules of institutional government. They are better conceived as instrumental rules of "organizations"—as instruments of power and not as normative restraints on power.[17] Being
wholly instrumental to ruling power, they are the hallmarks of
political authoritarianism, which is closely allied to personal rule.
In institutionalized systems personal political calculations are
made, but in terms of the universally accepted rules and requirements of the political game; in personal systems such calculations
are not mediated by reference to rules agreed to by all leaders and
factions. Thus, for example, while a governing party and its rivals
in a constitutional democracy will go to great lengths to win elections, they will not seek to abolish elections to stay in power or
manipulate the electoral rules or their supervision to the point
where they no longer are basically fair. By contrast, such manip-

which, as opposed to what may be called personal government, is based not on the
temporary caprice and whim of those who possess political power, but which, on the
contrary, is carried on in accordance with rules so clearly defined and so generally
accepted as effectively to control the actions of public officers" (Frank J. Goodnow,
Principles of Constitutional Government [New York and London: Harper & Broth-
ers, 1916], pp. 2–3).

16. John Rawls, *A Theory of Justice* (Cambridge, Mass.: Harvard University
Press, Belknap Press, 1971), pp. 55–56. See also F. F. Ridley: "Political Institutions:
The Script Not the Play," *Political Studies* 23, 2: 243–58, and *The Study of Govern-
ment* (London: George Allen & Unwin, 1975), esp. pp. 13–42.

17. In this regard, we believe that Huntington's outstanding and influential study
of "political order" is more about "organized" and "disorganized" states than institutionalized ones.

ulation is precisely what we should expect to see in personal, authoritarian regimes.

In advancing a theory of personal rule based on a traditional theory of comparative government, we do not wish to leave the impression that institutionalized polities have no problems of their own. Rules and offices can become ossified and stand in the way of necessary action. Institutions can decay and lose their effectiveness when people no longer value or utilize them. To maintain an ongoing and adaptive system of institutional government is obviously a continually demanding political task in constitutional states. But the problems of institutional government are not those of personal rule. They are problems, by and large, of conservatism and immobility in the face of demands for action. They are not, however, problems of imminent or persistent threats that powerful men or groups in an uninstitutionalized state present to the political order—the problems that personal rulers most often confront.

Here we arrive at the central feature of personal rule: it is a dynamic world of political will and action that is ordered less by institutions than by personal authorities and power; a world of stratagem and countermeasure, of action and reaction, but without the assured mediation and regulation of effective political institutions. Political power is capable of being checked and stalemated in Africa, as elsewhere, but less by institutions than by countervailing power. Mediation and regulation can take place, as they must in all political systems if these are to be kept minimally in order and at peace, but only at the instigation of the politicians themselves acting intelligently and wisely to avoid the political dangers of force, violence, and bloodshed. Perhaps the greatest of Africa's contemporary rulers are men, such as Senghor of Senegal, who have been able to perform this mediating role with accomplishment and civility.

Almost everywhere in Black Africa, systems of personal rule have come into existence. Where these systems have proved capable of providing political goods, it has been due almost entirely to the ability of leader-politicians to take firm control of the political situation. Personal rule tests the will, skill, and fortune of politicians—especially rulers—more than institutional rule, and one is struck by the number of remarkable politicians that the post-independence period in Black Africa has produced. There is reason to believe that the contemporary period of African history, when state institutions have been weak and the organizations of government limited in their capabilities, will be remembered primarily in terms of the exceptional politicians who had to contrive and manage personal systems of governance in the absence of effective institutions.[18]

18. Exceptional politicians in institutionalized states as well appear to arise during periods of crisis, when institutions have to be transcended or changed—such as during wartime or economic depression. Thus the constitutional crises of the Fourth French Republic called forth a Charles de Gaulle, who was the only political leader with sufficient personal authority to successfully undertake the reconstitution of the French state.

2

The Political System of

Personal Rule:

A Conceptualization

THE attractions of politics are many. Men have engaged in politics to pursue lofty ideals and ideologies, to serve a state or its people, to advance a cause or interest, to wield power, and to enjoy the fame, privileges, and honors that power brings. From an historical and a comparative view, of all these attractions the desire for power is the most ancient and persistent—especially when the state is the primary arena where power is secured.

The state in Africa in the late twentieth century is an arena in which individuals can obtain great power. What the church was for ambitious men in medieval Europe or the business corporation in nineteenth- and twentieth-century America, the state is today for ambitious Africans with skill and fortune. The political system in African states is more like a game or a market than a planning organization.[1] In regard to the game and its participants, contemporary Africa resembles early modern Europe, where the stakes of state power were high and the game of power politics was played not by philosophers, lawyers, or administrators, but by politicians of consummate skill and resourcefulness. However, state power in African countries has been the major arena of privilege—the religious, business, and other arenas provide fewer opportunities—and it has been more accessible to ambitious men of humble origin. The political capital of social standing and wealth has been useful but not essential to partake in the game or to win; personal strength, prowess, and popularity have been more important. In fact political activity has been seen by ambitious Africans as a way—indeed the most important way—of securing such capital.

1. F. G. Bailey, *Stratagems and Spoils: A Social Anthropology of Politics* (Toronto: Copp Clark Publishing Co., 1973), pp. 1–9.

14

While African independence from European colonial rule has justifiably been viewed as of little significance in terms of fundamental economic and social change, it has been of profound *political* significance. The administrative state introduced into Africa by European colonial powers (Britain, France, Germany, Belgium, Italy, Portugal, and Spain) mainly in the nineteenth century was placed in African hands starting in the late 1950s. Final responsibility for the actions of state agents was transferred from Europe, where it had been for almost a century and in some places longer, back to Africa. Africans could now enjoy the power and bear the burdens that powerholding entails in independent political systems. By 1980, when African independence from European colonialism was virtually complete, there were some forty sovereign states in sub-Saharan Africa. But the African state was not simply a colonial state in new dress; the transfer of authority from Europe to Africa—and especially the transformation of that authority— quickly made it a very different kind of state than its European-ruled predecessor had been.

Colonial rule in Africa had basically been bureaucratic rule. Colonial governments were run for the most part by administrative officials appointed by the imperial European authority to whom they were ultimately responsible. Not only the regular administrative staff, but also the colonial governor and other senior officials were appointees of the European authority. They were *officeholders* whose authority and powers were specified and delegated to them by the imperial authority (in the case of British colonies, for example, by the Colonial Office, the Cabinet, and ultimately the British sovereign). In the ordinary course of their careers they were subject to directives and orders such as transfers, promotions, reappointments, and even dismissals, which shaped their public and private lives, and which they might adapt to local conditions but could not wholly ignore or defy. If they did, they very likely would not occupy their offices for long. Not even the colonial governor was exempt. In the last analysis, all colonial officials were imperial servants and never fully independent statesmen within their jurisdictions.

African independence necessarily meant a fundamental change and reorientation of political authority. A new African ruler would not be occupying an office whose authority and power were delegated by a higher authority. The scope of his new office would be determined either by a new national constitution or, if it proved ineffective, by the ruler's personal domination. Almost everywhere in Black Africa new independence constitutions soon proved ineffective as either rulers or their opponents—often military leaders—acted in contempt of constitutional rules or arbitrarily changed them to expedite their goal of retaining ruling power or achieving it. Therefore, as was noted, independence involved not only the transfer of sovereign authority from European to African rulers, but also a fundamental change in the nature of that authority.

Independence brought a new and distinctive system of personal rule into being that was fundamentally different from the institutional-bureaucratic system of European colonialism. The new African statesman was a personal ruler more than a constitutional and institutional one; he ruled by his ability and skill (as well as the abilities and skills of those he could convince to be his supporters), by his personal power and legitimacy, and not solely by the title granted to him by the office he occupied and the constitution that defined it. Insofar as constitutions remained important features of rule, they were important less as constraints on the abuse of power and more as legal instruments that a personal ruler could amend or rewrite to suit his power needs. In taking such actions, the new ruler demonstrated that he regarded himself as being above his office and that the new political system was basically personal and authoritarian. Personalism did not usually stop with the ruler or even the oligarchy, but extended down the hierarchy of rule. Like the colonial governor before him, the personal ruler needed bureaucratic agencies—important if not vital instruments of rule and perhaps of growth and development, although their effectiveness varies from country to country and many are undermined by norms of personalism, overemployment, and corruption.

The colonial authorities were a guardian class not of the countries they ruled. The new African rulers and their lieutenants are of their countries sociologically and politically. The colonial state, which obtained its legitimacy from higher authorities in Europe, did not vest its authority in the African people, although it counted on their acquiescence. If Africans resisted, preponderant power and force lay with the colonial rulers; in a serious struggle between European rulers and African subjects, the former could bring in a reserve of power from abroad if necessary. Contemporary African rulers have no higher authorities to draw upon when legitimacy wanes and power is required; they must secure legitimacy or power by political or diplomatic means, either at home or from other independent statesmen in a position to aid them. As a consequence, it is possible for African rulers to fall from power in a way that colonial governors never could—that is, by their own miscalculations or because of a political situation that overwhelms them. Colonial governors could only fall from imperial favor and be removed from office or (more likely) be transferred elsewhere. When colonialism was at last brought to an end, it was the colonial *system* that was "defeated" and not the governors and their staffs.

When institutional rulers are replaced or removed from office, it is by higher authorities or by the constitutional rules of officeholding. But when a ruler places himself above the rules or personally tailors an office to suit his political needs, he cannot be made subject to removal or replacement by institutional means. If he loses the confidence and support of those he rules but is unwilling to step down, he can be dislodged only by superior power or fall from weakness, misfortune, inability, or miscalculation. Some of the African rulers we shall consider have held power successfully for decades; others have held it for a much shorter time. But whether power is held for years or only a few months, its holding depends very largely on the ruler, his skill, ability, and luck, and the ruling situation in which he finds himself. Some personal rulers have confronted difficult political situations and their powerholding has been adversely affected as a result, while others have brought greater skills and better judgment to bear on situations of comparable political difficulty, with the corresponding result of longer ruling tenures and enhanced rulership stability. Furthermore, some institutional rulers can confront difficult political situations and be defeated by them while others are not. A defeat may be very personal and humiliating, leading to a loss of the leader's honor and prestige. It may be brought about by his inability, miscalculation, or mistaken judgment, or by the ineffectiveness of the party or government he leads—as frequently happens to party leaders of Western democracies when they lose elections. But defeat consists in an adverse *opinion*—of the caucus, the party, the legislature, or the electorate—that cannot be disregarded by a ruler if rules prescribe his resignation in the event. To ignore or defy rules is unthinkable in an effectively institutionalized political system. A personal ruler may resign after an adverse opinion, but if he chooses to ignore it and hold on to his position, nothing can dislodge him but superior *power.*

The Character of Personal Rule

As we noted in chapter 1, we view personal rule as a distinctive kind of political system with generic characteristics and processes. During the past two decades scholars, journalists, and other observers of African affairs have noted the recurrence of such phenomena as "coups," "plots," "clientelism," "corruption," "factionalism," "purges," and "succession uncertainties" in numerous African countries. Some of these—such as coups and clientelism—have become subjects of considerable academic study and commentary; much attention has also been given to corruption and factionalism. However, as yet there has been little inclination to view such phenomena as *integral elements of a distinctive political system;* they are more likely to be seen as merely the defects of an otherwise well-established public order. In this study we shall attempt to show that these phenomena (and others like them), far from being extrinsic features of Black African countries, are constituent elements of a distinctive kind of political system that merit systematic analysis by political scientists.

Personal politics are "systems" insofar as they function to regulate power in the state and thereby provide political goods or carry out political functions (such as peace, order, stability, and nonmaterial security), but they are not systems of *public* governance or of *rationalist* decision-making. A political system of personal rule is not a system which responds to public demands and support by means of public policies and actions,[2] nor is it a system in which the ruler aims at policy goals and "steers" the governmental apparatus by information "feedback" and "learning."[3] Indeed, the concept of governance as an activity of guiding the ship of state toward a specific destination—the assumption of modern rationalism and the policy sciences—fits poorly with much political experience in contemporary Black African countries.

In African countries governance is more a matter of seamanship and less one of navigation—that is, staying afloat rather than going somewhere.[4] This is a source of considerable dismay to planners, economists, and policymakers (among others) who want African governments to initiate a rational and concerted assault on poverty, ignorance, disease, and other problems of underdevelopment. With a few notable exceptions, there is little governmental or even public organizational rationality in African states, although this is not the same as saying that there is little rationality

2. See David Easton: *A Systems Analysis of Political Life* (New York: Wiley, 1965), p. 32, and *The Political System: An Inquiry into the State of Political Science* (New York: Alfred A. Knopf, 1965), pp. 96–100, and Karl W. Deutsch, *The Nerves of Government: Models of Political Communication and Control* (New York: Free Press, 1966).

3. Ibid., ch. 5.

4. This distinction is taken from Michael Oakeshott, *Rationalism in Politics and Other Essays* (London: Methuen & Co., 1962), p. 127.

altogether. Active political interests exist in African states, but they tend to be more narrowly personal or factional than broadly organizational and social. As we have noted, the political system is more a game in which individuals and factions struggle for power and place rather than an arena in which groups or parties compete for policies and the constitutional right to command the ship of state. Although the system in Black Africa is like a game, it is not yet an institutionalized game. In the absence of effectively institutionalized rules, the players are not restrained from employing coercion, violence, and other harmful and unfair political means in their struggle for power and place. If such means are to be kept out of politics in personal systems, the players themselves must see to it without the assistance of a political culture with an institutional tradition.

As we have noted, a personal political system is not structured by impersonal rules that exist to uphold some conception of the public interest or the common good.[5] Personal rule is a system of relations linking rulers not with the "public" or even with the ruled (at least not directly), but with patrons, associates, clients, supporters, and rivals, who constitute the "system." If personal rulers are restrained, it is by the limits of their personal authority and power and by the authority and power of patrons, associates, clients, supporters, and—of course—rivals. The system is "structured," so to speak, not by institutions, but by the politicians themselves. In general, when rulers are related to the ruled, it is indirectly by patron-client means. Although it can be conceived as a political system of a distinctive kind, personal rule is less adequate than effectively institutionalized government in terms of the provision of political goods, and it is much more subject to disruptions caused by changes of personnel. The fact that it is ultimately dependent upon persons rather than institutions is its essential vulnerability.

Any political game can deteriorate into a fight, but the possibility is considerably greater in personalized regimes than in institutionalized ones. In the latter, fights are illegitimate by definition, and institutional rules and referees exist to prevent them from breaking out. In personalized regimes rules and authorities are not *effective* (although they are usually formally available); fights must be prevented by the players themselves. More often than not, informal understandings among them, as

5. In equating political institutions to the public interest, we are following Samuel P. Huntington, *Political Order in Changing Societies* (New Haven and London: Yale University Press, 1968), ch. 1.

well as self-interested concerns for the retention of political order, are sufficient to prevent fights. Personalized regimes can contain a pragmatic political knowledge concerning how to play the game without resorting to the risky and possibly costly stratagem of fighting. Players seek to avoid extreme risks and costs of severe loss—for example, loss of life, loss of personal freedom, loss of political privilege. Rational interests in security and stability are conducive to largely peaceful and orderly politics by insiders; rational fears of punitive actions and deprivations coerce outsiders into relative political quietude. However, there is a possibility— much greater in personalized systems than in institutionalized ones—that some players will resort to the use of violence for political ends, thereby threatening the game itself. In contemporary Black African countries the players most disposed to use violence have been soldiers.

In personal regimes the dark side of political life—behavior involving conspiracy, violence, and coercion—is much more evident than in effectively institutionalized regimes because the "game" of politics is without established rules and effective referees. Therefore, such behavior cannot be regarded as an aberration (as one is inclined to regard it in an institutionalized regime). Rather it must be viewed as generic to systems of personal rule (and the ample evidence of such behavior in Black Africa serves to underline the point). Furthermore, the game in personalized regimes is always nearer to becoming a "fight" than remaining a "contest" insofar as plots, purges, coups, and similar disruptions are ever-present threats that not infrequently surface (see "Plots, Coups, and Successions," below). Political insecurity is therefore far more prevalent, and in a climate of apprehension acts of political violence are to be expected. Those excluded from the game who wish to play or those who fear exclusion or the arbitrary loss of their political privileges may engage in plotting and conspiracies to safeguard their interests; those who are in control may be apprehensive of offensive attacks and may resort to purges against fellow players and acts of intimidation or overt coercion against opponents.

Some personal regimes are more prone to political deterioration than others. Fighting and other political evils are more likely to surface in personal systems that lack an effective ruler—a dominant political personage who is able to control the players. An effective ruler may be a political policeman with sufficient power and authority to preside over the game and keep it orderly—in a regime we shall term "princely rule." He may be a political strongman who at least temporarily succeeds in dominating everyone else and in effect transforming politics into administration—"autocratic rule." Or he may be a charismatic personality who can convert politicians into missionaries and politics into a crusade—"prophetic rule." The deterioration of some personalized games into fights can be caused by the rulers themselves and their supporters when they conduct themselves in a wholly abusive and unrestrained manner—the case of "tyrannical rule." It is possible, therefore, to conceive of different types of personal regimes that are distinguished basically by different patterns of rulership. Of the four types of personal regimes that we have identified, in contemporary Black Africa the most common has been princely rule; autocratic and prophetic rule have been less common and tyrannical rule quite uncommon.

(Let us here specify that by regime we mean the arrangement of authority, power, and political interests in a state. This arrangement may be constitutionally or institutionally governed or it may be informal, as it is in personal systems. If informal, it is likely to change when rulers change, in response to a new ruler's desires and aversions, interests and indifferences, strengths and weaknesses, and political formula—i.e., his ideas, procedures, and manner of ruling.)

A few remarks on the conditions that might give rise to personal rule may be worthwhile at this point, although we do not have the space to go into detail. Personal rule may be an adaptation to a comparatively low level of social and economic modernization in a country, and the transformation of personalized regimes into institutionalized ones may depend upon fundamental socioeconomic changes—as the theory of modernization suggests. However, personal authoritarianism has been present in relatively "developed" states in the twentieth century—such as Italy, Portugal, Spain, and (to consider non-European examples) Singapore and Taiwan. Furthermore, pre-modern societies have been as successful as modern ones—if not more so—in achieving political institutionalization, as Huntington has pointed out.[6] A more pertinent condition for personal rule may be an absence of a relevant and viable institutional tradition in the political life of a state. Modern states that have exhibited marked features of personal rule have often been newly formed, and their inhabitants have not shared a common political tradition or the political culture that inevitably upholds it—for example, modern Italy, Germany, and Yugoslavia. In Africa the colonial territories which became sovereign states

6. Ibid.

rarely corresponded with traditional African states; in consequence the citizens of new states did not have common political institutions that they could resurrect at independence. In addition, the political institutions and constitutions officially adopted by the vast majority of African states at independence were alien—specifically Western—in spirit and design. They were not founded on distinctively African political theory or political authority. In the absence of unifying indigenous institutions, politicians were left with the task of governing with their personal power and authority.

In sum, the existence of personal systems is dependent less upon the underlying socioeconomic environment and more upon the dispositions, activities, abilities, efforts, and fortunes of politicians—especially rulers. Politicians in uninstitutionalized systems largely determine whether the game of politics shall remain a contest with cooperation and restraint among participants or deteriorate into a fight. The ruler has the greatest influence in determining these issues in African personal regimes; how he chooses to perform his role, how well he performs, and with what degree of fortune are crucial to the stability of the polity and the persistence of the regime.

Personal Rulers and Authoritarianism

At the apex of all personal regimes is a ruler, a paramount leader who enjoys a position of uncontested supremacy as long as he succeeds in retaining power. The uncontested supremacy of African rulers is best seen in the fact that most rulers need not seek a contested reelection; most presidential elections are plebiscitarian in character. Furthermore, personal rulers are seldom subject to constitutional time limits on their incumbency.[7] Like monarchs of old, they stand above their subjects. In all save a very few states not only do they enjoy unrivaled power, privilege, wealth, and

7. Constitutional limitations have existed in Senegal and Rwanda (for example), but in 1973 Rwanda amended its constitution, ending restrictions as to the number of terms a president could serve (*Africa Contemporary Record: Annual Survey and Documents*; 1968–70, ed. Colin Legum and John Drysdale [London: Africa Research, 1969–70]; 1970–72, ed. Colin Legum [London: Rex Collings, 1971; London: Rex Collings, and New York: Africana Publications, 1972]; 1972–79, ed. Colin Legum [New York: Africana Publications, 1973–79]; on constitutional amendments, see 1973–74, pp. B 237–38). In 1976 Senegal removed all previous limits to presidential tenure (ibid., 1975–76, p. B 812). Liberia's constitution under President Tolbert provided that a president may serve only a single term of eight years.

honor—that is, overt public rewards—but also in some cases a kind of political divinity. In many an African country the ruler is portrayed as embodying the idea, dignity, and even the sacredness of the state—a concept most evident in countries with long-surviving rulers who have governed for a decade or more or have ruled continuously since independence. In those countries the idea of the state and the person of the ruler are intertwined to a degree that is difficult to imagine in institutionalized systems. For example, an Ivory Coast without Félix Houphouët-Boigny is difficult to visualize, even though one day it will be without him; when it is, the state is unlikely to be quite the same.

In personalized regimes the ruler is the pivot of state power, the commanding presence on the political stage. More than any other political actor, he captures and holds—or endeavors to hold—the attention of the audience that is "the people." But to hold the attention of the people and dominate the stage, the ruler need not actually be on stage. He may command even when off the stage by being a constant spiritual presence and consideration in the calculations and actions of all political actors. An all-imposing leader possesses a personal power and ability to focus the attention of lieutenants and subordinates on his wishes and dislikes, his interests and aversions, even when he is not present; this ability is the underpinning of his domination. Thus a strong personal ruler need not attend meetings of governing bodies, such as the cabinet or the ruling party executive, for those who attend will be careful to take account of his interests; he will be spiritually present even when physically absent. It goes without saying that a ruler who must assert and reassert himself presents at least circumstantial evidence that his personal domination may be flagging. (Weak rulers are often unwilling to leave their countries even for short periods out of fear of losing political control.)

Personal rule is inherently authoritarian. By "authoritarian" we mean an arbitrary and usually a personal government that uses law and the coercive instruments of the state to expedite its own purposes of monopolizing power and denies the political rights and opportunities of all other groups to compete for that power. The contemporary African state is marked by a preoccupation with questions of political position and control by a ruling class or party led by a dominant personality. Modern African authoritarianism is characterized by the removal of constitutional rights and protections from political opponents, the elimination of institutional checks and balances, and the centralization and concentration of state power in presidential offices, as well as the ter-

mination of open party politics and the regulation and confine-
ment of political participation—usually within the framework of
a single ruling party. Authoritarian government in Africa has
been severely restrictive in regard to political liberties while being
generally tolerant of non-political rights—such as the right to
worship freely, the right to possess private property, and the right
to choose one's occupation at will. It is specifically political rights
such as the right to form or join political parties of one's own
choice or to publicly criticize a regime or its ruler (i.e., the rights to
free speech and a free press) that have been severely limited and in
many countries largely eliminated.[8]

In sub-Saharan Africa the rise of political authoritarianism has
meant the narrowing of the public sphere and its monopolization
either by a single ruling party or a military oligarchy typically
under the direct control of a dominant personality. Among other
important effects, this narrowing and monopolization have transformed open politics with contested elections into intra-regime
factionalism and personal rivalry and have led to such clandestine
activities as plots and coups—that is, they have transformed the
public political process into a private struggle for power and place.
As a result, the process of government administration is often
much more a personal or private matter than a public one.

The authoritarian element in personal rule allows rulers to use
law virtually as a license of unrestrictive command. As early as
1964 Post observed that "with few exceptions the trend has been
for one man in each state [of West Africa] to be elevated to a position of great power. . . . Often the constitution reflects this domination of the state not only by a single party, but, within that
party, by a single man."[9] Instead of separating the office from the
incumbent, constitutions in Black Africa often have made it increasingly difficult to make a distinction. Not only constitutions,
but also other laws have been revised or rewritten to give African

8. On freedom of the press, see William A. Hachten, "Newspapers in Africa:
Change or Decay?" *Africa Report* 15, 9 (December 1970): 25–28; Dennis L. Wilcox,
Mass Media in Black Africa: Philosophy and Control (New York: Praeger, 1975).
For aspects of control of trade unions, see Jon Kraus, "African Trade Unions: Pro-
gress or Poverty?" *African Studies Review* 19, 3 (December 1976): 95–108. For a
study of student protest, see Michael Buraway, "Consciousness and Contradiction: A
Study of Student Protest in Zambia," *British Journal of Sociology* 27, 1 (March
1976): 78–98. On religious conflict with the state, see Kenneth L. Adelman, "The
Church-State Conflict in Zaire: 1969–1974," *African Studies Review* 18, 1 (April
1975): 102–16.

9. Ken Post, *The New States of West Africa*, rev. ed. (Harmondsworth: Penguin
Books, 1968), p. 96; see as well Aristide R. Zolberg, *Creating Political Order: The
Party-States of West Africa* (Chicago: Rand McNally & Co., 1966), pp. 108–14.

rulers the legal right to exercise exceptional powers. An emphasis on legality has been characteristically strong in Kenya, where constitutional amendments and statutory provisions gave former President Jomo Kenyatta virtually a "blank cheque" to bring emergency powers into operation anywhere in the country at any time.[10] Kenyatta enjoyed great discretion to have the constitution amended to suit his political needs. For example, in 1975 the constitution was changed to empower the president to pardon MPs who had been found guilty of violating electoral laws. Other African rulers have been granted similar discretionary powers. Both civilian and military rulers in contemporary Africa have employed law in a manner reminiscent of the royal use of edicts and decrees in absolutist Europe; to be the ruler in many African countries has been to enjoy very nearly unlimited legal competence; it has involved a degree of discretionary power that in some cases has added up to arbitrary rule.

While personal rulers may possess absolute legal competence, they are never wholly unrestrained or certain of their power. The restraints and uncertainties they confront, however, are not of a constitutional-legal character but of a personal-political one. Indeed, as a result of the weakness of institutions, personal rulers must deal more directly with other powerful men; they must more actively contrive to remove opposition or win cooperation and adherence to the regime. (Winning cooperation is necessary in institutional regimes as well in order to gain support for public policies, but the holding of power in the short and medium runs is not contingent on it. Institutional rules, not political wills, determine who holds power.)

As students of Machiavelli know, rulers may use stratagem as well as force to disarm opposition or secure cooperation from other political actors. In African states rulers use stratagem in the following typical ways: (1) co-optation and consultation, which in effect indicate that their power is legitimate and therefore a part of the state; (2) patronage, which may be seen as an exchange of state resources for political support; and (3) agreement and accord, between parties or countries, to perform certain activities or to forbear from performing them. Of course, African rulers may also employ intimidation and coercion. To secure cooperation and re-

10. H. W. O. Okoth-Ogendo, "The Politics of Constitutional Change in Kenya Since Independence, 1963–69," *African Affairs* 71, 282 (January 1972): 27. For a more general and comprehensive account, see Bereket H. Selassie, *The Executive in African Governments* (London: Heinemann, 1974), and B. O. Nwabueze, *Presidentialism in Commonwealth Africa* (London: C. Hurst & Co., 1974).

move opposition of domestic political actors, rulers in more open and relaxed oligarchical polities—such as Senegal and Kenya—have been inclined to employ non-coercive means such as co-optation and patronage, which are central features of political life in these countries. Rulers in more autocratic states are less inhibited from imposing their will by threats and coercion, while tyrants (in Africa no more than elsewhere)—such as the late President Francisco Macias Nguema of Equatorial Guinea or Field Marshal Idi Amin of Uganda—have had few compunctions about the use of outright violence and the exploitation of fear to intimidate opposition. However, the method of intimidation and coercion has a built-in cost: to the extent that opposition is suppressed, it is possible only to secure acquiescence, not active cooperation. But to survive, most personal rulers in Africa (as elsewhere) rely on the willing cooperation of other political actors, and generally they attempt to secure it by the stratagems of co-optation, consultation, agreement, and patronage—especially the last. In seeking to reduce opposition and increase cooperation by such means, personal rulers do not escape from an inherent characteristic of personal rule—that is, its vulnerability to, or dependency on, the wills, wiles, and abilities of others. This characteristic is nowhere more evident than in relations of the ruler to the military. Africa's rulers, soldiers and civilians alike, require the cooperation or at least the acquiescence of the military to remain in power, and at times they have been denied it. This vulnerability distinguishes personal rule from institutional rule and is yet another reason why personal systems are more subject to political uncertainty and instability. Almost everything depends upon the skills and fortune of the ruler.[11]

As we have noted, personal rule is marked by inherent uncertainty. At the best of times, when a ruler appears most firmly in control, there is nevertheless a possibility for fate or fortune to change things or, indeed, for the ruler himself unwittingly or incautiously to cause disruption. For instance, there is no way of accurately predicting military coups, and one could take place at any time, causing a change of ruler. The ultimate uncertainty in a system of personal rule lies in the key point of vulnerability: the ruler. His welfare and fortune are critical not only to the welfare of the political class that supports him, but often also to the political order in general. If he falls, his relatives, friends, lieutenants, clients, and followers also may fall, and the ensuing political dis-

11. For this reason Machiavelli's political theory is fresh and relevant in an attempt to understand this key characteristic of African politics.

ruption may threaten the political peace. Uncertainty associated with the vulnerability of the ruler is most sharply evident in questions of succession or in the general apprehension of coups. There is a lower degree of uncertainty within the personal networks and dyads that surround less important political men—that is, the smaller fry who are dependent for their fortune upon the "big man."

Clearly the uncertainty of personal rule affects the ruler more than anybody else. It is with him every day in the sense that he rules not by institutional right but by personal domination, intelligence, energy, and fortune. This is not to say that personal rulers may not be confident and relatively secure in their paramount position, but their confidence and security do not derive from their legal right to rule for a specified period recognized by all; they cannot take their political status for granted in the way that an institutional ruler can. If they possess confidence and security, it is their personal confidence in their legitimacy and ability, and security in the personal support and loyalty of lieutenants, clients, and followers. They may rule for many years, but there is always a possibility that legitimacy will be lost, that ability and loyalty will decline, and that misfortune will overtake them. Machiavelli counselled the Prince to build dikes against *fortuna,* that violent and impetuous river. Emperor Haile Selassie ruled Ethiopia with confidence for decades, but when he grew old and began to lose his grip, an assertive military establishment brought him and his empire down in 1974. A similar fate has befallen many less experienced rulers who have been overconfident in their power—as Haile Selassie never was—or who have alienated important clients, thereby causing a shrinking in their power base. Some have brought their own downfall and with them the fall of their regimes; others have been overwhelmed in a political situation calling for more skills and resources than they possessed.

In addition to domestic uncertainties, the power of Africa's personal rulers is subject to the restraints and uncertainties posed by foreign economic and political factors over which little if any control can be exercised. African economies are among the poorest and weakest in the world; in the 1970s twenty-three had per capita GNPs below $200. The dependency of many African countries on a few primary exports makes them especially vulnerable to uncontrollable changes in world prices and demand and to unpredictable fluctuations in weather conditions and harvest returns. Lacking industrial and manufacturing sectors of any size and importance and highly dependent upon imports from abroad, they are caught between the certainty of their demand for foreign goods and services and the uncertainty of their ability to secure the foreign exchange to pay for them. Furthermore, African economies are restricted by small domestic populations—in 1973 only eleven countries had populations in excess of ten million—which cannot provide the market needed to sustain large-scale manufacturing. In addition, most of these economies remain heavily dependent upon foreign experts and skilled manpower, not to mention foreign investment.[12]

The political fortune of a personal ruler may be directly affected by foreign economic and political circumstances; some of Africa's rulers have been brought down by economic misfortunes not of their own making. An economic windfall may help a ruler (as did an increase in African coffee exports following disastrous frosts in Brazil during the mid-1970s), while an economic windstorm may adversely affect his ability to rule (as did the combined misfortune of a dramatic rise in the costs of oil imports and a decline in both the price and demand for African exports in the later 1970s). Zaire and Zambia, Africa's major copper producers, were both severely affected by economic adversities in the latter half of the 1970s, and their rulers' political fortunes were also unavoidably and adversely affected.

Foreign political factors related to the economic ones can more directly and immediately affect the ability of a personal ruler to hold power and prolong his regime. External political actors can enhance the power of a ruler by providing the political resources to gain or hold power; they can also undermine his power by withholding the resources or providing them to opponents. The pretext of foreign powers in supporting a ruler—when the support is not clandestine—is often an expressed desire to assist his country and its people or to support their national interest, and they may do so with economic, military, and other kinds of foreign aid and assistance.

The political dependence of a personal ruler is most clear in connection with military power—specifically the provision by a foreign power of military equipment and assistance that a ruler can use to maintain his domination. A few rulers have been sub-

12. For two early studies of African economies, see Andrew M. Karmack, *The Economics of African Development* (New York, Washington, London: Praeger, 1967), and P. Robson and D. A. Lury, *The Economics of Africa* (London: George Allen & Unwin, 1969). For two studies of economic dependence, see Samir Amin, *Neo-Colonialism in West Africa*, trans. Francis McDonogh (New York and London: Monthly Review Press, 1973), and D. P. Ghai, ed., *Economic Independence in Africa* (Nairobi, Kampala, Dar es Salaam: East African Literature Bureau, 1973).

stantially assisted militarily—for example, the Amin regime in Uganda with Soviet military assistance. A dramatic beneficiary of military aid has been Angola, where the provision of Soviet arms and aid and especially Cuban troops enabled the Movimento Popular de Libertação de Angola (MPLA) regime of the late President Agostinho Neto to extend its control and domination much beyond what otherwise may have been possible. Some rulers and regimes who are supported by military and economic aid may face serious difficulties when the flow of aid is stopped, as did General Mohamed Siad Barre's regime in Somalia in the late 1970s. Ruler dependency on foreign powers can sometimes be seen best during crises; President Leon M'Ba of Gabon was saved from an attempted military coup in 1964 by French troops sent by Charles de Gaulle; General Gnassingbé Eyadéma of Togo was forewarned by British diplomats of a planned coup by hired British mercenaries in late 1977.[13]

It is usual to conceive of dependency relations between African rulers and non-African powers, especially the major powers. However, such relations can obtain within Africa itself. Following an attempted coup against the regime of President Gaafar Mohamed Numeiri of Sudan in September 1975, Numeiri accused President Moamar Gaddafy of Libya of "harbouring enemies of his regime."[14] In the early 1960s President Kwame Nkrumah of Ghana lent financial and material support to self-styled revolutionaries from other African countries who were seeking to overthrow conservative African regimes. Ideological considerations may have been behind Nkrumah's support, but this does not gainsay the fact that the targets of the revolutionaries would have been the rulers of other African regimes.

In contemporary African countries plots to overthrow rulers may be hatched from within or without, but external plotters are more likely to be favored with external aid. Support may be clandestine rather than overt—as in the case of the invasions of Zaire's Shaba Province (formerly Katanga) from Angola in the springs of 1977 and 1978 apparently by Katangan exiles and rebels identified with an opposition movement—the Front National de Libération du Congo (FNLC). Each invasion placed the regime of President Mobutu Sese Seko in jeopardy, due to the immobilism and incapacity of the Zairian forces, and the danger was removed only by the arranged intervention of trained foreign troops in support of the regime. A similar example was the support extended by

13. *Africa Confidential* 18, 24 (December 2, 1977): 5.
14. *Africa Contemporary Record*, 1975–76, pp. B 67–68.

the government of President Julius Nyerere of Tanzania to exiled Ugandan forces; mobilized and deployed in northwest Tanzania, these forces launched an unsuccessful attack on the regime of General Amin in September 1972 and a successful one—overwhelmingly aided by Tanzanian forces—in 1978–79. As some African countries become more economically and militarily powerful, thereby enhancing their ability to assist or undermine weaker rulers, we may expect an increasing degree of ruler dependency within the African continent. A country whose power may be increasing is oil-rich Nigeria, to which rulers of weaker and poorer countries may turn for assistance to safeguard their hold on government.

We noted above that personal rulers may have absolute legal competence but cannot act wholly unrestrained. Indeed, personal rule in Africa is characterized by the seeming paradox of relative autonomy or freedom for the ruler and his clique to make policies but great constraint and incapacity to implement or enforce them. In Africa the unpredictable changes and shifts in foreign policy may be largely attributed to a personal ruler's freedom to initiate policy. In the late 1970s this was made dramatically clear in the remarkable reversal of Egypt's Middle East policy—caused, it seems, by President Anwar Sadat himself. In Renaissance and absolutist Europe foreign policy was the prerogative of the ruler; diplomacy was a ruler's game. Foreign policy in contemporary Africa also tends to be associated strongly with the interests and concerns of the ruler. The foreign policy of Tanzania, for instance, is scarcely distinguishable from President Nyerere's international views. Personal rulers may abruptly intervene and decree changes in domestic policy as well, with little or no prior notice. Such was clearly the case in Kenya, when President Kenyatta announced in 1973 that henceforth the first three years of primary education in the country would be free—in direct contradiction of the existing government education policy. Notwithstanding tyrannical regimes—where policies may be changed completely at the whim of the tyrant, and where it may be misleading to speak of "policy" since extreme political uncertainty makes the existence of any plan or proposed course of action inconceivable—the more autocratic the system of rule, the more likely is policy to be determined by the ruler and therefore the more subject is it to a change in direction. Policy changes were particularly noticeable in Zaire during the 1970s, where President Mobutu frequently and unpredictably intervened in the policy process. In a ruler's freedom to initiate policy, personal rule stands in marked contrast with institutionalized and proceduralized regimes, where presidents and prime ministers may very well harbor desires to make policies alone and unannounced but where the structure of government and the institutional interests that have grown up around policymaking make this virtually impossible.

In spite of their freedom to initiate policy and to intervene in policymaking, personal rulers are often severely restrained in getting policies implemented—primarily because of the relatively limited capability of the agents and agencies of underdeveloped governments. In general, governmental capability is contingent upon two factors: the resources at the disposal of agents and agencies, and their efficiency and ability in using them. Unlike the governments of developed countries, African governments are seriously lacking in resources—for example, adequate finances, personnel, equipment, materiel, and technology—which must be considered in relation to the ambitious policies that underdeveloped African governments often seek to carry out. Moreover, the resources that are available may not be deployed efficiently, nor are public officials generally as able, well-trained, or diligent as their jobs require.[15] These factors contribute to the overall incapacity of government and its inability to realize its goals, including goals desired by the ruler. To be sure, there is considerable variation among African governments in these respects; some government apparatuses are more capable than others. For instance, one is struck by the much greater bureaucratic capability and efficiency of Ivory Coast in contrast to some of the other French-speaking African countries—most notably Togo, Benin, and Congo-Brazzaville. Among English-speaking countries the relative administrative effectiveness of Kenya or Malawi stands out, particularly when contrasted with the lamentable administrative decay of a country like Ghana, which at one time had a reputedly efficient civil service.[16] However, while obvious differences exist among African governments, limited policy capability and admin-

15. Ladipo Adamolekun, "Towards Development-Oriented Bureaucracies in Africa," *International Review of Administrative Sciences* 42, 3 (1976): 257–65; Jon R. Moris, "The Transferability of Western Management Concepts and Programs, An East African Perspective," in *Education and Training for Public Sector Management in Developing Countries*, ed. Lawrence D. Stifel, James S. Coleman, and Joseph E. Black (Special Report from the Rockefeller Foundation, March 1977), pp. 73–83.

16. For Ghana, see Robert M. Price, *Society and Bureaucracy in Contemporary Ghana* (Berkeley and Los Angeles: University of California Press, 1975); for Kenya, Goran Hyden, Robert Jackson, and John Okumu, eds., *Development Administration: The Kenya Experience* (Nairobi: Oxford University Press, 1970); see also Virginia Thompson, *West Africa's Council of the Entente* (Ithaca and London: Cornell University Press, 1972), pp. 216–22.

istrative ineffectiveness are common. It is these limitations that dispose African regimes toward and make them dependent on the aid and assistance of foreign powers.

Soldiers as Personal Rulers

Our image of Africa's rulers has undergone considerable change in the past two decades. Where once we thought of them as civilians—nationalist politicians who had successfully led the fight for independence—we now expect to find as many soldiers as civilians speaking and acting in the name of the state.[17] How significant is this change? Do Africa's soldier-politicians wield power in a manner basically different from civilians? We believe not. Indeed, we believe that in the character of their rule, soldiers and civilians differ very little. Both must rule without the benefit of institutionalized government; while the former may have somewhat greater coercion at their command, the effects of greater coercion on the character of the rule are slight. The possession of power cannot remove the preoccupation with retaining power that characterizes personal regimes. The power of soldier-rulers may not be as contingent as that of civilians, but it is nevertheless contingent. Soldier-rulers, like civilian rulers, may be and have been the victims of military coups; they may also be the targets of lesser plots and intrigues. Soldiers as much as civilians must rule as personal politicians. Some have been more adroit and successful personal politicians than others; the fact that they have been soldiers has had little to do with their success. Like civilian rulers, they have had to confront societal and cultural problems that almost everywhere in the sub-Saharan region have given rise to personal-factional rule.

17. For studies on the military in politics, see the following: Dennis Austin and Robin Luckham, eds., *Politicians and Soldiers in Ghana 1966–1972* (London and Portland, Ore.: Frank Cass & Co., 1975); Anton Bebler, *Military Rule in Africa: Dahomey, Ghana, Sierra Leone, and Mali* (New York: Praeger, 1973); Samuel Decalo, *Coups and Army Rule in Africa: Studies in Military Style* (New Haven and London: Yale University Press, 1976); Uma O. Eleazu, "The Role of the Army in African Politics: A Reconsideration of Existing Theories and Practices," *Journal of Developing Areas* 7, 2 (January 1973): 265–86; Edward Feit: "The Rule of the 'Iron Surgeons': Military Government in Spain and Ghana," *Comparative Politics* 1, 4 (July 1969): 485–97, and *The Armed Bureaucrats* (Boston: Houghton Mifflin, 1973); Kenneth W. Grundy, *Conflicting Images of the Military in Africa* (Nairobi: East African Publishing House, 1968); W. F. Gutteridge, *Military Régimes in Africa* (London: Methuen & Co., 1975); William Gutteridge, *Africa's Military Rulers—An Assessment* (London: Institute for the Study of Conflict, 1975; Conflict Studies No. 62); Morris Janowitz, *The Military in the Political Development of New Nations*

The usual concept of the "military" is of command and discipline, of organization and objective. Ideal military organizations are characterized by unified command structures, professionalism and *esprit de corps,* and commitment to the values of obedience, rationality, and efficiency. African military organizations have been viewed as carrying forward a military tradition implanted by colonialism.[18] Such prerequisites and background of African soldiers would seem to belie our argument that African soldier-statesmen are little different from civilian rulers.

It is important to note that African armies—like civilian structures of the state—have been Africanized not only within the ranks, but also at the officer corps level, providing a strong *prima facie* reason for believing that the effects of Africanization upon the military have been similar to its effects upon civilian state organizations—that is, African sociocultural norms have penetrated the military, reducing the level of organizational autonomy it enjoyed during colonial times.[19] We shall argue that African armies have not been immune to these effects because modern militarism and the profession of arms as we described them above have not been an authentic feature of traditional African societies—certainly not at the level of the territorial state.[20] Like almost everything else at this level, modern militarism has been imported from abroad. As

(Chicago: University of Chicago Press, 1964); J. M. Lee, *African Armies and Civil Order* (New York and Washington: Praeger, 1969); A. R. Luckham, "A Comparative Typology of Civil-Military Relations," *Government and Opposition* 6, 1 (Winter 1971): 5–35; Ali A. Mazrui, "Soldiers as Traditionalizers: Military Rule and the Re-Africanization of Africa," *World Politics* 28, 2 (January 1976): 246–72; Theophilus Olatunde Odetola, *Military Politics in Nigeria: Economic Development and Political Stability* (New Brunswick, N.J.: Transaction Books, 1978); Victor A. Olorunsola, *Soldiers and Power: The Development Performances of the Nigerian Military Regime* (Stanford: Hoover Institution, 1977); Keith Panter-Brick, ed., *Soldiers and Oil: The Political Transformation of Nigeria* (London and Totowa, N.J.: Frank Cass & Co., 1978); Robert M. Price, "Military Officers and Political Leadership: The Ghanaian Case," *Comparative Politics* 3, 3 (April 1971): 361–79; Claude E. Welch, Jr., ed., *Soldier and State in Africa: A Comparative Analysis of Military Intervention and Political Change* (Evanston: Northwestern University Press, 1970); Claude E. Welch, Jr., "Personalism and Corporatism in African Armies," in *Political-Military Systems: Comparative Perspectives,* ed. Catherine McArdle Kelleher (Beverly Hills: Sage Publications, 1974), pp. 125–45; Claude E. Welch, Jr. and Arthur K. Smith, *Military Role and Rule* (Belmont, Calif.: Duxbury, 1974).

18. Ruth First, *Power in Africa* (New York: Pantheon Books, 1970).

19. We set aside the question of whether the colonial tradition was more bureaucratic than militaristic.

20. There have of course been some traditional African societies organized along "military" lines, such as the Zulu; and some had "armies," as exemplified by the Kingdom of Buganda and the Empire of Ethiopia. But modern African territorial states have not built their armies along such lines. Even Ethiopia, which had a more developed traditional military foundation than other African countries, never saw fit to build its modern army on such a foundation.

with other imports, if it was to survive, it had to adapt to its new environment. In the process of adaptation, it undoubtedly was impregnated by African sociocultural norms.

Almost everywhere in sub-Saharan Africa independence was the achievement of nationalist politicians. Soldiers were not among the nationalists. Independence Day was a civilian political festival. Sudan was perhaps the only country with a strong tradition of militarism; at independence in 1956 the army was a well-trained, disciplined organization under the command of a Sudanese officer corps, and from independence the army was a significant force in politics. But Sudan was an exception. The only other major exceptions were the former Portuguese territories, where revolutionary nationalists achieved liberation from Portuguese domination principally by means of guerrilla armies which after independence were converted into state organizations.

In some African countries armies did not even exist.[21] The French-speaking countries came to independence without national armies owing to the characteristically centralist French policy of establishing regiments which were not identified with particular colonial territories. At independence national armies had to be created out of these troops. (As a result of the French centralist policy came one of the earliest signs of the future importance of the military in African politics: after independence the Togolese government of Sylvanus Olympio refused to employ disbanded African colonial troops in its new Togolese army, and it was overthrown by disgruntled, mainly unemployed soldiers who installed a new regime.) Partly because of their peculiar histories as traditional societies under British protection, Lesotho, Botswana, and Swaziland never had modern armies; only recently have they been created in response to an unstable political situation in southern Africa. The Gambia is still without an army. The British created some colonial regiments, such as the King's African Rifles and the Royal West African Frontier Force, but the officer corps remained largely European.

Military organizations stood at the political sidelines at independence, although the King's African Rifles regiments, which became the bases of the national armies of Tanzania, Uganda, and Kenya, mutinied shortly after independence in a "strike" for higher pay, promotions, and Africanization of the officer corps. In Zaire a large and apparently disciplined army existed at indepen-

---

21. For a concise early survey of African armies, see George Weeks, "The Armies of Africa," *Africa Report* 9, 1 (January 1964): 4–21. For an outstanding study of the development of the African military, see Lee, *African Armies and Civil Order*.

dence—the Force Publique—but it was completely under the command of a Belgian officer corps. In the face of Prime Minister Patrice Lumumba's initial indifference to demands for Africanization of the officer corps and resentful of having no benefits from independence, Zairian soldiers mutinied against the officer corps a mere five days after the country became independent, plunging the new state into a crisis that was to persist for several years. The entire officer corps had to be immediately replaced and the army reconstructed with international assistance over a period of three years. As in Togo, here was a portent of things to come: armies, or segments of them, would become politicized in search of their own interests. It was only a short step to the intervention of soldiers in the running of the state itself. Today all African leaders, civilian and military alike, must keep one eye on the army. This is nowhere more evident than in Nigeria, whose large army—built up during the Biafran crisis in the late 1960s but reduced afterwards—remains a cause of political uncertainty and potential instability. Constitutional restorations of civilian rule in Nigeria and Ghana in 1979 could founder if army interests are not properly taken into account.

It is evident that soldiers are no longer on the political sidelines in African countries. They have become increasingly politicized, and many of Africa's rulers are soldiers or ex-soldiers. However, the politicization of the army patently has not meant the militarization of the state. On the contrary, within the military political and personal considerations may very well get in the way of organizational hierarchy and the chain of command. Thus if the conditions of militarism are somewhat contingent even within the army, how much more contingent must they be within the government of the state? Under military rulers, most African governments have very little resembled a disciplined, praetorian agency—if at all. Seldom have soldiers ruled as a corporate entity; one of the very few examples of a corporate government was the second Ghanaian military regime of General Ignatius Kutu Acheampong (1972–78).

In sum, two general characteristics of the African military stand out and go some distance toward explaining why the African state under military rule has had so little militarism in it.[22] These are (1) the general absence of a modern military tradition in most African countries, and (2) the inability of military organizations to

22. John Ravenhill, "Comparing Regime Performance in Africa: The Limitations of Cross National Aggregate Analysis," *Journal of Modern African Studies* 18, 2 (1980).

withstand penetration by sociocultural norms any more successfully than most other state organizations.

(1) The military in most African countries has yet to establish
meaningful "traditions" based on past "glory," real or invented;
where traditions exist, they are usually colonial in character and
therefore somewhat tainted and suspect; there are few national
military traditions. The officer corps is not a military caste in the
way that it has been in militaristic societies—for instance, Prussia
or Japan. There is neither a history of military service by particular families—as there has been in Britain, the United States, or
the Soviet Union[23]—nor (with few exceptions) one in which particular ethnic groups monopolize the supply of recruits for the officer corps.[24] (Ordinary recruits are sometimes drawn from so-
called "martial tribes," a practice established during colonial
times and sometimes deliberately discontinued at independence.)
With the exception of the Sudanese, the officer corps of most African armies is largely a new class composed of first-generation
recruits drawn for the most part from different social strata.
(However, the "generation" is divided by "age-grades," which
can sometimes be a cause of conflict within the army.) The officer
corps of most African countries has been fully Africanized and is
now being staffed increasingly by young university and high
school graduates who view the military as a career promising income security and upward mobility. Older officers promoted from
the ranks at independence represent a diminishing segment of the
officer ranks.

(2) African military organizations exhibit many of the social
cleavages that disturb and sometimes disrupt the civil organizations of the state. It cannot be assumed that military training and
indoctrination in the ideals of discipline and obedience will take
precedence over ethnic, familial, or personal loyalty in situations
where soldiers are forced to choose between military duty and personal duty. The aforementioned intra-generational age-grade divisions within the officer corps also contribute to social cleavages.
Thus military commanders often cannot count on the obedience of
soldiers in a crisis situation, and command within military organizations—let alone the larger state organization under military
rule—must be exercised with the awareness and adroitness of a
politician if the command is to be obeyed. The general vul-

23. A movement toward the closure of the military elites (among others) in Soviet
society is analyzed by Alexander Yanov, *Detente After Brezhnev: The Domestic Roots
of Soviet Foreign Policy* (Berkeley: Institute of International Studies, 1977).

24. The domination of northern Kabré officers in the Togolese army is one of the
few exceptions. See Decalo, *Coups and Army Rule in Africa*, pp. 105–7.

nerability of state organizations and agencies to societal norms and influences does not stop at the barracks gates in Africa. In criticism of the portrayal of African military organizations as autonomous and instrumental in character, Dudley observes:

> The army officer or soldier is no more "detribalized" or "alienated" than the university don; no more modernity-oriented than the civil servant, nor is he more nationally conscious than the party-politician or the intelligentsia in general. . . . Apart from their overwhelming superiority in matters of force and violence and a special skill in the use of arms, the armed forces have no characteristics which are not shared by other members of the community. In the developing nations, it is this which constitutes the main weakness of the military in politics once they have seized power. The monopoly of force enables the military to intervene in the political process and to seize power. Their incapacity to rule derives, not from the fact that they lack legitimacy, but that, like the politicians they have ousted, they get caught in the cross currents of personal, lineage, clan, ethnic and other loyalties and sentiments which influenced and shaped the actions of the politicians.[25]

In an analysis of soldier rulerships in Africa—especially the more successful and enduring ones—it is impossible not to be struck by their strongly political and personal elements and easy to believe that the societies being ruled call for these. Successful soldier-rulers are political men. Mobutu of Zaire has managed to govern what in the early 1960s was widely held to be an ungovernable society, not because he is a skilled military commander, but rather because he is an accomplished practitioner of the ruler's craft. The differences separating civilian and military rule in Africa have been overdrawn and the similarities overlooked or underestimated.

The major problem that confronts soldier-rulers who desire to remain in power is similar to the problem civilian rulers face—that is, they must find power and authority beyond those their arms provide, and ultimately they must gather the wide political support and acquiescence necessary to rule.[26] In government "the military organization immediately becomes vulnerable to social and political pressures from which it was hitherto . . . protected, and is required to operate under conditions and for purposes for which it was not designed."[27] Soldier-rulers are no less dependent than civilian rulers upon securing the cooperation of the civilian

25. B. J. Dudley, "The Military and Politics in Nigeria: Some Reflections," in *Military Profession and Military Regimes*, ed. Jacques van Doorn (The Hague: Mouton, 1969), p. 208.

26. This is not the problem of military interlopers eager to hand power back to the civilian politicians.

27. Geoff Lamb, "The Military and Development in Eastern Africa," *Bulletin of the Institute of Development Studies* 4, 4 (September 1972): 21–22.

apparatus of government—the bureaucracies, the courts, the local authorities, and so forth—nor are they enabled by military might alone to enhance the power of the state and insulate its agents and agencies against the forces and influences of society. They cannot entirely ignore any influential group—not even the politicians. Acquiescence can perhaps be achieved solely by coercion, but support and acceptance cannot. Beyond a brief honeymoon period following a coup against an unpopular or discredited regime, support and acceptance must be cultivated by the only means possible— that is, political means of persuasion, promises, and inducements of whatever kind. A successful military ruler, like his civilian counterpart, must possess or somehow acquire the political arts. In political life, especially in African states, military power is not a substitute for political institutions any more than civilian power is. Like civilian power, it can be lost; military rulers are themselves victims of coups. General Yakubu Gowon, the ruler of Nigeria from 1966 until 1975, and in some respects a skilled practitioner of the political arts, was unable to prevent the takeover of his power by a more dynamic and popular military leader. Such is the uncertain stuff of African personal rule that military and civilian rulers alike must confront.

Clientelism, Corruption, and Pluralism

Personal rule, in contrast with institutional rule, needs arrangements by which uncertainty and potential instability can be reduced and some degree of political predictability obtained. Power itself is no guarantee of stability, for it depends on skill, resources, and fortune, and these can change. Something more than power is needed that can at least partly compensate for the absence of institutions.

Systems of personal rule are strongly marked by a desire for personal power—one might even say a love of power—and by the skills and constraints that affect the attainment and holding of personal power, but this is not the sole feature of such regimes. Although there is much personal power in these regimes, there is also some legitimacy in all but the most tyrannical. The game of personal politics is not an activity involving solely fortune and power; it is not a wrestling match engaged in by political strongmen. Rather it involves alliances, collaboration, and cooperation. Leaders in such a game have a need for lieutenants, clients, and other followers. It is certainly true that followers may be opportunists who attach themselves to leaders in anticipation of benefits to be derived from backing a successful political entrepreneur. Opportunism and expediency are important elements in the behavior of followers, but they do not account in full for the durability of some of Africa's personal rulers and the stability of their regimes because opportunism and expediency are notorious for their susceptibility to change. Personal rulers, we presume, sleep at night not only out of a knowledge that they have power, but also from knowing that followers are committed to their incumbency for reasons beyond pure expediency.

The arrangements by which regimes of personal rule are able to secure a modicum of stability and predictability have come to be spoken of as "clientelism"—a system of patron-client ties that bind leaders and followers in relationships not only of mutual assistance and support, but also of recognized and accepted inequality between big men and lesser men.[28] The ties extend usually from the center of a regime—that is, from the ruler to his lieutenants, clients, and other followers, and through them to their followers, and so on. The image of clientelism is one of extensive chains of patron-client ties. The substance and the conditions of such ties can be conceived of as the intermingling of two factors: first, the resources of patronage (and the interest in such resources, which can be used to satisfy wants and needs) may be regarded as

28. The literature on clientelism, the origins of which lie in social anthropology and history more than in political science, has grown enormously in recent years. We draw attention only to those studies which seem particularly perspicacious and which are more directly relevant to African political studies. For a recent outstanding compendium of articles on clientelism, see Steffen W. Schmidt, James C. Scott, Carl Landé, and Laura Guasti, eds., *Friends, Followers and Factions: A Reader in Political Clientelism* (Berkeley, Los Angeles, London: University of California Press, 1977). See also Elizabeth Colson, "Competence and Incompetence in the Context of Independence," *Current Anthropology* 8, 1–2 (February–April 1967): 92–111; Lloyd A. Fallers, *The Social Anthropology of the Nation-State* (Chicago: Aldine Publishing Co., 1974); Robert R. Kaufman, "The Patron-Client Concept and Macro-Politics: Prospects and Problems," *Comparative Studies in Society and History* 16, 3 (June 1974): 284–308; Keith R. Legg, *Patrons, Clients and Politicians: New Perspectives on Political Clientelism* (Berkeley: Institute of International Studies, 1975); René Lemarchand, "Political Clientelism and Ethnicity in Tropical Africa: Competing Solidarities in Nation-Building," *American Political Science Review* 66, 1 (March 1972): 68–90; René Lemarchand and Keith Legg, "Political Clientelism and Development: A Preliminary Analysis," *Comparative Politics* 4, 2 (January 1972): 149–78; Guenther Roth, "Personal Rulership, Patrimonialism, and Empire-Building in the New States," *World Politics* 20, 2 (January 1968): 194–206; Richard Sandbrook, "Patrons, Clients, and Factions: New Dimensions of Conflict Analysis in Africa," *Canadian Journal of Political Science* 5, 1 (March 1972): 104–19; James C. Scott, "Patron-Client Politics and Political Change in Southeast Asia," *American Political Science Review* 66, 1 (March 1972): 91–113; M. G. Smith, "Historical and Cultural Conditions of Political Corruption Among the Hausa," *Comparative Studies in Society and History* 6, 2 (January 1964): 164–94.

the motivation for the personal contracts and agreements of which patron-client ties consist; and second, the loyalty, which transcends mere interest and is the social "cement" that permits such ties to endure in the face of resource fluctuations.[29]

Both of these factors are important as an explanation for some of the stable elements in African personal rule. However, it is important to avoid succumbing to the temptation of sociological determinism which such an explanation contains: regimes of personal rule may to some extent be structured and stabilized by clientelist ties, but such ties are always conditional. Individual patron-client linkages are contingent upon the persons in a relationship and ordinarily cannot outlast them—unlike institutions. While systems of patron-client ties can survive beyond the lives or fortunes of the persons bound up in them—as do institutions— they are different from political institutions insofar as they are much affected by the power and fortunes of individuals. A change of ruler, as a result of a successful coup, for instance, can alter greatly both an existing clientelist pattern and the political fortunes of those entangled in it. Clientelist systems do not consist of legitimate and enforceable rules governing the exercise of power or the struggle for it. Clientelism is not a complete substitute for institutionalized politics, but neither is it merely a type of praetorianism. It is a structure between "civil society" and the "state of nature."

As we have noted, resources are necessary to respond to interests and to satisfy the wants and needs that stand behind them. For instance, in Congo-Brazzaville

> [President Fulbert] Youlou's political system [before he was deposed in 1963] depended heavily on large-scale finance to keep flowing the patronage on which it relied. . . . Since public funds and French subsidies were barely sufficient to keep the state intact, much less to sustain his broader ambitions, Youlou's foreign and economic policies were based on attracting more funds, and his support was available to the highest bidder.[30]

But resources alone are inadequate to operate a stable and predictable system of rule. If resources declined or interest in them increased, a system that was dependent on resources alone would be thrown into turmoil from the resulting dissatisfaction of those whose expectations had not been met. Since all political systems

29. See Carl H. Landé, "The Dyadic Basis of Clientelism," in *Friends, Followers and Factions*, ed. Schmidt, Scott, Landé, and Guasti, pp. xiii–xxxvii.

30. John A. Ballard, "Four Equatorial States," in *National Unity and Regionalism in Eight African States*, ed. Gwendolen M. Carter (Ithaca: Cornell University Press, 1966), p. 295.

are subject to unpredictable resource fluctuations in relation to the demand for them—especially those in poverty-ridden Africa—rulers and regimes that relied only on resources to achieve stability would find themselves in a kind of difficulty that perhaps even a resort to coercion could not overcome. Rulers require an allegiance that overrides dissatisfaction, disappointment, or disagreement and enables them to carry on during times of resource difficulty. They stand in need of loyalty—a steadying element that maintains organizations and relationships during times of trouble and over-rules the temptation to desert or "exit" (to borrow Hirschman's apt term).[31] Loyalty is tested in times of trouble—fair weather friends are opportunists, not loyalists.

In personal regimes loyalty understandably is a phenomenon more focused toward persons than organizations or institutions—particularly persons who share common ethnic or kindred bonds. But loyalty must be cultivated and earned. Resources will help rulers to build stable followings, but rulers must elicit devotion from their followers as well. To gain loyalty, leaders must deserve it. They must not appear weak, indecisive, or irresolute. If they do, not only will the confidence of supporters flag, but the ambition of opponents will increase; as a result, the balance of personal-factional power in the state may be threatened, with accompanying unpredictability and insecurity. Insofar as rulers appear strong, decisive, confident, and otherwise deserving of support, it is likely they will have the loyalty of followers and supporters and perhaps even the general public.[32] (The generalized loyalty of a wider public to a personal ruler is probably less important than the more immediate and direct loyalty of lieutenants and clients.) It may be suggested that by appointing clients to offices a ruler can make those clients personally loyal, but such clients may be merely dependent rather than loyal. To be loyal they must be steadfast in the face of temptations to desert; dependence means to be deprived of the freedom to leave.

In sub-Saharan Africa personal political loyalty, like social loyalty, is most likely to be cultivated and flourish in little societies such as communal or kinship groups, where members can exercise

31. Albert O. Hirschman, *Exit, Voice and Loyalty: Responses to Decline in Firms, Organizations and States* (Cambridge, Mass.: Harvard University Press, 1970), esp. pp. 76–105.

32. Loyalty and devotion can persist—and even intensify—in situations of great adversity, provided the leader remains confident and unperturbed. It is well known that military leaders of determination and courage have retained the devotion of their soldiers during times of great danger to all, even in the face of inevitable defeat by overwhelming enemy forces. The phenomenon of resolution and courage meriting loyalty and devotion must be known to all great commanders.

the responsibility of providing security and assistance to other members if called upon to do so and can personally experience their gratitude and devotion. In such contexts personal confidence in the faithfulness and steadfastness of others can grow; furthermore, it is reciprocal and mutually reinforcing. Members who need assistance can have confidence that it will be provided by other members in a position to assist; members who lend assistance can have confidence that their generosity will be recognized and that their standing, honor, and respect within the group will be enhanced thereby. Those who give will come to be looked upon as the "big men" of the little society; they in turn will be able to count on the support of the smaller fry and can call upon it when needed. The process by which responsibility is met with loyalty and devotion in little societies is probably very similar to the process by which political followings are built in the wider context of the state in Africa.

As we have noted, clientelism depends not only on loyalty, but also on patronage; in practice the two are undoubtedly interwoven and indistinguishable. Because of the general poverty and underdevelopment of African countries and the restricted scope of the private sector, government has become the main dispenser of patronage and is perceived as such. The interest in patronage resources is directed specifically at persons with power, positions, and influence in the ruling councils of the state—that is, officeholders in the cabinet, the party, the army, the civil service, and parastatal organizations. These officeholders tend to monopolize the kinds of goods and services that other individuals and groups need or want; a marked feature of pre-industrial societies is the treatment of governmental offices as entitlements. The discretionary control of patronage resources entailed thereby provides an appropriate context for the development of patron-client ties. Incumbents are able to use the resources within their discretion to assist clients and followers and thereby maintain—and perhaps enlarge—their political base. Personal political credit can be extended to clients and called in when needed. In this way patron-client networks are created and repeated over and over again in societies whose political cultures generally incline people not only to condone but also to approve of clientelist arrangements. The networks permeate the ruling oligarchy and political class and extend downward into society, constituting a "structure" linking rulers directly to their clients and indirectly to the ruled. An illustration of the pervasiveness of such networks in personal rule can be seen in Austin's remarks about Ghana:

If there is a pervasive concept in Ghanaian politics it is that of "patron-age," or "clientage," conveying the notion of dependence. Big men are patrons with followers. And the lines of patronage in what is essentially a world of distributory politics radiate out through fine-spun webs of influence from the centre to the districts; and, of course, from the local up to the national level, in a search for mutual benefits in the "trade-off" between national and local leaders which again is characteristic of a great deal of Ghanaian political life. People—that is to say individual families or the majority in a village, chiefdom, district, or even region— give their support to those who can look after them.[33]

Austin points out that a clientelist system is dependent for its successful operation on the availability of resources so that the wants and needs of political clients and supporters can be satisfied, and that in the Ghanaian case there has not been enough loyalty or affection to sustain ruling parties or patrons "when the goods run out."

There is therefore a need, most strongly felt by the ruler and the oligarchy, for resources to maintain the patronage system and political support. After independence this need initially contributed to the demand for Africanization of the civil service and other agencies of government (including the military) in all but a few countries (two notable exceptions were Malawi and Ivory Coast, which were much slower to Africanize and relied for much longer on expatriate manpower). When the Africanization resources were "spent," so to speak, African rulers who were short on loyalty had to search for additional resources by which the patronage polity upholding their rule could be fueled. A major reservoir of fresh resources has been the alien-dominated private economy, which most African governments have sought to bring under the control of state or private African agencies. The movement to indigenize and nationalize the foreign-owned private economy has been widespread throughout sub-Saharan Africa wherever such an economy has existed. (There have been some extremely poor countries where such an economy hardly existed—e.g., Chad, Burundi, Rwanda, Malawi, Niger—or where the state has so far refrained from taking action—e.g., Ivory Coast, Cameroon, and to some extent Gabon and Liberia.) For example, such major industries as copper mining and smelting in Zaire and Zambia have been nationalized, as have several mineral enterprises in Ghana, phosphates in Togo and Senegal, iron ore and copper in Mauri-

33. Dennis Austin, "Ghana and the Return to Civilian Rule: 1," *West Africa* 2851 (4 February 1972): 115; see also Robert M. Price, "Politics and Culture in Contemporary Ghana: The Big Man–Small Boy Syndrome," *Journal of African Studies* 1, 2 (Summer 1974): 173–204.

tania, and diamonds in Sierra Leone; in Nigeria petroleum has been partially nationalized. In addition, there have been socialist-oriented nationalizations in such countries as Tanzania, Angola, Mozambique, Ethiopia, Somalia, Congo-Brazzaville, Benin, and Guinea.

A more direct and politically popular method of securing patronage resources has been the indigenization of smaller alien-owned businesses. Typically, African governments either have required or encouraged the transfer of such businesses to Africans—for instance, by withholding business licenses from non-citizens and providing loans to Africans to purchase such businesses—or have insisted on a greater African share in their ownership, management, and employment. A problem with this method for creating patronage resources—like the strategy of Africanization of the public service—is that a transfer of opportunities or assets can take place only once (although the new African owners and managers are now themselves in a position to provide or withhold patronage—very likely to or from their friends and relatives), which means that the resources are perhaps better regarded as spent consumer goods than as political investments which can create further political utilities. Furthermore, the transfers of resources may create considerable resentment if certain classes or ethnic units are favored to the exclusion of others. In general, however, this method has been politically advantageous for African governments—especially against powerless aliens such as the Asians of East Africa (in particular in Amin's Uganda) and the Lebanese in West Africa, whose commercial predominance had been resented by Africans.[34]

The transfers of resources from foreign owners to African governments or their supporters have not been without adverse consequences. The principal disadvantage has been that some nationalized corporations or indigenized private firms have been badly managed and their resources effectively wasted, resulting in serious economic difficulties in the medium and longer runs. This has happened in Tanzania and more dramatically and destructively in Zaire, where it has led to attempts to secure new public and private foreign participation and investment in the economy. Quite clearly, there are economic limits to methods of creating patronage resources in African countries.

34. For a general review of indigenization, see Leslie L. Rood, "Nationalisation and Indigenisation in Africa," *Journal of Modern African Studies* 14, 3 (1976): 427–47, and Ghai, ed., *Economic Independence*. For Uganda see Justin O'Brien, "General Amin and the Uganda Asians: Doing the Unthinkable," *The Round Table* 249 (January 1973): 91–104.

Related to the system of patronage in African personal rule is the phenomenon of political and administrative corruption, which is probably quite widespread. Corruption constitutes an important means by which individual wants and needs in a personal regime can be satisfied; it is a black market mode of conduct quite consistent with personally appropriated government yet fundamentally at odds with state rules and regulations, whose violation or evasion corrupt conduct entails.[35] In many African countries (although in some more than others) corruption is a prominent feature of public life and appears to be sustained by established cultural attitudes and expectations. Moreover, it is invited by the state apparatus, which contains both resources and opportunities for corruption and rules and regulations which can be abused for personal or private advantage.

In African countries where corruption has been reported to be particularly widespread, such as Ghana, Zaire, Liberia, Amin's Uganda, Central African Republic, and Nigeria (to mention a few), it is regarded as "a way of life." As such, it is difficult to evade—for instance, by a refusal to make or receive bribes. It is a practical and acceptable stratagem which affords one a workable way of looking after one's needs and interests and achieving income and security. One Ghanaian scholar has commented that "bribery (or corruption) affords the individual the greatest possible security. At present [in Ghana] the risk of being charged with giving or receiving a bribe is one in ten thousand."[36] Corruption is personal; it is between "you" and "me," to the detriment of an invisible and impersonal third party—the state or the public interest. Indeed, where corruption is rampant, it is as if state institutions, offices, rules, or regulations did not exist. LeVine quotes a Ghanaian as saying: "We Ghanaians are so accustomed to bribing our officials, and they to stealing our rate-moneys, that it would be considered odd if we didn't bribe and they didn't steal."[37] In Nigeria corruption has been described as "built into the present accepted value system of Nigerian society."[38] When several prominent officials in Mauritania were given light or suspended sentences by a lenient court after being found guilty of serious

35. For a valuable introduction, see James C. Scott, *Comparative Political Corruption* (Englewood Cliffs, N.J.: Prentice-Hall, 1972).

36. Opoku Acheampong, "Corruption: A Basis for Security?" *West Africa* 3053 (5 January 1976): 5.

37. Victor T. LeVine, *Political Corruption: The Ghana Case* (Stanford: Hoover Institution, 1975), p. 12.

38. *Africa Contemporary Record*, 1971–72, p. B 653.

offenses of corruption, the judge "had to expel enthusiastic supporters from the courtroom."[39]

Students of African corruption have noted that its incidence varies directly with the size of the state. Thus writing of Ghana,
LeVine observes: "A factor that probably contributed as much as
any other to the increased incidence and generalization of corruption in the 1950s bears mention . . .: the growth of state corporations and marketing boards."[40] He also observes that corruption
has tended to increase in relation to "the increased Ghanaization
of the civil service and government."[41] In effect, Africanization has
meant the penetration of the state apparatus by sociocultural
norms and expectations favorable to corruption. Furthermore, it is
probably correct to suppose that an expansion of government regulations will lead to increased corruption as individuals have to
evade more rules. For example, African governments have a neo-
mercantilist penchant to regulate diverse aspects of economy and
society by means of licensing, a particular area where bribery and
corruption have probably flourished, although they are notori-
ously difficult to detect, let alone correct. In some areas the establishment of onerous regulations which lead to evasion or
corruption has been more clearly visible. In Tanzania the adoption
of the Arusha Declaration in 1967—which established a leadership code which sought to make the conduct of party and government leaders accord with socialist principles in respect of property
ownership, personal income, and the like—led to evasions which
led to further attempts by the National Executive of the ruling
party to establish effective procedures for the code's enforcement.[42]
Clearly, the establishment of an effective third-party regulator of
the personal contracts that characterize personal rule in African
countries is a difficult undertaking. In Nigeria a leading economist
claimed that corruption will continue to be a way of life until the
ruling "aristocracy" itself ceases to be corrupt.[43]

From our discussion, we conclude that two general conditions
are necessary for clientelism to emerge: states with (1) weakly institutionalized and highly personalized governments and (2) plu-
ralistic societies and particularistic cultures. Ineffective institutions provide incumbents with the discretionary license to
appropriate public powers and resources for personal-political

39. Ibid., 1972–73, p. B 664.
40. LeVine, *Political Corruption*, p. 17.
41. Ibid., p. 16.
42. *Africa Contemporary Record*, 1973–74, p. B 262.
43. Reported in ibid., 1972–73, p. B 687.

purposes. Some of the bounty of the state will be consumed by the leaders, their friends, and relatives, and some will be distributed to followers and supporters. Followers will be attracted and aroused by a chance to enjoy patronage either immediately or at some future time. If a leader or patron is politically responsible as well as astute, he will cultivate relations of opportunity and cooperation and ultimately cement them into ties of loyalty and devotion. Patrons and clients will be disposed to seek each other out in a mutual search for security and advantage since declared government legislation and policies based on universalistic principles of merit or qualification are neither widely appreciated nor adhered to, with the consequence that they are not reliably implemented or enforced; nor, therefore, do they prompt political support or gratitude.

Personal rule may be thought of as connected indirectly to the underlying social conditions of an ethnically divided society. Roth suggests that

> one of the major reasons for the predominance of personal rulership over legal-rational legislation and administration in the new states [of Africa and Asia] seems to lie in a social, cultural, and political heterogeneity of such magnitude that a more or less viable complementary and countervailing pluralism of the Western type, with its strong but not exclusive components of universality, does not appear feasible.[44]

The actions of political leaders—certainly in Africa—have an important effect on the activation or suspension of ethnic prejudice and hostility and consequently on the degree of conflict or harmony among ethnic groups. But the game of personal politics is not specifically and directly concerned with questions of ethnicity, at least not in any deliberate way; rather it is an adaptation to immediate and direct requisites of power at the center of a state. Personal rule itself is primarily about powerful men at the center of a polity and only secondarily about powerful ethnic groups at its periphery. This is not to say that personal rulers can overlook questions of ethnicity, which are among the most important political questions in African countries today. Insofar as African rulers deal with such questions, they do so in terms of the stratagems and resources of personal rule—that is, offering or withholding patronage mostly, coercing occasionally. However, ordinarily it is the elite representatives and fiduciaries of ethnic groups, more than the general members, who gain privileges or suffer punishments under systems of personal rule.

44. Roth, p. 203.

Factions, Purges, and Rehabilitations

The formula of personal rule in contemporary Africa, of both civilian and military rulers, has been authoritarian political monopoly. Monopoly may be defined as the absence of competition; political monopoly means the absence of leaders or parties contesting for the control of the state. Without a monopoly a personal ruler must struggle for supreme power with rivals who do not accept his uncontested supremacy; such a struggle is characteristic of personal regimes when established rulers begin to lose their grip on power through advanced age or infirmity; crises of succession then take place, and potential new rulers struggle for supreme power, as happened in the Soviet Union after the death of Stalin and in China after the death of Mao Tse-tung.

The establishment of political monopolies by paramount rulers implies the elimination or subordination of rivals, but it need not imply the elimination of all political participation. Those who accept the hegemony of the political monopoly and the supremacy of the personal ruler may compete for spoils and patronage within the state. Factional politics is not only possible in a personal regime but probably inevitable. Quite understandably, as Lewis has pointed out in his critique of one-party monopolies in West Africa, such competition can lead to schisms, to purges, and even to plots within the ruling group.[45] One of the major characteristics of African personal regimes is internecine struggles of leaders and factions jockeying for positions of advantage and security within the regimes.

Under conditions of political monopoly, factionalism is the predominant type of political conflict which stops short of the use or threatened use of violence. Since open, legitimate political competition is forbidden, competition for power and position must take the form of rivalry among politicians and factions within the monopoly. By its nature factionalism tends to be an internal struggle for power and position within a group rather than an open contest among groups. When a factional struggle is transformed into a public, non-violent contest for state authority among leaders and rivals, factions have been transformed into parties. Linguistic evidence of a transformation is found in the evolutionary distinction between the terms "faction" and "party" in our political vocabulary.[46]

45. W. Arthur Lewis, *Politics in West Africa* (London: George Allen & Unwin, 1965), pp. 55–63.

46. See Giovanni Sartori, *Parties and Party Systems: A Framework for Analysis* (Cambridge: Cambridge University Press, 1976), pp. 3–13.

The presence of a political monopoly is not a sufficient reason to believe that a factional political process must also be present. An autocratic ruler may be so strong or a ruling oligarchy so united as to totally dominate the political stage and prevent factional rivalry. A case in point is the rule of President Kamazu Banda of Malawi, who succeeded in virtually eliminating all factionalism and totally subordinating all would-be leaders. Some rulers encourage rivalry among lieutenants to prevent a too prominent potential successor from emerging. For much of their tenures of rule, Presidents Kenyatta of Kenya and Léopold Senghor of Senegal presided over the factional process with considerable advantage to themselves. If unchecked, factionalism within a monopoly may deteriorate into a struggle which could tear the state apart. Zaire, Chad, Benin, Burundi, Congo-Brazzaville, and Uganda have experienced particularly severe factionalism, with deleterious consequences for the operations and stability of government. We therefore agree with the proposition that factionalism is bound to be a variable phenomenon both among and within African monopolistic regimes. However, we argue that when non-violent politics takes place within such regimes it is likely to be a politics of faction, and that when the political process of factionalism breaks down (as it sometimes does), it very often leads to schisms, purges, and plots—outward signs that the factional struggle has exceeded the bounds of relatively peaceful rivalry.

Being a type of politics, factionalism involves the gaining and holding of political power. Ordinarily the objects—that is, the prizes or spoils—of factional conflict are political offices and the patronage they control. Donal O'Brien writes that factionalism in Senegal "exists above all to promote the interests of [faction or "clan"] members through political competition, and its first unifying principle is the prospect of the material rewards of political success. Political office and the spoils of office are the very definition of success."[47] Barker has aptly summarized how the competitive mechanism of intra-party factionalism operates in Senegal: "Factional fights . . . tend to spread downward as potential factions at lower levels ally themselves with the challenger to dislodge the incumbent at the higher level."[48] Within political monopolies (of both civilian and military regimes), the presence of factional-

47. Donal B. Cruise O'Brien, *Saints and Politicians: Essays in the Organization of a Senegalese Peasant Society* (London: Cambridge University Press, 1975), p. 149.

48. Jonathan S. Barker: "The Paradox of Development: Reflections on a Study of Local-Central Political Relations in Senegal," in *The State of the Nations: Constraints on Development in Independent Africa*, ed. Michael F. Lofchie (Berkeley, Los Angeles, London: University of California Press, 1971), p. 60, and "Political Factionalism in Senegal," *Canadian Journal of African Studies* 7, 2 (1973): 287–303.

ism corroborates the political no less than the economic truism that monopoly alone can do little to alter conditions of scarcity and the competition associated with it. In politics—whether factional, party-electoral, or otherwise—the number of contenders always exceeds the number of prizes; indeed without scarcity, the very idea of a prize is absurd. The only way to eliminate intra-monopoly factionalism is to make it normatively unacceptable or to suppress it.

The most important spoils of the factional struggle in African political monopolies are government and party offices, appointive as well as elective. Factional rivalry is likely for appointment to the National Executive of the ruling party or to the cabinet or promotions within such bodies, for the favor of electorates where intra-party electoral competition for party or government offices is permitted, for public patronage in the form of capital expenditures, and even for administrative posts within the regime. Factionalism is keyed to the personal drive for power of leading politicians and to the search for advancement, patronage, and protection of lesser figures. Whenever a measure of prominence is attained by a leader, clients tend to be attracted to him, and the ensuing patron-client networks tend to develop into political factions under his leadership.

The less autocratic and the more diplomatic the ruler, the more likely is factionalism, although it has been in evidence even in some of the most highly centralized ruler-dominated monopolies—for example, Gabon, where the ruling party has been purported to contain two broad factional groupings, one a "remnant" of former President M'Ba's "old guard" of conservative politicians, and the other a newly ascendant faction of young technocrats who were given place and prominence by M'Ba's successor, President Omar Bongo.[49] While a ruler's autonomous power and personal independence minimize the chances of factions to form, it is unusual in African monopolistic regimes for them to be absent altogether. Where rulers have not consolidated their hold on the political monopoly, serious internal factionalism and schisms have often resulted—for instance, in the early years of independence in Mauritania during the rise to power of President Moktar Ould Daddah,[50] in Chad throughout the unsettled regime of President Ngarta Tombalbaye (1960–75),[51] in Ethiopia both

49. *Africa Contemporary Record*, 1974–75, p. B 587.

50. Clement H. Moore, "One-Partyism in Mauritania," *Journal of Modern African Studies* 3, 3 (1965): 409–20.

51. J. F. Froelich, "Tension in Chad," in *Conflicts in Africa* (London: International Institute for Strategic Studies; Adelphi Papers No. 93, 1972), pp. 42–52.

before and after Haile Selassie's downfall in 1974, in Sudan and
Somalia under both civilian and military rulers, and in Congo-
Brazzaville, not only during the uncertain regime of President
Youlou (1960 until the "revolution" of August 1963), but also
since then under military rulers.[52]

In addition to political factors, factionalism can be encouraged
by sociological factors—particularly the mode of group affiliation
in a society. In many African states intra-monopoly factionalism—like the competitive party struggles of pre-independence
days—tends to be rooted in the kinship, clan, and ethnic patterning of social relationships. A paradigm is Senegal's "clan" politics,
by which established norms of friendship, clientelism, kinship,
and sectarian brotherhood serve as the models by which intra-
party factions are fashioned. In Congo-Brazzaville factionalism is
rooted in kinship, clan, and ethnic ties;[53] in Sierra Leone it grows
out of a similar social base—particularly chiefdoms—but religious sects and secret societies are important as well.[54] In Liberia
the factionalism of the former ruling True Whig Party was rooted
in the divisions among leading families of the Americo-Liberian
immigrant oligarchy.[55] In Zambia leadership and factional alliances within the ruling United National Independence Party
(UNIP) have had a strong basis in ethnicity and regionalism, as
they have in Kenya's ruling Kenya African National Union
(KANU).[56] Even in socialist Tanzania, where factionalism and
the particularism and personalism it implies are officially frowned
upon, evidence from the 1965 and 1970 elections suggests that kinship, clan, and ethnic considerations go some distance toward determining (among other things) the degree of support for
individual ruling party candidates for electoral office. As in other
East African countries, voting in Tanzanian national elections has
been strongly influenced by what Hyden and Leys call "the tradition of the 'big man' who can provide patronage and protection for
a local clientele, a tradition which accepts inequality as 'natural'
and sees politics as a means of solving individual and local prob-

52. Decalo, *Coups and Military Rule in Africa*, pp. 123–72.

53. J. M. Lee, "Clan Loyalties and Socialist Doctrine in the People's Republic of
Congo," *The World Today* 27, 1 (January 1971): 40–46.

54. Roger Tangri, "Central-Local Politics in Contemporary Sierra Leone," *African Affairs* 77, 307 (April 1978): 165–73.

55. Stephen Hlophe, "Ruling Families and Power Struggles in Liberia," *Journal of
African Studies* 6, 2 (Summer 1979): 75–82.

56. For other aspects of factionalism, see Dennis L. Dresang, "Ethnic Politics,
Representative Bureaucracy and Development Administration: The Zambian Case,"
American Political Science Review 68, 4 (December 1974): 1605–17.

lems through the provision of grass-roots support for the 'right' patron."[57]

Where intra-party electoral competition is permitted—for example, in Tanzania, Kenya, Zambia, and Senegal—it stimulates a type of factionalism resembling the party model of the "political machine," in which support for leaders is always conditional upon the tangible benefits or favors (i.e., the patronage) they promise to deliver to supporters.[58] Typically, the concept of "benefits" applies at a local-communal or a personal-tangible level or both, unlike the more abstract concept of a "policy" that is in line with one's ideological or class interests. It is quite likely that the concept of politics as a system of benefits is very widespread throughout the sub-Saharan region.

Political monopoly poses the problem not only of divisive factionalism, but also of how to control potential rivals who may exhibit excessive ambition, insufficient loyalty, or other dangerous or unacceptable behavior. The ruling oligarchy cannot operate in an arena of unlicensed political maneuver; some requirements must be placed on its members lest factional politics deteriorate into plots, conspiracies, or even civil war (between factions transformed into private armies—as in Chad after the fall of President Tombalbaye in 1975). If there is but one ruling group to which all leading politicians must belong, then the threat or use of expulsion may be a method of controlling them, while offers of rehabilitation may reduce their temptation to conspire against the regime from outside the ruling group. African rulers have resorted to both purges and rehabilitations to retain command of the somewhat uncertain situations that factional politics tend to foster.

Purges and rehabilitations are intimately associated with political monopoly. The two have been commonly associated with Communist parties—especially those of the Soviet Union, Eastern Europe, and China. With the rise of political monopolies in sub-Saharan Africa, there has been a corresponding rise of purges and rehabilitations as rulers have attempted to maintain control of regimes in which open political competition and criticism are forbidden. "To purge" is to remove from an organization persons

57. Goran Hyden and Colin Leys, "Elections and Politics in Single-Party Systems: The Case of Kenya and Tanzania," *British Journal of Political Science* 2, 4 (October 1972): 416.

58. Hyden and Leys regard the "political machine" model the most appropriate for understanding the 1969 and 1970 elections in Kenya and Tanzania respectively (ibid). The best account of this model in African political studies remains Zolberg, *Creating Political Order*, esp. chs. 1 and 5.

accused of being disloyal to the organization or ruler or undermining his authority or the unity of the regime; disobedience and excessive independence typify the grounds for purging. Purges may be concocted, as it were, to justify a removal for which there are no grounds other than the ruler's or some other important leader's displeasure. Webster defines a "purge" as "a ridding, as of a nation or party, of elements or members regarded as treacherous, disloyal, or suspect." The purge of members is a stratagem available predominantly to rulers of a single, closed membership unit; if the membership unit is a nation, one is "exiled" from it; if it is a court, one is "barred"; if a school, "expelled." The linguistic conventions governing the use of these cognates reveal that the actions conveyed are the prerogatives of the authorities in charge. In African systems of personal rule it is typically the ruler who enjoys the prerogative to purge as well as to rehabilitate—that is, to restore outcasts to political membership within the political monopoly.

In Africa the political monopoly is sufficiently attractive as a membership unit for purging and rehabilitation to be effective methods of ruler control. Where the prizes of politics are available only within one membership group, to be deprived of membership or to be restored to membership is to have one's political fortune greatly affected. To be sure, some leaders may enjoy sufficient prestige not to be totally deprived by purging or dependent on rehabilitation—for example, Oginga Odinga, who was excluded from the leadership of the ruling party of Kenya, yet who retained considerable status and power in the polity, but who nevertheless expressed a desire to be restored to a place of leadership within the oligarchy. For African politicians, no less than for politicians elsewhere, the political wilderness is an unhappy place.

As we have noted, in systems of personal rule rivals to the paramount leader cannot be condoned. Where independently powerful rival leaders emerge and are not purged, serious internal party difficulties may arise—for example, schisms—which may threaten not only the ruler, but also other members of the oligarchy and the monopoly itself. In Niger, for instance, the failure of former President Hamani Diori to purge the ruling party politburo of several strong-willed and independent leaders has been seen as a contributing cause of the downfall of his regime by a military coup in 1974.[59] Rival leaders can be threatened with removal or removed even for vocal criticism of the ruler, the re-

59. Richard Higgott and Finn Fuglestad, "The 1974 Coup d'Etat in Niger: Towards an Explanation," *Journal of Modern African Studies* 13, 3 (1975): 387.

gime, or its policies because such criticism may cause the ruler political embarrassment, or (more seriously) it may suggest that his authority can be defied. Clearly, in systems of personal rule public criticism cannot be tolerated, even if private criticism can be. In Zambia public criticism once provoked President Kenneth Kaunda to issue a thinly veiled threat of political banishment: "Some MPs," he is reported to have said in a 1975 speech to the National Assembly, "have . . . been speaking as if they were not members of the party and as if this Government was not theirs. Their anti-party and anti-Government mouthings have, I am afraid, left some of us with the impression that they are seeking to be an opposition party in our one-party participatory democracy."[60]

Ghana under Nkrumah presents the analyst with striking early evidence of the use of purges and rehabilitations in contemporary African politics. By 1960 effective party opposition had disappeared, and political conflict among rival leaders and factions increased within the ruling Convention People's Party (CPP). Apter writes that Nkrumah's famous 1961 "Dawn Broadcast" (in which the personal corruption and opportunism of party leaders were publicly criticized) enabled the militant socialist faction in the CPP to force the dismissal of some leading ministers. But in consequence "Party purges and attacks . . . so weakened the CPP that there were few on whom Nkrumah could rely for efficient and sensible administration and government."[61] Some of those purged were later rehabilitated; others remained in political limbo. The purges had been an attempt to purify the party as an ideological instrument of socialism, but the unintended effect was clearly that government operations were hampered by banishing talented persons. Eventually the incapability of government affected the power position of Nkrumah himself.

In Malawi the right to purge and rehabilitate has been an unquestioned and exclusive privilege of the ruler. President Banda has used his prerogative repeatedly and without hesitation since independence in 1964. High government and party officials have been purged for questioning Banda's policies, demonstrating a measure of independence, or not exhibiting sufficient personal devotion to Banda; lesser officials have been removed typically for failing to meet the President's avowedly puritanical standards of

60. Quoted in *Africa Contemporary Record*, 1975–76, p. B 383.
61. David E. Apter, *Ghana in Transition*, 2nd ed., rev. (Princeton: Princeton University Press, 1972), p. 348; also see Dennis Austin, *Politics in Ghana: 1946–1960* (New York and London: Oxford University Press, 1964).

morality. The most dramatic purge was in the cabinet in 1964, when six of the most talented and vigorous members challenged Banda's authority to determine policy. Three members were dismissed and three resigned, causing a crisis in the government. In the following purge of the ruling Malawi Congress Party (MCP), it was reported that "over a third of the country's district MCP committees were dissolved and successors [personally] appointed by the [then] prime minister."[62] Not only were dissidents purged from the party, but also a number of them were forced to flee the country and seek asylum abroad. Since the purges there has been repeated emphasis on the *personal* loyalty of party members to the ruler. MCP officeholders have almost always been removed by Banda on the grounds of "gross breach of party discipline"—a rule that is sufficiently flexible to include a variety of party offenses, ranging from personal opportunism and factional rivalry to moral or legal impropriety. In cases of local intra-party factionalism and rivalry, President Banda's tight personal rule has been evident in his prompt dismissal of officeholders and sometimes in his outright dissolution of local party committees without prior consultation with anyone. It is obvious from all accounts that the President runs his party the way he runs his country: with absolutely no patience for anyone who fails to exhibit total loyalty or who runs afoul of his personal moral standards.[63]

Leading politicians may be purged for a lack of ideological fervor or militancy as well. Understandably, these grounds are likely to be cited in more militant regimes. In Guinea President Sékou Touré has repeatedly reminded government officials and party cadres of their duty to serve the people and has warned irresponsible and undisciplined leaders of the penalties for their actions. In Mozambique the Frente de Libertação de Moçambique (FRELIMO) has been purged of leaders accused by President Samora Machel of corruption and opportunism—problems of new political monopolies, in which there is a rush for spoils. FRELIMO's post-revolutionary problems illustrate the vulnerability of even relatively well organized movement regimes to opportunism. In 1976 it was reported that "infiltrators" were being purged from the party.[64]

62. Samuel W. Speck, Jr., "Malawi and the Southern African Complex," in *Southern Africa in Perspective: Essays in Regional Politics*, ed. Christian P. Potholm and Richard Dale (New York: Free Press, 1972), p. 211.

63. See *Africa Contemporary Record*, 1973–74, pp. B 210–11, and 1974–75, p. B 233.

64. Ibid., 1975–76, pp. B 276–77.

In Tanzania attempts to transform the ruling party monopoly into a moral community have invited the use of the purge. It became apparent in the mid-1960s that under the influence of President Nyerere Tanzania was moving in a definitely socialist direction, and issues of leadership merit and probity arose. It became a conviction that a strong and ideologically disciplined party required exemplary leaders. In the words of Nyerere, "to build socialism you must have socialists."[65] Some leaders did not share this conviction either in their beliefs or in their actions, and were bound to arouse concerns about party loyalty and ideological commitment. Oscar Kambona, then Secretary-General of the party, was one such leader. When the Arusha Declaration with its stringent leadership code was adopted, Kambona was endorsing personal ambition and a leader's entitlement to accumulate wealth, creating pressures within the party for his removal. In an increasingly untenable position, he was forced to resign the secretary-generalship and leave the country. Later he was asked to return and face a judicial inquiry into his personal wealth, but he did not. In a 1970 treason trial he was accused in absentia of being the principal conspirator in a 1968–69 plot to overthrow the government.[66] The Kambona affair was the most prominent of a number of leadership purges and removals in Tanzania resulting from Nyerere's determination to move the country to the left. With the adoption of the Arusha Declaration, the National Executive Committee of the party was given powers to expel members who did not heed the party press exhortations to "measure up" to the new standards or "quit."

Africa's rulers have had recourse to the practice of political rehabilitations as often as to purges. Sometimes rulers have to purge previously loyal lieutenants whom they may wish to rehabilitate as soon as possible. This appeared to be the case in Malawi in the 1973–74 purge and rehabilitation of Aleke Banda (no relation to the President), an extremely able cabinet minister who found himself the unfortunate subject of press speculation that he was the most likely successor to the President. He was duly purged but was rehabilitated a year later, when the President was reported to have accepted his "apologies and plea for forgiveness."[67] In January 1980 Banda was purged again for violations of party disci-

65. Quoted in Helge Kjekshus, "Parliament in a One-Party State—the Bunge of Tanzania, 1965–70," *Journal of Modern African Studies* 12, 1 (1974): 31.

66. See John Dickie and Alan Rake, *Who's Who in Africa: The Political, Military, and Business Leaders of Africa* (London: African Buyer and Trader Publications, 1973), pp. 506–7.

67. *Africa Contemporary Record*, 1974–75, p. B 233.

pline. In Zaire, foreign minister Nguza Karl-I-Bond, a Lunda from Shaba Province, was sentenced to death at the 1977 "treason trials" which followed the humiliating invasion of Shaba by exiles opposed to the regime of President Mobutu. The sentence was not carried out, however. Partly in response to the wishes of Western countries and partly out of considerations for Lunda and Shaba informal representation in the government, Mobutu restored Karl-I-Bond to his former position in 1979.[68] In Ivory Coast prominent political leaders who were implicated in what is now referred to as the "bogus plot" of 1963 have been rehabilitated; principal among them is Jean-Baptiste Mockey—at one time Vice-Premier and Secretary-General of the ruling party—whose involvement was considered a "frame-up" by President Houphouët-Boigny.[69] Houphouët-Boigny has endeavored to restore the injured parties to their former status. Mockey repeatedly declined all offers of "political rehabilitation," but following the Sixth Party Congress in 1975, his name appeared among the newly appointed members of the party political bureau.

In one-party monopolies newly created out of formerly competitive political situations, personal rulers are sometimes faced with petitions for admission from leaders of former competing parties. For example, Simon Kapwepwe and his associates in Zambia petitioned for membership in the ruling party, but the central committee of the ruling party barred Kapwepwe's entry and denied membership to his leading associates and followers; "Simon Kapwepwe found himself virtually a non-person—unable to make his views known since the media refusal to print anything he has said."[70]

In some African one-party monopolies attempts have been made to proceduralize and routinize the purge process. For instance, in Congo-Brazzaville, a militant, socialist-style regime, criticisms of complacency and lethargy—indeed "morbidity"—of the party and state cadres resulted in the creation in 1975 of a "Purge Commission" with powers to investigate the conduct of cadres and remove all who failed to meet the party's standards or allowed themselves to assume bourgeois habits and attitudes. In November 1975, President Marien Ngouabi announced "a systematic purge" to be conducted by selected members of the party political bureau.[71] In Congo-Brazzaville, as well as in some other militant socialist-style regimes, purges have been resorted to in the hope of

68. *Africa Confidential* 20, 7 (March 28, 1979): 7.
69. *Africa Contemporary Record*, 1975–76, p. B 729.
70. Ibid., 1973–74, p. B 327. 71. Ibid., 1975–76, p. B 471.

restoring or improving party discipline. However, the effectiveness of purge measures in what are usually patronage-based and fairly corrupt regimes remains doubtful.

Plots, Coups, and Successions

The political uncertainty associated with personal rule gives rise to types of political calculation and action which have ancient origins and have featured in political life through the centuries. One is jockeying and maneuvering to influence a ruler and to increase one's political advantage and security in a regime; a second is scheming and plotting to hold power in the state. The first is inherently non-violent; factional politics in personal regimes is a characteristic example. The second has an inherent potential for violence and political instability: it aims at displacing personal rulers (through plots and coups), protecting them (when a ruler himself resorts to scheming and plotting against real or imagined rivals), or installing successors. This second type of political calculation focuses directly on the ruler and is therefore highly contingent on his personal-political skill, vigor, and fortune. As we have noted, since constitutions are not institutionalized in African personal regimes or have not had their provisions regarding succession tested, and since incumbent rulers are inclined to retain power, the death or disability of a ruler may result in serious uncertainty owing to the fact that power politics rather than institutionalized conventions and procedures may have to resolve the succession issue.

Individuals resort to clandestine politics either when they are deprived of opportunities of competing freely and openly for influence or power in politics but still crave the influence and power that politics holds out, or when they believe they cannot win by open competition. The latter will be recognized as a problem of institutionalized democracies when appetite for power overrides acceptance of the democratic rules of the political game. Plotting is of less moment in institutionalized systems because it cannot escape being tarnished with illegitimacy and because even a successful plot to kill a ruler may scarcely harm a regime. (Institutionalized systems, unlike personal ones, are more likely to be vulnerable to the clandestine politics of terror, in which acts of kidnapping or hijacking are undertaken to force particular concessions from a government.) In systems of personal rule the opposite effect is likely: by bringing down the ruler, the plotters may very

well succeed in bringing down the regime. In Africa military plotters have been highly successful in this regard. Since the ruler may
be the only obstacle in the way of powerholding, he becomes the
focus not only of calculations and actions to depose him, but also of
counter-stratagems to protect him.

In addition to plots, such calculations and actions as maneuvering, scheming, conspiring, and spying belong to the category of
clandestine politics. To plot is to plan and contrive in a secret manner. By definition, to plot is to place oneself outside the law and to
show contempt for institutions or authorities. All governments invariably view plots as evil and illegitimate threats or acts. If they
are seen rather as actions involving personal risk and courage,
then we have reason to doubt the legitimacy of the regimes that are
being plotted against. Doubtless in the view of most people, to
have "plotted" against the regime of Idi Amin was to have placed a
concern for justice and decency before considerations of personal
welfare and to have performed the very actions of which heroes are
made. On this view it would be legally and morally impossible to
plot against a tyrant. Since the term plot contains connotations of
treachery and conspiracy, it is understandably a favorite term for
rulers themselves to employ to label actions that displease or
worry them.[72] Personal rulers in particular have a certain penchant for discovering plots. Some African rulers—most notably
President Touré of Guinea, whom we shall discuss in detail in
chapter 5 below—have had a tendency to exploit the obvious legitimacy-conferring properties accruing to rulers who are victims of
plots. To label a real or imagined activity a "plot" or a "conspiracy" is to provide *prima facie* grounds for imprisoning the so-called
plotters.

In terms of political logic it is certainly possible for rulers to plot
and conspire against their personal enemies, and given the uncertain character of personal rule in Africa, it would be difficult not to
believe that many rulers do so. Indeed, insofar as plotting is generic to personal rule, a ruler may be no less tempted by it than his
rivals or opponents. However, the legal vocabulary of the state,
unlike the analytic vocabulary of political science, can impair our
appreciation of the extent of government plotting. All governments, legitimate or otherwise, have a police and investigation apparatus for the surveillance of individuals and groups. In
democratically institutionalized governments, it is expected that

72. See Niccolo Machiavelli, *The Discourses*, ed. Bernard Crick (Harmondsworth:
Penguin Books, 1976), pp. 398–424. Machiavelli devoted a discourse to the political
theory of conspiracies.

such an apparatus will be properly employed and that it patently will not be used against opposition politicians or parties. (Public indignation at the discovery that it can be improperly used—as has happened in some Western democracies recently—bears vivid testimony to this expectation.) In personal regimes, where the surveillance apparatus is often at the disposal of the ruler, the only restraint barring its improper use may be the ruler's self-restraint. If he believes that his enemies are plotting against him or is uncertain what to believe, it is unlikely that he will restrain himself for long. But he will not refer to his police activities as "plots" against political opponents; rather they will be portrayed as necessary "investigations" or "surveillance" of the enemies of the people and their government.

The legitimacy-conferring value to victims of alleged plots would lead us to expect that not all of the reported plots in contemporary Africa have been genuine. Some may have been—indeed are likely to have been—plots by governments to discredit opponents. The allegation of plotting is a strong temptation, especially in societies where an unsophisticated public may be susceptible to persuasion by news media totally under government control. A feature of personal rule in Kenya (and many other personal regimes) has been repeated reports and warnings against alleged plotters seeking to undermine the stability and unity of the regime. For example, a 1973 report illustrates that the government was aware of alleged clandestine activities aimed at provoking instability and disunity. In a speech President Kenyatta warned of "disgruntled people out to sabotage the stability and good government of the country." The government, he added, "was fully aware of the actions of individuals who preached disunity; when the time came, they would be 'picked up one by one.' "[73] Such warnings have not lacked conviction; individuals have been arrested and detained without benefit of trial under the provisions of preventive detention legislation. It is worth noting that the individuals who have been accused of conspiracy and treachery and placed in detention have often been prominent politicians—some of them members of Parliament—vocal in their criticism of the government.[74] Most telling of personal rule, the government has justified detentions by accusing such critics of being "disloyal" to

73. Quoted in *Africa Contemporary Record*, 1973–74, p. B 171.

74. Ladipo Adamolekun observes that in Guinea the targets of plot allegations have been the very individuals and factions who have had a falling out with the ruler (*Afriscope* 5, 3 [March 1975]: 49); also see Ladipo Adamolekun, *Sekou Touré's Guinea: An Experiment in Nation Building* (London: Methuen & Co., 1976), p. 151.

the ruling party, most of all to the President. In institutionalized regimes the ultimate political crime is to act in contempt of the law and the constitution; in systems of personal rule contempt for the ruler is the extreme disloyalty. As the contemporary record of African politics reveals, the *amour propre* of rulers and other big men is frequently liable to be injured or offended and innocent disagreement construed as treachery. Outspoken critics of government must tread warily if they are to survive. In Guinea the accusation of plotting may have been fastened upon by the government as a convenient device for discrediting political opponents, securing legitimacy for the regime and sympathy for the ruler, and justifying the banishment and exile of perceived opponents.

While it is clear that the bogus plot may be useful to rulers or perhaps certain elites, it is undoubtedly true that many African rulers are apprehensive of genuine plots.[75] Although there are no distinctive associations between the style of personal rule and the frequency of genuine plots—and we have no way of knowing the frequency of genuine plots because of their clandestine character—there is reason to believe that plotting and conspiracy against rulers will be less likely in regimes that permit legal opposition—as in The Gambia and Botswana—or where factional politics has been given some latitude—as in Senegal and Kenya. Guinea is an excellent example of a regime where attempted closure on factional politics has been accompanied by continuous reports of plotting. Ghanaian political life became more prone to clandestine and violent activities after the suppression of legitimate opposition in 1960. Two attempts were made to assassinate President Nkrumah, once in August 1962 and once in January 1964.[76] A recurrence of plotting was reported after a successful military intervention against the civilian government of Prime Minister Kofi Busia in 1972. In independent Angola, where the issue of leadership has not been settled among the factions of the MPLA monopoly re-

75. In 1963 it was believed that Houphouët-Boigny and his regime in Ivory Coast were seriously threatened by a major plot involving most of the prominent leaders of the party and government. By 1971 it was "openly admitted in the Ivory Coast that the chief of the 'Sûreté' [had] exercised the unlimited powers given to such organs in developing countries to frame people and place on them unfounded charges, to mount an atmosphere of fear and terror and to provide the President with fabricated evidence" (*West Africa* 2810 [23 April 1971]: 446–47). For a background and analysis of this plot, which turned out to be bogus, see Aristide R. Zolberg, "Political Development in the Ivory Coast Since Independence," in *Ghana and the Ivory Coast: Perspectives on Modernization*, ed. Philip Foster and Aristide R. Zolberg (Chicago and London: University of Chicago Press, 1971), pp. 15–21.

76. Dennis Austin, "Ghana: Recent History," in *Africa: South of the Sahara, 1976–77* (London: Europa Publications, 1976), p. 360; see also Austin, *Politics in Ghana*, pp. 409–10.

gime, plotting has taken place among rival leaders. Plotting has been frequently reported in Chad (under the uncertain regimes of President Tombalbaye as well as his successors), in Sudan (under the military regime of Numeiri—by both soldiers and civilians), in Congo-Brazzaville (especially after the overthrow of President Youlou by the military in 1963), and in Benin (plotting within the military). In each of these countries, as well as in ethnically divided and conflict-ridden Burundi, rulers have had to contend with highly divisive factionalism, both inside and outside the regime. In regimes of tyrannical or near tyrannical rule plots and alleged plots have been a feature of the political landscape, as in Amin's Uganda, Sheikh Abeid Karume's Zanzibar, Macías's Equatorial Guinea, and Jean-Bédel Bokassa's Central African Empire. However, in the absolutist autocracies of Malawi and Gabon, plots appear to be less significant in political life.

Plots are aimed at strategic vulnerabilities in regimes, which means that they are aimed usually at persons—most often the ruler, but secondary leaders as well. Successful plots may result in the removal of a ruler by assassination, as happened in Togo in 1963, when President Olympio was one of the first Black African statesmen to be murdered. Since that time political killing has increased. On January 15, 1966, junior army officers ended Nigeria's first experiment with constitutional government and caused the killing of the Federal Prime Minister, Sir Abubakar Tafawa Balewa, the Premier of the Northern Region, Sir Ahmadu Bello, and Premier of the Western Region, Chief Samuel Ladake Akintola. In reprisal on July 29, 1966, northern army officers killed Major-General Johnson Aguiyi-Ironsi, head of the Federal Military Government, as well as the military governor of the Western Region. In February 1976 General Murtala Muhammed, who had toppled the Gowon regime in July 1975, was himself killed in a counter-military intervention which failed. In Chad after fifteen years as the ruler of an increasingly unstable and faction-ridden regime, President Tombalbaye was killed during a military overthrow of his unpopular regime in 1975. In equally unstable and faction-ridden Congo-Brazzaville, President Ngouabi was assassinated in 1977 in a struggle for power that did not succeed but provoked the reprisal murder of the Catholic Archbishop of Brazzaville by ethnic supporters of Ngouabi. As we have noted, some plots are hatched by governments against their critics or opponents. In Kenya some leading political personalities—most notably Tom Mboya in 1969 and Josiah Kariuki in 1975—were murdered, allegedly by assailants under contract to unknown public authorities. Some conspiracies may be based less on political motives and more on private revenge, as appears to have been the case in the assassination of Karume, the near tyrannical ruler of Zanzibar, in 1972. (Even though the political motive was less important, there was nevertheless a notable change in the character of the regime.)

A *coup d'état* is a bid for government power, normally by a sudden seizure of strategic points of power in a state and by the removal of the ruler and his government. There may be both successful and unsuccessful coups.[77] The fact that a coup entails the seizure of government in a sudden assertion of power means that it is likely to be—and most often is—an act of the military or a segment of it, although by no means all coups, even in contemporary Africa, have been initiated by soldiers. In 1966 Prime Minister Milton Obote of Uganda deposed the presidential head of state, Sir Edward Mutesa (the Kabaka of Buganda—technically not a ruler but a constitutional head of the Ugandan state) and seized control of the state (using the army as an instrument of his power). Prime Minister Chief Leabua Jonathan of Lesotho in effect seized control of the state in 1970 by apparently defying the will of the electorate (the electoral results were never published) and refusing to step down. In Swaziland in 1973 King Sobhuza II abolished the constitution. In successful coups rulers may be killed—as in Togo in 1963, Chad in 1975, Ghana in 1979, and Liberia in 1980—but most often they are placed in some form of detention—as happened initially in 1974 to Haile Selassie of Ethiopia (who died nearly a year later in mysterious circumstances), Maurice Yaméogo of Upper Volta (1966), David Dacko of the Central African Republic (1965), Alphonse Massamba-Débat of Congo-Brazzaville (1968), Mohammed Haji Ibrahim Egal of Somalia (1969), Diori of Niger (1974), Grégoire Kayibanda of Rwanda (1973), Modibo Keita of Mali (1968), and Daddah of Mauritania (1978). Others have been exiled, some fled into exile, and some were out of the country when the coup took place. Indeed, a ruler's absence from the country may be an important contributing factor in a successful coup, as it was in the first military coup in Ghana against President Nkrumah (1966), Idi Amin's

77. By January 1980 there had been more than forty successful coups in some twenty-one countries of sub-Saharan Black Africa since independence; in addition, there have been numerous unsuccessful coups in more than a dozen countries that we know of and likely others that remain hidden. It is impossible to know how many abortive coups there have been, and some unsuccessful coups may be bogus.

coup against President Obote (1971), and the military coup against General Gowon of Nigeria (1975).

The intimate connection between personal, non-institutional rule and military coups has been given considerable emphasis in political analysis.[78] The absence of effective institutional restraints is a critical factor disposing ambitious individuals to contemplate and engage in bids for political control; in particular, it deprives military leaders of a strong sense of obligation to carry out their duty according to the spirit and letter of the civil law and military regulations. In sum, it is the absence of an ethos against political involvement by the military or an expectation of forbearance shared by the military and the wider society. The United States military has never intervened in government in an unlawful way, not only because the constitution forbids it, but also because the military and everybody else believe that it is its duty not to; indeed such an action would be unthinkable.

During the initial post-independence years in most African countries new military leaders were seldom in a position to take political action even if they wanted to. (The Sudan, with its tradition of militarism, was an exception.) Most often it was incumbent civilian rulers who violated constitutional and institutional rules—for instance, by transgressing them to suit their political convenience. Gradually, the expectation of forbearance by the military was replaced by an ambition for power and domination, and by the second half of the 1960s there was less and less hesita-

78. The most important and influential analysis of this connection remains Huntington, esp. ch. 1. For various accounts of military intervention in African politics see the following: Henry Bienen, ed., *The Military Intervenes: Case Studies in Political Development* (New York: Russell Sage Foundation, 1968); Henry Bienen, "Military and Society in East Africa," *Comparative Politics* 6, 4 (July 1974): 489–517; Thomas S. Cox, *Civil-Military Relations in Sierra Leone: A Case Study of African Soldiers in Politics* (Cambridge, Mass., and London: Harvard University Press, 1976); Robert E. Dowse, "The Military and Political Development," in *Politics and Change in Developing Nations*, ed. Colin Leys (Cambridge: Cambridge University Press, 1969); Garth Glentworth and Ian Hancock, "Obote and Amin: Change and Continuity in Modern Uganda Politics," *African Affairs* 72, 288 (July 1973): 237–55; Jay E. Hakes, *Weak Parliaments and Military Coups in Africa: A Study in Regime Instability* (Beverly Hills and London: Sage Publications, 1973); Ernest W. Lefevre, *Spear and Scepter: Army, Policy and Politics in Tropical Africa* (Washington: Brookings Institution, 1970); Robin A. Luckham, *The Nigerian Military: A Sociological Analysis of Authority and Revolt, 1960–67* (Cambridge: Cambridge University Press, 1971); N. J. Miners, *The Nigerian Army, 1956–1966* (London: Methuen & Co., 1971); Keith Panter-Brick, ed., *Nigerian Politics and Military Rule: Prelude to the Civil War* (London: Athlone Press, 1970); Robert Pinkney, *Ghana Under Military Rule, 1966–1969* (London: Methuen & Co., 1972); Robert M. Price, "A Theoretical Approach to Military Rule in New States: Reference Group Theory and the Ghanaian Case," *World Politics* 23, 3 (1971): 399–430; Claude E. Welch, Jr., "Soldier and State in Africa," *Journal of Modern African Studies* 5, 3 (November 1967):

tion by the military to assert its political power. In this regard some analysts of military coups in sub-Saharan Africa refer appropriately to the phenomenon of contagion: once coups began to take place, they tended to occur with increasing frequency.[79] In place of constitutionalism, there emerged contrary expectations of authoritarianism and personalism, in which the checks on powerholders became the power of others and the fear of that power or personal loyalty to one's superiors. In the absence of loyalty to one's ruler, one is restrained from making a bid for power by simple prudence—one might not succeed and failure may very likely bring reprisal. But if one calculates that more than sufficient power is in one's possession, or can be with suitable planning, and that given the right opportunity one may very likely succeed—the paradigm situation of military leaders in African countries—then (because of the absence of effective institutions) nothing but fortune stands in the way of action. Thus in a system of personal rule there is a stronger predisposition for planning and perpetrating coups.

In systems of personal rule there is a greater likelihood of direct personal confrontation among powerholders because relationships are not mediated effectively by institutions or offices, and in consequence policy differences tend to become personalized. When the interests of soldiers are not taken into account or are harmed, it may seem that the person in command—the minister of defense or (more likely) the ruler himself—is directly responsible. His personal indifference or ill will—rather than broad impersonal constraints such as budgetary limitations—may be perceived as the source of the difficulty. Certainly the unemployed soldiers who killed President Olympio could very well have perceived that he personally stood in the way of their employment and advancement in the new Togolese army. (In effectively institutionalized systems feelings of personal ill will may be present, but institutional restraint prevents action from being taken. In addition, it is likely that one's personal ill will toward a superior will be tempered by an understanding of the impersonal factors that obstruct one's interests—Congress, the state of the economy, East-West diplomacy, public opinion, etc.) The intervention of the military in African politics has sometimes led to a marked increase in budgetary allocations for the armed forces.

305–22; and Aristide Zolberg, "Military Rule and Political Development in Tropical Africa: A Preliminary Report," in *Military Profession and Military Régimes*, ed. van Doorn, pp. 175–202.

79. See Welch, "Soldier and State in Africa," pp. 318–19.

Personal rulers may be disposed to interfere in the military, thereby violating the trust and authority of senior officers and the military's corporate integrity. A ruler may wish to promote his own clients in the army in violation of military regulations, or he may be more ambitious and attempt to alter the general character of the military, as did Nkrumah by introducing new military concepts, calling in Soviet advisers, and creating a military formation separate from the established armed forces. If the ruler himself is violating rules and understandings, why should the military leaders not violate rules to defend their interests? Moreover, if there are serious divisions and factionalism in the state—especially when society is disunited and the ruler is only very contingently in control—the ruler may request the military's involvement in politics by ordering the army to take action against a political enemy. Gutteridge has pointed out that such a request may place the ruler at risk "because of the implicit admission of weakness which is involved."[80] A weak ruler may not be able to count on the obedience of the army, and an attempt to exercise authority over soldiers in a manner contrary to their perceived interests may provoke his downfall at their hands. Such a ruler is particularly vulnerable in a personal conflict with a military commander who may intervene for personal reasons. General Amin overthrew President Obote in 1971 when it became clear that Obote was seeking Amin's dismissal; General Eyadéma apparently seized the government of Togo in 1967 to prevent southerner politicians from assuming power and putting him on trial for his involvement in the murder of a southerner, former President Olympio. When the personal authority and command of a ruler show signs of weakness and if he becomes dependent upon the military for his power base, his survival may hinge on little other than the army's loyalty—particularly that of its officers.

In situations of weak rulership, extreme factionalism, and political instability, military leaders may not only be tempted, but even encouraged or obliged to intervene in politics through a coup. Sufficient historical time has elapsed since African independence that a correlation can be seen between political disunity and military intervention. Benin, one of the most politically divided countries in sub-Saharan Africa, has had six coups (between 1963 and 1972); Zaire has had two successful coups (both by General Mobutu), as well as at least one that was unsuccessful. General Mobutu's climb to power in Zaire took place within a context of

80. Gutteridge, *Africa's Military Rulers—An Assessment*, p. 7.

extreme political factionalism, regionalism, and governmental instability. The army served as a springboard to prominence and power for a man who was at most a novice soldier but had displayed political ambition and acumen from the time of his emergence on the political scene in the late 1950s in the Congo (later to become Zaire). Mobutu's Congolese experience is very near to the political scenario sometimes called Caesarism.[81] In a situation of a power vacuum in a state, the exercise of military power in politics may be seen as a burden that must be borne "for the sake of the state"—the classical justification of military intervention. In contemporary Africa it is significant not that many soldier-rulers have used this justification for their intervention, but that the justification has all too often appeared to be credible— that is, the civilian regime has been in disarray, leaving nobody to stabilize the state but soldiers. However, as we stressed earlier in this chapter, once in power, in sub-Saharan Africa the military has been as vulnerable to the norms of personalism and factionalism as its civilian counterparts. Soldier rule alone has not insured the polity against uncertainty; usually skilled and astute soldier-*rulers* have been required to accomplish this.

In established personal regimes succession or the prospect of succession is likely to be a serious political issue because the regime is tied to the ruler. When he loses his ability to rule or passes from the political scene, his regime is jeopardized. A change of ruler may very well mean a change of regime. Even if a succession does not fundamentally alter the regime, it alters at least some of the important relationships and standings among leaders and factions—for example, the standing of big men and the clan and ethnic communities they represent. It affects the power and privileges of individuals and groups as a result of changes in the membership of ruling bodies such as cabinets, party executives, and military ruling councils, especially at the political and senior administrative levels. Succession or its prospect can therefore provoke a climate of apprehension and even crisis.

Succession refers to the processes, manner, and methods by which one ruler replaces another, but it must be distinguished from replacement by democratic election, expiration of a term of office, or the restoration of civilian government after a military one. Specifically, a succession problem concerns how and with

81. For an account of Mobutu's rise to power in Zaire as an example of Caesarism, see Jean-Claude Willame, *Patrimonialism and Political Change in the Congo* (Stanford: Stanford University Press, 1972), pp. 141–46. Also see chapter 4 below.

whom to replace a personal ruler who has resigned, died, or become incapacitated. As we have noted, succession is important in contemporary African politics because rulers ordinarily cannot be replaced by democratic elections or by institutional rules governing terms of office. We do not consider the restoration of civilian government after an interlude of soldier rule a succession because it does not specifically relate to a change of rulers but rather to a deliberate (if problematic) change of regimes.

Almost all African countries have or have had constitutions that make provision for succession. (Keita's Mali was one of the few countries with a constitution that had no such provision; it turned out not to be needed with the intervention of the military in 1968.) Some African constitutions—like the United States Constitution—provide for the Vice-President to succeed the President in case of the latter's disability, death, or resignation. In Tanzania and Gabon Vice-Presidents have been constitutionally designated as interim successors as well;[82] in Senegal the Prime Minister is the designated interim successor.[83] Some constitutions which designate interim successors—most notably Kenya's—do not permit the interim successor to serve out the former president's term of office but provide instead for the holding of a presidential election within a specified time, while in some French-speaking countries the President of the National Assembly serves as the interim successor until a presidential election can be held—as in Ivory Coast as recently as the late 1970s. In Cameroon in 1979 the Prime Minister replaced the President of the National Assembly as the successor and would henceforth serve out the full presidential term.[84] In Guinea the constitution calls for an immediate election of a new president with the cabinet responsible for the procedures of the election. However, all these constitutional provisions belong to academic legal studies because as yet there is no basis in past political experience for being confident that they will be adhered to should the need for them arise. As constitutional procedures, they remain untested. It can only be a matter of speculation whether they will be used for the purpose intended; all that is certain is that it is uncertain whether they will be so used.

82. In 1975 a constitutional amendment abolished the vice-presidency in Gabon (*Africa Contemporary Record*, 1975–76, p. B 488).

83. A constitutional amendment of 1976 made the Prime Minister of Senegal the official successor in place of the President of the National Assembly.

84. In Cameroon the Vice-President was the constitutionally designated interim successor only during the period of the Federation, which ended in 1972. A constitutional amendment on June 9, 1979, provided for the Prime Minister to succeed the President and to hold office for the remainder of the presidential term (*Africa Research Bulletin: Political, Social, and Cultural Series* 16, 6 [July 15, 1979]: B 5297).

Because issues of succession contribute to uncertainty, political leaders (as distinct from rulers) must make contingency plans to attempt to prevent successions from adversely affecting their positions. We distinguish two basic types of plans: (1) political leaders may exploit their positions to acquire sufficient financial security (such as money or property) to not be dependent upon political or administrative office for income and advantage; (2) they may maneuver to be on the winning side after a succession struggle has ended, or avoid being identified with the losing side(s). Some leaders will view the prospect of succession as a chance to improve their power and advantage and increase their standing in the new regime. Thus the prospect of succession will provoke scheming and maneuvering and perhaps even plotting among rival political actors. In Ethiopia in the last years of Haile Selassie's reign, there was much plotting as power began to slip from his hands. Most of it was aimed at determining or at least influencing who would succeed the Emperor, but at least one plot—that of the Shoan establishment—was aimed at removing him.[85] As it turned out, the succession was resolved by the successful coup of the Ethiopian military, which assumed control of the government in 1974. The seizure of power by a faction-ridden military regime set in motion further rounds of plotting and violence, both within the regime by an array of radical civilian elements, and outside it by political forces such as the Eritrean separatists and Somali irredentists, whose ambitions for power and hopes for independence were temporarily enhanced by the ending of the imperial regime.

As long as a ruler retains command in African states, an overriding consideration in succession rivalries is that they be concealed from him. This consideration makes it difficult to study the subject of succession empirically with full confidence of achieving factual accuracy or specificity, but we can study the stratagems and calculations involved from reports of overt events in countries where the prospect of a succession has arisen. In Senegal and Ivory Coast it has given rise to speculation about the likeliest successor, as well as reports of behind the scenes maneuvering and jockeying for advantage and security; in Kenya there was considerable vying for power before President Kenyatta's death in 1978. In Ivory Coast it has been reported, on the one hand, that interest in succession has been encouraged by President Houphouët-Boigny's frequent remarks of being weary of ruling, but, on the other hand, it is speculated that the remarks are deliberately intended to identify

85. *Africa Contemporary Record*, 1974–75, p. B 161.

anyone who might harbor ambitions to replace him.[86] Only if a ruler himself names a successor can talk of succession openly take place (and only then if it supports the ruler's choice), but there is nonetheless no assurance that behind the scenes maneuvering will not continue. Seldom, if ever, can a political leader publicly claim to be the successor without leaving the impression of being disloyal and unfaithful to the current ruler. Not only must he avoid making such claims, but he must also insure that nobody else makes them in his behalf. To make such claims may adversely affect his chances and force a ruler's rebuke. The question of succession can be raised in public indirectly—for instance, by reference to the constitutional rules of succession. This has been done in Kenya, Malawi, Ivory Coast, Senegal, and Cameroon. In Tanzania it was raised more directly, but only after President Nyerere expressed a wish to vacate the presidency.

For analytical purposes, we distinguish three methods by which the issue of succession can be resolved. The first—and on almost any account the most certain—is the institutional method according to which rules and procedures prescribe how a transfer of power is to take place. These may be contained in a written constitution, or they may be conventions that belong to an established political tradition. The use of primogeniture in the succession of kings is such a convention. They may be common agreements that give an individual or a collective decision-making body (such as a council) the right to nominate a successor. An example of the latter is the right of the College of Cardinals to elect a new Pope. (Common agreement can be more tentative and uncertain and therefore more subject to political influence and conflict than unambiguous legal procedures, examples of which are most modern written constitutions.[87] However, if the decision of the body is authoritative, the method is institutional.) The second method is the personal designation of a successor by the current ruler. In a few regimes the ruler has attempted to designate a "Dauphin," usually by con-

---

86. Ibid., 1975–76, pp. B 728–29, and 1976–77, p. B 610.

87. In characterizing the issue of succession in pre-colonial Africa, Gluckman comments: "Rarely in Africa do we find rules which indicate clearly and definitely a single heir. In some kingdoms there was an open free-for-all struggle by princes for the kingship—like the dash for Winchester; in others there was a selection by commoner councillors from princes of the royal family; and in yet others the rules of succession contradicted one another. Or the kingship rotated through different houses of the royal dynasty. Or, if the rules themselves were clear, they operated uncertainly in practice. The result was that almost every succession could raise rival claimants, and after the king's death, when national strength was at its weakest, unifying wars for the kingship between claimants and their supporters might follow" (Max Gluckman, *Custom and Conflict in Africa* [Oxford: Basil Blackwell, 1955], p. 46).

stitutional amendment. The term, which denotes the heir to the throne of France, has been used in some French-speaking African countries in speculations about succession—most notably in Senegal, Ivory Coast, and Cameroon.[88] The idea of a Dauphin has obvious appeal to rulers who wish to settle the issue of succession in accordance with their own political or personal preferences. The third method is political intrigue and maneuvering—either by the factional political process or by plotting and more violent action if peaceful agreement proves impossible. The first method is by definition peaceful and orderly; the second could be peaceful and orderly to the extent that a ruler's designation of a Dauphin is found to be acceptable and legitimate; the third, which strictly speaking is no "method" at all, contains the greatest potential for disorder, disaffection, and instability. It is this method that primarily characterizes personalized regimes and prompts concern and interest in the succession questions in Africa.

The institutional method of arranging a succession of rulers through a written constitution is unusual and has been little tried in sub-Saharan Africa (although it has been successfully employed twice in recent years—Liberia in 1971 and Kenya in 1978), but this can come as little surprise for countries that on the average have had independence for scarcely two decades.[89] Institutional rules on succession require not only political agreement for the sake of expediency, but also acceptance and valuation for their own sake, and this takes time to develop. In other words, they must be tried and tested and found acceptable in practice as well as theory.

For most African personal regimes constitutional tests on succession rules have yet to take place. Where the question is beginning to arise, reports of behind the scenes intrigue and maneuvering do not augur well for an orderly constitutional succession. There appeared to be a good prospect for an orderly succession in Tanzania, where President Nyerere had in the late 1970s declared his wish to vacate the presidency, but the personal legitimacy and popularity of Nyerere himself, rather than the rules he is strongly committed to institutionalizing, could very well have been the determining factor. Outside of Liberia and Kenya, the only case of a tested institutionalized method of succes-

88. The *Oxford English Dictionary* defines Dauphin as "the title of the eldest son of the King of France."

89. We consider Botswana to be a constitutional government with the presence of competitive party politics. Following the death of Sir Seretse Khama in July 1980, the Vice-President, Quett Masire, was chosen the new leader of the governing party and was elected President by the Botswana legislature.

sion—and a special and somewhat uncertain case—is the traditional Kingdom of Swaziland. The case is special for several reasons. First, the traditional method of succession, which is by the decision of a royal council after a king's death rather than by primogeniture, has not been tested since Swaziland became independent in 1968. Second, the method is open to considerable personal and political influence, and there is no assurance that the next king will be allowed to dominate in the decision-making process as the present one has. Potholm points out the following:

> The next Ngwenyama [king] will be faced with the need to act from the moment he assumes office; and he will also be faced with an in-place, ongoing political system led by elites of experience and confidence, most of whom have been involved in political maneuvering for over a decade. It seems doubtful that either the Swazi National Council or the Imbokodvo [royal political party] will accept the dominance of the next Ngwenyama to the extent they have during the rule of Sobhuza II. It also seems likely that there will be increased strains within the Swazi traditional hierarchy as various individuals and groups seek to consolidate or gain power at the expense of the next Ngwenyama.[90]

The Swazi succession may give rise to as much factional intrigue and maneuvering as the succession in non-traditional personally dominated states.

Succession by a ruler's appointment of an heir is strongly characteristic of a stable, ruler-dominated regime in which his decisions concerning not only the present but also the future have legitimacy and are assured of acceptance. Most of Africa's present rulers, civilian and military alike, probably enjoy the authority to make short-term decisions, but it is uncertain how many can make them stick after their demise. Former President M'Ba of Gabon, who died in office in 1967, succeeded by creating a vice-presidency in 1966 and appointing a loyal and capable lieutenant, Bongo— the present ruler—to that office. It is probably true that Bongo's own political skills served him well during the transitional period, but this does not gainsay the fact that he was M'Ba's personally selected Dauphin and that he benefitted from the approval and legitimacy that such selection bestowed. During the 1977 coronation of "Emperor" Bokassa of the so-called Central African Empire, an attempt was made to establish a legitimate heir by naming Bokassa's young son the Crown Prince. The overthrow of Bokassa in 1979 ended this ludicrous experiment in neo-royalism. In other

90. Christian P. Potholm, "Swaziland Under Sobhuza II: The Future of an African Monarchy," *The Round Table* 254 (April 1974): 224. Also see Christian P. Potholm, *Swaziland: The Dynamics of Political Modernization* (Berkeley, Los Angeles, London: University of California Press, 1972).

sub-Saharan regimes the identification of a personally selected successor has been largely a matter of speculation. When constitutional provisions specifying procedures of succession are amended, they understandably give rise to speculation that the changes are deliberately intended by the ruler to favor particular lieutenants. Yet it clearly is not in the interest of rulers to create the impression of having designated a Dauphin by means of constitutional amendment since it may reduce the cooperation and loyalty of lieutenants who are not being favored. In this regard it is interesting to note that Presidents Senghor, Ahmadou Ahidjo, and Houphouët-Boigny have tried to avoid creating such an impression.

In many personal regimes in Africa, it is likely that the method of factional politics will settle the issue of succession. The likely successor will be the most able and resourceful politician—a "big man" capable of securing the support of other political big men and their factions, as well as the support of the military. In many countries soldiers may well be the most critical political actors influencing if not actually determining the outcome of a succession. Following the 1977 assassination of President Ngouabi of Congo-Brazzaville, Colonel Joachim Yhombi-Opango was appointed head of state by the ruling Military Committee of the Congolese Workers' Party.[91] There is no question that even in the relatively orderly and enduring personal regimes, if the skills and abilities of the players of the game of successor politics are found wanting, the outcome may be decided by the military. In addition to political ability or coercive power, fortune may count as a major factor. The man who is the most popular may be the most fortunate.

A Typology of Personal Rule

In setting forth our typology of personal rule, we have been influenced (like many others) by Weber's typology of legitimate domination. Since his typology is very familiar, we have not felt a need to recapitulate it; however, we would like to point out some similarities and some important differences between our categories of rulership and his. For Weber there were two basic subtypes of personal rule—traditional-personal domination and charismatic domination. These bear a resemblance to our concepts of "princely rule" and "autocratic rule" (or "lordship") on the one hand, and "prophetic rule," on the other.

91. *Africa Contemporary Record*, 1976–77, p. B 491. Yhombi-Opango was deposed in 1979.

We have departed from Weber's definitions and distinctions in two important ways, however. First, Weber bracketed the two sub-types of personal rule within an overall concept of "legitimate domination." In our survey of African rulership we identify a type of personal rule that is a familiar category in history and political theory but is outside Weber's theoretical framework—namely, "tyranny." (Weber did not consider tyranny—*tyrannis*—a type of legitimate domination and gave only the briefest attention to it in his famous study.)[92] We would find it difficult to write about rulers and regimes in contemporary Africa if we were restrained by our concepts from considering cases of political domination that appear not to be legitimate. Writing from his historical perspective of centuries, Weber could believe that illegitimate domination was inherently unstable and bound not to last. The perspective is different for the political analyst or historian of contemporary Africa, whose political systems include a few tyrannies that have lasted for some years.

Second, insofar as Weber's concepts of "patrimonialism" and even "sultanism" presuppose "traditional" norms that rulers and subjects can use to justify or criticize government acts or omissions,[93] they are of questionable value to students of African statecraft. In Black Africa it is the paucity of *political* traditions at the *territorial* level of new states, together with the failure of rational-legal offices and procedures to become fully institutionalized (as we have pointed out), that makes rulership so personal—that is, so contingent upon the skills, ability, and fortunes of the ruler. In all but a very few African countries there are no generally recognized political traditions at the territorial level that are valid and operative.[94] Among the countries which have such traditions are Swaziland, Lesotho, Botswana, and Somalia, and they seemed to exist in Ethiopia until the 1974 overthrow of Haile Selassie's regime.[95] Such traditions did not exist previously at the territorial level of

92. Max Weber, *Economy and Society: An Outline of Interpretive Sociology*, ed. Guenther A. Roth and Clause Wittich (New York: Bedminster Press, 1968), vol. 3, pp. 1315–17.

93. Ibid., vol. 1, p. 232.

94. There appears to be a further conceptual ambiguity in Weber's typology of legitimate domination that we do not have the space to investigate—namely, that the concept of "tradition" belongs, strictly speaking, to the category of "institutional" rather than "personal" rule. The uses of the terms "law" and "legal" in Weber's writings are also susceptible to this ambiguity.

95. Traditional norms were at the center of state authority in Rwanda and Burundi until independence, when the privileges and burdens they placed on different hierarchically arranged groups—castes—became the central issue of a violent political conflict that engulfed these countries. See René Lemarchand, *Rwanda and Burundi* (New York and London: Praeger, 1970).

most African states precisely because all but a very few states are novel political jurisdictions introduced by colonial rule. The political traditions that do exist are typically regional or local in character—as with the Hausa Emirates in northern Nigeria or the Kingdom of Buganda in Uganda—or the many traditions of large- or small-scale African communities. But these are norms valid for only a segment of the inhabitants of a country. Rather than traditional "patrimonialism," in most new African states (as Roth has pointed out),[96] we find forms of personal rule based on clientelism—some combination of personal-communal loyalty and patronage, but not a politically relevant tradition.

Our typology to analyze individual rulers and regimes in Black Africa raises the question as to why different types of personal rule emerge where and when they do. One might wish to explain different rulership types (dependent variables) in relation to underlying socioeconomic factors (independent variables)—for example—by seeing if there is a correlation between orientation of rule (e.g., radical versus conservative) and level of development or structural characteristics of the economy. Or one might seek to explain changes of rulership type as a consequence of underlying socioeconomic changes. In both cases one takes the approach that rulership is an adaptation to demands and restraints imposed by the underlying socioeconomic environment. Such an approach would adopt a conceptual framework based on sociological analysis that we find to be unsatisfactory for rulership studies. One cannot understand the whys and wherefores of personal rule by focusing upon underlying socioeconomic factors because such factors are by themselves too general to guide political choices in personal regimes. In advanced societies—especially democratic ones—where the choices and actions of governments are far more significantly (but by no means exclusively) policy and technical choices—such conditions can be very influential, and a study of them is important. But in underdeveloped countries where politics is more about power than policy—and where success or failure in policy is much less likely to bring direct political rewards or losses—the relationship between ruling and the socioeconomic environment is much weaker. One crucial factor reducing the importance of underlying socioeconomic conditions in political choices in African states is the usual absence of competitive elections in which governments can be replaced for their policy failures.

When we inquire into the relation between type of personal rule and the underlying socioeconomic environment in African coun-

96. Roth, p. 158.

tries, we are struck by a lack of correlation rather than by their interdependence. Nkrumah and Nyerere were alike in the character of their rule, yet in the 1950s when Nkrumah rose to power, Ghana was one of the most prosperous and modern countries in Black Africa, whereas Tanzania in the late 1950s and early 1960s, when Nyerere's regime emerged, was relatively poor and backward. Why do economically underdeveloped Tanzania and Malawi contrast sharply in their rulership types—that is, Nyerere the socialist prophet versus Banda the conservative autocrat? One cannot predict from a consideration of underlying sociological factors alone that the next ruler of Ivory Coast (for example) will be an autocrat as Houphouët-Boigny has been, or that the next ruler of Senegal will be a prince as was Senghor. As we noted in chapter 1, while we view rulers and other leaders as historical actors, we are interested not in political men in themselves but in the personal *systems* of conflict, reciprocity, obligation, influence, expediency, and sympathy in which they are entangled. We are therefore inclined to view a distinctive type of personal rule as the consequence of the patterning and evolution of specifically political factors at the center of the state.

The political factors that seem most to affect the type of personal system that emerges are the dispositions, activities, abilities, efforts, and fortunes of the key actors; the system is largely their political handiwork. The well-established personal regimes in Black Africa have to be seen as the creations primarily of African politicians; responsibility for failing to establish stable regimes likewise rests with political men. This is not to deny that some politicians are more fortunate in being in more governable countries. Clearly, The Gambia and Botswana are less difficult to govern than Nigeria, Zaire, and Sudan. Nor is it to deny that circumstances and contexts are important in affecting the choices of politicians, although only occasionally do they wholly determine actions. In addition to their roles in established regimes, rulers and other leaders figure prominently in changes of personal regimes, although such changes may be the unintended as well as the intended results of their actions. Malawi became an autocracy largely as a result of the determined, driving efforts of Banda in the face of ineffective opposition—mainly of younger and less skillful politicians. However, when Banda dies, it is far from certain that Malawi's autocracy will survive; whether it does or not will largely depend upon the actors involved. It is quite evident that the tyrannies of Amin in Uganda and Macías in Equatorial Guinea were brought about by the rulers' paranoid fears of the power of others, but neither Uganda nor Equatorial Guinea had to experience and endure their abusive rule for any compelling sociological reasons. In sum, whether abusive rule or constructive forms of personal rulership are practiced in a country depends less on underlying social conditions and more on the political actors, who must govern without institutions to assist them.

Let us now turn to a brief description of our sub-types of personal rule—princely (and autocratic), prophetic, and tyrannical. (Note that from here on we shall capitalize the ideal type in each category.)

Princely Rule and Autocracy

Since independence the majority of Africa's rulers have ruled in a way that exhibits caution, realism, and to some extent conservatism in the use of state power. Certainly many of the most successful—as measured by their years of incumbency—have. While some of these rulers preside over the polity, others dominate their countries almost as though they were personal estates, but they are neither Prophets bent on radically remaking the political and social order, nor Tyrants prepared to operate by fear and terror. They are not men of radical vision and ideological faith; they do not conceive of statecraft as a tool by which to reconstruct their countries. This is not to say that they are not builders or unconcerned with national development, but they are practical and circumspect builders generally without heroic socioeconomic goals or a master plan with which to pursue them. Among these rulers we distinguish two types on a continuum: the Prince and the Autocrat.[97]

The Prince.   This type of ruler is an astute observer and manipulator of lieutenants and clients. He tends to rule jointly with other oligarchs and to cultivate their loyalty, cooperation, and support. He encourages what President Senghor termed "politician politics":

> When I say "politics,". . . it is not a question of the *art of governing the state for the public welfare in the general framework of laws and regulations.* It is a question of politician politics: the struggles of clans—not even [ideological] tendencies—to place well oneself, one's relatives and one's clients in the *cursus honorum,* that is the race for preferments.[98]

97. One of the first distinctions between Prince and Autocrat in modern political thought can be found in Niccolo Machiavelli, *The Prince,* trans. with an introduction by George Bull (Harmondsworth: Penguin Books, 1975), ch. 4.

98. Léopold Senghor; cited in Edward J. Schumacher, *Politics, Bureaucracy and*

Thus to rule as a Prince is to preside over the struggle for preferments, to encourage it, to recognize that it is a source of the ruler's and the regime's legitimacy, but not to allow it to get out of hand, nor to let any leader emerge as a serious challenger. Unlike autocratic rule, princely rule is flexible enough to allow for a politics of accommodation (although not without the risk of clients becoming too independent and therefore too difficult to control). President Senghor has demonstrated princely rule with great success.

The Autocrat. This type of ruler tends to dominate the oligarchy, the government, and the state without having to share power with other leaders. Where the Prince presides and rules, the Autocrat commands and manages; the country is his estate; the ruling apparatus is ultimately his to deploy and direct, and the party and governmental officials his servants and agents. This type of personal rule is reminiscent of absolute monarchy. The African Autocrat faces limitations on his rule, but they are the limitations of resources and organizational capability—not of discretionary power. His power is limited by the relative "underdevelopment" of the ruling apparatus available to him, by limited finances, personnel, equipment, technology, and materiel, as well as by the limited skills and abilities of his officials. But his discretionary power to direct this apparatus is—in principle—unlimited. Presidents Bongo (Gabon) and Banda (Malawi) have exercised a type of personal rulership that has many of the earmarks of autocratic rulers.

Autocracy depends on the fortuitous confluence of circumstance and ability. Fortune favors an Autocrat in part by not creating rivals of comparable skill and determination to dominate. But autocracy depends most notably on the strength of will and ability of the ruler to dominate, as well as his ability to confine and largely limit the process of politics to issues completely within his immediate competence and control. The Autocrat is successful in eliminating the autonomous political power and influence of others, thereby inhibiting the development of politician politics and reducing politics to subordination and administration. Clearly, the main threats to the Autocrat are ambitious leaders who long to assert their own political power and privilege by building independent followings and political bases. While such leaders exist in all regimes, they constitute a serious potential for instability in autocracies, which by their nature cannot accommodate the political ambitions of such men. More than the Prince, the Autocrat

---

Rural Development in Senegal (Berkeley, Los Angeles, London: University of California Press, 1975), p. 5.

must endeavor to maintain a close identity with the "people," whose apparent or demonstrable support he may enlist to disarm or disdain independent-minded lieutenants, who themselves are never entitled to claim the "people's" support. If they do, the ruler is in a position to deride their claims as factional and divisive and therefore illegitimate.

Prophetic Rule

A minority of Africa's rulers—some civilian and others military—have been visionaries, wanting to reshape society in ways consistent with their ideology, which in Africa has been primarily socialist. The socialist visions of these rulers have not always been the same; some rulers have been strict Marxists, but others have wanted to adapt their socialist ideals to African conditions and circumstances. These rulers have been impatient with the social, economic, and political conditions about them, which they have seen—no doubt correctly—as obstacles to socialist progress. They have sought to eliminate these obstacles, but they have usually not possessed adequate political and economic resources to do so. Those who have persisted have been frustrated by their lack of success, and some have been defeated.

Because of their ideals, prophetic rulers have not been content simply to hold power or maintain the stability of their regimes or even to build in a piecemeal or pragmatic way. The least successful have spurned "politician politics"; others have practiced politician politics reluctantly and quietly; the most successful have understood it to be a necessity of rule, but none have regarded it as an adequate *raison d'être* of statecraft. To pursue an ideological vision of a better world is the only valid justification of rule for the Prophet. It follows that ideology is not separate from prophetic rule but essential to it and contained by it, although in practice it is often the "charisma" of the leader—his charm, mystique, and personality—that counts most in a prophetic regime—that is, not the ideology that he enunciates, but the fact that he enunciates it. Ideology remains intimately associated with the person of the ruler.

Prophetic rulers must lead in a manner that need never concern Princes and Autocrats. They must not only keep command of the ship of state and avoid mutinous challenges to their control, but they must also steer the ship in the direction of its ideological destination and mark off some recognizable progress on the chart along the way. Since ideology and rhetoric can inspire but cannot guide, these leaders must be concerned with plans, programs, and *dirigiste* politics for guiding the government. In a modern state the socialist Prophet must not only inspire others to believe in what he believes, but he must also lend what authority he has to the practical business of bringing about the desired future by state-directed action. The Prophet in Africa is confronted with the most serious obstacles to his vision at the practical level. The instruments and resources necessary for ambitious state planning are usually not available, and the government is sadly underdeveloped. If the government cannot implement his plans and designs, the vision will remain just that, and prophecy will fail. If a prophecy fails, there is disappointment and cynicism, and opposition usually develops—especially against individuals or groups who may be profiting from positions of responsibility and influence in the regime. The result may well be the disarming of the Prophet and his disciples and the toppling of his regime. The record of post-independence African politics contains instances of such an outcome.

Tyrannical Rule

An historic variant of personal rule that involves a high degree of uncertainty, insecurity, and at least potential instability has since ancient times been referred to as "tyranny."[99] Tyranny is a residual type of personal regime into which any or all of the other types may deteriorate. In a tyranny not only legal but also all moral constraints on the exercise of power are absent, with the consequence that power is exercised in a completely arbitrary fashion according to the impulses of the ruler and his agents. Historically, tyranny has been marked by particularly impulsive, oppressive, and brutal rule that has lacked elementary respect—and has sometimes shown complete disdain—not only for the rights of persons and property but also for the very sanctity of human life.[100] In addition to ruling through fear, Tyrants reward agents and collaborators and make mercenaries of them. Tyranny is a cunning kind of "Mafia" game, based not only on violence and fear but also on rewards and incentives, granting favors and accepting returns, extending credit and exploiting political and personal debts, and—of course—establishing personal dependence on the ruler.

Several caveats concerning the use of our typology should be noted. The forms of personal rule identified are ideal types. The

---

99. See Leo Strauss, *On Tyranny*, rev. and enlarged ed. (Ithaca: Cornell University Press, 1975).

100. On Idi Amin's impulsive rule, see Decalo, *Coups and Army Rule in Africa*, p. 222.

specific characteristics of each ruler that we consider will not conform exactly to the modalities of the category to which he is assigned. There are cases that would occupy a marginal position in
any category, not because of a lack of clarity in defining the categories, but because some rulers have exhibited characteristics of
more than one type of rule, usually brought about by a change of
rulership orientation over time. For example, we have classified
President Touré of Guinea as a prophetic ruler in recognition of
the great and continued emphasis he has placed on his socialist
doctrines, and despite his *realpolitik* or the fact that over the years
he has removed many suspected rivals and political enemies and
assumed the political mastery of a despot. We have classified President Mobutu of Zaire as an Autocrat for reasons of his political
mastery, and despite his evident indifference to the problems of
state economic management or the fact that in recent years his regime has come to the brink of tyranny.

It is necessary to note the considerations used to select rulers and
regimes for inclusion in the following chapters. Having satisfied
ourselves that the typology was properly cast to handle the wide
diversity of personal systems in contemporary Black Africa, we
selected countries that were representative and for which sufficient
information on leadership patterns was available. The largest
problem of selection was in the category of princely rule, where
more of Africa's contemporary rulers tend to cluster. However,
among the representatives of the princely category, we have been
able to include founder or successor rulers and new rulers. The
comparatively fewer autocratic, prophetic, and tyrannical rulers
eliminated the problem of selection for these categories; we were
able to include most of them.

Rulership studies contain an inherent historical dimension insofar as time is required before a leader of a country who is not an
institutional ruler can demonstrate the capacity, will, intelligence,
and ability to remain in power. Therefore, there is a bias against
considering political men who have exercised state power for only
short periods of time. This historical dimension illuminates an
important feature of personal rule in Africa—namely, by no
means all ambitious men who venture into the game of personal
politics and acquire the power of the state are successful in keeping it from other ambitious men. In addition, it underlines the fact
that without men of will, ability, and fortune who demonstrate
their capacity to rule and survive over a period of years—often
many years—systems of personal rule will scarcely evolve beyond
the "state of nature." Aside from African countries in which Ty-

rants have created situations of extreme apprehension and uncertainty where none existed previously, there have been countries that remained in a state of uncertainty for extended periods because an effective ruler and ruling class did not emerge; still other countries have been plunged into great uncertainty after a stable rulership was terminated, typically by military coup. Metaphorically speaking, in periods of unstable rulership the national political stage has been occupied by aspiring but novice actors seeking to give a commanding performance but unable to do so.

Our use of a typology makes it plain that we are more interested in explicating the theory and practice of personal rule than providing information on rulers. We have utilized the historical record of African politics to elucidate the logic of personal rule. We have not found it necessary to include the latest event—a succession or a coup—in order to complete the argument, and events have overtaken us since this volume went to press. Occasionally we have conjectured about the political future—particularly in connection with successions in specific African countries. But we make no bones about these being conjectures, and not predictions. Some conjectures will undoubtedly be cancelled by historical events, but we do not expect political history in Black Africa for the forseeable future to cease providing ample evidence of personal rule.

3

Princes

and

Oligarchic Rule

THE majority of Black Africa's new rulers, present and past, successful or unsuccessful, have exhibited the conservative characteristics of "princely rule." So far Africa has seen few Tyrants; there have been a number of Prophets, but these rulers have not been in anything like the majority; and of the conservative-type rulers, there have been many more Princes than Autocrats. We believe that the general category of conservative rulership is crucial to an understanding of personal rule in Africa. While it is often difficult, in practice, to draw a clear line between Princes and Autocrats, it is possible and essential to set out the conceptual distinctions. These we have tried to capture in the differences between such paired terms as "rulership" versus "lordship," "presiding" versus "managing" or "dictating," "rule" versus "command" or "order," "ruler" versus "master," and so on. In each pairing the first term applies to the Prince; the second, to the Autocrat. But these distinctions are conceptual only, and no African ruler has been so cooperative in his conduct to conform precisely to our concepts. However, most have tended to act more in one direction than the other over a period of time sufficient for us to classify them with some confidence.

Princes display royalist characteristics akin to those of a traditional monarchy, where the ruler is the personification of the state and the custodian of its political values and practices. But the new African Prince is obliged to conduct the affairs of state without the supporting normative framework of a political tradition: he is the custodian of present political values more than inherited traditions. However, there is a quality of princely rule, unlike the other

83

types that we consider in this study, that resembles institutional government in some of its features. Traditional rulers are, of course, institutional rulers; thus in resembling a traditional monarch the African Prince resembles an institutional ruler. But a more important resemblance has to do with the practice of political restraint on the part of the ruler and other leading and powerful political actors. "Traditions" are restraints of a distinctive kind. The legitimacy of both traditional rulers and modern constitutional rulers depends upon their acceptance of the limits placed on their actions by traditional norms or constitutional rules. But the legitimacy of the modern African Prince depends upon his respect for the *private* understandings and agreements he has made with other members of the oligarchy over whom he presides and with whom he rules. It is not only their power that he respects, but also his informal contracts with them. Such respect must, of course, be mutual. In characterizing princely rule in this way we are not characterizing institutional government because we are not describing a general acceptance of more or less permanent, widely understood, and *publicly* valued rules. We are referring only to political arrangements of an informal, temporary, and personal kind. They ordinarily do not outlive the persons who make them; if they do, it is evidence that they are becoming institutionalized.[1]

It is this incipient constitutionalism of princely rule—this emphasis on agreements, understandings, and promises—which suggests that it is long-standing princely regimes, more than any of the other forms of personal rule, that have the best chance to become institutionalized, for the private compacts between ruler and oligarchs can become the foundation of an institutional principle of government if the ruling class is prepared to accept them as such, and if these compacts can gain legitimacy from the larger society. But the African regimes that we consider in this chapter, excluding the two cases of traditional rule—Ethiopia under Emperor Haile Selassie and Swaziland under King Sobhuza II—and the ambiguous case of Liberia (prior to the 1980 coup), are not institutionalized: they are systems of personal rule in which political goods are dependent not upon functioning political institutions but upon the ruler and the oligarchs and, particularly, upon their personal/political restraint.

Before we turn our attention to some of the noteworthy princely rulers who have stood at the helms of Africa's post-independence ships of state, it may be helpful to comment briefly on the few

1. See chapter 7 below.

constitutional governments that remain in the sub-Saharan region and the fate of some earlier ones that failed.

The first wave of African independence, which grew out of the French, British, Belgian, and Italian decolonizations in the late 1950s and early 1960s, was by and large an attempt to establish constitutional governments: virtually all the new African governments began their independence with democratic constitutions. Few kept them for long: either the rulers began arbitrarily violating or changing the constitutions on grounds of expedience; or both governments and oppositions exploited the rules for their own advantages; or the military intervened to seize power. The fact that oppositions as well as governments have been responsible for the assertion of personal-party considerations in overriding the rules of constitutional government in Africa is sometimes overlooked. Sudan between 1956 and 1958, Nigeria from 1960 to 1966, and Somalia between 1960 and 1969 are examples of widespread abuses and exploitation of constitutions by opposition and governing parties alike, of anti-constitutionalism masquerading as constitutionalism. Military coups were often justified as efforts to rescue the state from such predatory action; these coups were themselves predatory. In Sierra Leone, the first ruler—Sir Milton Margai—appeared to be a constitutional ruler, but he did not have to face the constitutional test of reelection because he died in office in 1964 before his term had expired. His successor, Sir Albert Margai (a younger brother), was at best a dubious constitutionalist who tried unsuccessfully to create a one-party state; he was removed from office after his apparent defeat in the 1967 elections.[2] The current ruler and former leader of the opposition, Siaka Stevens, used the electoral victory to achieve what Margai had attempted: the suspension of competitive elections by the creation of a one-party state.

By 1979 there were only two of the original constitutional rulers of the 1960s left in Black Africa: President Dauda K. Jawara of The Gambia and Sir Seretse Khama of Botswana. In these cases it may be that constitutional government has been retained because the constitutions of independence contain a bias favoring the retention of power by these men and their parties, giving little chance to the opposition to win power electorally. Yet despite this dismal record, the attractions of constitutionalism have not been lost upon Africans. In the late 1970s attempts were made to re-

2. The actual results of the elections remain in doubt. See John R. Cartwright, *Politics in Sierra Leone 1947–1967* (Toronto and Buffalo: University of Toronto Press, 1970).

store constitutional government in Upper Volta, Nigeria, Ghana, and—incrementally—in Senegal. Some newly independent constitutional regimes have appeared. Djibouti became independent in 1977 with a national legislature elected from a single list of candidates freely agreed to by the country's five main political groupings; the legislature in turn elected the president (Hassan Gouled Aptidon). After a prolonged and oftentimes bloody civil war, Zimbabwe (formerly Rhodesia) became independent in 1980 under a constitution in which the Zimbabwe African National Union (ZANU), led by Robert Mugabe, won an overwhelming majority in a highly competitive election contested by several parties.

But personal rule, not constitutional rule, is the prevailing form of government in contemporary Black Africa, and most of Africa's personal rulers are more like Princes in their characteristics and methods of rule than any of the other types we deal with in this study. Among these African Princes, we can distinguish two subtypes: founder or successor rulers (among whom we discuss Senghor, Kenyatta, Tubman, and Tolbert) and new rulers who came to power by force (among whom we discuss Numeiri). We also include two traditional rulers in our analysis (Haile Selassie and Sobhuza II) to illuminate the resemblances between African traditional rule and princely rule.

The first sub-type of African Princes dealt with in this chapter, and the group that provides the key attributes that give the category of Prince its overall character, is founder or successor rulers: men such as Léopold Senghor of Senegal, Jomo Kenyatta of Kenya, and William V. S. Tubman and William R. Tolbert of Liberia, whose personal rule determined the character of the states over which they presided. In 1980 some of these rulers continued to govern—for instance, Senghor; others died in office—Kenyatta in 1978, after fifteen years of rule, and Tubman in 1971, after twenty-seven. Others remained in power for many years, but through growing weakness, miscalculation, or misfortune had power taken from them. Tolbert of Liberia promoted a policy of political liberalization and socioeconomic reform following his accession to power in 1971, but in the end he proved to be the victim of his own liberality. Diori ruled Niger from 1960 until 1974, but only from a narrow power base that he was never able to expand and with lieutenants whom he could not control.[3] From 1962 until 1971 Obote of Uganda was preoccupied with the centralization of

3. Richard Higgott and Finn Fuglestad, "The 1974 Coup d'Etat in Niger: Towards an Explanation," *Journal of Modern African Studies* 13, 3 (1975): 386–87.

the state against the resistance of powerful regional-ethnic interests. He made the fatal miscalculation of relying too heavily upon military force to achieve his aims.[4] Daddah ruled Mauritania—a state that he was largely responsible for creating out of an arid and unpopulated region that the French referred to as "the vacuum"— with considerable success from 1960 until 1978. When he became entangled in a conflict over the partition of the Western Sahara, he lost his authority and was overthrown by the military.[5] Some founder rulers had considerably shorter tenures; either they failed to develop the will and ability to govern or they confronted nearly ungovernable situations. David Dacko ruled the Central African Republic from 1960 until 1965 largely in a collegial fashion, which may have been a key factor in his downfall.[6] Youlou of Congo-Brazzaville is an example of an inexperienced ruler who confronted a nearly ungovernable situation of a faction-ridden, ethnically tense, socially mobilized society. He was overthrown by an urban mob of highly politicized youth in 1963 only three years after independence.[7]

Among the founder Princes who were still in power in 1980, at least brief mention should be made of Kenneth David Kaunda of Zambia, who has proved to be a princely ruler not from desire but of necessity: a political saint forced to become a Prince. Professing his faith in humanistic values and brotherhood, Kaunda believed that he could achieve the creation of a genuinely democratic one-party state with the consent of the Zambian electorate.[8] He was thwarted in his mission by his associates and their ethnic supporters, who proved to be interested in securing state patronage and political profits rather than in building a consensual party or a classless society. Of necessity, Kaunda was forced to impose a one-party state in 1972 without the consent of the Zambian electorate.

4. James H. Mittelman, *Ideology and Politics in Uganda: From Obote to Amin* (Ithaca and London: Cornell University Press, 1975); Ali A. Mazrui, "Leadership in Africa: Obote of Uganda," *International Journal* 25, 3 (Summer 1970): 538–64.

5. *West Africa* 3183 (17 July 1978): 1371.

6. Victor T. LeVine, "The Central African Republic: Insular Problems of an Inland State," *Africa Report* 10, 10 (November 1965): 18–19. Dacko was restored to power in 1979 when "Emperor" Bokassa was overthrown with the assistance of the French. (See chapter 6 below.)

7. René Gauze, *The Politics of Congo-Brazzaville*, trans. and ed. Virginia Thompson and Richard Adloff (Stanford: Hoover Institution Press, 1973).

8. Kenneth Kaunda, *A Humanist in Africa: Letters to Colin Morris* (London: Longmans, Green & Co., 1966); F. Soremekun, "Kenneth Kaunda's Cosmic Neo-Humanism," *Africa Quarterly* 12, 4 (January-March 1973): 285–313; Robert Molteno, "Zambian Humanism: The Way Ahead," *African Review* 3, 4 (1973): 541–57; Henry S. Meebelo, "The Concept of Man Centredness in Zambian Humanism," ibid., pp. 559–75.

A leadership code was established to regulate the conduct of party and government leaders, but since an elite more interested in their own advantages than in "socialism" had become entrenched, it was unlikely that "the high ethical standards demanded of prominent public figures" could be enforced.[9] Kaunda's political choices were further restricted by the abrupt downfall of copper prices—the backbone of the Zambian economy—in 1974, which robbed the political system, and specifically the ruling party and the ruler, of the patronage surplus that had helped them to rule democratically in an earlier period. Economic necessity dictated political authoritarianism, and in the new one-party constitution of 1972 Kaunda gave himself "virtually free rein over national and party affairs."[10] But in the world of practical politics the ruler of Zambia enjoyed no such power. He had to contend with not only a stagnating economy since 1974, which brought with it growing discontent and a general loss of national support because of declining opportunities and a lack of patronage for political distribution, but also an intense factional problem in his party. And to complicate his political life further, he found himself and his country—because of its strategic location—entangled in the southern African racial conflict, which had in it the potential to bring him down. Kaunda endured the difficulties and withstood the necessities—not by idealism, but by realism, political intelligence, and a measure of good fortune.

Of the traditional rulers in contemporary Africa, the two most important have been Emperor Haile Selassie and King Sobhuza II. Excluding the "constitutional" monarch in Lesotho, King Moshoeshoe II, the only other post-independence traditional ruler in Black Africa was *Mwami* (King) Mwambutsa II, who attempted to preside over the turbulent factional and caste politics of Burundi from independence in 1962 until July 1966, when he was deposed by his son, Prince Charles Ndizeye, who was himself ousted by a military coup in November.[11] Part of the reason for Mwambutsa's failure was a decline in the legitimacy of his office in the face of modern political norms and intensely politicized factions desperate to seize power.

9. *Africa Contemporary Record: Annual Survey and Documents*; 1968–70, ed. Colin Legum and John Drysdale (London: Africa Research, 1969–70); 1970–72, ed. Colin Legum (London: Rex Collings, 1971; London: Rex Collings, and New York: Africana Publications, 1972); 1972–79, ed. Colin Legum (New York: Africana Publications, 1973–79); on Zambia's elites see 1977–78, p. B 463.

10. Ian Scott, "Middle Class Politics in Zambia," *African Affairs* 77, 308 (July 1978): 330; for an excellent general study, see William Tordoff, ed., *Politics in Zambia* (Berkeley and Los Angeles: University of California Press, 1974).

11. René Lemarchand, *Rwanda and Burundi* (New York and London: Praeger, 1970), pp. 343–435.

A striking feature of African systems of personal rule over the past two decades has been the assertion of power, almost invariably military power, by new men with ruling ambitions against incumbents. The broad theme of such power assertions has been the attempt of the new men to achieve what their predecessors often were unable to—that is, the "normalization" of rulership, typically within the organizational framework of a one-party state. Like Numeiri, Maj. Gen. Juvénal Habyalimana of Rwanda, who came to power in a coup in 1973, proceeded to establish a one-party state and have himself elected President in December 1978; Gen. Moussa Traoré of Mali also founded a one-party state, and was similarly elected President in 1979. An exception to the "normalization" of soldier rule in this authoritarian way is the case of President (formerly General) Sangoulé Lamizana of Upper Volta, who was elected to office after presiding over the restoration of a system of constitutional government.[12] The tenures of other new rulers, who retained power only temporarily or who have come to power only very recently, have been too brief to qualify as established rulership for the purposes of our analysis.

Léopold Sédar Senghor, Senegal

Among the most sophisticated and enduring of contemporary Africa's founder rulers has been the scholarly president of Senegal, Léopold Sédar Senghor.[13] An experienced and consummate politician, Senghor has dominated Senegalese politics for nearly three decades and has achieved a position of virtually unrivaled authority over his government and the ruling Parti Socialiste (PS). During the course of Senghor's political career, other important Senegalese politicians have been defeated, outmaneuvered, or subordinated, and had their parties banned; some who have persisted in their rivalry have been excluded from the dominant party (and therefore the polity); and a few have been forced into exile or have had their civil and political liberties curtailed. Lamine Gueye, a leading politician in the era of nationalist politics and once Senghor's colleague, lost his paramount position when Senghor outmaneuvered him in a contest for the support of the powerful Mouride Islamic sect. Mamadou Dia, Senghor's confrere and his Prime Minister in the years immediately following independence in 1960, was defeated in a struggle for power in 1962. And Sheikh

12. See chapter 7 below.
13. For a study of Senghor's political beliefs, see Irving Leonard Markovitz, *Léopold Sédar Senghor and the Politics of Negritude* (New York: Atheneum, 1969).

Anta Diop, a recent rival, was unsuccessful in his bid to secure government sanction for his opposition party in the later 1970s, when Senghor's confidence in his own authority and the stability of his regime was demonstrated in his liberalization of the polity, allowing for the reemergence of approved rival parties to the PS within a semi-competitive party system.

Senghor's practical understanding of politician politics has contributed greatly to his success and survival as a ruler. Senegal has not been an easy country to govern. It has an unstable and dependent one-crop economy (peanuts), a complex and divided social structure, a strong, parallel religious authority (Islam), a rapidly enlarging urban sector with a tradition of civil liberty and political and intellectual discussion, and a history of intense political rivalry and jealousy—all of which have contributed to the difficulty of governance and influenced the character of government. Somewhat like Machiavelli's model Prince, Senghor has understood the skills and dispositions required to be successful on the Senegalese political stage: timing, adaptability, judgment; the ability to exploit the weaknesses of lesser politicians or potential rivals; the will to remain in control of the state even in the face of serious political problems and despite a professed and apparently sincere desire to retire to a life of poetry; and the confidence to allow a measure of political liberty. In Senghor we are presented with that rare politician who instinctively seems to understand the strengths and weaknesses of the society he rules, and therefore the possibilities and limitations of rule.

A central feature of Senghor's rule has been the development of his role as an arbiter of disputes among leading politicians, lieutenants, and their factions. For instance, he has employed his office as a "court" to give audiences to notables, to hear arguments and claims of rivals, and to receive pleas and appeals. Such conduct is very much in character with the magisterial and counselling function of traditional kingship. Employing the metaphor of interest politics, Edward Schumacher observes that

> Senghor has made direct personal access to the president's office the prime source of satisfaction for virtually all associational, nonassociational, and institutional interest group spokesmen involved in party politics and public policy formation. Indeed, the accessibility of the president to the numerous supplicants seeking his personal intervention on behalf of their individual or group interests is plainly seen in the well-publicized list of audiences daily accorded by Senghor.[14]

14. Edward J. Schumacher, *Politics, Bureaucracy, and Rural Development in Senegal* (Berkeley, Los Angeles, London: University of California Press, 1975), pp. 71–72.

Senghor has also enjoyed extensive constitutional and policy powers to rule directly by legislative initiative, and, if necessary, by decree. Before steps were taken to liberalize the regime, Senghor enjoyed, as Senegal's President, exclusive right to introduce legislation in the National Assembly and to make appeals to the Supreme Court on constitutional questions. Both privileges reflected, at least during the period of de facto one-party government from 1963 until 1978, a conception of the ruler as the highest source of law in Senegal. Despite the cautious liberalization (or perhaps because of it), the constitution was amended to give Senghor the effective right to name his own Dauphin: the new amendment declared that the Prime Minister, who is appointed by the President, shall automatically succeed him in the event of death or serious disability.[15] Presidential royalism has been evident in the setting aside of specific areas of government policy for Senghor's discretion alone, such as foreign policy (the traditional prerogative of the Prince) and cultural policy, which has been a particular concern of Senghor's both as an intellectual and as a politician.[16] Such constitutional and policy prerogatives have had the effect of subordinating not only cabinet ministers but also members of the Parliament to his personal rule.[17] Presidential royalism has also been revealed in the appointment of "courtiers," many of whom are bureaucrats and technocrats, to advise the ruler in matters of policy and to become ministerial executives themselves. Surrounded by courtiers of this type, the ruler has been shielded from ordinary political pressures and from the political rivalries of sectarian and clan notables. Adamolekun has argued that

> the presence of bureaucrats in large numbers in Senghor's Governments provided him with a kind of personal political strategy for survival, by removing a very important and sensitive area of government from internal conflict and controversy. Not only did bureaucrat-ministers constitute a protective shield against professional politicians, they also shielded the President from excessive exposure to public criticism and indignation arising from economic failures, as he could always argue that the best available brains in the country were handling the problem.[18]

Such courtiers are personally dependent on the ruler, and there-

15. *Africa Confidential* 19, 4 (February 3, 1978): 4–5.

16. " 'Reality' in Senegal," *West Africa* 3182 (10 July 1978): 1329.

17. Schumacher, pp. 70–72.

18. Ladipo Adamolekun, "Bureaucrats and the Senegalese Political Process," *Journal of Modern African Studies* 9, 4 (1971): 556.

fore easy for him to control. The Senegalese ruler is not alone in staffing his court and executive with such men.

While the President's court is the theater of high politics in Senegal, the system of politician politics is by no means confined to the courtiers, politicians, and petitioners in the court, but involves a broad spectrum of national and regional leaders. The growing number of appointed politicians, mainly bureaucrats, has not superseded the authority of national politicians in relation to regional and local constituents and supporters in all organized sectors of society.

Senghor's regime has been supported by two elements of Senegalese society, both of which exhibit basically a patron-client structure and a culture of personal or traditional obligation and deference—the Islamic religious brotherhoods of marabouts (religious leaders) and the political "clans" or factions. Exercising effective religious authority in a largely and thoroughly Moslem society, the brotherhoods have always been in a strategic position to thwart government policy. French colonial authorities knew it would be folly to alienate the marabouts and their devoted followers, and were prepared, therefore, to temper and adjust their policies for the sake of maraboutic support (or at least acquiescence). In the same cautious manner, Senghor also has recognized and cooperated with the Islamic leaders. His court is accessible to them, and he is reported to spend considerable time cultivating their support. Their influence, however, has been more negative than positive. They acquiesce in public policies rather than support them, but they block those they judge inimical to their interests and privileges.[19]

There are strong clientelist arrangements particularly in the organization and operation of the agricultural cooperatives in Senegal. Modelled on the "Providence Societies" established by the French colonial authorities, a structure of producer cooperatives and associated marketing boards was built up after 1962 by Senghor's government for the production and marketing of peanuts. The membership of the cooperatives is comprised mainly of Wolof peasants who plant peanuts, but effective authority within them is held by chiefs and marabouts—many of whom are politicians—who serve as patrons of their peasant followers. Nominally democratic in constitution and aim, the cooperatives have tended to be treated as the "property" not of the peasants but of their

19. William J. Foltz, "Senegal," in *Political Parties and National Integration in Tropical Africa*, ed. James S. Coleman and Carl G. Rosberg, Jr. (Berkeley and Los Angeles: University of California Press, 1964), p. 48.

leaders, who retain an important share of the agricultural surplus and who divert to their own use or give to selected followers government services allocated to the cooperative societies. Thus the powers and resources of the cooperatives have been appropriated, in a way reminiscent of feudalism, by chiefs and marabouts who in effect form the rural base of an alliance with national party and government leaders. This clientelist system based on the peanut economy and functioning through the cooperatives has formed the backbone of the national polity in Senegal under Senghor.

The Senegalese structure of co-opted traditional-religious authorities and commercial interests channels support for the central government and the President from those who count in rural society, but it requires his regime's acquiescence to the corruption of public officials having dealings with local leaders. The system and the regime derive legitimacy from the opportunity extended to patrons and clients at all significant levels of the polity to appropriate shares of its resources for themselves. Over the years, "corruption" has emerged as Senegal's national political style.[20] In his study of the cooperatives, Donal O'Brien reported that although peasant cultivators resented the flagrant corruption of superiors, they admitted they might behave in a similar manner if given the opportunity.[21] Not least because of the advantages (for some the riches) provided by a corrupt system of cooperative-government relations and by other sources of political and administrative largesse, Senghor's regime has retained the support of marabouts and other privileged rural leaders. In addition, the President has carefully avoided open competition with such elites for the support of the peasantry. Senegalese royalism has been built upon a system of essentially indirect personal rule. Says Markovitz:

> Senghor's generally élitist approach in politics, philosophy and the strategy of development meant that the secular leaders would not try to stir up crowds or appeal to the marabouts' followers directly, except on a level that would only emphasize their remoteness from the ordinary peasantry.[22]

The marabouts can be important auxiliaries of rule and order, but not of policy and change. They have been deployed for main-

20. Donal B. Cruise O'Brien, *Saints and Politicians: Essays in the Organisation of a Senegalese Peasant Society* (London: Cambridge University Press, 1975), p. 187.

21. Donal B. Cruise O'Brien, "Co-operators and Bureaucrats: Class Formation in a Senegalese Peasant Society," *Africa* 41, 4 (October 1971): 275.

22. Irving Leonard Markovitz, "Traditional Social Structure, the Islamic Brotherhoods, and Political Development in Senegal," *Journal of Modern African Studies* 8, 1 (1970): 96.

taining law and order, securing taxes and military service from
their followers, and mobilizing votes for the PS,[23] but they have
resisted most attempts by the government to reorganize rural life
in a developmental direction.[24] They have constituted, in other
words, powerful sources of tradition and conservatism in the Senegalese polity. But the relationship between mosque and state in
Senegal is not a constitutional union: it is a political alliance based
on expediency and interest for both parties, as the following remarks suggest:

> The Mourides and their Khalife General . . . still exercise an influence
> that can be measured negatively by the fact that if ever they told their
> followers not to vote for Léopold Senghor, it would be a serious political
> setback for the President. With the marabout as the intermediary be-
> tween the peasant and the administration, President Senghor has assidu-
> ously cultivated a reciprocal arrangement with the religious powers. In
> return for political support they are provided with economic facilities.[25]

The second pillar of Senghor's regime is the "clans" or factions,
which the ruler and other national PS leaders have found indispensable for the establishment and maintenance of their domination. The clan system is a network of national-regional-local
linkages that can be exploited for political and governmental purposes.[26] Often with the acquiescence, if not the active cooperation
of central authorities, some clan leaders of rural Senegal (typically
better-educated persons) have been able to penetrate the rural
state administration to extract resources for their own enjoyment
or for redistribution as patronage to their followers. Through
their control of local government and local PS offices, some have
gained access to municipal sources of patronage.[27]

Although centrally important to Senghor and his regime, this
dual clientelist system of Islamic authorities and clan politicians
accounts for only part of the political structure. Senegal is a more
complex and ambiguous society than this suggests, with an unusually strong tradition of political openness: electoral politics in
Dakar and some of the other urban communities date back to the

23. Ibid., p. 92.

24. O'Brien, "Co-operators and Bureaucrats," pp. 263–77.

25. " 'Reality' in Senegal: 2," West Africa 3183 (17 July 1978): 1383.

26. See a seminal article by William J. Foltz, "Social Structure and Political Be-
havior of Senegalese Elites," in Friends, Followers and Factions: A Reader in Political
Clientelism, ed. Steffan W. Schmidt, James C. Scott, Carl Landé, and Laura Guasti
(Berkeley, Los Angeles, London: University of California Press, 1977), pp. 242–49.

27. Clement Cottingham, "Political Consolidation and Central-Local Relations in
Senegal," Canadian Journal of African Studies 4, 1 (Winter 1970): 101–20.

late nineteenth century.[28] Senghor's ruling strategy has never been to close the polity entirely—to completely deprive individuals and groups of their liberties and opportunities to express their opinions and engage in politics. Intellectual and press freedom has generally been allowed during his rule, sustaining the lively activity and ferment of one of Africa's leading intellectual centers; political freedom has been more subject to control, but never with the aim of restricting it entirely. Had Senghor attempted to suppress it entirely, it seems unlikely, given the character of Senegalese society and history, that he would have succeeded. In fact, the recent liberalization of Senegalese party politics seems to have stemmed primarily from Senghor's recognition that a de facto one-party system brought with it underground and conspiratorial politics, especially in the urban centers, which were potentially more threatening to his regime than openly competitive party politics.[29] A politically sophisticated society, such as Senegal's, places constraints on statecraft and increases the contingencies of rule, and it is an astute ruler that recognizes this.

Senghor apparently hoped that renewed electoral competition, by enlarging political freedom, would provoke an "awakening" of his own party from the lethargy that ordinarily accompanies monopolism in politics no less than in economics.[30] In 1976 the constitution was amended to permit the existence of three (increased in 1978 to four) recognized parties, each with official labels to indicate their assigned positions on the left-right ideological spectrum. (The fact that the parties are officially recognized and classified is indicative of the qualified character of the new multiparty democracy in Senegal. Previously the constitution had placed no limit on the number of parties, although in practice none but the PS had been able to exist since the mid-1960s.) Senghor's party chose what was presumed to be the most widely appealing label—"democratic socialist"—which was also sought by other political parties; the remaining labels of "Marxist-Leninist," "liberal democratic," and "conservative" were reluctantly accepted by rival parties wishing to enter the political arena. One of these—the Parti Africain d'Indépendance (PAI)—chose to ignore its official label of "Marxist-Leninist" to avoid being stigmatized

28. G. Wesley Johnson, Jr., *The Emergence of Black Politics in Senegal: The Struggle for Power in the Four Communes* (Stanford: Stanford University Press, 1971).

29. *West Africa* 3183 (17 July 1978): 1381.

30. *Africa Contemporary Record*, 1976–77, p. B 695.

by an unpopular symbol in a predominantly Islamic society, preferring instead to use the label "scientific socialist." Other groups
refused to accept assigned labels as a condition of open participation and were denied official recognition in return: one of the most
important of these was Diop's intellectual-led but Moslem-based
Rassemblement National Démocratique (RND)—the unofficial
opposition in Senegal. Other political groups, some of them led by
important politicians, also refused to engage in the new political
game designed by Senghor.[31] To this extent, the constitutional
changes have not entirely eliminated clandestine politics from
Senegal; nor have they eliminated intra-party factional rivalries
and intrigues from the PS itself, which through most of 1980 continued to be fueled by the succession issue.

These electoral changes have failed to alter substantially (and
this was scarcely the intention) the dominant position of the PS in
the Senegalese polity. The semi-competitive elections of 1978 resulted in overwhelming victories both for Senghor in the presidential contest (82 percent of the votes cast) and for the PS in the
National Assembly contests (82 of the 100 seats): the consequence,
no doubt, of Senghor's historic cultivation of support from the Islamic and rural leaders of Senegal, although some complaints of
election irregularities were registered against the PS and the government.[32] The continued exclusion of important rivals and parties from the electoral arena (most notably Diop and his RND, as
well as Dia and the socialist elements that support him), along
with the fact that those included are handicapped by the system of
official labels, suggests that it is very unlikely for the foreseeable
future that the present regime can be altered or its ruler displaced
by electoral means. Moreover, constitutional amendments of 1976
authorized the President to seek reelection as often as he wished
(whereas formerly he would have had to stand down after 1978).[33]

It is unlikely, therefore, that the introduction of quasi-democ-
racy will remove the issue of the succession from the agenda of
Senegalese politics. The extent to which the issue remains salient
is an approximate indication of the difficulty of changing rulers by
electoral means. As was already noted, the constitutional changes
that ushered in the new era of semi-competitive politics were com-
plemented by changes in the procedures for succession, which in

31. See ibid., pp. B 694–97; *Africa Confidential* 19, 3 (February 3, 1978): 4–5; and
West Africa 3182 (10 July 1978): 1329, 1331; ibid., 3183 (17 July 1978): 1381–85;
and ibid., 3201 (20 November 1978): 2279–80.
32. See *Africa Contemporary Record*, 1977–78, pp. B 762–66.
33. "Senghor Makes Some Concessions," *West Africa* 3201 (20 November 1978):
2279.

effect permit the President to select his own successor, whereas
formerly new elections had to be called. There have been reports
of jockeying by rival leaders and factions within the PS for the best
position in any succession crisis that might develop: intense political interest and controversy have focused on appointments to the
office of prime minister.[34] Such interest is heightened by Senghor's
advanced age. (He was born in 1901.) It is a curious fact that the
parallel constitutional changes that liberalize the political arena
while enhancing the authority of the President to control succession are contradictory in their implications. The first suggest that
a process of political institutionalization is being fostered in Senegal which would permit a change of rulers by democratic electoral
means, while the second imply that elections are a less acceptable
method of choosing a presidential successor than selection by the
incumbent.

With his electoral reforms, Senghor has tried to disarm his critics who have complained of the undemocratic character of his regime. He has probably enhanced his international standing in the
West as a leader of a regime that respects civil and political rights:
his party was the first in Africa to be admitted into the ranks of the
moderate Socialist International.[35] Beyond the considerations of
political expediency, there is reason to believe that Senghor may
genuinely desire to introduce democratic reforms for the contribution they may make to the political development of Senegal. There
is little doubt that he will hold the center stage in Senegalese politics as long as he wishes—in part because so many political leaders
and factions are likely to insist upon it. Under Senghor, Senegalese democracy has been a controlled democracy, but the prospects of such a polity continuing after Senghor are uncertain. The
country has experienced one major coup attempt, and there have
been allegations of other plots over the years. There is no doubt
that powerful men and factions harboring a desire to rule will be
strongly tempted to seize control after Senghor is gone; what is
uncertain is whether they will be restrained from doing so by the
newly fashioned institutional rules of the game. Political disen-
chantment arising from the inability of government to protect people against inevitable cyclical losses in a vulnerable cash-crop
economy could provide the pretext for such action.[36] Clearly, the
testing time of Senegal's new political institutions will be after
Senghor.

34. *Africa Confidential* 19, 24 (December 1, 1978): 2–3.
35. Ibid., 19, 15 (July 21, 1978): 4.
36. See *West Africa* 3269 (17 March 1980): 471–74.

Jomo Kenyatta, Kenya

Until his death in 1978 at an advanced age, Jomo Kenyatta had been the dominant figure in Kenya's politics both as an anti-colonial nationalist and later as ruler of the new Kenyan state.[37] With national independence in December 1963, the ruling authority transferred from the British to the Africans was centralized in the hands of Prime Minister (later President) Kenyatta and his trusted advisors and powerful oligarchs.[38] To understand the character of personal rule in Kenyatta's Kenya, one must appreciate not only the ruler's pivotal role but also the relationships—with the oligarchs, with other important political leaders, with the provincial administration senior staff, with the people—which constituted his regime.

Kenyatta was like a presidential "monarch," elevated above all other politicians in Kenya, with rights and prerogatives not only to intervene in their factional political affairs, but also to require demonstrations of allegiance as well as specified forbearances from them. To remain within the Kenya African National Union (KANU) oligarchy, politicians had to demonstrate their loyalty to the President. In addition to commanding such allegiance from his political party, the ruler of Kenya was in command of the provincial administration, whose senior officers and their staffs were *his* servants and nobody else's. Finally, he served as a popular symbol of the new Kenyan nation: in the public mind it was difficult to distinguish between the two. For almost three decades Kenyatta and Kenya were as one, an identification made all the more natural by the likeness of names. The Kiswahili term of respect *Mzee,* meaning "wise old man," became Kenyatta's unofficial title as father of his country, with the connotation of paternal authority and

37. For a comprehensive biography of Kenyatta as a nationalist leader, see Jeremy Murray-Brown, *Kenyatta* (New York: E. P. Dutton & Co., 1973); see also Donald C. Savage, "Kenyatta and the Development of African Nationalism in Kenya," *International Journal* 25, 3 (Summer 1970): 518–37. For some of Kenyatta's views, see Jomo Kenyatta, *Suffering Without Bitterness: The Founding of the Kenya Nation* (Nairobi: East African Publishing House, 1968).

38. For a detailed political study of the early years of Kenyan independence, see Cherry Gertzel, *The Politics of Independent Kenya 1963–1968* (Evanston: Northwestern University Press, 1970); for collections of helpful documents, see Cherry Gertzel, Maure Goldschmidt, and Donald Rothchild, eds., *Government and Politics in Kenya: A Nation-Building Text* (Nairobi: East African Publishing House, 1969), and Donald Rothchild, *Racial Bargaining in Independent Kenya: A Study of Minorities and Decolonization* (London: Oxford University Press, 1968). For the colonial period, see George Bennett, *Kenya: A Political History: The Colonial Period* (London: Oxford University Press, 1963), and George Bennett and Carl G. Rosberg, *The Kenyatta Election: Kenya 1960–1961* (London: Oxford University Press, 1961).

sanctity. But more than the nation or its people, he symbolized the Kenyan state: the patriarch of Kenya.

Kenya was—and is—ruled by an oligarchy, but Kenyatta was more than *primus inter pares:* his position was virtually unassailable. But he was not an Autocrat, much less a Tyrant: he invited other men to become politicians too; he ruled *with* the political "barons" who constituted the oligarchy. The center of the regime was undoubtedly an inner "court" of fraternal Kikuyu politicians who rose to political prominence with him, and most of whom came from his home district of Kiambu, in Kikuyu country just outside Nairobi. Beyond this inner circle of intimate, trusted, and (a few) lifelong colleagues was a circle of important ministers in his government: some of them were members of the Kikuyu community, while others were independent "big men" or representatives of other ethnic communities. Another crucial circle of power and authority that was loyal to the ruler comprised select senior officials, especially the highest officers, of the provincial administration. The "royalist" character of Kenyatta's rule has been captured by such observers of the Kenyan political scene as Colin Leys:

> Kenyatta's court was based primarily at his country home at Gatundu, about twenty-five miles from Nairobi in Kiambu district; but like the courts of old it moved with him, to State House in Nairobi, to his coastal lodge near Mombasa, and his lodge at Nakuru in the Rift Valley.[39]

Like many other African Princes, Kenyatta held court for politicians, delegations, emissaries, and petitioners who came from various parts of the country—and from abroad—bearing gifts and seeking his support, assistance, or advice in matters of interest or concern to them:

> To the court came delegations of all kinds; district, regional, tribal, and also functional. Most of them came from particular districts, often in huge numbers, accompanied by teams of traditional dancers and choirs of school children, organized and led by the MP's and local councillors, and provincial and district officers from the area. They gave displays of dancing and singing; the leaders presented cheques for various causes sponsored by the President and expressed their sentiments of loyalty and respect; and would finally outline various needs and grievances. In return the President would thank them, commend the dances and songs, exhort them to unity and hard work, and discuss their requests, explaining why some could not be met and undertaking to attend to others.[40]

39. Colin Leys, *Underdevelopment in Kenya: The Political Economy of Neo-Colonialism* (Berkeley and Los Angeles: University of California Press, 1974), p. 246.
40. Ibid., p. 247.

Kenyatta held regular audiences, and evidently he regarded this activity as a most important one, the public face of which could be seen regularly on television. He used such occasions to make important pronouncements, quite frequently calling for unity and an end to political squabbling among KANU politicians and their factions, or warning usually unnamed individuals or groups of the harsh consequences in store for them should they persist in actions he claimed to be threatening to the regime. Such pronouncements were duly reported in the press or broadcast over radio and television; sometimes they carried the imprimatur of proclamations or decrees. On such occasions it was possible to discern Kenyatta's role as a plebiscitarian ruler speaking to, and on behalf of, the people.

Kenyatta's pronouncements sometimes had the effect of "edicts,"preempting the legislative role of Parliament and the policymaking role of government ministries. Among other things, it was this supremacy and independence of Kenyatta that contributed a highly personal quality to his rule. In his relations with Parliament, he was free to decide whether enacted legislation would be applied or not; similarly, if he desired a law but found it inconvenient to secure it from Parliament, then it would be secured by presidential decree. Sometimes he did not even bother with formal decrees, but would give private instructions that were treated as laws. For example, there was no public law preventing foreigners from purchasing coastal land in Kenya, but the administration, on the private instructions of Kenyatta, refused to accept transfers of title to foreigners, effectively preventing such transactions (with some rare exceptions).[41]

Kenyatta enjoyed great freedom to intervene personally in the policymaking process, at times overruling the technocrats and policy planners. Presidential intervention and preemption of government policymaking, with the effect of reversing or dramatically altering the direction of established policies, was evident in several major issue areas: the decision to adopt Kiswahili as the national language; the political attempt to establish levels of wage employment in the public and private sectors in 1970 (the second Tripartite Agreement); the determination of major agricultural pricing policies; the provision of free public education at the early elementary levels of schooling.

In these and other ways Kenyatta established in the public mind the relationship of the "king" and his "people." Observers have noted "the old man's . . . canny ability to identify and to meet criti-

41. See *Africa Confidential* 15, 18 (September 6, 1974): 4.

cal populist dissatisfaction."[42] On a number of occasions he deliberately adopted policies because they were popular. Among these were the redistribution of European settler-occupied land; the early and thoroughgoing Africanization of the civil service; and, perhaps most important, the gradual Africanization of the commercial sectors of the local economy by the government's withdrawing of commercial rights and privileges enjoyed by the Asian community. As Gertzel points out: "Kenyatta's responsiveness to populist pressures [was]. . . a critical element in diffusing factional and mass tension on a number of occasions."[43] He carefully and jealously cultivated his role as a popular African "king."

The major instrumentality of Kenyatta's rule, like that of colonial governors before him, was the provincial administration: a patrimonial organization established throughout the country and down to the local level whose officers are responsible not only for law and order but also for all important matters of government administration in the country. The intimate relations that existed between Kenyatta and the senior officers of the provincial administration, especially the provincial commissioners, was in the character of royalist administration. Unlike some other nationalist leaders in Africa, Kenyatta did not bring Kenya to independence at the helm of a nationalist movement united in opposition to colonial rule. He had been imprisoned by colonial authorities from 1953 until 1961 for his alleged leadership of the so-called "Mau Mau" movement, but factional rivalry among KANU leaders prevented anyone but Kenyatta from becoming ruler. (Kenyatta had been the undisputed leader of the post–World War II Kenyan nationalist movement—the Kenya African Union [KAU]—until it was banned in 1953 and its leading members jailed or detained.)[44] After preventing the establishment of a decentralized, regionally dominant state immediately after independence as specified by the independence constitution (an act of constitutional obstruction in which he was privately supported by many senior administrative officers of the central government, who had no desire to see their organizations dismantled), Kenyatta came to rely upon the provincial administration and to enjoy the confidence and loyalty of its senior staff. A tradition of imperial-bureaucratic rule was thereby maintained: President Kenyatta had taken the place of the colonial Governor. From this time onward, the provincial admin-

42. Cherry Gertzel, "Development in the Dependent State: The Kenyan Case," *Australian Outlook* 32, 1 (April 1978): 99.
43. Ibid.
44. Carl G. Rosberg, Jr. and John Nottingham, *The Myth of "Mau Mau": Nationalism in Kenya* (New York: Praeger, 1966), pp. 212–76.

istration came to be closely identified with the authority of Kenyatta. The identity was reinforced by the rapid Africanization of the civil service following independence and, in particular, by the rapid promotion of Africans to senior administrative posts.

Under Kenyatta, the provincial and district commissioners remained "political officers," as they had been during colonial times. The provincial commissioners in particular were extremely powerful and conducted themselves as the royalist officials they were: the authoritative representatives and agents of the ruler in the countryside.[45] They were directly responsible to the Office of the President, which in its day-to-day administration was in the charge of a brother-in-law of Kenyatta's. Some provincial commissioners were the final authorities within the jurisdictions they ruled, subject only to the directives of Kenyatta. As the king's men they were

> powerful vis-à-vis party people in their areas and vis-à-vis the representatives of the central ministries and elected officials like MP's, district councillors, and even ministers when the latter were operating in a commissioner's province or district and involving themselves in provincial affairs.[46]

The sometimes political character of the activities of the servants of the "crown" has been evidenced in their responsibilities for issuing "licenses" for the holding of public meetings,[47] or presidential "clearances" validating the nominations of KANU candidates prior to elections. Former opposition politicians on more than one occasion were prevented from participating in party politics by provincial officials enforcing government political regulations or the ruler's commands.

By his personal control of the provincial administration, Kenyatta was able to exercise effective authority throughout the country. The provincial administration, however, was—and probably still is—primarily an instrument of regulation and control which could operate routinely in respect to settled matters of policy and administration, but could not resolve controversial political ques-

45. *Africa Confidential* 19, 4 (February 17, 1978): 3. See also Cherry Gertzel, "The Provincial Administration in Kenya," *Journal of Commonwealth Political Studies* 4, 3 (1966): 201–15; Goran Hyden, Robert Jackson, and John Okumu, eds., *Development Administration: The Kenyan Experience* (Nairobi: Oxford University Press, 1970).
46. Henry Bienen, *Kenya: The Politics of Participation and Control* (Princeton: Princeton University Press, 1974), p. 38.
47. The "Public Order Act," *Laws of Kenya*, ch. 56, stipulates that all public meetings must be licensed by the district commissioner. See Gertzel et al., eds., *Government and Politics in Kenya*, p. 126.

tions involving the conflicts of powerful men or groups. In dealing with extra-policy political issues, the Kenyan polity, like any other, needs agents or institutions of adjudication. Kenyatta performed this function as final arbiter and grand political patron of Kenya. This function preeminently associated him with his "court," but it also associated him with the ruling party and with Parliament. KANU was not (and still is not) a political "organization" so much as a confederation of arenas where political bosses of rival factions collided and colluded in their perennial struggle for the power and patronage of party, governmental, and parastatal offices.[48] The intra-party struggle took place both in the various district arenas and in the national executive.

The struggle also took place, among generally the same political barons, within Parliament. To compete for a seat in Parliament an aspiring MP first had to obtain the permission of KANU, which in Kenya's de facto one-party system is the only political association with the right to present candidates for election. After opposition was effectively banned in 1969, the partisan divisions of the country tended to be contained within KANU itself, and within Parliament observers began to speak of KANU 'A' and KANU 'B' in referring to the major factional divisions that emerged within the party—almost like parties within a party. But in a competitive factional system, unlike a competitive party system that is regulated by institutional rules, the need for an umpire is great lest the factional struggle deteriorate into outright violence. Kenyatta presided over this personal-factional struggle, adjudicating disputes when called upon to do so and sometimes directly intervening to keep the peace and prevent some rivalries from getting out of hand—but he did not seek to eliminate the competition.

An unusual feature of politics in Kenya under Kenyatta was the freedom allowed to MPs to criticize the government and its policies. Kenya's Parliament has been exceptional in Africa in con-

48. See Joel D. Barkan, "Bringing Home the Pork: Legislator Behavior, Rural Development and Political Change in East Africa" (Comparative Legislative Research Center, University of Iowa, Occasional Paper No. 9, 1975); Alwyn R. Rouyer, "Political Recruitment and Political Change in Kenya," *Journal of Developing Areas* 9, 4 (July 1975): 539–62; and Goran Hyden and Colin Leys, "Elections and Politics in Single-Party Systems: The Case of Kenya and Tanzania," *British Journal of Political Science* 2, 4 (October 1972): 389–420. For an excellent study of a district, see Geoff Lamb, *Peasant Politics: Conflict and Development in Murang'a* (New York: St. Martin's Press, 1974); for a city environment, see Richard Stren, "Factional Politics and Central Control in Mombasa, 1960–1969," *Canadian Journal of African Studies* 4, 1 (Winter 1970): 33–56; and for trade unions, see Richard Sandbrook, *Proletarians and African Capitalism: The Kenyan Case 1960–1972* (Cambridge: Cambridge University Press, 1975).

tinuing to serve, with occasional difficulty and disruption, as a privileged forum of public comment, criticism, and debate. Kenyatta, of course, was above criticism, and it was clearly understood that even the mildest show of disrespect for the ruler would not be tolerated; in Kenya the "crown" was above Parliament. MPs and other leaders who made major criticisms of the government that could in any way be construed as criticisms of Kenyatta quickly found themselves in difficulty with the authorities. But ministers were known to be fair game, and criticisms of their policies or actions were permitted if they were clearly separated from the ruler and his regime. MPs generally knew the bounds of their parliamentary privileges and stayed within them, but occasionally they overstepped them. When Parliament as a whole became too vigorous or indiscreet in its criticisms of the government, and particularly when the regime itself appeared to be the target, the President took actions against it, including the exercise of his constitutional right to prorogue it. Presidential disloyalty was a serious crime, and MPs who deliberately or inadvertently *appeared* to exhibit disloyalty were sometimes punished severely. For declaring in Parliament that KANU was "dead" when President Kenyatta was maintaining the opposite, the Deputy Speaker of the National Assembly, John Seroney, and the MP for Butere, Martin Shikuku, were detained under the provisions of the Preservation of Public Security Act in October 1975.[49] In Kenya parliamentary privilege does not exempt MPs from preventive detention, and in making such allegations they presumably knew the risks they were taking.[50] Thus Parliament, for all its liveliness and independence, remained subordinate to the "crown" in matters of critical concern to Kenyatta.

Not far beneath the calm surface even of stable personal regimes, it is not surprising to find tensions and conflicts born of the jealousies and rivalries such regimes characteristically foster. Even a regime as durable as Kenyatta's, with its relative prosperity and stability since Kenya's independence, was no exception. On several occasions Kenyatta's regime was disrupted when major leaders were excluded from the ruling oligarchy or withdrew, carrying not only clients but also at times ethnic segments away with them. This happened when a leading Luo politician, Oginga

49. *Weekly Review* (Nairobi), October 20, 1975, pp. 4–9. Seroney and Shikuku were released, along with all others detained under the act, in December 1978 on the order of Kenyatta's successor, Daniel arap Moi.

50. A leading constitutional lawyer, Mr. J. P. W. B. McAuslan, gave this opinion in an interview with the press in 1967. See Gertzel et al., eds., *Government and Politics in Kenya*, p. 221.

Odinga, was excluded in 1966,[51] and it has happened with less prominent leaders before and since. The greatest disruptions, however, were caused by acts of political murder against leading politicians. The two most unsettling episodes were the 1969 assassination of Tom Mboya,[52] a brilliant nationalist politician, and the 1975 murder of Josiah Mwangi Kariuki, a populist Kikuyu leader who had fallen out of favor with the oligarchy.[53]

Political disruption of personal regimes is caused not only by the fall of a man, or even by the fall of other men and followers who have tied their careers to his. (In both the Mboya and Kariuki cases, entire political factions, and the communities and groups they represented, suffered a political fall.) It is also caused by the insecurity that political violence inevitably produces; public confidence and the stability of political and social expectations are dramatically undermined for some time afterwards. In both the Mboya and Kariuki cases personal violence was followed by disruptions and dislocations that extended far beyond the oligarchy and had effects on the political system as a whole. With the fall of Mboya, many of the Luo people became disaffected from the regime, having already lost their other major representative in the regime—Odinga. A major realignment and narrowing of the ruling ethnic coalition resulted. In Mboya the country lost one of its most talented leaders and perhaps the most likely successor to President Kenyatta at that time.[54] In the aftermath of his death there was violence based on ethnicity in the urban areas of Nairobi and Kisumu, as well as a resurgence of ethnic political consciousness, particularly by the Kikuyu people, who engaged in forced oath-takings reminiscent of the "Mau Mau" oath-takings of the early 1950s. The murder of Mboya raised to the level of public notice the specter of "tribalism" that had haunted Kenyan political life since independence.

The fall of Kariuki led to a different result, but it also had significant social and political repercussions. In this case it was not an ethnic community, but a subordinated and impoverished lower class, both Kikuyu and non-Kikuyu, which was deprived of a very significant and prominent spokesman. There is some irony in this: Kariuki was a very wealthy man, very much a "big man" in the eyes of his followers and admirers. The poor were deprived of the

51. *Not Yet Uhuru: The Autobiography of Oginga Odinga* (London: Heinemann, 1967).

52. *Africa Contemporary Record*, 1969–70, pp. B 122–26.

53. Ibid., 1975–76, pp. B 215–18.

54. See Tom Mboya, *Freedom and After* (London: Andre Deutsch, 1963).

hope he held out for them to realize a greater stake in the country: perhaps a more equitable distribution of opportunities, if not for themselves, then for their children. Kariuki was an ambitious politician who undoubtedly saw in the mobilization of popular support from among Kenya's poor his opportunity for greater power and national prestige. But he must have known the risk he was taking—that by voicing the discontent of the numerous poor he could be perceived as dividing the people and alienating them from the ruler and his regime. By persisting in his populist opposition he gambled and he lost.

His bloody elimination probably reflected the political fact that the regime could not tolerate public rivals to the ruler (especially a rival speaking in the name of "the people" or "the poor") and the economic fact that the government had only limited opportunities and benefits to extend to politically conscious individuals and groups. Politicization could only increase a sense of deprivation and alienation. Little land remained in alien hands which could be effectively and productively distributed to Africans; the Africanization of the public and to some extent the private sectors had pretty much run its course; the possibility of creating new jobs was limited to what could be obtained by economic growth, which was being robbed of much of its wealth-creating potential by a birth rate of over 4 percent—one of the highest in Africa.[55] All that was left as a possible policy to ameliorate the conditions of the poor was the redistribution of resources and opportunities from one African group or class to another. Since this would mean redistributing the wealth and opportunities of the oligarchy and its supporters, it was unlikely to be considered, let alone implemented in any substantial manner. The nationalization of foreign and domestic business, even if it were a practical possibility, would not have benefitted the poor, but only the state bureaucratic class that would have run the nationalized firms. All that remained as a response to the demands voiced by Kariuki was to ignore them or suppress them; by removing Kariuki the populist demands he represented were in effect suppressed. Kariuki's popularity among the poor is reason to believe that the demands and grievances he voiced were genuinely held by many, but it is not reasonable to

55. For a critical account of the economy, see *Employment, Incomes and Equality: A Strategy for Increasing Productive Employment in Kenya* (Geneva: International Labour Office, 1972). For critical reviews see David G. Davies, "A Critical Discussion of the ILO Report on Employment in Kenya," *Pakistan Development Review* 12, 3 (Autumn 1973): 283–92, and Colin Leys, "Interpreting African Underdevelopment: Reflections on the ILO Report on Employment, Incomes and Equality in Kenya," *African Affairs* 72, 289 (October 1973): 419–29.

assume that he was the only authentic spokesman for the poor. Many individuals among the poorest strata of Kenyan society may have admired Kariuki but may have believed that they were primarily responsible for their own welfare.

It is still not known exactly who ordered or instigated these political assassinations. However, in the case of Kariuki, a select committee of the Kenya Parliament inquired into the affair and published a report of its findings. High officials in the government were implicated, but immediately prior to the submission of the report to Parliament the committee was summoned by President Kenyatta. It was later reported that two names were removed before the document was tabled in the National Assembly. One of the names was that of a minister of state: only one member of the government held such a title at the time, and he was an intimate colleague and close relative of the President. Apart from this intervention, the committee was not prevented from releasing its findings, which were particularly unfavorable to the regime. The committee believed that its inquiry had contributed to relieving the tensions surrounding the affair and had prevented a more serious political conflict.[56] (This, of course, is one important reason for having Parliaments.)

Kenyatta died in office on August 23, 1978, and was succeeded by longtime Vice-President Daniel Toiritich arap Moi, a Tugan from western Kenya. Despite the fact that Kenyatta had personified the Kenyan state and dominated the political life of the country from its very inception, and despite the widespread apprehension of political breakdown without his stewardship (which was widely expressed and lasted at least for the final decade of his rule), the succession was constitutional. It may be worthwhile to examine the succession because it defied the expectations of many observers. Was this a "straw in the wind" signalling a process of political institutionalization in Kenya?

Toward the end of Kenyatta's rule, the question of succession, although it could not be discussed or speculated about publicly on threat of severe punishment, began to loom large, bringing with it growing political uncertainty and factional regrouping and jockeying. Indeed, more than anything else it was the succession question that provided the primary organizational stimulus for the two major factions—KANU 'A' and KANU 'B'—led by rival contenders for the throne (neither of which Kenyatta publicly identified with). Insofar as these two factions cut across ethnic lines, and

56. *Africa* (An International Business, Economic and Political Monthly) 47 (July 1975): 24.

as their leaders attempted to build up support from wherever and whomever they could secure it, they contributed to a major regrouping of political forces in the country and an apparent decline in the saliency of ethnic divisions. But the rival factions could not compete openly and directly on the succession issue. Instead, their competition took the form of a struggle for the best position—the highest and most defensible ground, so to speak—from which to secure the ruler's mantle when it fell. The best position came to be defined in institutional terms: primarily in terms of the advantages and disadvantages conferred by the constitutional rules in respect to succession, and secondarily in terms of controlling positions in the ruling party.

The faction in the best strategic position was the one controlling the constitutional successor's office—the vice-presidency of the country—and the National Executive of the ruling party: on both counts the political advantage rested with the faction associated with a triumvirate which included Moi—KANU 'B.' The succession strategy of Moi's faction was therefore to adhere to the rules. KANU 'A'—comprising a number of Kikuyu politicians, relatives of Kenyatta, and others, and centered upon Dr. Njoroge Mungai—sought to reduce its disadvantages first by trying to change the constitutional rules on succession and second by attempting to win an intra-party electoral contest for membership on the National Executive of the ruling party. In late 1976 the opposition faction attempted to change the rules which provided for the Vice-President to succeed the President as a caretaker and for a presidential election to be held within ninety days. Reflecting the logic of personal rule, their reasoning was that the Acting President would be tempted to perpetuate his own rule by invoking emergency powers and even by detaining rivals for the presidency.

> Like a football team which does not seem able to score a victory under existing rules, they seem to be calling for a change in the rules of the game so that their chances of victory might be boosted. The game, however, is not an ordinary soccer match and the rules happen to be the country's very constitution.[57]

It is speculated that the Attorney-General, who happened also to be perhaps the key member of the Moi triumvirate, convinced Kenyatta not to allow such a change. The proposal was brought to a resolute end when the Attorney-General announced and Kenyatta's cabinet confirmed at a special meeting that even "to imag-

---

57. "A Boon for the Constitution," *Weekly Review* (Nairobi), October 18, 1976, p. 21.

ine" the death of the President would be treated as a criminal offense.[58] The second stratagem of KANU 'A' also failed (it is conjectured) when it became clear that KANU 'B' would win the party elections. The elections were cancelled at the last moment. It was speculated that the cancellation was due to the fact that Kenyatta was ill at the time, and it was feared that he would be unable to perform his customary role as arbiter between the factions to prevent overt conflict and the threat of instability.[59] However, it was never in Kenyatta's interest as a ruler to see either faction predominate.

The succession of Moi to the presidency following Kenyatta's death was entirely orderly. Fears that he might abuse his interim powers and seize control unconstitutionally proved unfounded, but the Kenyan newspapers were instructed that his title henceforth would be President, not Acting President![60] Subsequently, Moi was elected to replace Kenyatta as President of KANU, which was tantamount to being elected President of the country in Kenya's de facto one-party system. Shortly afterwards a slate of candidates, reflecting at least in part Moi's choices, was elected to occupy controlling party offices. (Some of them were later defeated in the 1979 parliamentary elections, suffering a loss of authority from the electorate's rebuff.)

Outwardly these events appeared to be a demonstration of constitutionalism. In the face of general apprehension that the passing of Kenyatta would bring serious political instability to Kenya, how can this peaceful transition be explained? Was it because the constitutional rules had become fully accepted by all factions in the Kenyan polity? The attempt of KANU 'A' to change the succession rules in 1976 would appear to belie such a simple explanation. Was it because the entire political oligarchy in Kenya— KANU 'A' and KANU 'B'—feared political disorder more than they feared any loss of political advantage that might result from following the rules? There is some evidence to support this explanation: a meeting of all the ministers, assistant ministers, MPs, and top civil servants was held in January 1978—the first of its kind in fifteen years—in which it was resolved that incumbent politicians should not jockey for personal power and advantage.[61] Was it because the Moi faction was virtually guaranteed of success, and that any bid by others to seize power very likely not only would fail but also would lose them any chance of future patron-

58. *Africa Contemporary Record*, 1976–77, p. 219.
59. *Africa Confidential* 19, 17 (August 25, 1978): 2.
60. Ibid., 19, 21 (October 20, 1978): 6.
61. Ibid., 19, 4 (February 17, 1978): 1.

age and favors that could be claimed in exchange for a current show of loyalty and support? A leading Kenya weekly suggested that the suddenness of Kenyatta's passing and the smoothness of the early days of transition signalled a peaceful change to Moi: "All leaders had rallied behind Moi as the new president, [and] . . . the mood of the country was such that it was not possible for a challenger to emerge at that hour."[62] In a similar vein, the *Times* noted: "The openly expressed grief at Kenyatta's death was transformed into warm expressions of loyalty to Mr. Moi . . . who wisely announced that the policies of the late President would be faithfully continued. It was quickly apparent that in such an atmosphere no other challenger would try his luck."[63] Was the successful transition a matter of luck in that Kenyatta died suddenly, enabling the country to escape the scheming and plotting that a lingering illness might have invited?[64] The contemporary historical evidence is too ambiguous for these questions to be answered. All that can be said is that rules were complied with, and that one possible reason is that they had gained a sufficient measure of legitimacy that no faction would risk violating them.

Moi was elected to the presidency, unopposed, before the ninety-day interim period had expired, and on October 10, 1978, he was inaugurated as Kenya's second President in a public ceremony, with Mwai Kibaki, a prominent Kikuyu, as his Vice-President. Of course the succession was not completed solely by the constitutional transfer of the presidential office to Moi; in addition, he had to consolidate his power and position in the new regime. Kenyatta had dominated the country for so long and so thoroughly that Moi had to be concerned with establishing his personal authority. A number of actions had to be carefully planned and executed to rearrange the powerful politicians and officials in the party-government oligarchy in such a way as to create a new stable and workable ruling coalition. During the first year Moi ruled with essentially the cabinet he had inherited from Kenyatta (except for the demotion of a minister of state who had been Kenyatta's hatchet man). Stressing continuity, he adopted the slogan that all should follow in his *nyayo* (Kiswahili for

62. *Weekly Review*, December 29, 1978, p. 5.
63. *Times* (London), November 23, 1978.
64. As suggested in *Weekly Review*, December 29, 1978, p. 5. In fact, there appears to have been much idle scheming, and afterwards the Attorney-General claimed that a plot to seize power by force did exist but failed, in part because Kenyatta died not at his lodge in Nakuru, where the plotters were located, but on the coast at Mombasa. However, this may have been a ploy to discredit any critics of the new regime. See *Africa Contemporary Record*, 1978–79, pp. B 267–68.

"footsteps") in the same way he was treading in those of Kenyatta. Initially, he moved slowly and cautiously, removing some district commissioners in the provincial administration and shifting some permanent secretaries in the national government. But below the oligarchy, he moved much faster—with an eye on public opinion—and declared his determination to stamp out nepotism, corruption, and other legal abuses; he took steps to shake up the police force, the army, the immigration department, and the diplomatic service; he released all political detainees, extended free public schooling to the sixth grade, and decreed that the private sector increase its number of employees by 10 percent.[65]

Under the Kenyan parliamentary system, with the election of a new parliament, the President has to renew his mandate. Moi had to do so in the general elections in November 1979, but as President of KANU he stood unopposed. Moreover, it was Kenya's system of one-party elections that furnished Moi with the strategic opportunity to consolidate his position and establish an oligarchy identified with him. The system is remarkable for the intensity of its personal-factional competition and the regularity with which it decapitates incumbent MPs, including ministers and assistant ministers of the government. In the November election more than 740 parliamentary candidates competed; 72 out of a total of 158 elected incumbent MPs were defeated, including 7 ministers and 15 assistant ministers.[66] The defeat of the 22 front benchers gave Moi the opportunity to appoint new ministers of his own; in addition, he appointed a larger number of ministers and assistant ministers than in the previous Kenyatta government, partly by reorganizing and adding seven new ministries. For example, instead of one minister of agriculture with two assistant ministers, there were now two ministers and six assistant ministers—an almost threefold increase in front bench representation. Of the 158 elected MPs, 73 were appointed by Moi to the front benches; in addition, the constitution gave him the right to nominate a further 12 MPs who are totally dependent upon his patronage. Effectively, he was guaranteed a near permanent majority in Parliament by his use of patronage and appointment powers. In selecting ministers he was careful to include all the ministers who had been reelected, including three prominent members of the old anti-Moi faction of KANU.[67] By the time he formed his own gov-

65. See ibid., pp. B 266–76.

66. *Africa Research Bulletin: Political, Social, and Cultural Series* 16, 11 (December 15, 1979): 5466.

67. See *Weekly Review*, November 16 and 30, 1979.

ernment, he had changed three-fourths of the ministries' permanent secretaries in a search for both new talent and loyalty.

Moi took great care (as Kenyatta had done before him) to maintain proportional regional representation in his government, thereby appealing to the sense of regional-ethnic equity which is such an important criterion for justifying governmental organization in African countries. As if to complete the political succession and give his regime the final stamp of its own identity, he rehabilitated Kenyatta's toughest and oldest opponent, Odinga, appointing him chairman of the Cotton, Lint and Seed Marketing Board—a post with not inconsiderable patronage powers. In January 1980, perhaps in gratitude, the new President was given a public reception by Odinga's numerous supporters among the Luo people, a political event that could not have happened while Kenyatta ruled. Finally, Moi's identity as Kenya's new ruler has been marked by his assertive role in foreign policy; in 1981 Nairobi will host the summit of the Organization of African Unity (OAU). However, while the Moi era has been dubbed "Chapter Two," a climate of political certainty and calm is by no means assured.

William Tubman and William Tolbert, Liberia

For more than a century national politics in Liberia was the privileged occupation of the Americo-Liberian community, and particularly of prominent families within it—the descendants of a charter group of liberated slaves from the United States who had settled on the windward coast of West Africa early in the nineteenth century.[68] Liberia became a sovereign state in 1847, with a constitution modelled on that of the United States. However, between 1877 and 1980 the True Whig Party (TWP) enjoyed an unbroken tenure of political monopoly as the ruling vehicle of the Americo-Liberian community. The community had all the earmarks of an "aristocracy": it was an establishment of not only privileged but also "superior" self-regarding families whose power and wealth derived directly from the control of government; its dominant standing was supported by a system of laws and rules that sustained its power and privileges; and while open to the absorption of some indigenous Liberians into its families, it was

68. For three recent studies of Liberia, see J. Gus Liebenow, *Liberia: The Evolution of Privilege* (Ithaca and London: Cornell University Press, 1969); Christopher Clapham, *Liberia and Sierra Leone: An Essay in Comparative Politics* (Cambridge: Cambridge University Press, 1976); and Martin Lowenkopf, *Politics in Liberia: The Conservative Road to Development* (Stanford: Hoover Institution Press, 1976).

hegemonic in relation to other communities. During much of this period Liberian politics was exclusively a factional conflict within the Americo-Liberian community, whose members, because of their wealth and privileges, were the only ones able to engage in political activity. Liebenow notes:

> An analysis of the genealogies of the political leadership of Liberia over a period of years provides the objective observer as well as the active participant with an explicit map of the Liberian political terrain, plotting not only the immediate strength of a given family and its patrons but also a history of the upward and downward movement of various families in the political scene.[69]

No more than a dozen or so families dominated the Liberian state in recent decades, controlling the leadership of the politically important Masonic Lodges and the TWP.[70] The leading family was, of course, the current ruler's: from 1944 to 1971, this was the Tubmans; from 1971 to 1980, it was the Tolberts.

In recent decades leaders of subordinated African groups were incorporated into the regime on a basis of clientage and patronage, and some indigenous leaders and their families entered the familistic polity as more peripheral players. Many of these changes occurred during the long regime of William V. S. Tubman (1944–71). In the 1970s the successor regime of William Richard Tolbert took some hesitant steps in the direction of more progressive social policies and political liberalization. However, this had the unintended effect of creating a performance gap between public expectations and governmental accomplishments. At the end of the decade long-standing rumblings from within the subordinated groups manifested themselves as open opposition movements demanding revolutionary change and promoting public protests against the regime. During the same period, in the face of these changes the TWP began to lose its cohesiveness, with right-wing members strongly opposed to changes. In April 1980, following a year of political uncertainty and tension, the Tolbert regime was overthrown in a coup of non-commissioned officers and soldiers led by Master Sgt. Samuel K. Doe.

William Tubman was the President of Liberia for nearly three decades—an era that saw the rise of some Americo-Liberian families from outside the Monrovia inner circle that had previously controlled the presidency and the country.[71] As patriarch as well

69. Liebenow, p. 137.

70. *Africa Confidential* 20, 6 (March 14, 1979): 4.

71. For a view of Tubman's presidency as ending the "politics of elite families" of an earlier era, see Stephen S. Hlophe, "Ruling Families and Power Struggles in Liberia," *Journal of African Studies* 6, 2 (Summer 1979): 75–82.

as President, Tubman used his position to regulate personal and factional disputes within the aristocracy and to maintain its position in the country at large. Maintaining aristocratic privileges was tantamount to ruling the regime: Liberia *was* the aristocracy, and the indigenous African societies were little more than client communities under its *imperium*. Writing before Tubman's death in 1971, Liebenow said: "While he is the dominant figure in Liberian national politics, the President is not a dictator. A more accurate description would be that he has been the presiding officer of the Americo-Liberian ruling class."[72] Tubman's position as President enabled him to keep other men dependent upon him by his control of virtually all significant offices in the government. His powers of patronage were strengthened by his astute use of corruption: he could offer "his appointees opportunities for corruption which they could scarcely decline, but which could be held against them should any excuse be needed for their dismissal."[73]

For the greater period of his rule, Tubman did not rely heavily upon coercion to maintain the subordination of Liberian groups and communities—unlike some of his predecessors. But during his last years, at an advanced age, he grew apprehensive of opponents, especially from among modernist indigenous African circles and from among younger, discontented, more radically inclined Americo-Liberians. His use of a special security police resulted in a number of political arrests and imprisonments.[74] It was at this time that a more politically conscious class of Africans was emerging in Liberia who were capable of comparing the slow evolution of political change at home with the swift decolonizations taking place in neighboring West African countries, most notably Guinea and Sierra Leone. This class became available for political mobilization by any radical opponents of the regime who were prepared to take risks.

Undoubtedly influenced by the rise of African nationalism in neighboring countries, Tubman began to co-opt indigenous Liberian leaders into his regime. But such patronage was seldom extended to the highest government and party offices, which continued to be regarded as the exclusive entitlements of Americo-Liberians. Indigenous Liberians were brought into the apolitical organs of the state—the civil service, the fledgling technical ser-

72. Liebenow, pp. 152–53. For a view of Tubman as a despot, see Tuan Wreh, *The Love of Liberty . . . ; The Rule of President William V. S. Tubman, 1944–1971* (London: C. Hurst & Co., 1976).

73. Clapham, *Liberia and Sierra Leone*, p. 59.

74. *Africa Contemporary Record*, 1971–72, pp. B 600-1.

vices, the district administrative apparatus. (Under Tolbert the appointment and election of indigenous Liberians to some of the highest state offices began to take place. Evidently he believed that it was important to increase their representation in his regime, but as recently as 1979 there was only a small number in leading roles.)[75]

In 1971 Tubman died in office; Tolbert, a Baptist minister of strong religious faith, had served as Vice-President for almost twenty years. To the surprise of some observers, his succession was entirely constitutional and orderly, but as Vice-President, Tolbert had built up a political base within the aristocracy second only to Tubman's,[76] and this undoubtedly assisted the transition. It was rumored that the transition had also been assisted by a powerful kingmaker within the aristocracy, the national chairman of the TWP, "who more than anyone ensured a peaceful succession to President Tubman by refusing to accept any candidate but Vice-President Tolbert."[77] Not only had Tolbert placed himself in a strong political position to succeed, but he was also careful to cultivate the loyalty and allegiance of powerful individuals and groups after Tubman's death, not least the leaders of the country's armed forces.[78] If power and political skill were on the side of Tolbert, so also was the Liberian political tradition and the historic place of the aristocracy. The constitutional rules governing succession could be followed to the letter because the aristocracy stood behind them: in an atmosphere of rumblings within the subordinated African groups and classes, the aristocracy could not afford an internecine struggle over the succession.

Tolbert endeavored to distinguish his regime from that of his predecessor by adopting a populist style for his personal rule and a reform style for his government, but stopping short of basically altering the political status quo. He took immediate steps to disband the paid political informers that Tubman had employed in his last "paranoid" years and released and rehabilitated political prisoners. He also announced a campaign aimed at stamping out the abuses that had long been associated with government in Liberia: corruption, graft, embezzlement, and various other practices. The TWP "tithe," which deducted 10 percent of every government employee's salary, was abolished, to the dismay of the more conservative, right-wing stalwarts of the party, who feared the weakening of party strength that such a loss of resources might

75. *Africa Confidential* 20, 6 (March 14, 1979): 4.
76. Clapham, *Liberia and Sierra Leone*, p. 47.
77. Ibid., pp. 53–54.
78. Ibid., pp. 60–61.

entail. But Tolbert inherited and basically sought to work within the personal and factional polity of the Tubman era.

Tolbert's style of rule was especially pronounced in his accessibility to all groups—people from all over the country and any station in life who came to petition for some form of aid. He would generally respond by promising to fulfill their needs and then tell his ministers to carry out his promises. While this aspect of personalism made possible a short-term and direct "connection" with the people (and which most African rulers seem to feel uncomfortable without), it made more difficult the development of a routinized rational planning and provision of goods and services through a technically oriented ministry. In addition to this inhibition of planning, Tolbert also had to contend with the long-standing Americo-Liberian factional politics. Disputes and alliances in the ministries were very apparent, forcing Tolbert to shuffle key ministries and deputy ministry personnel around in order to keep his intra-elite factional opposition from getting control over resources in the ministries.

Tolbert's populist style of rule characteristically involved the use of catchy slogans and a rhetoric intended to appeal to the ordinary Liberian. He spoke of progress in the homely terms of "from mats to mattresses," and in what was to be his final address he declared expansively: "We stand upon the premise of liberty. We search for the true circle of unity and we seek a new cadence of mutuality, by which our continent can march towards brighter horizons."[79] His political rhetoric was flavored with biblical phrases and injunctions; in 1979 he declared a "War on Ignorance, Poverty and Disease," but he also designated 1979 the "Year of Discipline and Responsibility." In practice, social progress and responsibility proved difficult to achieve separately, let alone in combination. Under the influence of President Kaunda of Zambia, Tolbert coined the slogan "humanistic capitalism" stressing the suitability for Liberia's history and economic conditions of private ownership tempered by social altruism.[80] An economics of aggrandizement and personal acquisitiveness could appeal to the aristocracy, while the notion of altruism and social responsibility introduced an element of "social justice" that could be seen to transcend privilege and class.

The Tolbert regime took initial steps to introduce reform measures of "policy government" (as distinguished from the historic Liberian pattern of patronage government). Among others, these

79. Quoted in "Matchet's Diary," *West Africa* 3274 (21 April 1980): 690.
80. *Africa Confidential* 18, 5 (March 4, 1977): 6.

measures included (1) civil service reforms and—most important—the attempt to introduce a merit system in civil service appointments and promotions;[81] (2) the formulation of public
policies and programs based upon impersonal "social" criteria—
qualification, need, and so forth—with little evidence of an ability
to implement and enforce such policies; (3) the promotion of a foreign policy with Liberia's "national" interest and not merely that
of the aristocracy in mind. Under Tolbert Liberia entered into a
customs union with neighboring Sierra Leone providing for common tariffs and the free movement of goods between the two countries (the "Mano River Union"); in addition, Liberia became
prominent in pan-African affairs, and in 1979 Tolbert became
chairman of the OAU.

In addition to these policy changes, Tolbert promoted constitutional and political changes. In January 1975 a Constitutional
Commission was appointed to recommend changes to the constitution that would eliminate features that "may suggest class distinctions, separateness or sectionalism."[82] The commission's report
recommended both symbolic and substantive changes, including
the following: (1) that the slogan in the preamble "The Love of
Liberty Brought Us Here" be replaced by "Love, Liberty, Justice
and Equality"; (2) that references to the "enlightenment of the
benighted continent" be deleted from the preamble; (3) that the
hinterland, indigenous Liberian regions be incorporated into the
system of electoral constituencies, the property qualification for
voting be eliminated, and the secret ballot introduced; (4) that constitutional provision be made for the protection of a minority party
in the House of Representatives should a two-party system emerge
in Liberia; (5) that freedom of worship be guaranteed to non-
Christian communities (Moslems had enjoyed such a right only on
a de facto basis); and (6) that a previous constitutional amendment
limiting the President to one eight-year term be reaffirmed.

Among the important changes proposed and cautiously initiated
was the inclusion of more indigenous Liberians at the senior levels
of government and party. Tolbert appointed a non-Americo-Li-
berian to the vice-presidency in 1977 following the death of the
incumbent, and was reportedly grooming him as a successor. He
also stated, forcefully and on several occasions, his intention to
abide by the constitutional restriction of the presidency to one term
(included at his own insistence in reaction to the twenty-seven-

81. The enforcement of these reforms may have been confined only to the middle
and lower levels, at the cost of some resentment by individuals in these ranks.
82. Cited in *Africa Contemporary Record*, 1977–78, p. B 693.

year incumbency of President Tubman) and step down in 1983, while repeatedly refusing to seek any constitutional changes that would enable him to stay on. However, the clause in the constitution which restricted voting to the owners of property was not changed in the face of opposition by the Americo-Liberian-dominated Senate. This continued restriction had enormous potential for further alienating those excluded from the purportedly democratic regime; at the same time, any steps taken to implement it would have aroused serious opposition within the ruling class.

Toward the end of the 1970s, there were some signs of further political change. Americo-Liberian privileges remained basically intact, but a new political awareness and resentment of them was developing under the influence of a small group of young, educated, and politically conscious intellectuals who were increasingly vocal in their criticism of the regime. Opposition groups appeared, and the prospect of increased political freedom and constitutional reform was giving them the coloration of political parties. One such group was the Movement for Justice in Africa (MOJA), led by local young academics with support among students, urban workers, and poor farmers; another was the Progressive Alliance of Liberia (PAL), founded by Gabriel Baccus Matthews and other expatriate Liberian youths living in the United States. The activities of such organizations provoked the reactive opposition of right-wing elements in the TWP.

On April 14, 1979, riots occurred in Monrovia when PAL called upon people to protest against government pronouncements that the price of rice would have to be increased. A police force inexperienced in crowd control and caught unawares fired upon the demonstrators; forty-nine people were killed (the unofficial figure was over one hundred) and many others wounded.[83] Tolbert spoke of the episode as the "most regrettable and unprecedented in the history of our country,"[84] and he seemed to be making amends by allowing (if not actually encouraging) the registration of PAL as a political party: the Progressive People's Party (PPP). He also expressed the "hope that all of us have learned well our lessons from these unfortunate events, and would in the future strive to avoid them."[85] Tolbert's Liberia seemed about to follow in the steps of Senghor's Senegal, where liberalization had led to the emergence of a semi-competitive party system: MOJA unofficially supported a candidate to stand in the mayoralty elections in Monrovia, and

83. *West Africa* 3274 (21 April 1980): 687.
84. In an interview with *West Africa* 3265 (18 February 1980): 289.
85. Ibid.

the PPP had declared itself to be a "loyal opposition." However, perhaps fearing MOJA's greater organizational strength in any future liberalized polity, Matthews—in a rambling and contradictory speech on March 7, 1980—demanded the resignation of the President and Vice-President and called for a general strike. The challenge was clear, and Tolbert had little alternative but to reply with decisive action. The government arrested PPP members and sympathizers and brought charges of treason and sedition against its leaders, while formally banning the party. Right-wing members of the TWP called for the legalization of a one-party state in Liberia. Then, on April 12, just before the PPP leaders were to go on trial, the government was toppled in the coup by Doe, who apparently had ties with the PPP leaders. Tolbert was assassinated during the coup, and leading members of his government were executed shortly afterwards in a carnival atmosphere following speedy and summary trials by military personnel. Prominent members of MOJA and the PPP as well as military officers were named to the cabinet of Doe's government, but real power was placed in the hands of the soldiers' ruling People's Redemption Council.

Tolbert was not a determined modernizer, much less a radical. He was a conservative reformer who, by initiating or allowing certain changes, had brought about political demands that he later found impossible to control. He was the product of a paternal, aristocratic society, and his remarks about the April 1979 disturbances reveal an expectation that the young and inexperienced intellectuals who promoted them would heed the wise counsel of their elders and mend their ways. He failed to appreciate the potential power held by the young intellectuals and the discontent of the ordinary Liberians, to whom the new radical ideology was designed to appeal. He seemed unconcerned about the possibility of a military coup, and he underestimated the emotional power of radical ideology in a hierarchical society while overestimating the loyalty of the young Americo-Liberian intellectuals to his regime. The intellectuals' explanation of the changes that were taking place before the coup was characteristic: one of MOJA's most articulate leaders, Dr. H. Bioma Fahnbulleh, observed that "The society is in a state of ferment because the developing consciousness of the people has outstripped the institutions which were designed to cater for the consciousness of a different historical era."[86] Thus, while the immediate cause of Tolbert's downfall was un-

86. Quoted in ibid., 3274 (21 April 1980): 687.

doubtedly guns in the hands of young soldiers prepared to act, the more general one may have been the relaxed and indulgent paternalism of the ruler himself.

Of the once numerous traditional African kingdoms, few survived European colonization or the assaults of new nationalist elites.[87] Many were incorporated into overarching colonial states by European powers, becoming part of the infrastructure of colonialism. Other kingdoms were tolerated as dependencies during the colonial period, but were overthrown or abolished by African nationalists at independence or shortly afterwards. In general, one may say that traditional political systems in Africa have been vulnerable to the normative assault of modernizers and have usually lost their legitimacy as a result. By 1970 only Haile Selassie's Ethiopian empire and Sobhuza II's Swazi monarchy had survived as independent African states.[88] In both of these cases, but especially in the case of Ethiopia, we have perhaps the closest contemporary African approximations of Weber's ideal-type of traditional patrimonial rule. Strictly speaking, these rulers are not personal: they are institutional. But we have included them along with the non-traditional Princes for two basic reasons: first, they are closely akin to the Prince in many characteristics, and help to illuminate the category accordingly; second, both have been vulnerable to the loss of legitimacy in the face of modernization— imperial Ethiopia being destroyed in the encounter and royalist Swaziland threatened.

Haile Selassie, Ethiopia

Never the victim of full European colonization, Ethiopia as an independent African state was entangled in the fortunes (or rather misfortunes) of Mussolini's pre–World War II colonial adventure in Africa. Italy ruled Ethiopia as an African colony for a brief period (1936–41), forcing the Emperor into exile, but with the military support of the Allied forces, he was able to resume his

87. For an analysis of a number of these kingdoms, see René Lemarchand, ed., *African Kingships in Perspective: Political Change and Modernization in Monarchical Settings* (London: Frank Cass & Co., 1977).

88. The Kingdom of Lesotho became independent as a constitutional monarchy in 1966, with the crown reduced to a symbolic role. See B. M. Khaketla, *Lesotho 1970: An African Coup Under the Microscope* (Berkeley and Los Angeles: University of California Press, 1972); Richard F. Weisfelder, "The Basotho Monarchy," in *African Kingships in Perspective*, ed. Lemarchand, pp. 160–89.

throne in 1941 and to rule Ethiopia until he lost control of state power in a military rebellion in 1974.[89]

Leul Ras (literally "Prince") Haile Selassie's prolonged, if briefly interrupted, rulership, which began in 1930, is a fascinating African example of traditional "patrimonialism" as defined by Weber:

> The patrimonial office lacks above all the bureaucratic separation of the "private" and "official" sphere. For the political administration, too, is treated as a purely personal affair of the ruler, and political power is considered part of his personal property. . . . The office and the exercise of public authority serve the ruler and the official on which the office was bestowed, they do not serve impersonal purposes.[90]

Ethiopian patrimonialism reflected "traditional" norms which were given formal constitutional recognition at the midpoint of Haile Selassie's reign. In 1955 the newly adopted Constitution of Ethiopia "legalized" the traditional principle of divine emperorship, vesting sovereignty in the person of the Emperor, who alone exercised "supreme authority" over "all the affairs of the empire" (Art. 26).[91] The patronage (appointive) powers of the Emperor over the government and the administration were extensive, enabling him to treat state affairs as exclusively his own. He was empowered to determine the "organization, powers and duties" of all the ministries, departments, and branches of the government, as well as to appoint, promote, transfer, suspend, and dismiss "the officials of the same" (Art. 27). The rights and powers that enabled Haile Selassie to preside over the Ethiopian empire for almost half a century were also sanctified by the religious traditions of the Coptic Christian Church.

Enjoying traditional or constitutional rights to power and holding power or being able to use it effectively are distinctly different. Although the late Emperor of Ethiopia had traditional and con-

89. See the following studies: Christopher Clapham: *Haile-Selassie's Government* (London: Longmans, and New York: Praeger, 1969), and "Ethiopia," in *African Kingships in Perspective*, ed. Lemarchand, pp. 35–63; Patrick Gilkes, *The Dying Lion: Feudalism and Modernization in Ethiopia* (London: Julian Friedman Publishers, 1975); Peter Schwab, *Decision-Making in Ethiopia: A Study of the Political Process* (Rutherford and Teaneck, N.J.: Fairleigh Dickinson University Press, 1972); Richard Greenfield, *Ethiopia: A New Political History* (London: Pall Mall Press, 1965); Robert L. Hess, *Ethiopia: The Modernization of Autocracy* (Ithaca and London: Cornell University Press, 1970); and Margery Perham, *The Government of Ethiopia*, 2nd ed. (London: Faber and Faber, 1969).

90. Max Weber, *Economy and Society: An Outline of Interpretive Sociology*, ed. Guenther A. Roth and Clause Wittich (New York: Bedminster Press, 1968), vol. 3, pp. 1028–29, 1031.

91. See Amos J. Peaslee, *Constitutions of Nations*, vol. 1—*Africa*; rev. 3d ed. (The Hague: Martinus Nijhoff, 1965), pp. 167–90.

stitutional powers and rights, his long-term success depended more on his ability to use his office and impose his authority in the practical struggle for power among leaders and groups. In a political system noted for its Byzantine intrigues and personal alignments, Leul Ras dominated the Ethiopian political stage (even playing a prominent role on the world stage for a time), the master of the art of powerholding. Personal domination of a complex traditional polity for a long period of time could only have been accomplished by remarkable will and by the mastery of the skills and wiles of politician politics: shrewd judgment, careful timing, subtle maneuvering, and, above all, acute perceptions of the strengths and weaknesses of others. Writing in the late 1960s just before Haile Selassie's personal grip on power began to weaken, Clapham drew the following portrait of his rule:

> He combines his appeal to divine right with an intense personal grasp of power, in much the same way as symbols and controls are combined in the emperorship itself. . . .
>
> Highly personalized control is the essence of his style. . . . High on Haile-Selassie's list of essential skills is his ability to play on the aims and characters of others in order to secure their dependence on himself—for example, by appointing antipathetic rivals to complementary posts, or encouraging officials to appeal direct to the palace over the heads of their superiors. Information services work in a similar way, through rival politicians reporting on one another's activities, so that the Emperor stands at the centre of a web of competing intelligence networks.[92]

While earlier emperors had always to contend with a semi-feudal polity, with strong regional notables who possessed their own armies and autonomous bases of wealth and power, Haile Selassie presided over a successful process of administrative and military centralization aimed at reducing regional power and enhancing royal power and the central authority of the Ethiopian state. The powers of provincial governors to collect their own revenues and maintain autonomous police and military forces were curtailed, and the regional arrangements were replaced by a central system of national revenues, a national *gendarmerie*, and the subordination of the provincial administration to the Minister of the Interior—the Emperor's appointee. The royalist centralization of the Ethiopian state in this century is reminiscent of state-building by the monarchs of sixteenth- and seventeenth-century Europe. But in Ethiopia the process was never completed (perhaps it never was in Europe either, if contemporary demands for devolution and de-

92. Christopher Clapham, "Imperial Leadership in Ethiopia," *African Affairs* 68, 271 (April 1969): 115–16; see also John H. Spencer, "Haile Selassie: Triumph and Tragedy," *Orbis* 18, 4 (Winter 1975): 1129–52.

centralization are any indication), and at the end of Haile Selassie's reign, political fissures based upon regional and historical particularisms, most dramatically evident in the emergence of an organized Eritrean separatist movement in the 1960s, began to reappear in the state.

After World War II the Emperor began to staff his administrative service with graduates of Western schools and universities: men possessing technical and professional qualifications, but not authority derived from traditional standing or political followings—that is, men dependent upon the Emperor, whose continued favor would be essential for promotion to senior administrative posts and to ministerships.[93] Possessing the extensive and pervasive patronage powers set forth in the constitution, the Emperor was the strategic player in an intensely personal game of politics. Provincial governors, court and administrative officials, military officers, and the higher clergy were all permitted to join in the game, but the Emperor was the final arbiter in political conflicts and disputes. By encouraging the politically astute and ambitious to consult the palace directly (thus ignoring their hierarchical superiors), by setting rivals in competition for his favor and encouraging them to report on one another's activities—in such ways he undermined the ability of rivals to unite against him. He would privately encourage the policies of certain ministers, then stand back and see if they were successful: "If all goes well, the Emperor claims the credit; if not, others take the blame."[94] Under Haile Selassie, Ethiopian politics resembled a grand stage play, with the characteristic supporting roles of courtiers, noblemen, senior officials, army leaders, and high-ranking clergy played by capable actors, but with the commanding role reserved for the Emperor himself.

Despite his extensive personal power to stage-manage the political drama, Haile Selassie's authority was not absolute. Although politically preeminent, he could not ignore with impunity the wishes of other men or the interests they claimed to represent; the regime depended on the cooperation of such men and on the contributions they could make to it in exchange for power and place within it. Neither could the Emperor abandon the essentially diplomatic and intensely personal style of conciliar government that

93. Writing at the time of Haile Selassie's reign, John Markakis and Asmelah Beyne stated that "although a civil service has been formally established, appointive power is still widely exercised by the Emperor personally, and he is still the only source of honours and titles" ("Representative Institutions in Ethiopia," *Journal of Modern African Studies* 5, 2 [September 1967]: 196).

94. Clapham, "Imperial Leadership in Ethiopia," p. 116.

has been such a prominent feature of imperial rule in Ethiopia. The basic character of such a government was not to promote any kind of public or national interest, but to recognize and honor, and where they conflicted to reconcile, particular interests. Because the senior imperial service was a locus of patronage, or at most the imperfect instrument of the ruler's will, more than an impersonal agency of policy, it was exceedingly difficult for even the most determined public-policy-minded officials to function effectively. Under Haile Selassie the Ethiopian state remained (to quote Clapham) "an absorptive polity, which can find room for modernisers on much the same basis as it finds room for other pressures, but which is quite unadapted to any goal-oriented development programme."[95] The fact that it could not formulate and implement policies to ameliorate social problems—an incapacity born both of its agents' lack of competence and of their overall failure to conceive of themselves as agents rather than as components of the regime—has been seen as an important factor in the regime's collapse. John Harbeson has argued that the fall of the *ancien régime* "preceded the emergence of rebels committed to destroying and replacing [it]," and that the two major precipitants of its collapse were the drought and famine of 1972–73—one of the most serious the African sahel had suffered—and the subsequent inflation: in both crises the government proved helpless.[96] It was not organized to deal with modern "social" questions, as distinct from traditional regional-political questions that called simply for domination or reconciliation. While unable to respond, the government could not dismiss these problems—especially the famine, which had captured the attention of international public opinion. Price increases caused by inflation led to urban unrest and the resignation of the Prime Minister and his cabinet: an unprecedented action and the first public sign of immobilism in the regime.

   In the end Haile Selassie's efforts at state-building and modernization had not proved successful, even if he had wanted them to be. At the best of times the state was no more than a coalition of notables, regions, institutions, and groups subordinated to the throne and placed under imperial administration, but never fully integrated into a state. The new modern sectors—such as the students or the trade unions—could never reconcile themselves to a polity rooted in monarchical principles; on the other hand, the

95. Ibid., p. 119.

96. John W. Harbeson, "Socialist Politics in Revolutionary Ethiopia," in *Socialism in Sub-Saharan Africa: A New Assessment*, ed. Carl G. Rosberg and Thomas M. Callaghy (Berkeley: Institute of International Studies, 1979), p. 352.

government could not reconcile itself to the demands or ideals of such groups. In the final analysis, Haile Selassie was the Ethiopian state; when his grip on power weakened, the state was also weakened. In the uncertain regime of a weak and indecisive ruler, if plotting is not suppressed, the strongest among the plotters gain in confidence and boldness, and the weaker grow apprehensive and fearful; to borrow from Hobbes, the psychology of the state of nature begins to take possession of all men. Under an aged and weakened emperor, the absorptive polity in Ethiopia began to deteriorate into a paralyzed state.[97]

The deterioration of sovereignty into political uncertainty and then into disorder and violence took place in Ethiopia at the very end of the Emperor's reign. Personal rivalries grew among the ruling class, and non-ruling groups and classes began to protest and agitate for reform. Not only general political authority but also the social authority of major institutions of society began to be questioned and then attacked. Rivalries within the military led to a weakening of command within the officer corps and then to outright mutiny by soldiers among the ranks. The nobility, historically deriving its wealth from the surplus produced by a passive and ignorant peasantry, became the target of political agitation by the intelligentsia, particularly students. The privileges of the Coptic clergy and the extensive landholdings of the church also came under attack. The regions of the empire, never fully integrated into the regime, grew restless as they once again became conscious of their separate identities, and some (like Eritrea) became the sites of stepped-up campaigns for greater autonomy and even independence.

The political and natural world of Ethiopia appeared to be coming apart, and Ethiopia was ripe for a violent change of regime. Indeed, what appeared to exist in Ethiopia in 1974 was an historic "revolutionary situation" somewhat reminiscent of France in 1789 or Russia in 1917: a rare moment in history when existing political and social authorities are discredited and irresolute and the state is vulnerable to expropriation by the boldest and strongest adventurer. In Ethiopia in 1974 the boldest and the strongest were soldiers with arms. As in the other two great revolutionary situations, the period following the collapse of the *ancien régime* was disorderly and bloody, as rival groups attempted to claim revolutionary legitimacy and to gain control of the situation. Lt. Col.

97. See *Africa Contemporary Record*, 1974–75, p. B 161; see also Gilkes, pp. 227–67.

Mengistu Haile Mariam, a prominent leader of the military junta, or Dergue, successfully consolidated his personal power in 1977 and gained the exclusive right to speak and act in the name of the Ethiopian state. His political success was due in part to his intelligence and ruthlessness and in part to the expertise, heavy weapons, and men provided by the Soviet Union and Cuba to support his regime against Somali irredentist and Eritrean separatist forces. This technical and military assistance gave him the coercive means necessary to maintain the integrity of the Ethiopian state and his personal supremacy within it.

Sobhuza II, Swaziland

With the collapse of the Ethiopian empire, King Sobhuza II of the Kingdom of Swaziland became sub-Saharan Africa's last ruling traditional monarch.[98] In acquiring independence as a monarchy at the eleventh hour of colonial rule (with a parliament constitutionally grafted to the reemerging traditional state), the royalist elements in Swaziland succeeded in gaining sovereign powers, while elsewhere in British Africa (e.g., northern Nigeria and the Kingdom of Buganda), they had to settle for the much less satisfactory solution of constitutional protection under a federalist political arrangement.

Swaziland's 1968 independence constitution provided for parliamentary government on a modified Westminster model, but the imported institutions were not expected to displace the traditional institutions of the Swazi state—especially the kingship, the Ngwenyama. It was hoped, rather, that both sets of institutions could be made to work in harness. Traditionally the King presided over a royalist administration of chiefs, of both common and royal lineages, who provided his regime with a substructure not unlike the British system of indirect rule. In colonial times the kingship was maintained with popular approval under overall British protection, but in response to the competitive political situation created by decolonization, the King assumed the leadership of a royalist party—the Imbokodvo National Movement (INM)—that brought the country to independence by gaining control of all the

98. See the definitive study by Hilda Kuper, *Sobhuza II: Ngwenyama and King of Swaziland* (London: Gerald Duckworth & Co., 1978); see also Christian P. Potholm: *Swaziland: The Dynamics of Political Modernization* (Berkeley, Los Angeles, London: University of California Press, 1972); "Swaziland Under Sobhuza II: The Future of an African Monarchy," *The Round Table* 254 (April 1974): 219–27; and "The Ngwenyama of Swaziland: The Dynamics of Political Adaptation," in *African Kingships in Perspective*, ed. Lemarchand, pp. 129–59.

seats in the lower House of Assembly in pre-independence elections and outmaneuvering both militant pan-Africanists and European settler interests—the other major political forces. The traditional symbols, institutions, and loyalties of the Swazi people were exploited by the royalists, and all but the most modernist elements among the Swazis were successfully appealed to for support. The British had also played their part by encouraging the survival of traditional political institutions and sentiments during the colonial era.

Always a traditional ruler and then a party leader, the King now became a kind of constitutional head of the new state with his own party in control of Parliament. Constitutionally, he was empowered to appoint six of the thirty members of the House of Assembly as well as six of the twelve members of the upper house, the Senate. He was also empowered to appoint the members of the cabinet, appointments that ordinarily took account of such critical facts as personal loyalty to the crown or royal kinship or both. He was obliged to appoint the leader of the majority party in Parliament as Prime Minister, in keeping with British parliamentary practice, but since it was *his* party that had the majority, he had considerable power over the Prime Minister, rather like the substantive power British monarchs once held. (Members of the royal extended family have held the office of Prime Minister, and while one of the King's sons was a minister, another son was an appointed member of Parliament.) In addition, the King was granted specified legislative and executive powers, unlike a constitutional monarch. In practice, if not in theory, the crown was supreme.

Once in authority, the royalist party could tolerate modern political institutions—for instance, the constitution and parliamentary democracy—so long as they served its corporate interest of upholding the authority of the King; when the same institutions generated opposition, as they were bound to do, they could be discredited as inconsistent with Swazi traditions. The royalists regarded opposition as a demonstration of disloyalty to the King. This conception was not entirely at odds with a constitutional instrument that had assigned to the Ngwenyama important executive and legislative powers that made him much more than merely a constitutional head of state. Consistent with the Swazi tradition of monarchy, when opposition asserted itself in April 1973, the King seized power, abolished the constitution, dissolved Parliament, banned the opposition, and restored the *ancien régime*. Now that imported institutions were no longer instrumental to royal power (in fact were being used to undermine that power), they were dispensed with. More in character with personal rule, the issue was not policy or ideology but authority and loyalty. Hence no opposition party or politician could be permitted to engage in Swazi politics. Parliament could only be a royal council where private discussion of government policies would be allowed, but not public disagreement. When the King's interest was declared, it was final: it was the *only* public interest and as such could not be criticized.

The Swazi people are bound together by kinship ties and a system of hereditary chieftaincy at the regional and local levels, but these characteristics do not define the status of the Swazi "subject." That is defined solely by allegiance to the Ngwenyama. It is this political principle of personal loyalty that originally was used to build the Swazi state from diverse cultures in the pre-colonial era, and has been used to maintain it under Sobhuza II. The Swazi equivalent of "fealty" makes it possible for non-Swazis, including European residents of Swaziland, to become subjects of the neo-traditional state and for the state to absorb these new subjects. The fact that the state is not based on ethnicity—on race or culture or language—enables it to adapt to social changes and movements of people in ways that more culturally or ethnically homogeneous regimes could not. This is an enormous advantage for the survival of the royalist tradition in Swaziland; a disadvantage is that there is no way to distinguish between loyal opposition to royal policy and acts or utterances of disloyalty. The King is the government as well as the state, which has made the Swazi kingdom—unlike a modern constitutional monarchy, such as Britain, which resolved the issue during a lengthy and intermittently violent struggle between crown and Parliament for control of the government—vulnerable to the crises of disloyalty that historically have beset absolutist monarchies.

The suspension of the independence constitution and the banning of opposition in 1973 was such a crisis. The anomalies of the constitution on the question contributed to it: in theory, the King as head of state was above criticism, but his government was not. In practice, this came to mean that opposition views on public policy could be expressed in Parliament, but could not be pressed beyond the point at which the government declared a consensus had been achieved. The issue did not arise immediately, since Sobhuza's royalist party had initially succeeded in gaining a monopoly position in Parliament. Without party and partisan divisions, Parliament posed no threat to the traditional order. But in the national elections of 1972, a small, urban-based opposition party—the Ngwene National Liberation Congress Party—won three seats and formed a "ginger group" in Parliament. Without power

to block government policies, it nevertheless challenged fundamentally the unitary and hierarchical ideal of the neo-traditional
state. The initial reaction of the King's government was to have
the election of the three opposition members nullified by claiming
electoral irregularities. A special tribunal was established to hear
some of the charges, but the Swazi appellate court found the stat-
ute establishing it to be unconstitutional. It was now quite clear
that the new constitutional order could be used to thwart royal
power.[99] The King reacted swiftly, announcing his intention to
rule by decree until a new constitution could be written that would
"take full notice of the circumstances in Swaziland and of Swazi
culture and tradition."[100] A royal constitutional commission was
then established for that purpose.

Following the "royal coup" of 1973, Swazi affairs were conducted exclusively by the King and his council. But in October
1978, indirect elections of a bicameral Parliament were held, as
recommended by the constitutional commission (and reflecting
Sobhuza's ideas of kingship and royalist government). By means
of a traditional electoral process known as the "Tinkhundla" poll,
Swazi voters elected an 80-member electoral college (from among
160 district candidates), who in turn elected 40 and 10 members
respectively to a reconstituted National Assembly and Senate. The
King later appointed 10 additional members to each body, including 4 "White Swazis." To complete the process, the now 50-mem-
ber Assembly was required to elect an additional 10 members to
the Senate.[101] The King appointed the Prime Minister and the
cabinet ministers. Moreover, he retained the power to veto legislation. It remains to be seen whether this attempt to modernize
Swazi political traditions will last beyond the reign of the present
Ngwenyama, who was eighty years old in 1979 and the world's
longest reigning living monarch.

Political events in the late 1970s cast a shadow of doubt on the
prospect. Tensions were reported between the older, traditional
elite—especially the ruling Dlamini clan—and younger, educated
Swazis who not only desire greater influence but also are likely to
be disrespectful of traditional political norms. In 1977 student
riots and protests occurred: the first serious popular challenge to
the authority of the present ruler and his regime. Then in 1978
some members of South Africa's Pan African Congress living in

99. See P. H. Proctor, "Traditionalism and Parliamentary Government in Swaziland," *African Affairs* 72, 288 (July 1973): 273–78.
100. *Africa Research Bulletin: Political, Social, and Cultural Series* 14, 4 (May 15,
1973): 2818A.
101. Ibid., 15, 10 (November 15, 1978): 5024B; ibid., 16, 1 (February 15, 1979):
5124A, B.

exile in Swaziland were arrested and expelled. The geopolitics of Swaziland, in particular its contiguity with South Africa and Mozambique, may eventually prove the chief source of difficulties for Swazi royalists. South Africa has now entered an era of radical confrontation and conflict between opposed and mutually exclusive black and white nationalisms. This conflict will inevitably influence the thoughts and actions of the younger, more radical Swazis and perhaps even the government. And the fact that an alternative neo-Leninist state exists in neighboring Mozambique can only add to the tensions between old and new, between royalism and radicalism in Swaziland. There have been reports that FRELIMO in power in Mozambique has emboldened some Swazi radical politicians to speak out against the government, which has prompted warnings that seditious actions of any kind will not be tolerated.

One of the most striking features of African politics since independence has been the seizure of state power by aspiring new rulers—almost always military men—who have attempted to impose their domination, often by force, upon a political situation that other rulers proved unable to control. Not all of them have succeeded in their political ambitions, and some have been defeated by the very instrument—force—that was used to launch them upon a political career. Others have seen a gradual attrition of their military-based domination as political opposition to their rule grew in strength and determination; such was the case of General Acheampong of Ghana after several years of his fruitless attempt to restore economic and social prosperity to that West African country. Still others have withdrawn to the barracks once the state had been rescued from its predators—as did the first military rulers of Ghana (1966–69). The successful new rulers have had to find legitimacy and political power beyond those which arms can obtain. The most successful have left their military careers largely behind them and have become political men, demonstrating their mastery of the ruler's craft. One of the most prominent of these military-cum-political men is the current ruler of Sudan.

Gaafar Mohamed Numeiri, Sudan

Since 1969 Sudan has been ruled by President Gaafar Mohamed Numeiri, a professional soldier who, at the relatively youthful age of thirty-nine, came to power in a bloodless coup against an immobilized civilian regime. The successful coup had been carefully planned by a politically conscious faction of younger army officers—the Free Officers Movement—of which Numeiri was the acknowledged leader. This seizure of state power by a faction of the military was in character with the dynamics of Sudanese politics since independence in 1956: a politics of persistent and intense factional, sectarian, regional, and ideological rivalry, with repeated plots and coups, a major north/south regional conflict, and a succession of regimes led by civilians and soldiers.[102]

Although Numeiri achieved power through the military, and remains something of a "soldier prince," he has derived little political advantage or comfort from his background. He has had to subdue military plots to overthrow him on more than one occasion. Like the other rulers of Sudan before him, he has had to contend with a highly complex country that is very difficult to govern: a country whose religious, political, social, racial, and regional-ethnic divisions and tensions have stood in the way of the development of a stable and organizationally effective system of government, placing the burden of ruling squarely in the hands of the ruler. What is distinctive about rulership in Sudan under Numeiri, and what separates it from the rule of a Senghor or a Kenyatta, is its much more contingent nature. Numeiri has managed to retain power since 1969, and has shown himself to be one of the masters of political survival in Africa. However, his political and personal survival has been due to his good fortune as well as his political skills; indeed, his luck has enhanced his personal legitimacy by convincing many ordinary Sudanese that he leads a charmed life.

While fortunate as well as skillful in maintaining his personal control of Sudan, Numeiri has also recognized the need for viable political structures of some kind, and has promoted efforts to bring them into being. One of the most important of these has been an effort to build a new political framework around a single political party—the Sudanese Socialist Union (SSU)—which he has envisaged as the central pillar of a reformed Sudanese state. To date, this effort at organizational and political engineering has not been entirely successful, if success is indicated by the ability to canalize in a new direction the political attitudes and activities of the Sudanese, especially the politicized among them. The lack of success reveals an important paradox that is not confined to Sudan and may be a generic feature of efforts of personal rulers to found new organizations based on modern, rationalist principles— namely, that neither the ruler nor his organizational builders or-

102. For a study of Sudanese politics in the post-independence period, see Peter K. Bechtold, *Politics in the Sudan: Parliamentary and Military Rule in an Emerging African Nation* (New York: Praeger, 1976).

dinarily are free of the personal-factional forms of suspicion and rivalry that the organizations they are attempting to build are intended to supplant. Why should the ruler trust his organizational builders any more than he trusts others? In practice he cannot place his full confidence in them, nor they in him.

It is true that some new structures have been created and have operated: elections have been held within the overall framework of the ruling SSU;[103] elected members of the ruling party have taken their places in a new National Assembly; and the functions and relations of these bodies vis-à-vis each other and the presidency have been set down.[104] But these structures are far from being "institutionalized" in the sense that they have an independent life of their own beyond the ruler's power: they remain dependent on the ruler for their continued existence and use. The old and divisive political culture is not far below the surface in Sudan. In parliamentary elections some old political faces have reappeared, although in the new garb of the SSU. The Sudanese ruler has enjoyed the legal powers, and so far he has possessed the will and the ability, to prevent the old-style politics from reappearing within the National Assembly; but it is clear that his extra-parliamentary rivals and enemies, such as the Islamic Ansar (Mahdist) and other sectarian forces as well as the Communists, have only been contained. They have not disappeared, even though some of their leaders have been jailed or gone into exile and renewed attempts at national reconciliation have taken place. So long as such forces and rivals exist, the ruler can have no assurance that attempts will not be made against his regime: this is one of the distinctive contingencies of personal rule. In addition, the international politics of the Middle East, which have been complicated by Soviet and Cuban involvement in the Horn of Africa, contribute to the uncertainty of Sudanese political life. The character of Sudanese politics has not changed in any basic way during Numeiri's tenure: some of the actors in the play have changed, but the script remains essentially the same. High politics in Sudan remain the authoritarian and personal politics of the Prince in his relations with collaborators, rivals, and the people. Since no one

103. The intent of the new rules to override the old personal-factional norms is indicated in the report that "candidates are forbidden to promise the voters any specific services if successfully elected, may not raise tribal, racial, or partisan issues, and must refrain from attacking rival candidates" (*Africa Research Bulletin: Political, Social, and Cultural Series* 9, 9 [October 15, 1972]: 2603C).

104. Timothy C. Niblock, "A New Political System in Sudan," *African Affairs* 73, 293 (October 1974): 408–18.

can trust others to act in accordance with the new constitutional rules, they stand little chance of being instituted.[105]

The problems confronted by the personal ruler of a highly divided, faction-ridden society (who of necessity must accept the norms of personal rule while seeking to be an organizational modernizer) can be explored by considering very briefly the political history of Sudan since it became independent. Unlike some other African and Arab countries, Sudan did not benefit politically from the integrating effects of a united nationalist movement mounted against colonial rule. Indeed, no popular, integrative nationalism arose. Such political sentiments as initially arose were mobilized and canalized by the historic Islamic rivals—the Mahdist and Khatmiyya sects—whose leaders were in a position to dominate Parliament when representative institutions were introduced late in the colonial period. Later, a regional African nationalism arose in the southern Sudan, but in the face of an intransigent Arab government in Khartoum, it developed into a movement for separate independence of the region that sparked a prolonged military conflict between government forces and armed separatists.[106] Doctrinally and politically opposed, the sectarian parties in Parliament were unable to form an alliance and agree on a constitution, a requirement the British normally imposed before granting independence. However, for purely expedient reasons of gaining independence, they agreed to a joint declaration of independence in 1956; for equally expedient reasons, the condominium powers found this acceptable. Thus in place of a united nationalist movement, at independence Sudan was governed by two rival and fundamentally opposed sectarian parties, each bent upon displacing the other. While a Communist party and other secular parties existed in urban centers, mainly in Khartoum, they had neither the leadership, the organization, nor the popular support to be of major importance in shaping political events in the late 1950s.

The first period of civilian rule (1956–58) was characterized by endless parliamentary maneuverings among leaders, factions, and parties, each aiming at securing advantages and power for itself. The political process conformed closely to the classic factional pattern: people "voted to assert their adherence to personalities rather than programmes. Hence, the political parties were groups attached to leaders, or temporary alliances, rather than stable,

105. This is a curious variant of the "prisoner's dilemma" and a common problem of normative and institutional change in underdeveloped countries.

106. Dunstan M. Wai, "Revolution, Rhetoric, and Reality in the Sudan," *Journal of Modern African Studies* 17, 1 (1979): 72–75.

well-organized groups with definite and distinctive objectives."[107]
The result was disillusionment and the withering of extra-parliamentary support on any kind of general basis; there was little hope
of producing good government by reshuffling parliamentary factions or parties—only the leading actors in a bad play could be
changed this way. Thus a November 17, 1958 army coup led by
General Ibrahim Abboud met with no opposition; indeed, the climate of opinion seemed to favor it. As early as November 11, the
independent Khartoum daily *al-Ayam* had editorialized: "Nobody
will be sorry to see the present government go. It has given this
country instability, misrule, disunity, and economic disaster."[108]
Sudan appeared to be returning to its colonial tradition of authoritarian government: Parliament was dissolved, parties were
banned, the statutory authority under which the civilian government operated was suspended, and a state of emergency was declared restricting civil rights.

The main thrust of colonial rule in the Sudan had been the creation of a civil service and an army to administer and secure the
territory. These structures in particular embodied the governmental tradition of authoritarianism central to the political history of
Sudan. Through the rapid "Sudanization" of the civil service just
prior to independence, and the more gradual indigenization of the
army officer corps, these two structures were place in Sudanese
hands. It is possible that the pre-independence Sudanization of
these structures denied to the secular nationalist movements an
important source of potential recruits and party cadres: some of
the most able young men found their way into the military, from
within which their political consciousness would be formed and,
for some, their political activities launched. Since 1958 there has
been abundant evidence of the politicization of the army in Sudan,
and particularly of factions within it which have been important
politically. Numeiri himself has insisted that soldiers in Sudan
ought to be viewed as having full and equal political rights with
their civilian counterparts. There is no question that the army (or
parts of it) has in some ways taken on the appearance of a kind of
political "party" with a specific interest not only in defending the
state and maintaining its integrity, but also in guiding it. In this
respect it is not inappropriate to argue that the army in Sudan,

107. P. M. Holt, *A Modern History of the Sudan: From the Funj Sultanate to the
Present Day* (London: Weidenfeld & Nicolson, 1961), p. 180. For the pre-indepen-
dence period, see L. A. Fabunmi, *The Sudan in Anglo-Egyptian Relations: A Case
Study in Power Relations, 1800–1956* (London: Longmans, Green & Co., 1960).

108. Cited in Helen Kitchen, "The Government of General Abboud," *Africa Report* 4, 1 (January 1959): 3.

before independence and since, has been a kind of "guardian" class with a presumptive sense of its entitlement to rule. But it would be a mistake to conclude from this that the army has been a cohesive political class: far from being united, it has contained the same sectarian, ideological, and ethnic divisions that have plagued the larger society.[109] Its capacity to serve as the representative and prime agency of the Sudanese state was therefore limited by these internal weaknesses. In addition, authoritarian government in Sudan was limited by the very society it had to govern:

> If past history is anything of a guide, the power of the government, so vast in appearance, will be greatly checked in practice by the geographical and social circumstances in which it has to work. The inherent complexity and ancient traditions of Sudanese society, rather than the paper safeguards of any constitution, are its best safeguards against oppression.[110]

The limits to military authoritarianism in Sudan were first dramatically demonstrated against the first post-independence military-led government by a massive uprising among diverse groups and classes in Khartoum in October 1964. What became known as the "October Revolution" began among students and faculty at the University of Khartoum, who were joined by a range of professional groups—lawyers, judges, doctors. With the active involvement of political parties, including members of the Communist party, the protests increased, and the demonstrators became determined to bring down the military rulers and institute some form of popular democracy in Sudan.[111] Factors internal to the military contributed to the success of the rebellion, with army officers sympathetic to the aims of the demonstrators pressing for and obtaining a negotiated settlement. Thus the first military government in Sudan proved to be no more successful at founding a durable political order than its civilian predecessors.

The urban rebellion of 1964 produced a United National Front, composed of the professional groups who had initiated the protests and the established sectarian and secular parties (including the Communist party), who formed a new civilian government. This "transitional government" could not be effective: it contained too many incompatible elements representing divisive sections of society. The aim of professional groups to found a new progressive

109. Ruth First, *Power in Africa* (New York: Pantheon Books, 1970), p. 144.
110. Holt, pp. 186–87.
111. See Robert W. Crawford, "Sudan: The Revolution of October, 1964," *Mawazo* 1, 2 (December 1967): 47–69, and Yusuf Fadl Hasan, "The Sudanese Revolution of October 1964," *Journal of Modern African Studies* 5, 4 (December 1967): 491–509.

political order was blocked by the old parties, who called for new elections knowing that the progressives could not oppose the demand and that only the parties could win, since each had an established bloc of popular support. Thus the Spring 1965 elections returned Sudan to the old civilian pattern of rival, factional politics dominated by the sectarian parties. From the Spring of 1965 until the military coup of 1969, four different coalition governments attempted to govern Sudan without creating a new constitutional framework to avoid the excesses of factional, parliamentary politics.[112]

Following the bloodless military coup on May 25, 1969, its leaders quickly gained control of power in Khartoum, and an attempt was made to resurrect the progressive forces of the transitional government, free of sectarian elements and guided and protected by radical, middle-ranking army officers seeking to fulfill the political and social hopes of the 1964 rebellion. All senior military officers were arrested and shortly thereafter retired; leading politicians of the former regime were detained and their organizations proscribed; and a Revolutionary Command Council headed by Numeiri was proclaimed as the supreme authority in the country, henceforth to be known as the Democratic Republic of Sudan. Promoted immediately to the rank of Major General, Numeiri also became commander-in-chief of the armed forces.

Without previous government experience, the new military rulers chose to rely upon progressives, including Communists, to staff a cabinet that included only two soldiers. A former chief justice with close Communist party connections was made a member of the Revolutionary Command Council and appointed Prime Minister. In a radio broadcast immediately after the coup, Numeiri stated that since independence "Sudan had not known stability, only a series of tragedies because of a multiplicity of parties in power acting in their own interests. . . . The Revolutionary Command Council will direct Sudan's affairs from now on, with its only aim the country's interests."[113] In pursuing stability and unity, the government adopted a political strategy of denying any political role to organized groups while encouraging individuals to take an interest in politics. Clearly, the aim was to deny the underlying social "constitution" of Sudan any place in the new political order. The regime hoped to supplant it with new national struc-

112. John Howell, "Politics in the Southern Sudan," *African Affairs* 72, 287 (April 1973): 174.

113. *Africa Research Bulletin: Political, Social, and Cultural Series* 6, 5 (June 15, 1969): 1404.

tures that might prove capable of giving voice and expression to general social interests—to do the organizational engineering that had never been done before.

Events since 1969 have proved the difficulty of carrying out such a project. The underlying political forces of Sudanese society have not proved tractable, nor have the agencies and agents of the new government proved capable and resolute in their efforts at organizational engineering. The exigencies of personal rule, of not only wielding but also holding on to power, have relegated the concern with structures to secondary importance. Numeiri has appeared genuine in his professed desire to build new political structures in Sudan, but he has known that the establishment and holding of power come before the building of new structures. With the passage of time, the aims of political engineering have receded in importance to such an extent that it appears rather doubtful that they are any longer seriously entertained.

The old political forces have asserted themselves on numerous occasions. Since 1969 there has been almost continuous reporting of rebellions, attempted coups, plots, and other conspiracies against the ruler and his regime. Some of these have involved considerable bloodshed and disruption and come very close to overthrowing the government. Within the first two years two major challenges were mounted against Numeiri's regime. The first was by conservative forces, including a private army loyal to the Mahdi, the sectarian Islamic leader; the second was from Communist elements.

While the Mahdist-supported political party—the Umma of the Ansar sect—had been banned along with all other parties, Numeiri's cooperation with individual Communists, development of closer ties with Egypt, and consideration of a regional approach to the southern separatist problem contributed to growing alarm among the Mahdists as well as other Moslem groups. A military confrontation occurred in March 1970 at Abba Island, 150 miles south of Khartoum, where the private army of the Mahdi was destroyed and the then Mahdi—Imam al-Hadi al-Mahdi—was killed while attempting to escape to Ethiopia. As one observer noted, no effective ruler could have condoned "a relatively reactionary state within a state over which he had no control."[114] The conservative forces of the Moslem brotherhood, devoted to the creation of an Islamic state of Sudan, have continued as an underground right-wing opposition to Numeiri's regime.

114. Peter Kilner, "The Sudan: A Year of Revolution," *African Affairs* 69, 277 (October 1970): 375.

On July 19, 1971, a military faction supported by the Communist party (and led by an officer who had previously been dismissed from the Revolutionary Command Council for providing confidential information to the Communist party) was temporarily successful in capturing power in Khartoum, posing an extremely dangerous threat to Numeiri personally and to his regime. Numeiri, along with other members of his government, was arrested, and a new regime was proclaimed. According to one account, the plotters made a serious miscalculation in allowing a Communist demonstration to parade through the streets of Khartoum, thereby identifying the incipient regime with the Communists: "Immediately the enormous anti-Marxist sentiment within the Sudan and in neighboring countries sprang to life and eventually rescued a regime which otherwise almost certainly would have been doomed."[115] The Soviet embassy in Khartoum may also have been involved.[116] Forces loyal to Numeiri counterattacked, including a strategic tank brigade once commanded by Numeiri, and defeated the armed forces supporting the coup. While Iraq supported the coup, Egypt and Libya actively assisted Numeiri in the crisis.

Behind the nearly successful bid for power was a widening rift between the regime and one section of the Communists who refused to accept the dissolution of their party. During the year prior to the coup, the Communists had increasingly come under attack, and officers with Communist sympathies had been dismissed from the army. The secretary-general of the Communist party, Abdel Khalek Mahgoub, and other leading members of the party were detained in a general political crackdown that continued into the Spring of 1971. In the aftermath of the coup attempt, the army officers held responsible were executed, many others found guilty by military tribunals were imprisoned, and the Communist leadership was rooted out and virtually destroyed. Mahgoub along with two other Communist leaders was hanged, and during the next six months the regime sought to eliminate all vestiges of the party. Asked about his feelings while under arrest during the crisis, Numeiri is reported to have said: "I felt perfectly calm and confident. I had no fear for myself although I realized I

115. Peter K. Bechtold, "Military Rule in the Sudan: The First Five Years of Ja'Far Numayrī," *Middle East Journal* 29, 1 (Winter 1975): 24.

116. Numeiri has been quoted as saying: "Russia, of course, was behind the coup attempt. . . . The Russian Ambassador in Khartoum went personally to see the rebel leadership. Our people interpreted this as official Soviet endorsement of the new regime" (cited in Anthony Sylvester, *Sudan Under Numeiri* [London: The Bodley Head, 1977], p. 69).

might die any moment. What mattered was that I was thoroughly convinced that the communists would not win and that my side would soon be in control of the situation."[117]

On several occasions since 1971, Numeiri's government has been confronted with conspiracies and attempted coups. The most serious was an attempted coup in July 1976 which came close to succeeding. Except for the good fortune of arriving back in Khartoum earlier than scheduled from a visit to the United States and France, and thereby avoiding capture by soldiers who had plotted to seize him and his associates at the airport, Numeiri would very likely have fallen from power. Much bloodshed and property damage followed in the wake of the coup attempt (it is estimated that as many as one thousand people were killed and £150 million worth of property destroyed), as forces loyal to the ruler crushed the conspiratorial military group. The punishment meted out to plotters not killed in the fighting was severe.[118]

Numeiri has been not only a master of political survival, but also a statesman. Perhaps his most enduring act of statesmanship has been the resolution of the southern separatist problem within the framework of the Sudanese state. After seizing power, his regime held out the possibility of southern regional autonomy within a single Sudan. New policy initiatives were taken, including the creation of an Office of Southern Affairs headed by a southerner and the promotion of greater social and economic development in the region. While these policies perhaps laid the foundation for a future accommodation, they did not allay the suspicions of the southern Anya Nya guerrilla movement or bring its leaders to the conference table; nor did they lessen Sudan's isolation from the OAU. It became clear to Numeiri that a successful initiative would require a basic reorientation in the manner in which the Arabic north approached and dealt with the Black African south. In place of an exclusively Arab-Islamic foreign policy, a dual policy was adopted which de-emphasized and postponed Sudan's joining an Arab federation and aimed rather at securing new workable relationships with Black African countries. The biracial and bicultural character of Sudan was given official recognition. In this way Numeiri was able to secure the cooperation of other African countries, particularly Haile Selassie's Ethiopia, which played a key role—along with the World Council of Churches—in establishing serious negotiations that led to a settlement. There were important compromises on both sides:

117. Cited in ibid., p. 68.
118. Ibid., pp. 77–78.

while the southern leaders gave up their demand for complete independence, the Numeiri government accepted an arrangement that gave the south greater internal autonomy than it had previously been willing to consider.[119]

Governance in the Sudan has become centered on the ruler. Numeiri has sought to build up structures that in the long run will be able to operate independently of his personal mastery and manipulation. At the same time in the context of a political situation and culture that have prevented him from doing otherwise, he appears to have increased his capacity for personal rule. Observers have been struck by his sense of personal power and his ability to assert it. He is reported to believe that politics are primary, and that everything else—including economic development—"must take second place." "Politics" means, above all, "power . . . and he has a very fine understanding of that."[120] In addition to personal politics, he has cultivated his role as a plebiscitarian leader. Soon after the unsuccessful coup attempt of 1971, he held a national referendum on his leadership; it received overwhelming popular support, much of it undoubtedly genuine. Afterwards he abolished the Revolutionary Command Council, indicating that the legitimacy of the regime henceforth would no longer be based solely on the military as a collegial body, but rather upon his authority as elected President and upon the authority of the newly founded SSU. Subsequent events seem to indicate that his power and legitimacy are probably more important to his regime than any the party might possess. He has taken considerable pains to become a genuinely popular Islamic ruler: he makes regular radio broadcasts to his people that air public grievances; he tours the country regularly, seeking contact with the ordinary people of the Sudan (it is reported that his quest for popular support is not impaired by any personal concern for his own safety);[121] and he has cultivated his role as a devoted follower of Islam, announcing regularly the towns or villages in which he plans to offer up his Friday prayers. The sense of his populism is conveyed in the following message he broadcast over television: "I am with you in the markets and pub-

119. For a helpful study of the problems of the southern Sudan, see Dunstan M. Wai, ed., *The Southern Sudan: The Problem of National Integration* (London: Frank Cass & Co., 1973); see also Richard P. Stevens, "The 1972 Addis Ababa Agreement and the Sudan's Afro-Arab Policy," *Journal of Modern African Studies* 14, 2 (1976): 247–74; Nelson Kasfir, "Southern Sudanese Politics Since the Addis Ababa Agreement," *African Affairs* 76, 303 (April 1977): 143–66.

120. Sylvester, p. 72.

121. Ibid.

lic places, in the villages and the towns. . . . I feel close to your living problems. . . . I hear and learn and see more from people than I learn from any reports."[122] Sylvester's study of Numeiri gives an intimate portrait of his relationships with his colleagues and his people:

> Seeing him talk to his Ministers I thought the relationship was remarkably easygoing. It was like the captain of a football team discussing a point with his mates. But everyone knew that he was also the club manager, as ruthless as any. He was also the star player who drew all those crowds.[123]

This puts as fine a point on his ruling style as any description could.

The Prince is a ruler who presides over the polity but refrains from suppressing politics, even if he were in a position to do so. He is prepared to rule with his oligarchs—to recognize their authority and to secure their cooperation. The Prince stands above politician politics, especially in his role as arbiter of the disputes between other powerful men, but he also stands among such politicians who extend to him cooperation and deference in exchange for the political rights and privileges of belonging to his regime. If the political system of personal rule appears to be a historical adaptation to the conditions of an underdeveloped society, of all the personal rulership types that we identify, the rule of the Prince appears best adapted to such a society and most prepared to accommodate its pluralism, particularism, and localized norms and traditions. In seeking political mastery rather than oligarchical cooperation, the Autocrat resists such adaptation and accommodation; in wishing to escape from such conditions, in viewing their elimination as his mission, the Prophet is ideologically disposed to reject such accommodation; and in fearing all power save his own, and wishing to destroy such power that he is unable to possess, the Tyrant is incapable of making such an adjustment. Thus we are left with the Prince: an arbitrating, compromising tactical ruler who seeks power and authority, but not to the point of denying the political and ideological independence of others. Unlike the Autocrat, he is a political man more than an organizational man; unlike the Prophet, he is an accommodator rather than a mobilizer. For those who believe that the political problems of underdeveloped countries require rationally organized governments guided by scientific or ideological goals, the improvised political system that the Prince creates (usually without deliberate intent) will have little attraction. But for those who believe that politics is a practical and demanding art learned from experience, his political handiwork is likely to be of considerable interest and value.

4

Autocrats

and Lordship

IN a number of African countries the ruler is less fettered than the rulers we have considered so far by the power of other political men or by the tacit understandings and agreements that exist among them. The men who govern Ivory Coast, Cameroon, Gabon, Malawi, and Zaire have enjoyed a greater measure of autonomous power and independence of personal entanglements. These are autocratic rulers. The African Autocrat is to be distinguished from the African Prince not by ideology or ruling style but by his greater freedom to act as he sees fit. He is freer to break agreements (or not to make them in the first place) because those with whom he may have them are in no position to enforce them. There are no powerful rivals with whom he must contend.

The African Autocrat dominates the state to a greater extent than the African Prince. Lieutenants remain far more dependent on him and are prevented by him from acquiring an independent power base. It is only a slight exaggeration to suggest that the "state" under autocracy of the African type is more the ruler's private domain than the public realm; he conducts himself and is treated like the proprietor of the state. Autocratic "proprietorship" frequently results in a "bureaucratic management" approach to rulership. A concern with managerialism, we shall see, is particularly evident in Houphouët-Boigny's Ivory Coast and Banda's Malawi, and to a somewhat lesser degree in Ahidjo's Cameroon and Bongo's Gabon. But this approach is not the only one. The Autocrat can also issue to political clients what amount to conditional licenses to do his bidding and can recall them whenever it suits his interests or needs. The conditional licensing approach is much in evidence in Mobutu's relations with lesser men in Zaire, where the ruler's concern for bureaucratic and managerial efficiency is less apparent. Whether by bureaucratic management or by conditional licensing, Autocrats in Africa dominate their governments much more than they preside over them, corroborating a historic distinction between "lordship" and "rulership" recently resurrected by Oakeshott.[1]

Autocracy is absolute government by right (distinguishing it from tyranny—see chapter 6 below); the Autocrat is a ruler of unlimited authority (but not, as we noted in chapter 2, unlimited power). Burke thought that despotism (basically the same as autocracy, but heavier and more burdensome) was the simplest form of government; we consider that autocracy is as simple as despotism because the national political stage is dominated almost entirely by one man—a strongman confident in his power and authority and firmly in control. Because the Autocrat is the only legitimate national politician, autocratic regimes are lacking in politics—not only public politics, but politician politics also. Autocracy is not a school for training national leaders in the demanding political art of cooperative rulership. However, it may be a training ground for administrators. In the more bureaucratically organized autocracies administration has largely displaced politics as the principal method of governance.

When the state is virtually one man, the death or disability of the ruler and the problem of succession loom large. Traditional autocracy resolved the problem—insofar as it can be resolved—by the simple institutional mechanism of primogeniture (which still did not prevent disputes about who was the *rightful* heir). With the possible exception of the farcical experiment with neo-royalism in Central African Empire (discussed below), modern African autocracy has sought no such mechanism. Perhaps the current strongman in each of the five countries we discuss will be responsible and astute enough to name a Dauphin, and perhaps his choice can be made to stick. However, abilities are specifically personal and cannot be passed from one man to another—except perhaps by instruction, which usually is not offered in autocracies. Furthermore, specifically personal relationships built up by the old ruler cannot endure wholly uninterrupted without him—for instance, Houphouët-Boigny's intimate ties with old comrades-in-arms in Paris. Finally, because under autocracy all other political men have been strictly subordinated to the ruler or have been driven out of politics (possibly into exile), the lack of an obvious successor within the regime is a major problem.

1. Michael Oakeshott, *On Human Conduct* (Oxford: Clarendon Press, 1975), esp. pp. 218-19, 268-70, and 286-87.

A related problem is that politicians who were driven out by an Autocrat may try to fight their way back in; exiles may desire to seize the throne from abroad. Thus the problem of succession could grow from a factional struggle at the center of the state into a broader political struggle among both clients and enemies of the former Autocrat. Of all the countries considered in this chapter, this possibility is perhaps greatest in Malawi; Kamazu Banda is an old man who has made many political enemies over the years, some of whom are reported to have organized and armed themselves in neighboring countries. In Zaire and Cameroon, there is a possibility that the disappearance of the incumbent rulers from the political scene could result in reassertions of regionalism and struggles by long-frustrated politicians to carve out smaller regional-ethnic states for themselves—for example, in Zaire's unsettled Shaba Province. In other words, the suppression, if not actual suspension of all politics in autocracy is an invitation for political trouble when the reigning Autocrat passes from the scene. Unless a new Autocrat emerges or the potential rivals can make an effective compact among themselves, political factionalism will likely ensue, very possibly threatening or breaking out in violence.

Félix Houphouët-Boigny, Ivory Coast

The government of Ivory Coast has been the government of virtually one man: Félix Houphouët-Boigny, *"le vieux."* An astute and realistic conservative, he has ruled that country since independence in 1960 and dominated Ivorian political life since the first stirrings of nationalist politics in 1946. In seeking to describe the particular style of Houphouët-Boigny's rule, one fastens upon words such as "assured," "dignified," "austere"—but totally "colorless" and lacking in "flamboyance" or "charm." Houphouët-Boigny is a remote eminence, an elder statesman with the stature of Senghor of Senegal. Perhaps for that reason (not less than for policy reasons), he has been an historic rival of the Senegalese ruler. Unlike Senghor, Houphouët-Boigny is an anti-politician, an administrator's politician and not a politician's politician. During the long and successful tenure of his rule he has virtually suspended public politics in Ivory Coast and subjected what remains to his stern and unrelenting control.

Houphouët-Boigny is above all a believer in management and organization. He had an opportunity to gain respect for Cartesian managerial government by serving for thirteen years in the French cabinet during the Fourth Republic. Here he developed a distaste for faction-ridden parliamentarism and an admiration for strong, capable bureaucratic rule. In governing, Houphouët has relied almost entirely on the agencies of the state bequeathed to him by the French, and he has largely maintained the efficiency and capability of these agencies. Bureaucratism in the state is unmistakable. It is evident, for example, in the incorporation of military men into important "command posts" in the cabinet and within the civil administration; officers now serve as prefects and sub-prefects in the politically important Ministry of the Interior.[2]

Almost twenty years after independence, the French bureaucratic and commercial presence was still pervasive in Ivory Coast. Indeed, the French population in the country had grown from about 12,000 in 1960 to more than 50,000 by the late 1970s.[3] There is no question that the ruler has relied upon their managerial, technical, and business expertise—and their investments—to help produce the impressively high rate of economic growth that Ivory Coast has achieved since independence.[4] Although at one time the French presence extended to non-technical, middle-management posts, the French managerial elite in particular has provided loyal and capable agents who have contributed greatly to the overall effectiveness of both the state and the private sectors of the economy and enabled Houphouët to monopolize political power. The positive effects of high growth, and the ruler's political longevity, have no doubt contributed greatly to Houphouët's belief

2. *Africa Contemporary Record: Annual Survey and Documents*; 1968–70, ed. Colin Legum and John Drysdale (London: Africa Research, 1969–70); 1970–72, ed. Colin Legum (London: Rex Collings, 1971; London: Rex Collings, and New York: Africana Publications, 1972); 1972–79, ed. Colin Legum (New York: Africana Publications, 1973–79); on bureaucratism in Ivory Coast, see 1974–75, p. B 685, and 1978–79, p. B 663.

3. "Ivory Coast: France's Place in the Sun," *The Economist*, January 28, 1979, p. 10. In addition to the French, there are some 100,000 "Syrian-Lebanese," who are mostly urban merchants, and more than a million non-Ivorian Africans—mostly Mossi from Upper Volta.

4. For two sharply differing analyses, see Elliot J. Berg, "Structural Transformation versus Gradualism: Recent Economic Development in Ghana and the Ivory Coast," in *Ghana and the Ivory Coast: Perspectives on Modernization*, ed. Philip Foster and Aristide Zolberg (Chicago and London: University of Chicago Press, 1971), pp. 187–230, and Samir Amin, *Le Développement du capitalisme en Côte d'Ivoire* (Paris: Les Editions de Minuit, 1967). See also Bonnie Campbell, "The Ivory Coast," in *West African States: Failure and Promise: A Study in Comparative Politics*, ed. John Dunn (Cambridge: Cambridge University Press, 1978), pp. 66–131.

that economic growth and its corollary benefits—especially employment and increased personal income—are not only essential
for political stability but may also serve as substitutes for political
participation. By providing tempting opportunities, economic
growth has generally served the interests of the ruler and his regime. However, by the same token, an abrupt decline or even a
serious falling off in the rate of economic growth could make the
regime vulnerable to political uncertainties that it has thus far
been able and fortunate to avoid.

(The neo-colonial bureaucratism of French nationals has become politically costly in recent years. Until the late 1970s with
steady economic growth the state sector could expand to guarantee
all qualified Ivorians some kind of civil service appointment [or
they could find a corresponding position in the private sector].
"Each and every young Ivorian knows that if he conforms to the
rules he is sure to be adopted by the system—and thus be able to
enjoy all the 'fringe benefits.' . . . So high is the prize of becoming
part of the system that very few can resist the temptation."[5] In
recent years there has been a dramatic increase of young, well-
educated Ivorians in management and executive posts in private
firms—some coming out of government administration and causing considerable concern in government circles. Furthermore, although the expanding economy could contain the demands for
full-scale Ivorianization, positions at the lower or middle levels do
not assuage the desire for promotion to senior posts, nor do they
come to grips with the public attitude that the continued presence
of aliens—who happen to be the former rulers—is intolerable. In
the late 1970s the government found it politically expedient to initiate an extensive Ivorianization of the private as well as the public
sector at all levels. French nationals have suffered in consequence.
For example, in 1978 the French manager of the Michelin company was expelled for advertising a position that was open only to
French nationals.)[6]

The National Assembly has been a passive instrument that con-
sents automatically to executive decrees and instructions. The cabinet is less a collegial body of powerful and independent
incumbents and more a technical and political advisory body to the
ruler. In recent years there has been an increase of young technocrats both in the cabinet and in the bureaucracy. Of the thirty-
six ministers in 1974, only six were Houphouët's old political

5. *West Africa* 3088 (6 September 1976): 1288–89.
6. *Africa Contemporary Record*, 1978–79, p. B 669. Also see *West Africa* 3248 (8
October 1979): 1912, and ibid., 3250 (29 October 1979): 1977.

party colleagues— *"les anciens."*[7] The increased presence of technocrats—all appointed by the ruler and personally dependent on
him—is consistent with the autocratic view that government is
solely the ruler's agency rather than an arena where political differences are resolved and agreements secured for laws and policies. Technocrats are facilitators rather than deliberators, agents
rather than representatives.

In making cabinet appointments, Houphouët-Boigny has been
careful to insure that all major ethnic groups are represented—but
not by their most prominent politicians. Young, less experienced,
and less well known men have received the nod. The Ivorian ruler
has shown a marked preference for "courtiers" rather than "barons"—that is, men who are prepared to serve devotedly and perhaps with ability but who lack independent political means.[8] In
such a regime "representation" obviously is more nominal than
real. The *modus operandi* of autocracy—personal dependence on
the ruler—has been described particularly well by *West Africa:*

> How often has one heard that the future of the Ivorian success saga
> depends on one man and one alone—Felix Houphouet-Boigny? . . .
> Nearly all members of the elite were creations of the Head of State.
> The President has long been the man who makes and unmakes the lead-
> ers. With the exception of perhaps one man—Jean Baptiste Mockey—
> they owe all they have to "the Old Man." He has brought them into the
> system, provided them with all their needs—and he is the man who
> could exclude them from the system. And although this exclusion has
> mostly been smooth, and rather non-violent, the sheer threat of it has so
> far acted as a magnificently efficient preventative.[9]

In the Ivorian state "free floating" political resources do not exist. The centralization of the state, concomitant with its depoliticization and the expansion of the "administrative" and "technical"
within it, has left few mobilizable or usable political resources
outside it.[10] For example, there are no large-scale, potentially
powerful ethnic groups that ambitious political men could use for
a political base independent of the offices and patronage of the
state. Other political resources, such as wealth, tend to require the
cooperation of state authorities before they can be obtained. More
important, state agents—particularly the prefects in rural areas—

7. *Africa Contemporary Record*, 1976–77, p. B 610.
8. See *West Africa* 3089 (13 September 1976): 1323.
9. "The Iceberg That Is Ivory Coast: 1," *West Africa* 3088 (6 September 1976):
1289.
10. See Michael A. Cohen, *Urban Policy and Political Conflict in Africa: A Study of
the Ivory Coast* (Chicago and London: University of Chicago Press, 1974); also see
Robert D. Tree, "Administrative Structure, Ethnicity, and Nation-Building in the
Ivory Coast," *Journal of Modern African Studies* 12, 2 (1974): 211–29.

effectively enforce bans on political freedom and thereby prevent an autonomous mobilization of potential resources. Local party leaders of the sole legitimate party, the Parti Démocratique de Côte d'Ivoire (PDCI), exercise little authority and less power vis-à-vis state agents. For all intents and purposes, the Ivorian state is an administrative-technical agency devoid of structures of representation or participation. There are few nationally important politicians. Among these are Philippe Yacé, the President of the National Assembly, and Jean-Baptiste Mockey, a former rival of the President whose long-standing reluctance to be "rehabilitated" suggests that he may have some political status independent of the ruler's control.[11]

The late President Nkrumah of Ghana once admonished Africans: "Seek ye first the political kingdom." President Houphouët-Boigny holds the conviction that salvation, if it is to be found anywhere in an underdeveloped African country, is to be found only in an apolitical government that is prepared not only to permit but also to encourage economic growth by private means. The ruler has chosen and been able to govern without politics—certainly without public contestational politics, which are associated in his mind with ethnic and generational conflict, instability, and disorder. By "postponing" politics, as Stryker puts it,[12] Houphouët has had to provide compensating opportunities, as well as exercise effective control to forestall discontent. As was noted, successful economic growth has greatly aided the ruler in his efforts to depoliticize the state by providing such opportunities.

Of course, the skillful use of state patronage—especially in the form of well-paying jobs made available by economic growth—has been a very important means of enforcing political quiescence among the elite. In addition, patronage to selected local areas—for example, the allocation of regional or local development projects—has been distributed as presidential favor or gratitude to faithful local notables. Presidential favor is evident also in the selection each year of a different site for national independence day, the preparations for which involve considerable public expenditure which directly benefits the chosen community.[13] On occasion the President has responded directly to petitions from neglected

11. See *West Africa* 3088 (6 September 1976): 1289; *Africa Contemporary Record*, 1976–77, p. B 610.
12. Richard E. Stryker, "A Local Perspective on Development Strategy in the Ivory Coast," in *The State of the Nations: Constraints on Development in Independent Africa*, ed. Michael F. Lofchie (Berkeley, Los Angeles, London: University of California Press, 1971), p. 124.
13. Michael A. Cohen, "The Myth of the Expanding Center—Politics in the Ivory Coast," *Journal of Modern African Studies* 11, 2 (1973): 231–45.

regions and communities and has made funds available for social and economic infrastructure—as he did during a tour of northern Ivory Coast in 1975, for instance. He has adopted the practice of touring the country seeking direct "dialogue" with local leaders without the intervention or intermediation of political brokers. From time to time he has convened in Abidjan a kind of "Estates General" attended by as many as 2,000 local leaders, who gather to give praise, air grievances, and receive the assurances and instructions of the ruler. In the event of local political trouble—as occurred in the prefecture of Man in 1976—the Ivorian ruler has been known to dispatch "special missions, often headed by several cabinet ministers, to investigate the incident, dismiss the guilty, and restructure the local organization."[14] If such measures have failed, the President has been known to use sterner means.

The ruler's anti-politics stance and the "administrization" of the state have combined to reduce the former commanding importance of the ruling PDCI. What was before independence a fairly lively "political machine"[15]—especially in the urban centers and in particular around Abidjan—has atrophied. Much of the party's decline may be attributed to the ending of competitive politics by Houphouët during terminal colonial rule and to the infrequency of intra-party elections since then. Although the PDCI was declared "a single party, for a single people, with a single leader" at its 1965 Congress, it seems to have become a somewhat tarnished symbol of statehood and a channel of patronage, especially for old guard politicians who stood with Houphouët during the fight for independence and who lack the ability to hold government office yet have remained personally loyal to the ruler. Many of these men serve as regional secretaries-general or members of the Political Bureau. They resemble a kind of political gentry with modest privileges, but they are in fact a client class totally dependent upon the ruler for their position and perquisites. The party has been described as a kind of Ivorian "House of Lords," where old political cronies of the President can be retired with dignity and without political loss of face.[16]

The lordship of personal rule in Ivory Coast is evident in a number of features of the state. It is particularly evident in the extensive, privately owned presidential domains. The President's

14. "Ivory Coast Looks Ahead: 2," *West Africa* 3117 (4 April 1977): 647.
15. Aristide R. Zolberg, *Creating Political Order: The Party-States of West Africa* (Chicago: Rand McNally & Co., 1966), pp. 14–15; see also Zolberg's earlier study, *One-Party Government in the Ivory Coast*, rev. ed. (Princeton: Princeton University Press, 1969).
16. *Africa Contemporary Record*, 1972–73, p. B 628.

personal estate at his birthplace of Yamoussoukro is reported to be one of the largest in all of Africa; it may very well be one of the most prosperous. It has been expertly managed by agriculturalists from abroad—most notably from Israel and Taiwan.[17] With the strong backing and personal interest of the ruler, it has been the site of important experiments in crop cultivation and in the development and application of new agricultural techniques. Here Houphouët's belief in pure managerialism has been personally rewarding. In addition, on his domains and in Yamoussoukro there are imposing new edifices—including the Maison du Parti (an impressively styled palace of the people), the luxurious Hotel President, and of course the President's palace with its surrounding moat containing the sacred crocodiles. (The ruler also owns a small castle in Geneva, a luxurious apartment in Paris, and a house in Abidjan.) It is in the palace that the Ivorian autocrat receives important emissaries and visitors from home and abroad.

Like Machiavelli's Prince and personal rulers in general, the Ivorian ruler has treated foreign policy as his personal domain. The independence of mind that Houphouët-Boigny has demonstrated in his domestic policy of unbridled capitalism has been equally evident in a foreign policy of cautious and quiet "realism."[18] Like another African Autocrat of independent spirit, President Banda of Malawi, Houphouët has shown disdain for the main currents of international opinion within the African continent. Out of a profound suspicion of Marxist ideology and Communist states, he has remained utterly aloof from the Eastern bloc countries and China, which do not have embassies in Abidjan. At the same time, he has acted in defiance of the OAU and intra-African public opinion by initiating trading and diplomatic contacts with South Africa; he has even held personal discussions with former Prime Minister Vorster at Yamoussoukro. For such foreign policies, as well as for his domestic economic policies, Houphouët-Boigny has become something of an anathema not only for Africa's radical governments and intellectuals, but for many Western intellectuals also. However, Houphouët has made absolutely no public demonstration of ill-feeling—let alone defiance—toward the more radical African statesmen with whom he disagrees; in character with his particular ruling style, he has steadily maintained ties with all who will maintain them with him, obviously believing in the traditional concept of diplomacy as an expedient, amoral activity of statesmen.

17. Ibid., 1975–76, p. B 726.
18. See *West Africa* 3117 (4 April 1977): 646–49.

Since Ivory Coast is Houphouët's personal government and since he alone represents the people, only he is entitled to voice legitimate criticisms against government policies and actions. He is skillful in playing the people's spokesman against the oversights and failures of government officials. However, it is a stratagem that can work better in local communities where wrongs can be righted and expectations fulfilled; it works less well at the national level, where large-scale issues or concerns are not recognized as political and so cannot receive the genuine attention of government. Houphouët sees to it that national problems remain unarticulated and their causes suppressed.

Houphouët-Boigny is evidently aware of the problems of a nonpolitical state despite the fact that he has often fixed his public criticisms on political rivalry. While he has maintained opposition to competitive politics—declaring that "competition is healthy for sport, but in politics, what must triumph is team spirit"[19]—he has recently shown an inclination to allow some politics in Ivory Coast. For example, hesitant steps were taken in the late 1970s to replace appointed mayors by elected ones.[20] In addition, the possibility of competitive elections in the PDCI for National Assembly seats has been explored.[21] These were perhaps the most prominent signs of a political awakening in Ivory Coast.

As we have noted, one-man politics raises the question of succession, and Ivory Coast lacks capable politicians with demonstrated public support. Houphouët-Boigny is in his seventies, and there is no clear successor. Although the President of the National Assembly (currently Yacé) is constitutionally entitled to succeed in the event of the death or incapacity of the President, it is speculated that Yacé is not the President's personal choice. Mockey, the only other independent national leader, appears not to be politically ambitious.[22] Thus it is impossible to know who is most likely to succeed Houphouët-Boigny; it is certain, however, that the issue will loom very large in the future.

Ahmadou Ahidjo, Cameroon

In Cameroon (as in Gabon) a highly centralized and firmly controlled regime exists under a civilian ruler who is without doubt a

19. Quoted in ibid., 3274 (21 April 1980): 694.
20. *Africa Contemporary Record*, 1978–79, p. B 664.
21. *West Africa* 3274 (21 April 1980): 696.
22. Ibid., 3250 (29 October 1979): 1977. At the 1980 Party Congress Yacé was effectively eliminated as a designated successor by the abolition of his party post as secretary-general.

political strongman. President Ahmadou Ahidjo has been resolute, tough, and uncompromising. He has exercised great discretion in choosing whether, how, and when to act. He has been remarkably successful in eliminating rivals and suppressing opposition—in fact, in depoliticizing the regime. He effectively claims to be the sole representative of the people, exclusively entitled to speak in their name; more important, he has appropriated the state, becoming ruler-manager with the exclusive right to issue commands and give political instructions.

The emergence of autocracy in Cameroon was in part conditioned by internal strife that arose during the end of the colonial period and was not finally resolved until a decade after independence (1960). Since his government's suppression of regional rebellions, particularly among the Bamiléké peoples of southwestern Cameroon,[23] Ahidjo has ruled with an exceedingly tight rein. He has been likened to a stern father unwilling to brook even the slightest degree of political independence among his "children." To speak of Ahidjo as a father or patriarch is not simply to employ a metaphor; he has deliberately sought to cultivate this view of himself. On the occasion of Cameroon's Tenth Anniversary of Independence from France (1970), the following poem was read to the President:

> The voice of the child-people echoes with pleas for
>   your help and your pardon. . . .
> Only you do we hear, for sky and earth no longer
>   remain unaware of your vocation.
> Give counsel to us, as a father to his erring children.[24]

Bayart has remarked that "power [in Cameroon] is in considerable measure personalized in the popular mind: not only M. Ahidjo but also, in the rural context, the prefect and sub-prefect assume the character of father-figure."[25] In other words, the parallels between father and Autocrat are well exploited in Cameroon. The rights and responsibilities of fathers are extensive and ordinarily cannot be interfered with; certainly children cannot claim reciprocal rights. In like manner the Autocrat possesses rights and responsibilities in relation to his people, while they should possess only gratitude and the obligation to obey. The state is the family writ large; as such it gives to a ruler the power to instruct subjects and to punish disobedience. President Ahidjo is

23. Richard A. Joseph, *Radical Nationalism in Cameroon* (Oxford: Clarendon Press, 1977).

24. Quoted in J. F. Bayart, "One-Party Government and Political Development in Cameroun," *African Affairs* 72, 287 (April 1973): 142.

25. Ibid.

not in any way an inspirational leader; he possesses nothing in the way of charisma. However, through shrewd maneuver, skillful manipulation and timing, and the will and ability to use power and force, he has acquired complete personal mastery of the state apparatus, and he is an effective manager of the economy.

Like all strong rulers, Ahidjo has a clear sense of the state as his personal agency, from which he exercises rightful power. What he called the Cameroonian "revolution" in a speech in 1973 was not a revolution of ideology but of the state: "There is no question of our leaning to the Left or to the Right. . . . It is a question of being faithful to the mission of a State which is worthy of that name and which is aware of its responsibilities."[26] In a 1977 address to the National Council of the ruling party, the Union National Camerounaise (UNC), he called upon the people to exhibit greater "duty consciousness" in their public and private lives: "There is no dignity for those who await everything from others."[27] At the 1980 Congress of the UNC, where he accepted the nomination as the sole candidate for the next presidential "election," Ahidjo warned against the "subversive activities" of those who hope to bring "the collapse of the fine structure of unity, stability, and progress which we are constantly struggling to build."[28] According to Ahidjo, the only worthwhile state is a unitary state; Cameroon became a federation shortly after independence, but Ahidjo has since centralized it.[29]

Like all stern and demanding fathers, Ahidjo relies substantially on the instruments of permission and punishment at his disposal, and he requires obedience without exception. The President personally commands the *gendarmerie* and the *sûreté nationale* (secret service), while his old friend and trusted advisor, Sadou Daoudou, who hails from the same northern district as Ahidjo, has been his Minister of the Armed Forces for many years. As is characteristic of autocracies, Ahidjo's essentially bureaucratic-prefectural rule includes a form of newspaper censorship and an efficient system of political security and personal surveillance, making government in Cameroon something of a "police state" somewhat reminiscent of Russian tsarism.[30] It has been reported that the se-

26. Quoted in *Africa Contemporary Record*, 1973–74, p. B 554.

27. Quoted in " 'Self Reliance' in Cameroun," *West Africa* 3111 (21 February 1977): 374.

28. Quoted in ibid., 3266 (25 February 1980): 374.

29. For the federation period, see Willard R. Johnson, *The Cameroon Federation: Political Integration in a Fragmented Society* (Princeton: Princeton University Press, 1970); Victor T. LeVine, *The Cameroon Federal Republic* (Ithaca and London: Cornell University Press, 1971).

30. *Africa Confidential* 17, 1 (January 9, 1976): 5.

cret service is highly efficient and that it is aided by a network of informers;[31] in consequence, Cameroonians are particularly discreet and circumspect when it comes to political talk.[32] Nonetheless, it has been estimated that from 10,000 to 30,000 "political prisoners" have been detained—remarkably high for a country of about seven million. Yet Cameroon cannot reasonably be regarded as a tyranny (see chapter 6 below). "There are no Cameroonian refugees living in camps in other African countries, nor are there wanton massacres of people as seems to be [sic] the case in Idi Amin's Uganda."[33] But it is an authoritarian state with an autocratic ruler who is prepared to rule severely.

Ahidjo has been likened to de Gaulle and is known to be a great admirer of the former French statesman. However, he is not a ruler in the mold of de Gaulle; he does not preside over a realm as a Prince, the conscience and embodiment of a people, the custodian of a great political and cultural tradition. Bayart has described Ahidjo's preoccupation with control and his desire to eliminate all particularist loyalties as Jacobin: "Particularist loyalties (identifications) are systematically suppressed in the interest of national consciousness."[34] His fear and suppression of political particularism is a legacy of the bitter internal struggle that Cameroon endured before and after independence, as well as a characteristic of a ruler jealous of his powers. Some of Cameroon's laws and decrees reflect Ahidjo's fears. For instance, not only all political groups, but also ethnic associations that are not specifically permitted are banned by the government. The Law of 12 June 1967 banned "any associations exhibiting an exclusively tribal or clan character."[35] Rule by decree, by general ban, and by specific permit is a bench mark of autocracy and authoritarianism.

In Cameroon the subordination by the ruler of the ruling class has been accomplished in a number of ways. From time to time Ahidjo has demanded and received oaths of personal loyalty from members of his government—especially on ceremonial occasions (such as the fifteenth anniversary of his accession to power in 1973), in which the oaths have recalled the acts of fealty of vassals to their overlords in a distant European past. At other times he has exercised his discretionary right to nominate, rotate, or replace members of the political oligarchy. In this way he has succeeded in

31. *Africa Contemporary Record*, 1976–77, p. B 463.

32. "Many Cameroonians are afraid to criticize the government even in front of their wives and children, as families have been known to betray their husbands and fathers to security officials for financial or other benefits" (Sammy Kum Buo, "How United is Cameroon?" *Africa Report* 21, 6 [November–December 1976]: 18).

33. Ibid., p. 19.   34. Bayart, p. 127.   35. Ibid., p. 128.

completely dominating the ruling party and the government, transforming all other "leaders" into his underlings. In addition, he has seen fit to amend the constitution to create new offices that are clearly and unambiguously subordinated to the presidency, and he has filled these offices with loyal servants. In 1972 a Supreme Court was established to try (*inter alia*) "political crimes," but ministers and vice-ministers could be brought before the court only with presidential permission.[36] In 1975 constitutional provisions for the creation of an office of prime minister were decreed, but the powers of the office were clearly subordinated to the presidency, and Ahidjo granted himself the discretion to appoint the new officeholder. As it turned out, he selected Paul Mbiya, who had spent the seven previous years working in the Office of the President.[37]

Omar Bongo, Gabon

The ruler of Gabon, Omar Bongo, is cut from a similar cloth as Ahidjo, although Gabon is quite different from Cameroon. South of Cameroon, Gabon is a small country with a population of less than one million. It is rich in natural resources; in colonial times Gabon was exploited economically more than politically, and the same remains true today. Extensive foreign investment in its abundant oil, mineral, and timber resources—now with increasing state participation—has given Gabon (albeit somewhat artificially) the status of having one of the highest per capita incomes in sub-Saharan Africa. In important ways the country remains an economic estate to be managed rather than an arena of politics. Cooperative arrangements between Bongo's government and foreign investors—mostly from France—have proved to be workable so far.

It would be a mistake to view Bongo merely as some kind of neocolonial "puppet," however. He is a tough politician with a marked belief in managerialism and an impatience for both politics and socialism (somewhat like Houphouët-Boigny). He is a statist, a mercantilist, and an economic nationalist, as revealed in the following remark: "Each country does what is necessary and profitable for its own interests."[38] (By "interests" Bongo meant

36. *Africa Contemporary Record*, 1972–73, p. B 502.
37. Ibid., 1975–76, pp. B 440–41.
38. Quoted in Anthony J. Hughes, "Omar Bongo: President of the Republic of Gabon," *Africa Report* 22, 3 (May–June 1977): 3.

economic interests.)[39] In large measure, statecraft is the managing and guidance of economic interests, and the Autocrat is better placed strategically to control such interests than the Prince. Distressed at the cost of servicing the public debt, Bongo declared in 1976: "Our loans are too short-term. I've made a decision: until 1979 I will not pay anyone, nor will I pay anything."[40]

Omar Bongo became ruler of Gabon in 1967, following the death of President M'Ba, who had selected Bongo as his successor and had amended the constitution in Bongo's favor.[41] One is struck by the assertiveness, outspokenness, and flamboyance of Bongo's rule; the Gabonese autocrat is much given to publicity. Furthermore, he has demonstrated a penchant for state and personal grandeur that is unusual even among Africa's personal rulers. For example, for the OAU summit in Libreville (the capital city) in 1977 (at which time Bongo became chairman of the OAU), the ruler allocated funds for the refurbishing of the capital, including the construction of divided highways and grand ocean-front hotels; for the personal use of the African statesmen in attendance he provided an unspecified number of imported limousines; for himself he authorized the building of a marble-floored palace with sliding doors and walls, rotating rooms, and a private nightclub (among other things); much to his disappointment, the palace was not finished in time.[42]

Yet Bongo is a dedicated and effective personal ruler. Still only in his forties, he is as much a strongman as Ahidjo. He is in total control; he has no rivals, only subordinates who are fully dependent upon his favors. He rewards or punishes as he sees fit. He views the "people" as pliant subjects, innocent of partisan interests and free of corruption. (The party banner, an open hand on a white field, represents "the disinterestedness, sincerity and clear conscience expected of the people.")[43] Bongo does not recognize any temporal superiors. When asked to explain his conversion from Catholicism to Islam, he pointed out that it removed intermediaries between himself and God: "I do not have to appear in front of a Monsignor or Bishop in order to render account of what I have done."[44]

39. Ibid., p. 4.
40. Quoted in *Africa Guide, 1978* (London: Africa Guide Company, 1977), p. 127.
41. For the colonial and early independence period in Gabon, see Brian Weinstein, *Gabon: Nation-Building on the Ogooué* (Cambridge, Mass., and London: MIT Press, 1966).
42. *Africa Contemporary Record*, 1977–78, pp. B 573–74.
43. Ibid., 1973–74, p. B 600.
44. Quoted in Hughes, "Omar Bongo," p. 5.

The running of virtually the entire government is subject to Bongo's personal instructions. Bongo issues decrees and orders. Reserving the most important cabinet portfolios for himself, he has assigned trusted relatives to strategic positions in the armed forces and the civil administration; for expertise and efficiency he has placed French officers and *coopérants* alongside them.[45] Even the post of Mayor of Libreville, once an elective office, has come within the President's patronage. Bongo not only handpicks both cabinet ministers and governors of the provinces with an eye to their subordination and loyalty, but also subjects them to frequent and unpredictable rotation, promotion, or dismissal. However, the highest offices—including that of prime minister—involve largely administrative functions and are devoid of autonomous political power. These are "ministers of the crown" in a way that no British government officer has been for centuries. A former technocrat himself, Bongo has sought to increase the presence of technocrats in the government, coincidentally with a desire to Gabonize the state apparatus and the managerial positions of the economy. The ruler has appointed the entire membership of the National Assembly by his discretionary right as Secretary-General of the ruling Parti Démocratique de Gabon (PDG) to nominate candidates in single-list elections.[46] Furthermore, he has required all members of the party's Political Bureau—whom he appoints—to swear an oath of loyalty to him, in his capacity both as Head of State and as Secretary-General. He has required pledges of loyalty and obedience from the police force and instructed its members never to complain to deputies or ministers, only to their commander or (if necessary) to him personally. Should they disobey, he has threatened to dissolve the force.[47] When once confronted with a mild show of independence by members of the National Assembly regarding a piece of minor legislation, Bongo stated simply: "If you refuse to fulfil your obligations, I will not hesitate to assume my responsibilities."[48]

Bongo can and does exercise his prerogative of mercy, but in a political fashion typical of authoritarianism. In other words, mercy is the handmaiden of coercion. Although in Gabon nobody

45. *Africa Contemporary Record*, 1977–78, pp. B 572–74.

46. For the February 1980 elections to the National Assembly (whose membership was increased from seventy to eighty-nine), in place of a single list of candidates, there were provincial lists which permitted local electors to choose from among several candidates. To the extent that politicians are now permitted to campaign individually for electoral support, it would appear to be a movement away from autocracy and toward princely rule.

47. *Africa Contemporary Record*, 1974–75, p. B 589.

48. Quoted in ibid., 1972–73, p. B 550.

is entitled to publicly criticize the conduct of government officials, Bongo has commuted death and prison sentences for political crimes—for example, releasing opponents of former President M'Ba from prison. "Pardon," Bongo has declared, "is the best revenge."[49] At the same time, the ruler of Gabon has enacted unusual legislation providing for "civil death sentences." According to one report, "Those sentenced to 'civil death' would lose all civil rights and be cut off by society. They will be listed as dead in civil registers, and their property will be handed over to their heirs."[50] Political dissidents are undoubtedly the targets of such legislation.

As we have indicated, autocratic rule in Gabon is a matter not only of political control, but of economic control as well. Bongo is a "modernizing" autocrat in a restricted technical-economic definition of that term. This does not mean he is interested in issues of equity distribution of wealth among the Gabonese; he is not even a mild redistributivist. However, he strongly believes in a Gabonese national interest in economic growth and in an increasing control of that growth by the Gabonese themselves, which in the absence of indigenous private enterprise means control by the Gabonese state. He has seriously pursued a policy of increased Gabonization of the economy by insisting upon state equity participation and the employment of Gabonese nationals in the management of foreign enterprise as a condition of foreign investment. He believes in managerialism in the pursuit of economic prosperity and in the "national" definition of the wealth of nations—which in the late twentieth century, an era of international capitalist enterprise, means that he believes in "nationalizing" enterprises without "socializing" them. He is not unlike a growing number of other non-socialist African rulers who have opted for a kind of neo-mercantilist growth strategy aimed at siphoning off as much profit as possible from foreign investment without frightening investors away. Gabon's undeveloped rich natural resources make this stratagem a particularly practical and plausible one.

H. Kamazu Banda, Malawi

The personal rule of President H. Kamazu Banda of Malawi has been described as "rule with an iron hand," and the ruler himself as a "paternalist despot."[51] The paternalist elements can be seen in the ruler's strong sense of personal responsibility for the

49. Quoted in ibid., p. B 551.   50. Ibid., 1970–71, p. B 320.
51. Ibid., 1975–76, pp. B 249–50. For accounts of Banda's rule, see Philip Short,

security and welfare of his subjects; the despotic elements, in his intolerance of rivals or opponents and his willingness to use force (if necessary) to suppress them. A politician showing even the mildest form of independence can suffer the ruler's rebuke, be it merely a warning or a more substantive punishment. To receive the ruler's praise or favor, demonstrations of loyalty verging on servility are expected and given. The official watchwords of Banda's regime are "Unity, Loyalty, Obedience, and Discipline." They succinctly sum up the personal autocracy that is Banda's Malawi, where the ruler's edicts and instructions must be accepted without question and where his personal desires and aversions in matters of morals set the national standards. As a result, Malawi is one of the tightest autocracies in Africa, and although it is in one of the most backward parts of the continent, it is a ruler estate that has been managed with fair economic success.

Banda is the *Ngwazi* (Conqueror, Champion) of Malawi—that is, a man of exceptional valor and achievement.[52] He dominates the public affairs of his country in a manner reminiscent of European absolutism; as Life President, he enjoys the tenure of a monarch; as author of the government's policies (including its foreign policy), his will and idiosyncracies are stamped on the regime; as the sole manager of the Malawian state, he personally involves himself in the supervision and implementation of policy, often attending to quite small details. Like Houphouët, Ahidjo, and Bongo, Banda makes all of the important political and governmental appointments in the country, frequently rotating, promoting, or dismissing men in a manner calculated to remind them of their total dependence upon his continued favor. His rule is absolute insofar as no important jurisdictions of law or policy—including the courts—are secure from his intervention or meddling.

President Banda's political domination of Malawi is due in no small or coincidental way to his remarkable life Odyssey. Malawi is a land of migrants—or what might be called "industrial pilgrims"—many of whom travel great distances to secure employment in the mines of the Zambian copperbelt and in South Africa; Dr. Banda has been the most illustrious of the migrants. He was absent from the country of his birth for forty years, during which time he became a medical doctor as well as an active pan-African-

Banda (London and Boston: Routledge & Kegan Paul, 1974); T. David Williams, *Malawi: The Politics of Despair* (Ithaca and London: Cornell University Press, 1978); and Richard Hodder-Williams, "Malawi's Decade Under Dr. Banda: The Revival of Politics," *The Round Table* 252 (October 1973): 463–70.

52. Victor T. LeVine, "Changing Leadership Styles and Political Images: Some Preliminary Notes," *Journal of Modern African Studies* 15, 4 (1977): 635.

ist and lived for an extended period in England and a shorter one in Ghana. He returned to Malawi in 1958 at the invitation of local nationalists who wanted him to assume the leadership of their independence movement. He quickly eclipsed these much younger and less worldly leaders and became the dominant figure in Malawian politics. Since Malawi's independence in 1964 Banda has steadily elevated his status and powers while subordinating those around him. He was made Life President of the ruling Malawi Congress Party (MCP) in 1960; he was Prime Minister of Malawi from 1962 until 1966, became President of Malawi when it was declared a republic in 1966, and has been Life President since 1970. In his regime there is no office of vice-president or prime minister, nor are there any recognizably prominent ministers or oligarchs. Dr. Banda is the state.

In addition to his lifetime title to rule, the "royalism" of Banda's presidency is cultivated by slogans such as "Kamazu knows best," by extensive display of his portrait in the press and elsewhere, by public demonstrations that celebrate his comings and goings, by popular songs in his praise, and by the celebration of Kamazu Day, which has replaced the Queen's Birthday as an annual occasion of national festivity. (In most other countries in Africa, celebrations at least officially pertain to the country, the people, or the party—not to the ruler.) Observers have been struck by the extent to which Banda has encouraged the cultivation of royalism: "Within the 'Malawi tribe,' the position Banda had come to hold was like that of one of the old *Maravi* kings, complete with divine right and absolute authority. So, at least, he saw himself, and so he wanted to be seen."[53] In addition, the trappings of chieftaincy have been put to use—for example, Banda carries traditional staffs of authority (such as the fly-whisk), and his entourage is "preceded by a modern version of the praise-maker—a Land-Rover fitted with loudspeakers—and welcoming groups of ululating women symbolically sweeping the ground with brushwood in front of his path."[54]

The royalism of Banda's rule is matched by a complementary plebiscitarianism. The possessive character of Banda's relations with "his people," the endless "meet the people" tours, the ceremonial populism—all are in character with royalist plebiscitarianism. Banda conceives of himself as the sole legitimate representative and protector of Malawians—particularly those of

53. Short, p. 281.
54. John G. Pike, *Malawi: A Political and Economic History* (London: Pall Mall Press, 1968), p. 171.

his ethnic group, the Chewa, who make up 46 percent of the population. He once remarked:

> When I say "for my people," . . . I do not mean clerks in the offices here in Blantyre [the former capital] and Zomba. I mean the ordinary people in the villages—farmers. I must create a situation for them in which they find not only peace and tranquility, but have something to eat, something to put on their backs, on their wives' heads, and if possible, shoes.[55]

In addition to extolling the people's simple virtues and wanting to attend to their basic material needs, Banda has declared his concern for their moral protection—particularly from the "decadent" influences of the West and the Westerners in their midst. He has dealt harshly with "corrupters"—typically foreigners or youth who have adopted Western moral practices or habits of dress. Moreover, he has taken steps to bolster the rights and powers of chiefs, which had declined under the influences of rising African nationalism just prior to independence. "Since 1965 the position of chief . . . has been gradually restored."[56] At the same time, Banda has sought to diminish intermediate authorities. In particular, he has drawn a clear line between his rights and those of all other politicians—for instance, he has granted MPs the very restricted right to lobby only in behalf of the parochial interests of their constituencies,[57] reserving for himself the right to speak on national issues. No political barons between the ruler and the parochial lobbyists are allowed; the kingdom comprises the ruler, courtiers without independent power bases, parochial spokesmen, and the people. Parliament has not been a national assembly for the debate of national issues, but a house of local spokesmen, all of whom had been appointed by Banda until 1978, when he permitted the first general elections since independence.[58] Banda has displayed great jealousy of his role as ruler and great displeasure at politicians who might wish to be something other than parochial spokesmen or subservient courtiers. He has repeatedly emphasized that he alone can represent all the people and declare national policy, and that all other leaders derive what rights and

55. Quoted in Samuel W. Speck, Jr., "Malawi and the Southern African Complex," in *Southern Africa in Perspective: Essays in Regional Politics*, ed. Christian P. Potholm and Richard Dale (New York: Free Press, 1972), p. 217.

56. Richard Hodder-Williams, "Dr. Banda's Malawi," *Journal of Commonwealth and Comparative Politics* 12, 1 (March 1974): 103.

57. Ibid., p. 101.

58. *Africa Contemporary Record*, 1978–79, pp. B 302–4. A certificate of proficiency in English was required for candidacy; as a result, seven constituencies had no candidates, and in another thirty-three of the total eight-seven constituencies only one candidate succeeded in obtaining a certificate. All candidates had to be members of the MCP.

powers they enjoy directly from him. (One of his closest lieutenants is reported to have said, "We feel that he should be allowed to
do pretty much as he sees fit, so long as he has the support of the
people."[59] The word "allowed" was clearly ill chosen, since it is
the autocrat of Malawi who is exclusively entitled to give or withhold permission.)

Banda's feelings of responsibility and paternalism in respect to
the rural people are matched by a disrespect—even a contempt—
for urban and modern people—in other words, for people like
himself who have sought a place in the modern world. He has
demonstrated public disdain for such persons, from clerks to cabinet ministers, and there have been numerous reports of his referring to the latter as his "boys." Banda has reserved his greatest
contempt for African "intellectuals"—those with a claim to educational, professional, or technical competence—whom he apparently distrusts and may refuse to consult even on technical
questions where his own competence is seriously limited. Hodder-
Williams notes that Banda has been "neurotically distrustful of
Africans as ministers or senior civil servants," preferring to rely
upon expatriates for expert advice precisely because they have no
separate interest in power or clients to satisfy.[60] Expatriates could
be made much more dependent upon the ruler than Africans, and
they posed no threat of disloyalty.

Shortly after independence in 1964 a number of fundamental
disagreements arose between Banda and a majority of his cabinet—most of them university-educated "intellectuals"—in connection with foreign and domestic policy. At issue was Banda's
right to personally dictate policy and overrule cabinet opposition;
also at issue was the direction his policies had been taking. At
home Banda had been reluctant to rapidly Africanize the civil service, while abroad he seemed to be turning away from neighboring
black African countries and toward some kind of *rapprochement*
with the white-ruled colonies and states of southern Africa.
"Banda's arrogance and high-handedness provoked the young
ministers' challenge; these same qualities ensured that Banda
would be infuriated by the challenge to his authority."[61] He demanded the resignation of those cabinet ministers who opposed his
policies (most of them the very same young nationalists who had
been responsible for bringing him back to Malawi after his long
absence and placing him on "the throne"); those who refused were

59. Quoted in Speck, p. 210.
60. Hodder-Williams, "Dr. Banda's Malawi," p. 96.
61. Ibid., p. 93.

summarily dismissed and publicly rebuked. He asked members of the National Assembly for a vote of confidence; having personally nominated them all for election in 1964, his appeal was assured of success. An attempt against his regime early in 1965, led by former education minister Henry Chipembere, proved to be a failure, and opponents of Banda's rule were either detained or forced into permanent exile. In 1967 a former home affairs minister was killed by Banda's soldiers when he attempted with his comrades to overthrow Banda. For well over a decade and a half Banda has been exclusively in command of his country's affairs, but the threat of plots against his regime has remained.[62]

Presidential patronage is a central feature of the regime. Banda's powers of appointment are extensive: he enjoys the sole right to appoint members to the National Executive Committee of the MCP; as was noted, until 1978, he alone made the final selection of party candidates for Parliament; he has exclusive powers to discipline and dismiss MPs; he nominates the Speaker, as well as a number of "Nominated Members" (of whom several usually have been Europeans); and he appoints, rotates, and dismisses cabinet ministers. One commentator has summed up Banda's rule as follows:

> Although the government is composed of ministers who theoretically report to a cabinet headed by the President, which in turn proposes legislation to the Parliament, in practice, the ministers, who are appointed and dismissed by the President at will, report directly to him. Once the President has made a decision, everything else becomes a formality.[63]

Cabinet appointments and rotations have taken place so frequently as to have created "an atmosphere of perpetual musical chairs."[64] Periodic abrupt dismissals of senior party, governmental, and administrative officials have long since ceased to surprise observers of Malawi's political affairs. In July 1977 Banda was reported to have dismissed his entire cabinet as well as all deputy ministers and parliamentary secretaries, and to have dissolved the National Executive Committee of the MCP.[65] These are clearly the acts of a powerful, strong-willed, and independent-minded ruler.

62. A former Secretary-General of the MCP, Albert Muwalo Ngumayo, was found guilty and executed in 1977 for plotting to kill Banda (see *Africa Contemporary Record*, 1978–79, p. B 302).

63. Henry J. Richardson, III, "Malawi: Between Black and White Africa," *Africa Report* 15, 2 (February 1970): 18.

64. John Dickie and Alan Rake, *Who's Who in Africa: The Political, Military and Business Leaders of Africa* (London: African Buyer and Trader Publications, 1973), p. 259.

65. *Africa Contemporary Record*, 1977–78, p. B 303.

Banda's judgment has been the final and most important deter-
minant of policy in Malawi. More often than not, he has shown
himself to be far out of step with other African rulers and the
OAU, marching to his own tune.[66] Prior to the collapse of Portugal's African empire, he had cultivated friendly relations with
Lisbon. He established diplomatic ties with South Africa in 1967,
receiving Prime Minister Vorster in Malawi in 1970 and becoming in 1971 the first African ruler to travel to Pretoria. Diplomatic
and economic ties have developed between Malawi and South Africa since then. Following the defeat of the Portuguese and the establishment of the FRELIMO regime in Mozambique, Banda
took steps toward a *rapprochement* with Maputo. It is evident that
Banda treats foreign policy as his prerogative, to direct and alter
according to his will and judgment and with little seeming regard
to other African rulers.

In determining both domestic and foreign policy, the ruler of
Malawi has often relied on his own judgment against the advice of
senior civil servants, although he has been reported "susceptible"
to arguments if he judges them "sound."[67] (The fact that he listens
to arguments at all distinguishes his rule from the largely impulsive and cunning rule of a Tyrant.) Banda has held a number of
ministerial portfolios—among the most noteworthy have been the
ministries of external affairs, works and supplies, agriculture and
natural resources, and justice—and has taken a keen personal interest in supervising much of the activity of others. Short writes
that everything of any importance has come before him, and no
decision of the least importance has been taken "without his first
having approved it."[68] "Nothing is not my business in this country," President Banda declared in 1972. "Everything is my business. Everything. The state of education, the state of our economy,
the state of our agriculture, the state of our transport, everything is
my business."[69] Here is perhaps one of the most candid claims to
lordship and to a proprietary interest and right of control made by
a contemporary African Autocrat. In the autocratic state the ruler
has a right to take an interest in whatever he wishes; everything is
his business, even if he is unable to bring everything under his
control. Banda's autocratic self-image was once strikingly revealed when he declared to the directors of a large British multina-

66. For a summary of Banda's foreign policy until 1973, see Carolyn McMaster,
Malawi—Foreign Policy and Development (New York: St. Martin's Press, 1974),
esp. pp. 162–76.
67. *Africa Digest* 20, 1 (February 1973): 18.
68. Short, p. 278.
69. Quoted in *Africa Contemporary Record*, 1973–74, p. B 210.

tional company: "Anything I say is law. Literally law. It is a fact in this country."[70]

Banda's quest for absolute control has extended particularly to the courts. He has given his attention to matters of both civil and criminal law, as well as to questions of trial and punishment. Important conventions of British law introduced during colonial times and retained in the independence constitution have been altered at his insistence—particularly rules concerning the admissibility of evidence and the grounds for conviction and acquittal. Banda has given himself the discretion to interfere with legal tribunals and proceedings—a kind of arbitrary "royalist" involvement that recalls the long-abolished Court of the Star Chamber used by English kings for imposing their domination. The President's powers to detain political enemies—to whom he is fond of referring as "subversive elements"—have been used against any and all he regards as disloyal. Political or treason trials have taken place in traditional African courts,[71] and "evidence" of very questionable validity or relevance has been allowed. The very establishment of these courts reveals an important dimension of Banda's autocratic rule—that is, his ability to tamper with justice or adjust it to his specifications. Furthermore, Banda instructed Parliament to pass the Local Courts (Amendment) Act, which empowered him to permit specified traditional courts to try serious criminal cases and to pass the death sentence; it also empowered him to direct that no appeal on a death sentence be allowed to any higher court. In one High Court trial, Banda not only refused to accept the ruling of its English judge—who, for reasons of insufficient evidence, had dismissed charges of murder brought against five men—but also blocked the release of the men and proceeded to give the traditional African courts the right to retry the cases and to pass sentences of death upon conviction. When asked to comment on the High Court judge's action, Banda warned: "They [the five men] are not going to be let loose, I can tell you that. . . . Never, never, never. No matter what anyone says or does. . . . Those people are not going to be let loose. . . . I am in charge, and I am not from England, either."[72] In addition, Banda secured from Parliament a Forfeiture Act, which empowered him to withhold the personal property of all persons whom he judged to be "subversive." An amendment permitted the law to be used

70. Quoted in Short, p. 254.
71. *Africa Contemporary Record*, 1976–77, p. B 268; also ibid., 1975–76, pp. B 249–50.
72. Quoted in Short, pp. 270–71.

against allegedly corrupt or negligent officials, and no prior conviction had to be obtained in the courts.

When we observe the autocracy in Malawi, we cannot avoid noticing that Banda either has caused independent-minded individuals or groups to be suppressed or has driven them into exile. Reports indicate that political detention is a fact of life, serving as a reminder of an Autocrat's determination to remain totally in charge. Individuals and groups (among the latter most notably the Jehovah's Witnesses) who have either defied Banda or overlooked his insistence on obeisance have suffered from his wrath.[73] A sizable group of exiles—many of them associated with leaders who were dismissed and driven away in the mid-1960s—are reported to be living in the neighboring countries of Tanzania, Zambia, and Mozambique. Such suppressed or exiled opposition, along with Banda's open fear of "plots,"[74] suggests that a potential for instability exists in Malawi. Should Banda, who is now an old man, lose his capacity to dominate, the political affairs of the country could be thrown into considerable turmoil as old foes reassert their claims upon the state and faithful clients attempt to inherit the ruler's mantle.

Mobutu Sese Seko, Zaire

In turning to Zaire, the political analyst is confronted with a form of autocracy that began as "Caesarism" in 1965, when Mobutu Sese Seko—the "Caesar"—rescued the state from predators, but by 1980 had evolved into a particularly severe and rapacious despotism. Caesarism refers to rule (usually of a military leader) seized in a "post-constitutional" state with widespread public disorder, institutional decay, and corruption; the Caesar is a strong ruler who is called upon to save the state from those who would destroy it, and his domination is accepted out of a recognized necessity of reestablishing some form of public order and predictability.[75] Under Caesarism the consolidation and ex-

73. A large group of Asians were expelled from the country in 1976 for turning off a radio carrying a speech by the President during an Asian wedding reception (reported in *Africa Contemporary Record*, 1976–77, p. B 271).

74. Ibid., p. B 269.

75. For a critical discussion of Caesarism, see Leo Strauss, *On Tyranny* (Ithaca: Cornell University Press, 1975), pp. 190–97. For a more historical account, see Robert G. Wesson, *The Imperial Order* (Berkeley and Los Angeles: University of California Press, 1967), pp. 53–76. For an analysis of Caesarism in Zaire, see Jean-Claude Willame, *Patrimonialism and Political Change in the Congo* (Stanford: Stan-

pansion of power in the hands of the ruler and at the expense of other powerseekers is its own justification because the misrule of a strongman, no matter how despotic, is preferable to the non-rule and disorder of a stateless situation. However, in fifteen years of personal domination the Zairian Caesar has not created an orderly (if rigorously controlled) autocracy, but a despotism founded on widespread coercion and rampant corruption. The extensive coercion and corruption distinguish the Zairian autocracy from those considered above and identify the degree to which Zaire under Mobutu has approached a state of tyranny.

Zaire (formerly Congo) gained independence in 1960 following a very abrupt transfer of power from Belgium.[76] For five years it was a country without a single, effective political authority to govern it, barely existing in a pre-civil condition in which the shape and size as well as the control of the state were at issue. Very briefly, Zaire's statelessness (or at most its status as a very contingent state) could be identified as follows: (1) the offices of president and prime minister were largely treated by incumbents as political bases from which to assert their personal control; (2) other governmental and administrative offices were largely appropriated by incumbents, effectively resulting in the immobilism of state agencies; (3) the army collapsed into either mutinous or conflicting groups; (4) movements for regional autonomy or secession arose to challenge the territorial integrity of the state; (5) political-religious uprisings and rebellions broke out.[77] In general, a state of internal warfare existed in Zaire among conflicting groups and authorities, while the state apparatus was riddled with conflict and effectively immobilized.

Zaire obviously presented an opportunity for the ablest and most daring powerseeker. General Mobutu, a young man who had briefly seized power in September 1960 to resolve a conflict between President Joseph Kasavubu and Prime Minister Patrice

ford University Press, 1972). Nzongola-Ntalaja employs a "Bonapartist model" in "The Continuing Struggle for National Liberation in Zaire," *Journal of Modern African Studies* 17, 4 (1979): 595–614.

76. For a definitive account of colonial rule and initial post-independence politics in Zaire, see Crawford Young, *Politics in the Congo: Decolonization and Independence* (Princeton: Princeton University Press, 1965). For the nationalist period, see Herbert Weiss, *Political Protest in the Congo: The Parti Solidaire Africain During the Independence Struggle* (Princeton: Princeton University Press, 1967).

77. Thomas Turner, "Congo-Kinshasa," in *The Politics of Cultural Sub-Nationalism in Africa*, ed. Victor A. Olorunsola (Garden City, N.Y.: Anchor Books, 1972), pp. 197–265; Charles W. Anderson, Fred R. Von der Mehden, and Crawford Young, "Domestic Violence in Africa: The Congo," *Issues of Political Development* (Englewood Cliffs, N.J.: Prentice-Hall, 1967), pp. 120–42. See also Jules Gérard-Libois, *Katanga Secession*, trans. Rebecca Young (Madison, Milwaukee, and London: University of Wisconsin Press, 1963).

Lumumba, proved to be that person. In November 1965, during one of a series of constitutional stalemates and associated political disorder, Mobutu staged a coup, dismissed Kasavubu, and proclaimed himself President, with a promise that he would remain in office for five years.[78] According to Kitaka, not only did many people consider Mobutu a messiah, a "savior" who would lead his country away from chaos, but Mobutu as well saw himself in that role. He has on occasion compared his work in Zaire to a "mission" like that of Moses or Jesus Christ. Part of that mission has been to insure law and order, political unity, and administrative services.[79]

In real world situations, the seizure of power is one thing, and its effective use is another. In systems of personal rule generally, the consideration of the loyalty of a ruler's agents must weigh more heavily than the consideration of their competence. (Of course, in specific situations competence must take precedence— e.g., in warfare. A loyal but ineffective commander is of little use to a ruler. In the 1977 invasion of Shaba Province, the commander of the Zairian army, who was personally loyal to Mobutu, proved wholly ineffective and had to be replaced. However, a competent commander who is successful may pose the risk of a potential rival.) The dilemma faced by an Autocrat confronting a "post-constitutional" situation is that in cultivating the personal trust of subordinates, he may have to totally disregard merit, experience, or expertise. This has largely happened in Zaire: personal-familial governance, royalist-style patronage, and administrative venality and corruption—on a scale that is nearly impossible to imagine—have assumed great prominence in the ruler's quest for control. The outcome has been the creation of a "state" whose agents are either loyal to Mobutu or totally dependent upon him, and are in either case totally dedicated to self-enrichment. "In fact," Jean Rymenam writes,

> the President of the Republic finds himself at the head of all important political institutions and treats the country as if it were his private patrimony. All revenue, all appointments, all promotions depend in the last analysis upon the pleasure of the President. No fortune, no undertaking, no position is possible without the decision of Mr. Mobutu.[80]

78. A. P. J. Van Rensburg, "Mobutu Sese Seko, Zaire: Africa's Machiavelli and Bismarck Rolled into One," *Contemporary Leaders of Africa* (Cape Town and Pretoria: Haum, 1975), pp. 486–92. For Mobutu's links to the U.S. Central Intelligence Agency, see René Lemarchand, "The C.I.A. in Africa: How Central? How Intelligent?" *Journal of Modern African Studies* 14, 3 (1976): 410.

79. E. B. Z. Kitaka, "Mobutu's Rule in the Congo"; unpublished ms., n.d., p. 2.

80. Jean Rymenam, "The Zairian Fiction," *Le Monde Diplomatique*, May 1977 (unofficial translation). See also Ghislain C. Kabwit, "Zaire: The Roots of the Continuing Crisis," *Journal of Modern African Studies* 17, 3 (1979): 381–407.

From 1965 until 1970 Mobutu consolidated and expanded his power. Potential rivals were either eliminated or subordinated, the instruments of state power were centralized and placed under the ruler's personal control, regional opposition was suppressed, and steps were taken to found a party under the ruler's command. Opposing politicians were purged, and four who were accused of plotting against the new ruler were publicly hanged in April 1966. The military had been used as the primary vehicle for Mobutu's coup, but with only one exception soldiers were not placed in positions of authority in the new regime. Rather, civilian associates of the new ruler—among them members of the so-called Binza group (which had provided Mobutu with an important political base during the years of disruption from 1960 to 1965)—were given the principal positions of confidence and responsibility. The new leaders began to alter the existing constitutional and organizational framework—which had emphasized a division of authority in the state, both in respect of a separation of powers among the President, Prime Minister, and National Assembly, and in respect of independent jurisdictions between the center and the provinces.

In March 1966 Mobutu began to rule exclusively by decree. Scheduled presidential elections were cancelled, the powers of the Legislature were removed, and the Prime Minister was dismissed in October 1966. Early in 1967 Zaire effectively became a unitary state, and shortly afterwards regional administration was centralized in Mobutu's hands, with all provincial governors henceforth his appointees and with the powers of the provincial assemblies greatly reduced. In June 1967 a national referendum was held which affirmed the changes that the new ruler had instituted; the referendum was the first indication of Mobutu's penchant for the engineering of consent and his strong disposition toward methods and symbols of plebiscitarianism. It was in 1967 also that the word *Zaire* was first employed for the basic denomination of the currency. In the same year the giant Belgian mining consortium Union Minière du Haut Katanga was nationalized, further enhancing Mobutu's image as a popular hero. More important, a new party, the Mouvement Populaire de la Révolution (MPR), was officially launched, but without any serious attempt at making it popularly based. The MPR belonged not to the "people" of Zaire but to its ruler, who conceived himself to be the sole rightful representative of the people.

Central power was extended to dominate groups that heretofore had enjoyed considerable autonomy, if not privilege. Regional rebellions were gradually put down, and either the remaining resistance was destroyed or the rebels were driven across Zaire's borders into neighboring states. In the industrial urban sector, a state trade union organization was imposed by the forced amalgamation of existing unions, and the right to strike was suspended. Students—especially university students who had begun to protest one-man rule—were made subject to harsh measures of repression, which included the use of military force against student protests, the closing of the university, and the forced conscription of students into the army. Student associations were disbanded, and all students were required to join the youth section of the MPR. Finally, Mobutu's old political allies—particularly from the Binza group—who exhibited the slightest sign of independence were purged from the regime. By 1970 Mobutu's personal autocracy was firmly established.

Since 1970 Caesarism in Zaire has been deliberately enhanced by the ruler. The glorification of Mobutu has accompanied his efforts at increasing the cultural and economic independence and stature of Zaire. The image of himself and the conception he wished to project of the Zairian state became increasingly indistinguishable: a cult of "Mobutuism" was matched by a program of Zairian "authenticity"; the power and fame of the ruler were pursued parallel with a dramatic gamble to enhance the wealth of the economy while at the same time a diplomacy calculated to appeal to other African and Third World leaders was promoted. Yet, beneath the drama and rhetoric, the characteristic underworld of personal rule has continued, and Mobutu has retained his acute sense of power and control and demonstrated his intuitive grasp of Machiavellian statecraft. He is in many ways *the* African Prince—a ruler who must ultimately rely on his cunning and scheming to remain in command. The situation he confronts is more demanding and complex than that faced by any other African Autocrat, not only because his political estate is a vast empire of diverse regions and people, but also because Zaire has had a chaotic history since independence.

Mobutu's bid for power and glory may be considered as it relates both to Zaire and to the international politics of Africa.[81] In practice the two are intertwined, although the former is much more crucial to his *realpolitik,* while his international standing can undoubtedly enhance his standing among his countrymen. In Mobutu's bid for national glory, three stratagems stand out: his encouragement of the cult of Mobutuism, his promotion of the

81. For a perceptive analysis by a leading authority, see Crawford Young, "Zaire: The Unending Crisis," *Foreign Affairs* 57, 1 (Fall 1978): 169–85.

MPR as the central political agency of the state, and his pursuit of cultural and psychological decolonization represented by the policy of "authenticity." Let us briefly consider each of these.

First, many of Africa's rulers have tended to encourage a "cult of personality" by having their portraits prominently and widely displayed, assuming folk titles, and fostering the use of slogans, demonstrations, and legends that promote their mystique. Mobutu has simply carried this tendency much farther than most. The cult of Mobutuism, defined simply as the thoughts, words, and actions of Mobutu, has involved (among other things) acts of fealty, such as the requirement that all officials take a formal oath of loyalty to Mobutu; praise-words in referring to the ruler, such as "Guide," "Messiah," "Founding President," and "Grand Patron" (in a more populist phase Mobutu insisted on being called "Citizen" rather than "Excellency"); signs and symbols to popularize and publicize his rule, such as praise-songs, dances, lapel badges with his miniature portrait, and large public portraits ("The television news [has been] preceded by the image of the President, as it were, descending from the clouds, with his recorded voice booming out a message of hope");[82] and a decree that no ideology but Mobutuism be taught in the schools. In fact, Mobutu created a party school—the Makanda Kabobi Institute— to preach the ideology, or rather the political religion of Mobutuism to cadres and important individuals. An interesting attempt to glorify Mobutu was the censorship of all Zairian names in the press—except those of the President and the country's soccer players. One diplomat was reported at the time to have said: "We have reached the cult of anonymity."[83] Indeed, Mobutuism was made the official ideology in 1974. In an important respect it represents the outer limits of the cult of personality: it can be changed from day to day, from one political contingency to the next.

The second stratagem in Mobutu's bid for power and glory at home has been his promotion of the MPR. As we have noted, the MPR is not a political party in the ordinary sense of being an arena of representation or a state instrument of political mobilization and support. Rather, it is the ruler's personal political vehicle, a royalist party. During the 1970 MPR Congress, the party was officially declared the supreme political instrument and sole party of the country. Prior to the Congress, Mobutu had arbitrarily altered the electoral laws of the country to make party representatives and officials totally dependent upon him, and the MPR

82. The Style of Mobutu," *Africa Report* 20, 2 (March–April 1975): 2.
83. Quoted in ibid., p. 3.

manifesto declares that the party "will adhere to the political policy of the Chief of State and not the reverse."[84] The Congress affirmed that

> only one man, previously noted for his outstanding services to his country, can assure the well-being of each one of us and create the conditions propitious for the people's moral and spiritual growth, and offer them a common ideal, the feelings of a joint destiny and the knowledge of belonging to one country.[85]

The Congress also affirmed Mobutu as the sole candidate for the presidency. In organizational terms, the party is indistinguishable from the government; important functionaries have overlapping roles, and all are subordinated to the same master. In important respects, the party simply validates the ruler's rhetoric of "revolution" and "the masses" in a way that lordship without a symbolic party would not permit. For example, Mobutu could claim that the MPR was "our national Party, . . . the foundation of the peace which we have established. Even though all Zairians do not speak the same language, the MPR does so. The MPR *is* the people, and my people will never hesitate to give me their support." Furthermore, he could criticize party "cadres" for their lack of "militancy" and their separation from "the masses," whom they should serve. In other words, by creating a nominal party and a rhetoric of revolution, the ruler of Zaire has been able to proclaim the legitimacy of "the people" and criticize elites in their name.[86]

Mobutu's third stratagem has been a pursuit of the elusive goals of cultural and psychological decolonization through what he has called a policy of "authenticity." He has declared an intent to fashion "the authentic Zairian personality" by the manipulation of symbols, signs, and names. The effort has mainly involved a widespread change of place names and Christian names into purportedly "authentic" indigenous ones. The change of Christian names understandably provoked dismay and opposition from the Catholic Church (as did an attempt to establish local branches of the MPR in Catholic seminaries). Conflicts with the Church have been serious and somewhat reminiscent of the struggle between church and state at an earlier era in royalist Europe.[87] However, the ruler of Zaire has not allowed rhetoric and symbolism to inter-

84. Quoted in *Africa Contemporary Record*, 1968–69, p. 441.

85. Quoted in ibid., 1970–71, p. B 288.

86. Independence Day Speech by President Mobutu Sese Seko, July 1, 1977, delivered at MPR National Headquarters at N'Sele (outside Kinshasa), passim (unofficial translation).

87. Kenneth L. Adelman, "The Church-State Conflict in Zaire: 1969–1974," *African Studies Review* 18, 1 (April 1975): 102–16.

fere with his *realpolitik*. He needs the Church for the educational and welfare services it provides—especially in the countryside—and so at critical junctures Caesar has astutely rendered unto Rome. For the elites (who are in a position to afford it) "authenticity" has required special dress, following the example of the ruler—for men, an "Abaco," or two-piece suit cut to be worn with an open collar and an ascot.

In economic matters authenticity figured in a decree in 1973 to Zairianize and "radicalize" large sectors of the economy which remained in foreign (mainly Belgian) hands, including many firms in the important trading and service sectors. On a massive scale Mobutu simply redefined property rights, arbitrarily transferring title from one category of owners (aliens) to another (citizens). In one stroke firms were expropriated (initially without compensation)—not by the state, however, but by favored members and friends of the ruling class who were given title to them. The economic effects of the decree were serious and harmful. The unanticipated effects included much economic dislocation, bottlenecks, shortages (of foodstuffs, among other things), and inflation, as the critically important factor of management and entrepreneurship was precipitously removed from the economy. By 1976 the decree was recognized as a mistake, yet subsequent steps by the government to deal with the damage—including permission for foreign owners to have initially 40 percent and later 60 percent of their assets restored to them and the right to select African partners to hold the remainder—could not repair it. It is difficult to know whether the government—and more specifically the ruler of Zaire—learned anything from the fiasco. It is also difficult to know what significance ought to be attributed to the authenticity movement. On one view, it is the farcical publicity stunt of an African despot.[88] On another, it is the plan of a political messiah with a genius for promoting unity and development.[89] What alone seems clear is the instrumental value for Mobutu of authenticity as a visible public demonstration of his authority over and devotion to the nation.

In the international context since 1970 Mobutu has wanted to establish Zaire, which is large, rich in resources, and strategically located, as a leading African country and himself as a major African statesman. He has sought political fame from economic achievement. His principal effort entailed a bold but ill-consid-

88. V. S. Naipaul, "A New King for the Congo," *New York Review of Books*, June 26, 1975, pp. 19–25.
89. "The Style of Mobutu," *Africa Report* 20, 2 (March–April 1975): 3.

ered plan to dramatically expand the infrastructural and industrial base of Zaire by 1980, primarily by developing the enormous hydroelectric potential of the lower Zaire River and investing heavily in the mineral economy—especially by expanding copper production. (Copper is Zaire's principal export.) In economic terms, the plan rested on a dangerously one-dimensional assumption that the international market in copper would continue to be buoyant. The plan was to be funded by Western loans, which would be repaid out of copper earnings, and it was to be supported by Western expertise as well as capital.

The plan was a total failure. The price of copper took an unforeseen plunge in 1974 from which it had not recovered by 1980. At the same time, the global oil crisis hit Zaire (along with other Third World oil-importing countries), with adverse consequences for its balance of payments. Zaire was burdened with an enormous national debt whose interest repayments would have to be taken out of other sectors of the economy under a program of austerity. As almost nothing else could, the failure of Mobutu's plan exposed the vulnerable, dependent nature of the Zairian economy and showed how unsophisticated economic policy in a less developed country is at the mercy of unstable international economic forces and events. However, the economic debacle was of sufficient magnitude, and Zaire of sufficient strategic importance, that its rescue by Western creditors was certain: "Zaire's survival was due to unashamed exploitation of the old business adage that if you fail in a sufficiently massive way, your creditors will have no option but to rescue you from your own ineptitude."[90] In economic matters, it seemed, President Mobutu could have his cake and eat it too.

In matters of policy, a corruption-ridden and personally appropriated government such as that of Zaire cannot be an effective instrument of the ruler's will for progress. One of the most important facts of autocracy in a country such as Zaire is that while the ruler can effect the adoption, declaration, and publicity of policies, he cannot insure their success. However, as we have seen in the case of Mobutu, he may be able to secure backing from other governments and agencies to insure his regime against the consequences of failure. Thus to some extent the political arts of stratagem and maneuver can make up for a lack of policy expertise and organizational capability—as was dramatically revealed in

90. *Africa Contemporary Record*, 1976–77, p. B 526. For an analysis of the economy until 1974 see J. Ph. Peesmans, "The Social and Economic Development of Zaire Since Independence: A Historical Outline," *African Affairs* 74, 295 (April 1975): 148–73.

the abrupt reversal of Mobutu's fortunes in the invasion by rebel forces of Shaba Province in the Spring of 1977. The Zairian army was incapable of stopping the invasion, and the credibility of Mobutu's power was placed in serious jeopardy. With an acute understanding of existing political enmities and alliances among African states and their supporters, Mobutu secured military assistance from Morocco and France; Morocco provided battle-tested troops, while France, recognizing an opportunity to extend its influence in central Africa, provided air transport. The rebel invasion was repulsed, and Shaba Province was securely placed under Zairian control. The remarks of one commentator are particularly apt:

> The invasion showed Zaire's excessive political centralization and military weakness, while simultaneously highlighting the President's political brilliance. The crisis also validated the ancient Greeks' ranking of politics as the "queen" of the sciences; political skills in Kinshasa quite literally snatched victory from the jaws of economic and military defeat.[91]

In 1978 there was a second rebel invasion of Shaba Province, and a Franco-Belgian military expedition, supported logistically by the United States, was required to bring it to an end. The fact that it proved necessary to secure foreign power to enforce the "sovereignty" of the Zairian state demonstrates vividly the organizational incapacities of the government.[92]

In sub-Saharan Africa, a world region of organizationally and militarily weak states, tests of sovereignty will continue to be made, and international statecraft will be important, not only to obtain aid and resources, but also for a ruler to gain recognition and prestige. It is largely international recognition and forbearance by powerful states that permits African states to exist. Mobutu has demonstrated his awareness of the importance of diplomacy and intrigue. In particular, he has been aware of the advantages and disadvantages of different kinds of international ties. Ties with developed Western states may be of crucial importance

91. Kenneth L. Adelman, "Zaire's Year of Crisis," *African Affairs* 77, 306 (January 1978): 41.

92. In this respect the government of Zaire is not unique; many other African governments—such as Angola, Chad, Ethiopia, Mauritania, and Uganda—would prove similarly vulnerable to invasions. An OAU agreement on the sanctity of existing state boundaries has prevented more frequent invasions. However, there now reportedly are as many as twenty African states that face the threat of invasion by armed exiles, increasing doubts about the effectiveness of the agreement in the future. Ironically, the first major violation of the OAU agreement was by Africa's "man of peace," Julius Nyerere, whose forces invaded Uganda to overthrow the Amin tyranny (see chapter 6 below).

for obtaining economic and military aid, but they may negatively affect relationships with the Eastern or non-aligned blocs. In his bid for international standing, the ruler of Zaire has taken the calculated risk (so far without penalty) to accept Western aid while at the same time engaging in symbolic attacks upon some of the suppliers. In 1975 Mobutu expelled the American Ambassador on grounds that he was implicated in a plot against the Zairian regime, presumably to impress upon African and Third World countries that he was not an American or a Western puppet but a genuine member of the non-aligned bloc. Mobutu apparently recognized that his bid for African leadership could be credible only if he conformed to the values of the non-aligned club of the great majority of African states. The pull of the club, and the reference group behavior associated with it, can perhaps explain the panegyrics of the Zairian autocrat.

As we have indicated, the panegyrics of populism and plebiscitarianism are the forte of President Mobutu. His praise of the "Great People" of Zaire is matched only by the praise he arranges for himself. As the representative and *voix du peuple,* Mobutu has established a safe distance between himself and the government, permitting him to denounce the notorious conduct of government officials. Among other abuses, he has pointed at the diversion by army officers for "their own personal profit the supplies intended for front-line soldiers," the refusal of rural development officials to leave their "air-conditioned office[s] in Kinshasa," and the "misuse of judicial machinery for revenging private disputes, abuse of power, selective justice depending upon one's social status and wealth (*justice à la tête du client*)." He has concluded: "If we want to be taken as a modern and organized country . . . it is time . . . that we have a system of justice that is just."[93] The greatest advantage of such panegyrics is not the popularity they may bring the ruler, or even the political distance they create between him and his officials; rather they justify his actions against the oligarchy—particularly those who discredit him or constitute a possible threat to his power. Of the successful Prince, Machiavelli observes: "As long as he does not rob the great majority of their property or their honour, they remain content. He then has to contend only with the ambition of a few, and that can be dealt with easily and in a variety of ways."[94] A modification of

93. Independence Day Speech by President Mobutu Sese Seko, July 1, 1977, passim (unofficial translation).
94. *The Prince,* translated with an introduction by George Bull (Harmondsworth: Penguin Books, 1975), p. 102.

Machiavelli's precept that Mobutu seems to be following is that an exposure of the oligarchy's corruption may effectively conceal the ruler's own. The ruler of Zaire has exploited his position as people's representative to rotate and remove many officials and to put many others on notice. In addition, he held national elections in 1977 and created a measured opportunity for the entry of new members into the political class.

Mobutu has appointed technocrats to the government for many of the same reasons that other African rulers have done so—that is, they are not only likely to be more efficient, but are also more dependent on him and less threatening politically. But in a state that is overwhelmingly characterized by the exploitation of the people by the government, the chances of installing new norms of efficiency and capability—even if they were desired—seem minimal. Corruption in Zaire has been termed a "structural fact": it is part of the very constitution of the state, and to change it would entail changing the present makeup of the state and the way in which power is exercised and devolved.[95] It has been estimated that as much as 60 percent of the annual national budget has been misappropriated by the governing elite. One International Monetary Fund team dispatched to investigate the economic crisis in Zaire in 1975 was dismayed that complete facts about the national debt were impossible to determine: "This is perhaps not surprising in a country where the precise dividing line between private and public sectors (or between the public treasury [and] . . . the ruling oligarchy's personal assets) has never been very clearly drawn."[96]

The extravagance and opulence of Mobutu and the ruling class of his dependents are exceptional. Mobutu himself is reputed to be one of the world's richest men with an enormous personal fortune that was accumulated by directing a large segment of the annual national budget into "Presidency services," where funds not only are amassed for self-enrichment, but also are used for creating personal dependency among associates and clients:

> Mobutu has built for himself and the Zairian elite a life of opulence and corruption, bolstered by an excessive desire to acquire as many material

95. *West Africa* 3255 (3 December 1979): 2224. See also "Unrest in Zaire: Anti-Mobutu Feeling Swells Among the Masses Living in Destitution," *Wall Street Journal*, June 25, 1980.

96. *Africa Contemporary Record*, 1976–77, p. B 528. According to Young, "One recent study showed that the Shaba Regional Commissioner was grossing $100,000 per month in 1975, of which only two percent was his nominal salary" ("Zaire: The Unending Crisis," p. 173). In 1980, Zaire's foreign debt was 6.4 billion U.S. dollars (*Wall Street Journal*, June 25, 1980).

possessions as possible. These include palatial residences not only in France, Belgium, and Switzerland, but also in all eight Zairian Provinces, including a magnificent building at Nsele, 40 miles from Kinshasa, which has a swimming pool described as Africa's largest. The President frequently uses the national airline, Air Zaire, as a personal service.[97]

In addition to appropriating his economic fortune by political fiat, Mobutu is a leading businessman with a personal financial interest in banks, wholesale and retail trade, taxi companies, apartment buildings, and sporting events—for example, "40 per cent of the gross world receipts from the highly publicised 1974 fight in Kinshasa between Mohammed Ali and George Foreman are said to have wound up in Mobutu's pocket."[98] The rapaciousness of the Zairian ruler is imitated, on a declining but nevertheless exceptional scale, down the civil and military hierarchy of the Zairian autocracy. Among the most rapacious are soldiers, who are reported to enjoy virtually "a license to steal."[99] So unusual is the corruption in Zaire that observers have virtually had to invent new phrases to describe it; Zaire is referred to in the press and in scholarly journals alike as "an extortionist culture" in which bribery is practiced among diverse strata of society and often assumes the form of "economic mugging."[100] For a despot like Mobutu, who is determined to retain power at all costs, the venal system of government provides a device of personal control: by inviting his officials to be corrupt, he stakes them to an interest in the perpetuation of his rule, and he holds the trump card of sanctions should they waver in their loyalty or support.

Under Mobutu, not only had Zaire been thoroughly corrupted by 1980, but its general population, resigned to political apathy, had been reduced to living under conditions of servility and fear. The fear has been justified. As early as 1969 students at the University of Lovanium who were demonstrating against government educational policy were fired upon by undisciplined soldiers, and some were killed. Regional rebellions have been violently suppressed by the government, and local people in the regions suspected of harboring sympathies for rebels have been brutalized by

97. Kabwit, p. 398. Young adds: "The size of the presidential fortune . . . has been a matter of controversy in and out of Zaïre: a South African publication recently listed his property holdings in Switzerland, Belgium, and elsewhere as $25 million, and cash holdings in Swiss banks at about $70 million" ("Zaire: The Unending Crisis," p. 173).
98. Kabwit, p. 398.
99. Ibid., p. 399.
100. Ibid., p. 397.

Mobutu's soldiers. On several occasions the Mobutu regime has been cited for gross violations of human rights; the execution of political opponents has not been unknown, and repression with violence has extended to members of the Kimbanguist Christian sect. Following an alleged coup attempt in 1978, to which the government responded in part by the execution of thirteen military officers and the imprisonment of others, Mobutu appeared on television and issued a warning to political opponents: "I solemnly declare that from now on, I will be without pity against all attempts of that kind. In the past executive mercy has been mistaken for weakness. But now whoever tries again to use the sword will perish by the sword."[101]

Western observers have been amazed at the docility of Zairians confronted by the abuses of civil and military authorities. Typical was the remark of a United States diplomat in reporting reactions when an abrupt change of currency forced people to stand in long lines in the hope of being able to bribe bank officials to exchange their old banknotes for new ones: "I can't understand it. These people are so hopeless they'll take anything."[102] Reporting on the loss of $350,000 by his mission society in the currency exchange, an American missionary exclaimed: "The people get screwed to the wall and just turn the other cheek."[103] It is clear that as a result of the excesses of the Mobutu regime, Zaire is a country that has come to the brink of tyranny, and rule is ultimately based on fear of the government, its agents, and the ruler himself.

The Autocrat and the Prince represent opposite poles on a continuum of personal rulership that is marked by the absence of political religion or ideology and the presence of an almost exclusive preoccupation with questions of personal power. As we have seen, the Prince is a political man who does not pursue his own interests to the exclusion of the interests of others, but accommodates other political men and not only tolerates but also uses politician politics for his own purposes. The Autocrat is much less a political man in this sense: he is antagonistic to politician politics and to the autonomous power and authority of others, and he desires to rule alone; he is an absolutist. In the African autocracies that we have examined, politics are undeveloped and the ruler is very nearly the only legitimate politician. Those who persist in opposing him and refuse to become merely his political dependents are forced to be-

101. Ibid., p. 396.
102. *Wall Street Journal*, June 25, 1980.
103. Ibid.

come conspirators and plotters—or exiles. In effective autocracies politics are dishonored and forced underground, where they assume the more dangerous and volatile characteristics of violence-prone activities. The restrictions upon and suppression of legitimate political activity are the crucial weakness of autocracy as a political system. Sooner or later the sole master politician must exit from the stage, and when he does, a political struggle for the succession is likely to take place—very likely involving violence—unless a capable successor can be named before the Autocrat has gone. Since Autocrats are disposed to suppress politician politics and since their own political abilities and experience—and probably their authority also—are specifically personal and cannot therefore be transferred to another, it is not likely that capable and experienced politicians will be available to insure a peaceful succession and a stable political climate afterwards. It is more likely that the succession will usher in an unstable political world which will be governed, if governed at all, by inexperienced clients of the old ruler or by former conspirators—political amateurs whose education in the art of statecraft will have to be acquired at the possibly painful expense of the ruled.

5

Prophets
and Leadership

SUCCESSFUL prophetic leaders have been very rare in history. This is because of the goal they set for themselves: to build the new Jerusalem. The Prophet, political or religious, is a revolutionary—that is, one who prophesies a better future, whose attainment requires the radical transformation of the present.[1] The Prophet can be distinguished from the three other types of rulers we have considered insofar as power—its gaining and holding—is not his final concern. The mission of the Prophet is to foretell a new and better world and to inspire and guide others toward its attainment. Like the other ruler types, the Prophet is a political agent, but he is also a moral agent—a political-religious man. Unlike the pragmatic politician of change, the Prophet does not merely promise or undertake to provide "more"; he deals not only in quantitative change but also in qualitative transformation. For the political Prophet of the twentieth century, as for religious prophets of earlier centuries, power must be exercised in the service of a higher goal or authority: perhaps an ideology (such as Protestantism or Socialism) or a moral community (the Faithful, the People, the Proletariat) and most likely both. When power is used in the service of such higher goals or authorities, it can be wielded with great conviction and with ruthlessness, if that is believed necessary to fulfill the Prophet's vision. The goals can justify the means and thereby excuse any actions, however ruthless or brutal they may be. The political failure of a prophetic leader is a lack of dedication and faith, not a lack of sensibility. The political

1. The *Oxford English Dictionary* defines a "prophet" as "one who speaks for God or for any deity, as the inspired revealer or interpreter of his will; one who is held or (more loosely) who claims to have this function; an inspired or quasi-inspired teacher." This is the traditional religious meaning of "prophet," but it also has acquired a political meaning as "the 'inspired' or accredited spokesman, proclaimer, or preacher of some principle, cause or movement."

challenge is to maintain a following of devoted disciples dedicated to the cause. To write of "prophets" in either the religious or the political sense is to write also and necessarily of their "disciples": the "pupils or followers of any teacher or school." Disciples must not succumb to ambition or acquisitiveness; if hardships arise, they must remain steadfast and not desert. If the disciples become merely politicians, preoccupied with political interests and personal appetites, the Prophet's mission can be placed in jeopardy. If the Prophet cannot keep their allegiance (perhaps because he exhibits moral failings in his own conduct), there is the likelihood that faith and loyalty will lapse into cynicism. If and when his disciples desert, the Prophet will have failed, or in Weber's terminology, his "charisma" or the power of his vision will have been lost.

The religious sphere and the political-religious sphere, as Weber and other social theorists have pointed out, are much alike in being collective in character. In colonial Africa, religious movements of a prophetic nature were spawned alongside the nationalist movements and in response to many of the same aspects of subordination within the colonial situation. In writing about African religious prophets, Michael Banton has argued that "political sentiment may receive expression in religious guise";[2] the opposite is unquestionably also possible. Religious prophecy and political prophecy are much alike: they express a vision that represents salvation insofar as it is held out as an escape from the present (that one kind of salvation is secular, as in the political religions of modernity,[3] makes little difference to the mechanism, which is grounded in belief and faith); they appeal to the ideals and the moral passions, not to cold calculations of narrow political or economic interest; they arouse faithful followings and employ devoted disciples; they utilize ideology that is often codified as a text or testament.

The political and the religious strands have been entwined in the rulerships of two of the prophetic African leaders to be considered in this chapter: Kwame Nkrumah and Julius Nyerere. In the page facing the title page of his autobiography, Nkrumah addressed his prospective disciples by quoting Walt Whitman:

2. Michael Banton, "African Prophets," *Race* 5, 2 (October 1963): 45; Thomas Hodgkin, *Nationalism in Colonial Africa* (London: Frederick Muller, 1965), ch. 3: "Prophets and Priests," pp. 93–114.

3. The theme of "political religion" is discussed in David Apter, *The Politics of Modernization* (Chicago and London: University of Chicago Press, 1965), ch. 8. See also Edward Shils, *Center and Periphery: Essays in Macrosociology* (Chicago and London: University of Chicago Press, 1975).

Who is he that would become my follower?
Who would sign himself a candidate for my affections?
The way is suspicious, the result uncertain, perhaps destructive,
You would have to give up all else, I alone would expect to be
    your sole and exclusive standard,
Your novitiate would even be long and exhausting,
The whole past theory of your life and all conformity to the
    lives around you would have to be abandon'd.[4]

And *Mwalimu* Nyerere, the teacher-president of Tanzania, once remarked: "I should have been a preacher in a pulpit instead of the president of a republic."[5]

Prophetic leadership does not function through adjudication and political compromise, as does princely rule, nor through control and management, as does autocratic rule. Neither has it the amoral characteristics of pure power-hunger distinctive of tyranny. Quite the opposite: it is founded on morality, but the morality of ultimate ends—a teleological morality. It is autocracy with a mission. The leader himself must be a moral exemplar: an inspiration to his disciples and followers and yet a severely demanding taskmaster. The prophetic leader deals in norms—in "faith" and "belief," "devotion" and "sacrifice," "right" and "wrong," even in "needs"—but not in interests and certainly not in happiness. (When preaching of the value of sanitation and the necessity of clean water and being told that "the Masai are completely happy," Nyerere is reported to have remarked: "It's not a question of whether they are happy. . . . I'm not trying to make them *happy*! But there is a difference between clean water and dirty water. My problem is to get a woman clean water. My problem is to get her a healthy child. Happy! I'm not involving myself in that.")[6] In the case of the African Prophets being considered in this chapter, all of their regimes reveal the manifold problems that can arise when radical plans and policies are imposed upon a largely conservative socioeconomic environment, and how strong the temptation is to use coercion in trying to deal with them. Although prophetic rule has as its *raison d'être* the creation of a radically transformed order that has the character of a "utopia," it remains personal rule insofar as its ideology is intimately associated with the ruler himself.

The emergence and survival of prophetic leadership, as Weber

4. Kwame Nkrumah, *Ghana: The Autobiography of Kwame Nkrumah* (New York: Thomas Nelson & Sons, 1957).

5. Quoted in "Profiles: President Nyerere of Tanzania, Part I," *The New Yorker*, October 16, 1971, p. 42.

6. Ibid. (original emphasis).

pointed out in connection with "charismatic" leaders, is difficult because it demands the suspension (or at least the postponement) of the ordinary interests and appetites of political men. For this reason it is likely to be associated with unsettled times (such as revolutionary situations). For prophetic leaders to be successful without falling prey to the temptations of power politics, they must suppress the natural political dispositions of their followers while retaining their devotion.

Of the prophetic leaders that have emerged in Africa before independence and since, very few have managed to persist in their prophecy and to continue to hold power. It may well be an axiom of leadership studies that prophetic leaders are more likely to be opponents of regimes than to be rulers. As opponents they are in a position to exploit the perceived "oppression" of evil and unjust rulers and thereby to prompt people to make the kind of sacrifices that moral leadership requires. Prophetic leadership thrives on evil times. In terms of the theory of political choice, for prophetic leaders to gain a significant following, public evils (negative political goods) must be sufficiently in evidence and their authors sufficiently identifiable for people to conclude that the efforts and risks involved in attempting to eliminate them are worth taking. Once prophetic leaders are in power, they still maintain the opposition in relation to other evils: "capitalism" perhaps, or "neo-colonialism." But the practical, day-to-day contingencies and requirements of rule are not favorable to visionary, inspirational politics. In Black Africa, Nyerere has been the exception in reconciling the business of practical politics with the moral requirements of his socialist vision.

While most of Africa's ruling Prophets have been socialists, and therefore statists who have preached social revolution, often with great personal charm and conviction, they have seldom seen their visions translated into realities. They have usually been frustrated by the fact that the apparatus of government has not possessed the financial and material resources, the organized and rational agencies, or the competent, diligent, and dutiful agents required by socialism to succeed. In other words, the gap between the ideological goals and the governmental means has been too great. Thus the Prophets have not begun to achieve what they set out to accomplish. Some have lost power as a result; some have reverted to holding power like a despot; some have scaled down their expectations and preached patience and perseverance. After as much as two decades of rule, in some cases, the future they have foretold remains distant and elusive. In 1977 Nyerere confessed:

I am a very poor prophet. In 1956 I was asked how long it would take for Tanganyika to become Independent. I thought 10 to 12 years. We became independent 6 years later! In 1967 a group of the Youth who were marching in support of the Arusha Declaration asked me how long it would take Tanzania to become socialist. I thought 30 years. I was wrong again: I am now sure that it will take us much longer![7]

Prophetic leaders usually emerge during periods of crisis, when norms become uncertain and the authority to determine and enforce them is in question. The African anti-colonial revolution was such a situation. African nationalists saw themselves as engaged in a fundamental political struggle for "freedom" and "independence" and against "racial subjection" and "colonialism." The political vocabulary of nationalism was a fundamentally moral one: nationalists fought against the "injustice" and "indignity" of alien rule and for the "right" of self-rule. Colonialism lost its justification and eventually its claim to authority in the face of rising moral arguments against the idea and practices of colonial rule, but not necessarily its power, which was the continuing power of a European state. Only the Portuguese (for a time) and the white regimes of southern Africa proved willing to ignore this new "universal" moral principle, justifying their rule in terms of colonialist and racialist principles. Moral struggles tend to call forth exemplary leaders—politicians who appear as heroes. Many of the most successful African nationalist leaders were capable politicians who assembled anti-colonial coalitions by appealing to the political interests of various ethnic groups. But their appeal to the larger population was moral as much as or more than political. Because he controlled few resources, the nationalist leader was in no position to purchase support on a wide scale, but he could prophesy a free and independent future and identify the immoral power that stood in the way of its attainment. The nationalist prophecy was believable because independence was attainable: the colonial enemy could be defeated. Often, though, victory consisted less in overcoming the power of alien rulers than in convincing them to leave. The battle was as much a struggle of moralities and authorities as of anything else; only in a few countries was it a struggle of arms.

Africa's nationalist leaders in the 1950s and early 1960s were visionaries almost by definition. They held in common the vision of an independent Africa, although they differed in their view of

---

7. Julius K. Nyerere, *The Arusha Declaration Ten Years After* (Dar es Salaam: Tanzania Government Printer, 1977), p. 1.

its political framework. It might correspond with the territorial boundaries of the colonial state, with some larger regional unity, or even with some kind of pan-African political entity.[8] Keita's vision of a greater Mali arising within the framework of a former French West African empire,[9] Nyerere's hopes for a greater East African political community,[10] and Nkrumah's dream of a United States of Africa[11] are merely the most dramatic and memorable visions of African nationalists.

Independence has tended to change the requirements and relative value of different types of leadership. In general, the post-independence period has required political stability and control more than mass exhortation or mobilization. This has placed a premium on the more conservative skills of statecraft—on building and maintaining political coalitions, on domination and subordination. The stratagem of political mobilization might very well be seen by the astute personal ruler in the 1980s as risky in the extreme and capable of backfiring by causing political unrest, increased instability, or even a loss of power. For most of Africa's new rulers, political independence transformed future-oriented politics into activities concerned with holding power and managing the affairs of state on a day-to-day basis. For only a small number has independence involved the replacement of one vision, now realized, with another still to be achieved. In a minority of African countries, the vision of political independence was replaced by a vision of socioeconomic independence. And this new socialist vision appeared even nobler than the old one, for only by its consummation could "true" independence and freedom finally be realized.

There have been many prophetic leaders in modern sub-Saharan Africa who have held socialist visions but have failed to achieve command over the state. Two of the most prominent of these among the first generation of nationalists were Barthélemy Boganda of Central African Republic, who was killed in an air-

8. See American Society of African Culture, ed., *Pan-Africanism Reconsidered* (Berkeley and Los Angeles: University of California Press, 1962); Colin Legum, *Pan-Africanism: A Short Political Guide* (New York: Praeger, 1962); and Claude E. Welch, Jr., *Dream of Unity: Pan-Africanism and Political Unification in West Africa* (Ithaca: Cornell University Press, 1966).

9. W. J. Foltz, *From French West Africa to the Mali Federation* (New Haven and London: Yale University Press, 1965), esp. pp. 210–11.

10. J. S. Nye, Jr., *Pan-Africanism and East African Integration* (Cambridge, Mass.: Harvard University Press, 1966), p. 175.

11. Amirudha Gupta, "Kwame Nkrumah: A Reassessment," *International Studies* 12, 2 (April–June 1973): 207–21.

craft accident in 1959 on the eve of independence,[12] and Lumumba, who failed to gain control of the turbulent political situation in Zaire during the first year of its independence (1960).[13] There have been other prophetic leaders emerging from the era of West African anti-colonial nationalism who *did* become rulers; of these the most notable are Nkrumah, Touré, and Keita. The personal rule of Nkrumah and Touré will be considered in some detail later, but at this point let us turn our attention to Keita.[14]

Modibo Keita, it is reported, was directly descended from an ancient chief of Mali—a status undoubtedly of political value to him first as a nationalist leader and later as the ruler of a new African state (1960–68). But Keita was a modernist rather than a traditionalist—a socialist in the white flowing robes of a traditional leader. In the words of Francis Snyder: "His outlook . . . is basically optimistic. Progress means movement and attainment of future goals. . . . The utopia at the end of evolution is one of economic equality."[15] According to Snyder, Keita's thought was influenced by Marx, Lenin, and Rousseau. But it also reflected the moral values and teachings of Islam: the virtues of "austerity, discipline, individual responsibility, criticism and self-criticism; the *tradition étatique* and a historical sense of identity."[16] Keita believed that the attainment of a Malian utopia would require considerable struggle and hardship,[17] which he also believed the people could be persuaded to endure. This belief was to be severely tested during his tenure as Mali's first ruler.

12. See Pierre Kalck, *Central African Republic: A Failure in De-Colonisation*, trans. Barbara Thompson (London and New York: Pall Mall Library of African Affairs, 1971).

13. *Patrice Lumumba* (London: Panaf Books, 1973); Washington Okumu, *Lumumba's Congo: Roots of Conflict* (New York: Ivan Obolensky, 1963); G. Heinz and H. Donnay, *Lumumba: The Last Fifty Days*, trans. Jane Clark Seitz (New York: Grove Press, 1969).

14. For useful accounts of Keita's Mali, see Francis G. Snyder, "The Political Thought of Modibo Keita," *Journal of Modern African Studies* 5, 1 (1967): 79–106; Frank Gregory Snyder, *One-Party Government in Mali: Transition Toward Control* (New Haven: Yale University Press, 1965); Guy de Lusignan, *French-Speaking Africa Since Independence* (London: Pall Mall Press, 1969), pp. 231–49; Helen Desfosses and J. Dirck, "Socialist Development in Africa: The Case of Keita's Mali," in *Socialism in the Third World*, ed. H. Desfosses and Jacques Levesque (New York: Praeger, 1975), pp. 163–79; Guy Martin, "Socialism, Economic Development and Planning in Mali, 1960–1968," *Canadian Journal of African Studies* 10, 1 (1976): 23–47.

15. Snyder, "Political Thought of Modibo Keita," p. 81.

16. Ibid., pp. 102–3.

17. Ibid., pp. 89–92.

Keita's utopia had two dimensions that were almost identical to Nkrumah's: one of socialism, the other of internationalism. His vision of African unification was shaped by the universalist and rationalist assumptions of French colonial administration and political thought. There was in Keita an element of the *philosophe*—that is, a strong Enlightenment belief in the possibility of building political units by rational agreements—but he had little appreciation of the political problems that might stand in the way of their implementation even if they could be attained.

In 1959, Soudan (as Mali was then known) united with Senegal—but without the hoped-for participation of the other French-speaking West African territories—to form the Mali Federation.[18] Soon thereafter, the many political, economic, and administrative difficulties that ordinarily arise in such ventures made themselves felt; instead of a joint struggle, mutual sacrifice, and compromise by the parties to the accord, divorce resulted. The federation had lasted little more than a year, and the divorce was far from amicable: both parties sued, causing each side considerable difficulties, but those affecting Mali were greater and contributed to a series of costly political choices involving the reorientation of traditional lines of communication, transportation, and trade away from Senegal. Disregarding economic considerations, Keita severed the railroad link with Senegal, depriving Mali of its major channel of access to world markets. Assisted by Eastern bloc aid and Western credits, Mali established an alternative truck route to the Ivory Coast–Upper Volta railroad. It was a costly alternative that priced Mali's peanut exports above those of Senegal and other producers. At about the same time, public pronouncements from Bamako provoked Paris to deny Malian exports favored access to French markets. (In 1962 on the advice and urging of Moscow, the government decided to leave the Franc zone—with serious consequences for the economy.) In sum, flowing out of an initial desire to achieve a broader political unity, Keita's regime succeeded only in exacerbating Mali's problems of development.

Keita also entertained a vision of an egalitarian, socialist society. He and his disciples believed that socialism was like a military campaign—something that could be accomplished in a reasonable length of time with the appropriate strategy and resolution on the part of the leaders and their followers. The socialist state was conceived in the same terms as the Islamic conquest state of the Sudanic past. A five-year plan was adopted (1961–1966), proposing that the structure of the economy could be fundamentally

18. See Foltz, *From French West Africa to the Mali Federation.*

changed without any of the costs one would expect from a major economic reorientation in which private traders would be displaced by a state trading monopoly and rural cooperatives. The plan was ambitious and comprehensive:

> The five-year plan was to impinge on, and was to be effected by, every sector of the nation. . . . At the national level government controls covered every aspect of the development programme. . . . Mali aimed at a truly Socialist society, not one dominated by the middle class. The first concern of every social group was to be the welfare of the people. Such measures were to ensure that the middle class of traders would never again flourish in Mali.[19]

Not only the politicians supporting Keita but also the planners believed that the proposed measures were practical and attainable within the plan period; indeed, they believed them to be economically beneficial in the short run as well as the long. As William Jones puts it: "Far from expecting the structural transformation to impose economic costs on society, they thought it would start paying its way immediately and provide a surplus to finance other investments."[20] An annual growth rate of 11 percent was anticipated (later reduced to 9 percent), but during the early years of the plan the economy actually grew at a rate of less than 2 percent. Since this was lower than the rate of population growth, the wealth of the country was declining on a per capita basis.[21] (Meanwhile, the costs of an expanded government apparatus increased by 77 percent at a time when revenue increased by only 12 percent.)

The Keita regime made a belated attempt to confront the serious difficulties that arose from its socialist development strategy. In 1967 Mali's currency was devalued by 50 percent to make its exports more competitive and to stem the importation of expensive luxury goods from abroad—the major condition of its reentry to the Franc zone. Public salaries were not increased, with the result that civil servants and other state agents had to pay double the previous price for imports. State enterprises were instructed to increase their financial discipline and operational efficiency to reduce the drain on the national treasury. The testing time of sacrifice and hardship, of which Keita had spoken so eloquently in

19. Lusignan, pp. 237–38.
20. William I. Jones, "The Keita Decade, 2: Economics of the Coup," *Africa Report*, March–April 1969, p. 26. For a more elaborate account, see his *Planning and Economic Policy: Socialist Mali and Her Neighbours* (Washington: Three Continents Press, 1976), esp. ch. 6.
21. Jones, "The Keita Decade," pp. 26 and 51.

the past, had arrived. In a 1967 speech to the National Assembly acknowledging that the government had been living beyond its means, he introduced a range of stringent economy measures. But Malians were not in the mood for sacrifice—least of all the political-bureaucratic class who had become accustomed to their privileges. When these measures proved inadequate and growing opposition to them developed, the full powers of the National Assembly were transferred to the President, and a "Committee for the Defense of the Revolution" was established. It turned out that sacrifice could no more be coerced than commanded. In November 1968 Keita was overthrown and his ruling Union Soudanaise party dissolved by the military. He was kept under house arrest until his death in somewhat suspicious circumstances in 1977.[22]

Many of the leaders who oppose the current regimes of sub-Saharan Africa (most of them secretly or from exile) claim to do so on grounds of principle. They usually see the current rulers as too conservative and lacking in vision, or as "neo-colonial" puppets standing in the way of socialism. At present few of the opposition leaders have much chance of gaining power. Among those who have a somewhat better chance are some revolutionary leaders in southern Africa who have long stood in opposition to white rule, typically envisaging a future that is both nationalist and socialist. Other opposition leaders are representatives of historically defunct radical movements from earlier eras which lost in struggles with more conservative rulers—for instance, the Union des Populations du Cameroun (UPC), which was suppressed by the French colonial authorities and later crushed by the government of President Ahidjo; the political millenarian movements that rebelled against the government of Zaire in 1964–65; or the many radical leaders and parties that have been defeated, suppressed, or banned in most of the monopolistic regimes of Africa. Many of history's political losers in Africa have been men and parties of radical vision.

During the first wave of constitutional nationalism (1950s and early 1960s) only a small minority of the new African rulers were

22. *Africa Contemporary Record: Annual Survey and Documents*; 1968–70, ed. Colin Legum and John Drysdale (London: Africa Research, 1969–70); 1970–72, ed. Colin Legum (London: Rex Collings, 1971; London: Rex Collings, and New York: Africana Publications, 1972); 1972–79, ed. Colin Legum (New York: Africana Publications, 1973–79); see the report of Keita's death in 1977–78, p. B 702. There was some speculation that he was murdered by the military rulers. The large size of the crowds at his funeral suggests that some of his earlier popularity had survived or had been restored, perhaps owing to his long period of detention and the political difficulties of his military successors.

socialists, but during the second wave of *revolutionary* nationalism in the late 1960s and 1970s (involving many fewer countries), a larger proportion were radical.[23] The termination of Portuguese rule in Guinea-Bissau, Mozambique, and Angola was brought about by radical leaders bent on implementing socialist policies once installed in power. Two of these movement regimes came into power under a unified leadership in full political command of the state apparatus (Guinea-Bissau and Mozambique); the other (Angola) has taken longer to settle the issues of territorial control and political unity. During the period since independence in these countries, major steps in state reorganization have been taken under a vanguard party whose function is to exercise political control over governmental and administrative structures on the principle of "democratic centralism." The ultimate aim is the Leninist one of gaining control of the state in order to take command of society and the economy. Sufficient time has not yet passed to permit a confident judgment of the degree of success of these political experiments.

Socialist and visionary rulership in contemporary Black Africa has not been confined to civilian rulers. Soldiers have sought to employ the agencies of the state to pursue socialist visions in Benin, Congo-Brazzaville, Ethiopia, and Somalia. The rulers of Benin and Congo-Brazzaville have professed Marxist ideology and employed its rhetoric, but unresolved questions of state unity and elite discipline have rendered the socialist efforts of these regimes largely ineffective. In Benin the military elite that came to power in 1972 discovered Marxist ideology only after it gained control. Its doctrines and policies have been incoherent: governance has been mainly the ad hoc issuance of decrees. While the rhetoric of Benin-style "socialism" sets off the post-1972 military clique from the many previous regimes, the primary political problems that have plagued the country since independence—regionalism and factionalism—have persisted, although in a muted form. The Parti de la Révolution Populaire du Bénin (PRPB), established in 1976, appears to be a legitimation device of the President—Lt. Col. Mathieu Kerekou. The so-called revolution lacks substance and social roots. In Congo-Brazzaville, more than a decade of professed Marxism-Leninism has scarcely affected the factional-regional character of politics. Personal rivalries and plots have been

23. For an analysis of the first wave of African socialism, see William H. Friedland and Carl G. Rosberg, Jr., eds., *African Socialism* (Stanford: Stanford University Press, 1964); for the second wave, see Carl G. Rosberg and Thomas M. Callaghy, eds., *Socialism in Sub-Saharan Africa: A New Assessment* (Berkeley: Institute of International Studies, 1979).

a persistent feature of political life, and in March 1977 the then President (Ngouabi) was assassinated, creating considerable insecurity and further violence. Ethnic factionalism has persisted throughout the entire post-1963 period of "revolutionary" socialism, as has welfare factionalism, which is not unrelated to ethnic divisions, and is based upon the struggle for jobs and sinecures—especially among the youth—in a highly urbanized country. The economies of Benin and Congo-Brazzaville have continued to be dependent on French aid, with no apparent effort to change the situation. In sum, socialist ideology has largely played a symbolic rhetorical role in both countries: it is a currency of revolutionary political discourse devoid of purchasing power.[24]

Post-imperial Ethiopia since 1974 has been undergoing turbulent general revolution (in combination with several violent regional conflicts) during which attempts have been made by several different revolutionary groups at the center to gain control. The ideology of socialism has been adhered to by virtually all of the revolutionary factions, civilian and military, that have sought to fill the political vacuum left by the collapse of Emperor Haile Selassie's regime and has not been a subject of dispute.[25] The central issue of contention has been whether the military should lead the march from "feudalism" to "socialism" or give place to the civilians. The conflict over this issue has involved widespread and reckless violence and bloodshed. The violence committed by the ruling military junta, or Dergue, and its agents (some of them self-appointed) has been justified as being against the "enemies of the revolution," while their opponents have justified their own violence on similar grounds.[26] In February 1977, Mengistu seized power within the Dergue by killing rival officers. Power was now in the hands of a single ruler who was not only determined to suppress opposition and maintain the territorial integrity of the formerly imperial state, but also was apparently committed to transforming Ethiopian society in conformity with the principles

24. See Samuel Decalo, "Ideological Rhetoric and Scientific Socialism in Benin and Congo-Brazzaville," in *Socialism in Sub-Saharan Africa: A New Assessment*, ed. Rosberg and Callaghy, pp. 231–64. See also Dov Ronen, *Dahomey: Between Tradition and Modernity* (Ithaca and London: Cornell University Press, 1973), and René Gauze, *The Politics of Congo-Brazzaville*, trans. and ed. Virginia Thompson and Richard Adloff (Stanford: Hoover Institution Press, 1973).

25. See Marina Ottaway, "Democracy and New Democracy: The Ideological Debate in the Ethiopian Revolution," *African Studies Review* 21, 1 (April 1978): 19–31, and Marina and David Ottaway, *Ethiopia: Empire in Revolution* (New York and London: Africana Publications, 1978).

26. *Africa Contemporary Record*, 1976–77, pp. B 178, B 186–88.

of "scientific socialism." (How the Ethiopian regime differs from a tyranny will be discussed in chapter 6 below.)

The most noteworthy of the efforts of military rulers, in terms of substantive programs, have been in Somalia, where Mohamed Siad Barre, himself a devout Moslem, has attempted to join "scientific socialism" and Islam to promote the transformation of a nomadic pastoral society. The case is unusual and of particular interest insofar as the key elements in the experiment—the military, a pastoral society, Islam, and "scientific socialism"—seem quite incompatible. In some respects the experiment has not gone beyond political symbolism, and Siad has shown himself to be a gifted rhetorician. It has produced some substantive socioeconomic changes, but it cannot yet be determined how significant and permanent these are likely to be.

The civilian regimes of the first decade of Somali independence (1960–69) were increasingly corrupt. The political corruption reached its highest point in the 1969 national elections, when a thousand candidates representing 62 parties, most of them "one-man lineage parties," competed for 123 seats in the National Assembly—not by making policy or interest group appeals but by openly buying votes. I. M. Lewis reported that "in a nation where the annual budget runs at approximately £15 million, some candidates are estimated to have spent as much as £15,000."[27] For the unfortunate many who were unsuccessful, the outcome was substantial financial loss. For the fortunate few who won, electoral victory meant an opportunity to make windfall profits by agreeing to cross the floor of the National Assembly and support the government in return for financial and other rewards. The reported cost to the national treasury of forming a grand coalition government was £500,000 in public funds in 1969 alone.[28] It was such circumstances that provided the opportunity and the justification for a military coup by Siad in October 1969, who later observed that "there was no longer a sense of confidence in the national will, not even a minimum basis for national cooperation was established, and there was a high degree of moral decay."[29]

27. I. M. Lewis, "The Politics of the 1969 Somali Coup," *Journal of Modern African Studies* 10, 3 (October 1972): 397–98. For an early account of Somali political parties, see A. A. Castagno, Jr., "Somali Republic," in *Political Parties and National Integration in Tropical Africa*, ed. James S. Coleman and Carl G. Rosberg, Jr. (Berkeley and Los Angeles: University of California Press, 1964), pp. 512–59. For an outstanding general history, see I. M. Lewis, *The Modern History of Somaliland: From Nation to State* (New York: Praeger, 1965).

28. Lewis, "Politics of the 1969 Somali Coup," p. 398.

29. Quoted in David D. Laitin, "The Political Economy of Military Rule in Somalia," *Journal of Modern African Studies* 14, 3 (1976): 453.

The extreme venality and privatism that characterized the Somali state under civilian rule afforded an opportunity for collectivism in their repudiation. Not only could Siad expose and decry the extreme self-interestedness and divisiveness of his predecessors (condemned as "tribalism"), but also he could promote their opposites: public spiritedness, national service, and unity. The Devil has always performed exemplary services for the Saint. Warnings against the evils of tribalism could be accompanied by exhortations to seek the benefits of the nationalist (and later the socialist) collective. In 1974 Siad declared:

> We continue to seek vigilance and if it requires even a death penalty to prevent a revival of tribalism we will enact the law. . . . We have overcome colonialism and we have the imperialists at bay. The only internal obstacle is tribalism and this we have faced with courage.[30]

As for the obverse of tribalism, shortly after the coup in 1969 he had declared:

> The purpose of the Revolution is to guide us back to our true Somali characteristics. . . . We have to embark upon the task of creating a nationalism that will not detrimentally differentiate the rich from the poor, and the educated from the illiterate, the urban from the nomad, and the high from the low. In sum, what we are striving to create is a nationalism of oneness.[31]

Under Siad's leadership, steps were taken to promote a renewed Somali nationalism. A significant action with not only symbolic but also important practical implications was Siad's declaration in 1972 that henceforth the Latin alphabet would be the official working script of the Somali language. In this act Siad resolutely cut through years of controversy over the script issue and succeeded in generating a broad consensus.[32] Another significant measure, but whose success is not yet clear, was a national literacy campaign that involved the closure of all secondary schools for a year in 1974 and the mobilization of their students, aged fifteen and older, to teach the new Somali script throughout the countryside. As many as 25,000 students and hundreds of thousands of nomads were drawn into the campaign. As befitted the campaign's Spartan and collectivist spirit, those students who refused to participate were penalized by being excluded from the educational system for three years.[33]

---

30. Quoted in *Afriscope* 4, 7 (June 1974): 48.
31. Quoted in Laitin, "Political Economy of Military Rule in Somalia," p. 455.
32. David D. Laitin, *Politics, Language, and Thought: The Somali Experience* (Chicago: University of Chicago Press, 1977), pp. 84–136.
33. Philippe Decraene, "Scientific Socialism—African Style," *Africa Report* 20, 3 (May–June 1975): 49.

Siad's search for a socialist framework led to the founding of the Somali Revolutionary Socialist Party (SRSP) on the sixteenth anniversary of Somalia's independence in 1976. The military Supreme Revolutionary Council, established after the coup, was abolished and replaced by a party Political Bureau under the chairmanship of Siad, who was named Secretary-General of the new party. In character with militant socialist regimes elsewhere, the government established "orientation" centers throughout the country to propagate socialist ideology. In regard to social policy, a large number of self-help projects were initiated (their impact on material welfare is not fully known), and legal measures pressing in the direction of greater civic equality were also implemented, though not without some resistance. The most noteworthy of these was the provision of equal rights for women, which was opposed by some members of the Islamic priesthood. In one of the isolated cases of extreme punishment for political crimes in Siad's Somalia, ten minor Islamic leaders were executed for preaching against this measure.

In his efforts to demonstrate the compatibility of Islam and Somali socialism, the Somali ruler has declared:

> Islam and socialism supplement each other because both advocate the advancement of the interest of the people, of mankind—justice, dignity, prosperity and equality. The Islamic tenets are the utterances of God and socialism is the sum of the constructive thoughts of mankind and one can say in essence socialism is a supplement to Islam.[34]

Probably more important than the rhetorician's gift of being able to unite in language what cannot be joined in strict logic, let alone in fact, has been the promotion of socialist slogans. How attractive "socialism" can be in the Somali linguistic context is to be seen in its name, which signifies "the richest grazing grass in the country."[35] Because we do not yet know the effect of these words and symbols on the social and political attitudes of the Somali people, we cannot assess their significance for socialist change.

There is one additional component of Somalia's experiment with rural socialism that may prove to be of considerable significance: the resettlement schemes of the mid-1970s, in which a relatively large number of nomadic Somalis left their traditional way of life to take up a new one in state-organized agricultural and fishing settlements. Resettlement schemes are not distinctive

34. Quoted in Anthony J. Hughes, "Somalia's Socialist Road," *Africa Report* 22, 2 (March–April 1977): 41.
35. David D. Laitin, "Somalia's Military Government and 'Scientific Socialism,' " in *Socialism in Sub-Saharan Africa: A New Assessment*, ed. Rosberg and Callaghy, pp. 200–1.

to Somalia, but the conditions under which they took place and the nature of the social choice that led to them may well have been unique. Somalia was among the countries most seriously affected by the devastating drought in the African sahel during the early 1970s. (In Somalia the greatest devastation occurred in 1973–74.) Since virtually half of the population—one and a half million people—was directly affected by the disaster, it could not be ignored by Siad's government. By 1975 some 300,000 people had been "moved into [relief] camps and were totally dependent upon government efforts, supported by outside assistance."[36] (In relocating such large numbers of drought-stricken Somalis, the government was assisted by the Soviet Union, which had established a presence in Somalia and was in a position to furnish critically important logistical support. Without such outside assistance, upon which the government's program was considerably dependent, it is doubtful that such large numbers could have been moved.)

Of those made destitute by the drought, half volunteered to be resettled in state agricultural and fishing projects, while the remainder chose to return to their nomadic way of life. Hughes observes that "whichever decision was made, the choice in all cases does seem to have been freely made."[37] There is evidence that the socialist government saw in the disaster a unique opportunity to promote socialism: "The calamity from which we suffer," said a Somali army captain involved in the mass resettlement of victims, "must give us an opportunity to re-balance the local economy. . . . The government wants to modify the economical structures of Somalia"; a civil servant said: "At the same time as we come to the assistance of the victims, we bring them some education and thus set the basis for solving the problem of nomadism."[38]

A country like Somalia, with the pastoral economy very exposed to the powerful effects of nature, may provide a situation in which a choice in favor of collectivism can be made with minimal political persuasion, inducement, or compulsion. But it is still too soon to know how enduring this attempt at reorienting society and economy in Somalia will prove to be. Much will depend on the capacity of the settlement schemes to provide concrete advantages and promote the welfare of the nomads in comparison with their former way of life. When the climate improves, will the traditional way of life once again become attractive? Or will life in the settlements begin to take hold and become permanent? Or will some

36. Hughes, "Somalia's Socialist Road," p. 48.
37. Ibid. See also I. M. Lewis, "Somalia," in *Africa: South of the Sahara, 1976–77* (London: Europa Publications, 1976), p. 764.
38. Quoted in "Scientific Socialism—African Style," p. 48.

unforeseen development, natural or man-made—such as repeated drought or continued violent conflict in the Ogaden and the pouring in of hundreds of thousands of political refugees—determine the final outcome of the experiment?

But there are disquieting signs of the government's incapacity as a socialist agency. While Siad initiated his regime with a strong condemnation of "tribalism" in all its forms, there is reason to believe that clan and ethnic influences continue to play a significant role in his government.[39] And if the power and authority of Siad rest on such a base, then there is good reason to be skeptical about the moral force of his personal authority and ideological vision. If there are such influences, it would suggest that Siad has not succeeded in suppressing the selfish dispositions of at least some of his followers, and that he has acquiesced to a less morally strict and more instrumental type of rule—at least with regard to them.

In the remainder of this chapter we shall discuss three Black African regimes whose rulers have sought to bring into existence socialist "utopias" that would require a fundamental transformation of the society and the economy. Nkrumah's Ghana, Touré's Guinea, and especially Nyerere's Tanzania have been socialist experiments inspired, and to a considerable extent directed, by the prophetic ruler himself. Nkrumah and Touré have been in the forefront of socialist experimentation in Africa; indeed, they were the leaders of the first major attempts to introduce socialism into post-independence Africa.

In Ghana (as in Mali) the political prophet was eventually removed by the military and his regime was abolished, leaving little trace of socialism and a legacy of economic travail. But Nkrumah is remembered less for what he did than for what he represented: more than any other leader of his era, he personified Africa's hope for a future of peace, justice, and prosperity. Nkrumah was the New African Man representing Africans to themselves and to the world. His politics were mass politics, and his skills were those of arousing mass popular support: inspiring rhetoric, mastery of political and ideological language, and virtuoso political acting. His ineffectiveness as a ruler after African independence was due largely to his lack of the more mundane and practical skills of governing.

In showmanship and rhetoric, Sékou Touré has skills equal to Nkrumah's and, in addition, a profound sense of personal power.

39. See *Africa Confidential* 20, 23 (November 14, 1979): 7–8.

Perhaps even more than Nkrumah, Touré gained international fame—certainly in the French-speaking world—as an uncompromising opponent of colonialism. He had stood up to de Gaulle in Guinea's 1958 independence referendum. In this episode Touré demonstrated his distaste for political compromise and his desire not only for national independence but also for his personal independence of other political men. He has continued to believe in the power of ideology to change the political and social consciousness of men, thereby moving them to do what otherwise they would not have done. But ideology has never been allowed to fetter his own personal power or prevented him from using coercion when it has suited his purposes.

While the regimes of Nkrumah and Touré captured much of the initial interest in state-sponsored social and economic transformation in Black Africa, there is little doubt that it has been Nyerere's experiment with agrarian socialism in Tanzania that has commanded the greatest long-run attention. More than any other African statesman, past or present, Nyerere has embodied the hope for a socialist Africa that will be both developed and democratic. He has become Africa's political saint: a "philosopher-king" whose authority does not depend upon Plato's noble lie. Nyerere is a rare political animal indeed: one who displays a sure sense of power and dedication to his principles and also the strongest possible sense of honesty and integrity. These virtues have not only enhanced his personal status, but have also been reflected in the large amounts of aid that Tanzania has received from abroad during his period of rule. In the late 1960s and 1970s Tanzania came to embody the hopes of many that a policy of agrarian socialism might succeed in providing poor rural peasants with a decent life. Tanzania may be the test case of whether agrarian socialism can be successful in Africa, but the question must be raised whether—and how far—socialism in that country can be separated from the remarkable person and role of its ruler.

Kwame Nkrumah, Ghana

Kwame Nkrumah remains one of the most fascinating of Africa's political visionaries.[40] Our characterization of him as a political Prophet rather than as a despot is consistent with his elevation to the pantheon of modern Africa's martyrs and saints since

40. The best standard political studies of his rule are David E. Apter, *Ghana in Transition*, 2nd rev. ed. (Princeton: Princeton University Press, 1972), and Dennis Austin, *Politics in Ghana: 1946–1960* (New York and London: Oxford University

his death.[41] More than any other leader, Nkrumah represents Africa's encounter with the modern world, Africa's revolution,[42] which so far has been fundamentally political in nature. His admonition "Seek ye first the Political Kingdom!" expressed a conviction that only political action could bring about a new Africa that was socialist. This was not the belief of a purely instrumental politician, but of a prophet in politics—a political-religious man. While not for a moment overlooking his considerable organizational and manipulative skills, his awareness of the interests and appetites that move men in newly liberated and rapidly changing societies—Nkrumah was first of all a politician[43]—one cannot fail to see the intimate connection of the religious and the political-ideological in his speeches and writings (especially his autobiography). After all, he had been educated in schools strongly tinged with a religious as well as an educational mission. In his autobiography he declared: "Today I am a nondenominational Christian and a Marxist socialist and I have not found any contradiction between the two."[44] Nkrumah's religiosity was traditional as well as Christian—he was a Ghanaian. To be a Prophet is to engage in a role that is clearly recognized by the categories of traditional African belief, most certainly in Ghana. It should not be assumed that modern, universal religion or ideology is necessarily at odds with traditional beliefs; indeed, many of the best studies of African religious movements point to a syncretic intermingling of Christian and traditional African beliefs and practices.[45] For example, Austin has reported a "substantial increase in prophet-healing cults" among students at the University of Legon, Ghana.[46]

Press, 1964). An important recent study is Trevor Jones, *Ghana's First Republic: 1960–1966* (London: Methuen & Co., 1976). For an early biography, see Bankole Timothy, *Kwame Nkrumah: His Rise to Power* (London: George Allen & Unwin, 1955).

41. His rule is characterized as "despotic" in Henry Bretton, *The Rise and Fall of Kwame Nkrumah* (New York: Praeger, 1966).

42. This view is presented with great passion and conviction by an obvious admirer and personal acquaintance—C. L. R. James—in *Nkrumah and the Ghana Revolution* (Westport, Conn.: Lawrence Hill & Co., 1977).

43. The theme of politics in Ghana as "the politics of the marketplace" is explored with much insight by Dennis Austin, *Ghana Observed: Essays on the Politics of a West African Republic* (New York: Africana Publications, 1976), ch. 13, and by Maxwell Owusu, *Uses and Abuses of Political Power* (Chicago and London: University of Chicago Press, 1970).

44. *Ghana: The Autobiography of Kwame Nkrumah*, p. 13. For a very helpful account of Nkrumah's Marxism, see Jon Kraus, "Socialism and Political Economy in Ghana," in *Socialism in the Third World*, ed. Desfosses and Levesque, pp. 180–215.

45. The best-known study of these movements is B. G. M. Sundkler, *Bantu Prophets in South Africa* (London: Oxford University Press, 1961); see esp. ch. 7.

46. Austin, *Ghana Observed*, pp. 186–87.

As we noted above, the earlier nationalist victories were basically moral in character: the victory of the principles of national self-determination and racial equality over those of colonial tutelage and paternalism. Nowhere was the victory of national independence in Africa more of a moral victory, and for that reason more of a symbolic event of international interest, than in Ghana (1957). In the event a minor British colony became a new African state of international renown; simultaneously, Kwame Nkrumah was promoted from the status of a relatively unknown colonial agitator into a world leader. The victory was scarcely the achievement of Nkrumah alone, or even of the Convention People's Party (CPP). But it is impossible to overlook the extent to which his early vision of independence and his determined pursuit of the goal justified his newly acquired stature. Of all the Ghanaian nationalists of the time, he best understood—and arrived at this understanding earlier—the great power to be unlocked from the symbol of African freedom; he understood (to borrow Murray Edelman's helpful phrase) "the symbolic uses of politics."[47] He was portrayed as the *Osagyefo* (Redeemer):

> To millions of people living both inside and outside the continent of Africa, Kwame Nkrumah is Africa, and Africa is Kwame Nkrumah. When the question was asked: "What is going to happen in Africa?" it is to one man that everyone looks for the answer: Kwame Nkrumah. To the imperialists and colonialists his name is a curse on their lips. . . ; to Africans suffering under foreign domination, his name is a breath of hope and means freedom, brotherhood and racial equality; to us, his people, Kwame Nkrumah is our father, teacher, our brother, our friend, indeed our very lives, for without him we would no doubt have existed, but we would not have lived; there would have been no hope of a cure for our sick souls, no taste of glorious victory after a life-time of suffering.[48]

The tension between political appetites and political religion in Ghana began to appear in a significant way after independence was won and the CPP was installed as the first African government of the country with Nkrumah at its head. Prior to independence, the political wants and interests and political religion of Ghanaians were for the most part compatible because they were really two sides of the same coin: independence meant both freedom and opportunity—two values that were probably indistinguishable in the minds of ordinary Ghanaians. The promise of

47. Murray Edelman, *The Symbolic Uses of Politics* (Urbana, Ill.: University of Illinois Press, 1964).
48. Tawia Adamafio, *A Portrait of the Osagyefo, Dr. Kwame Nkrumah* (Accra: Government Printer, 1961); quoted in Apter, *Ghana in Transition*, pp. 325–26.

independence was the promise of African self-government, which implied African opportunity—most certainly increased political and bureaucratic opportunities and, to some extent as a result, economic opportunities. The fact that independence was first claimed by the most strident and vigorous African nationalists—in this case, Nkrumah and his CPP—made it appear that independence was solely the achievement of nationalist power rather than, to a considerable extent, the grant of colonial authorities. What African could not support a movement and a leader whose vision promised, once the colonial authorities accepted the principle of political independence for Ghana, racial dignity and personal or familial opportunity? And all with little or no genuine sacrifice: the political struggle was largely among the nationalist parties and leaders for the spoils of independence.[49]

The theme of the "man of the people" becoming the ruling politician—with all that that can imply in terms of the decline of virtue, the rise of acquisitiveness, the worldly temptations of corruption, and the intensified competition for power and its privileges—has been widely used not only in African political studies but in African literature as well.[50] It is certainly a theme that can be applied to the transfer of authority in Ghana to Nkrumah and the CPP. It applies because of the sharp contrast between the moral symbols and the political reality in Ghana—between the ideal of continued devotion and sacrifice for the common good and the reality of post-independence politics as a rush for political spoils. With independence there came a sharp conflict between moral standards and material wants. Increasingly during the period of transitional government and extensively in the post-independence period, there was a stampede for jobs and opportunities of all kinds that made a mockery of the political ideals of sacrifice and struggle.

While there remain benefits and opportunities to be secured, such acquisitiveness is merely a corruption of ideals, but when opportunities are exhausted—as they soon must be in an economically underdeveloped country—dissatisfaction and discontent will very quickly arise. This problem has been confronted by all of Africa's new rulers. For the Prince or the Autocrat, the challenge has been to keep the rush for spoils within limits and not to allow

<hr/>

49. Nkrumah and some of his colleagues were imprisoned by the British for their agitational activities, but being a "prison graduate" proved to be a political advantage for Nkrumah. See Nkrumah's own account in *Ghana: The Autobiography of Kwame Nkrumah*, pp. 121–35.

50. See, for example, Chinua Achebe, *A Man of the People* (New York: Anchor Books, 1967).

it to undermine the ruler's power, authority, and control. Some Princes, like Kenyatta, have achieved this by controlling the allocation of the political spoils and investing their distribution in their own authority. Some Autocrats, like Houphouët-Boigny, have achieved it by holding down demands for political and bureaucratic spoils while providing opportunities in the economic sphere. But the Prophet cannot rest content with such solutions even if he can achieve them: he must speak of higher, moral goals and political struggle—that is, of continued discipline, devotion, and sacrifice—not self-indulgence. When Nkrumah's disciples began to lose faith and become preoccupied with political interests, a change came in Ghana perhaps nowhere better symbolized than in the cynical remark: "Nkrumahism [is] the highest stage of opportunism."[51]

There is no way to know if Nkrumah would have survived longer had he become a Prince or an Autocrat. Whether he chose not to change his basically moralistic and messianic orientation to leadership, or was unable to change, or did not consider the possibility of changing, we cannot say. He continued to speak of visions and to prophesy a nobler, greater, and more powerful Ghanaian and African future; ultimately he foresaw a politically unified, socialist Africa. (On this view, independence was at best only a preliminary stage.) Here indeed was a new vision, a new expression of symbolic politics, but one that was utterly unattainable.

The new vision of African political unification and socialism was enormously ambitious and very different from the old goal of independence, which was a politically practical aim. In principle a unified African state could be agreed to in a compact of preexisting African states, and the agreement could even declare such a state to be "socialist" in the legal arrangement of its institutions and in its goals. But it requires only a very limited imagination to foresee the manifold difficulties and obstacles that would stand in the way of concluding such an agreement—in particular, the numerous vested interests that have been built into the existing arrangement of a continent of independent African states, most of which had become or were becoming independent as Nkrumah described his vision. And one can readily imagine the difficulties of implementing such an agreement if it were signed.

Nevertheless, African political unification became the cornerstone of Ghana's foreign policy under Nkrumah and his fondest vision for Africa's future.[52] For nationalism and "Self-Govern-

51. Cited in Apter, *Ghana in Transition*, p. 327.
52. Kwame Nkrumah, *Africa Must Unite* (London: Heinemann Educational Books, 1963).

ment Now" (the earlier nationalist slogan) were substituted conti-
nentalism and "Union Government Now." Nkrumah spoke and
wrote of a United States of Africa as if it were not only a practical
possibility but an urgent necessity:

> The emergence of such a mighty stabilising force in this strifeworn world
> should be regarded . . . not as the shadowy dream of a visionary, but as a
> practical proposition which the peoples of Africa can and should trans-
> late into reality. There is a tide in the affairs of every people when the
> moment strikes for political action. We must act now. Tomorrow may be
> too late.[53]

Nyerere shared Nkrumah's goals, but as a gradualist believed
that they could only be achieved painfully by a long step-by-step
process. Thus Nyerere could support regional associations such as
an East African Federation as initial steps, whereas Nkrumah saw
such intermediate associations of states as standing in the way of
greater unity. It is true that Ghana, with Nkrumah's blessing,
participated in the Ghana-Guinea-Mali Union, but this union
was seen as an open association with invitations for all African
states to join: it could be enlarged easily and could be the nucleus
of African unity, especially since it bridged Anglophone and Fran-
cophone Africa. Despite Nkrumah's enormous investment in his
diplomacy, by 1962 he had become "virtually the only prominent
exponent in Africa" of continental union government.[54] Nkrumah's utopianism was sharply revealed at the May 1963 conference of African statesmen which established the OAU: he
proposed "a formal declaration that all the independent African
states here and now agree to the establishment of a Union of African States" and "machinery for the Union Government of Africa."[55] The comments of Austin are apposite:

> Here was a vision indeed! But Nkrumah was in a minority of one. The
> Addis Ababa states drew up a modest "Charter of the Organization of
> African States" which stressed the sovereignty of the individual mem-
> bers, and reached agreement on the principle of non-interference in the
> territorial integrity of the existing states.[56]

Instead of utopianism, the practical realism of the protection of
state interests was going to govern the relations of African states.
  But what of socialism? The unreality of the goal of a united
African state makes the discussion of socialism within it fanciful,[57]

53. Quoted in Legum, *Pan Africanism*, p. 57. 54. Ibid.
55. Austin, *Politics in Ghana*, p. 399. 56. Ibid.
57. Nkrumah continued to speak and write about the necessity of a united African
society based on socialism, as though it were ever anything but chimerical: "At the
core of the concept of African unity lies socialism and the socialist definition of the

but what of socialism in Ghana? Nkrumah believed that "capitalism is too complicated a system for a newly independent nation. Hence the need for a socialistic society."[58] The opposite is nearer the truth. The policy of socialism presumes major efforts at government reorganization and actions whose rationality and reliability are commensurate with the requirements of state plans and designs. Nkrumah may have been equating "capitalism" with the "modern capitalist societies of the West," but their essential complexity is due less to their capitalist character than to their modernity. Historically, capitalist or market economies have been large and small, rich and poor, industrial and commercial, technically advanced and relatively simple. Adam Smith could enunciate the principles of market economies without ever having seen the highly industrialized, technically complex versions of modern capitalist economies.

The practical possibilities of a circumspect and modestly ambitious government appear never to have been appreciated by Nkrumah. Instead, very ambitious plans and policies were adopted and actions taken—some of them sufficiently unrealistic to jeopardize the economic foundation that had been inherited from colonial rule. Part of this irrational policymaking—no doubt a considerable part—can be attributed to the relentless rush for political spoils after independence which, among other things, inflated the government bureaucracy in order to provide jobs and sinecures. Many of the new government officials were bound to be inexperienced, perhaps incompetent, and probably with a limited sense of public service and duty. Looking back on this period Nkrumah himself had to admit that many of his civil servants "had no loyalty to the state or understanding of the social purposes which we were attempting to achieve. . . . In the old days popular opinion forced me to maintain in positions of authority individuals who were well-known in their localities through their local families and tribal influences."[59] This was one of the great dilemmas confronted by Nkrumah, who needed an effective and loyal government if he was to have any chance of realizing his socialist goals. Such a government has another defect: it is very likely to "consume" a much larger proportion of public funds than it "invests." In Nkrumah's Ghana there was a marked tendency for

new African society. Socialism and African unity are organically complementary" (Kwame Nkrumah, *Handbook of Revolutionary Warfare: A Guide to the Armed Phase of the African Revolution* [London: Panaf Books, 1968], p. 28).

58. *Ghana: The Autobiography of Kwame Nkrumah*, p. xvi.

59. Kwame Nkrumah, *Dark Days in Ghana* (London: Lawrence & Wishart, 1968), p. 74.

consumption expenditures in the government budget to increase and for capital expenditures to decrease.[60] Socialism has the effect of exacerbating this tendency by providing the justification for an expanded and powerful *dirigiste* state.

What is the reality of economic management of a dependent, single cash crop economy (cocoa in the case of Ghana) with at best a marginally competent and not wholly reliable government apparatus to do the managing? It is surely that such an economy, simple in structure and based only on a few major factors of production and highly vulnerable to external economic forces—even to the fickleness of nature, such as the weather—is essentially fragile and prone to instability.[61] The economic managers must walk a tightrope if they are not only to avoid economic difficulty but also to advance. So variable and unpredictable are the economic forces that conduce to production and growth, and indirectly to government revenue, that non-prudential policies must assume the character of "gambling" with the wealth and welfare of the nation. Variability and unpredictability in the economics of cocoa are to be seen right down the line: production may be up or down; the international market price may be high or low; the total foreign exchange earnings and government revenues must consequently fluctuate, having effects on future investment and government expenditure. The effects upon government revenues and policies are pronounced; Killick comments: "In the eight financial years ending in 1962–3 the average year-to-year fluctuation in revenue from export duties was plus or minus 28 percent."[62] He adds: "The implication of this is that it renders the pursuit of a reliable and moderately sensitive fiscal policy extremely difficult,"[63] making it impractical for government to attempt to vary its expenditures to the same degree as its revenues. Realistic economic principles were never understood by Nkrumah; if anything, his tenure of rule in Ghana seems to prove the unfortunate truth that political men and their ideas can ruin as easily as they can build.

Even if the most rational policies are adopted, there still remain problems of implementation. Killick observes that "the most appropriate policies . . . can only succeed if the authorities are prepared to put their entire weight behind them"[64] (and, we would add, if they are able to). There is evidence to suggest that the nec-

60. Tony Killick, "The Possibilities of Economic Control," in *A Study of Contemporary Ghana*, vol. 1: *The Economy of Ghana*, ed. Walter Birmingham et al. (London: George Allen & Unwin, 1966), p. 420.

61. Ibid., p. 412. 62. Ibid., p. 434.

63. Ibid., pp. 434–35. 64. Ibid., p. 438.

essary power and authority were not available to Nkrumah even if he had understood their importance. In a study of the Ghanaian public service carried out shortly after the fall of Nkrumah's regime, Price found a marked discrepancy in the attitudes and role expectations of civil servants between the official requirements of the bureaucracy and its policies and rules and the unofficial requirements of Ghanaian society and its norms.[65] The result was an overall incapacity of the civil service to effectively implement public policy.

Along with the public service, the other agency of state control—the ruling CPP—was similarly ineffective. In the first place, Nkrumah never exercised full control over the CPP (or even the government ministries that came under the influence of party "barons"), so it could not serve as an organizational extension of his will. Moreover, the CPP never came close to being an "organizational weapon" of the sort that Leninist-type states have found indispensable for implementing and enforcing socialist policies. The party structure did not accord with Nkrumah's own leadership style, which placed personal loyalty above the development of a competent, disciplined body of party cadres. Ever fearful of conspiracies from among his lieutenants, Nkrumah spent much time and effort manipulating his close associates. The party remained an uneasy coalition of sometimes unpredictable and often opportunistic fair-weather supporters. As Selwyn Ryan has observed, it was scarcely the kind of organization out of which a socialist state might develop:

> One cannot build socialism without socialist cadres, nor can the ideology of one or a few men be imposed on an entire nation without coercion or the technology to engineer consent. . . . In Ghana . . . cadres were scarce, and those that were on hand were fractious and unreliable. There was no revolutionary experience to cauterize them against the temptations of office. . . . The transition to socialism required a secure base of power and Nkrumah had none outside of those who benefitted directly from his regime.[66]

Nkrumah was overthrown by the military in February 1966 while visiting Peking. (He died in exile in Guinea in 1972.) The excesses and mismanagement of his regime created a legacy of economic stagnation and decay. Successive governments, military and

65. Robert M. Price, *Society and Bureaucracy in Contemporary Ghana* (Berkeley and Los Angeles: University of California Press, 1975).

66. Selwyn Ryan, "The Theory and Practice of African One Partyism: The CPP Re-examined," *Canadian Journal of African Studies* 4, 2 (Spring 1970): 169.

civilian alike, have been unable to restore the country to a sound economic footing. Ghana continues to stagger from one economic problem to the next, lacking in elementary economic functioning—let alone progress. Whereas the West in the 1950s looked upon Nkrumah's Ghana as the new Africa, and was prepared to offer it various forms of aid and assistance, in the 1970s Ghana had to compete with numerous other African countries—many of them far better economic prospects—for help. Since Nkrumah's time, if not since independence, very little if any real progress has taken place in what was once the most prosperous country of West Africa.

Sékou Touré, Guinea

In turning to Sékou Touré's Guinea, we encounter one of the most durable personal regimes in independent Africa and one of the most despotic. Touré's rule has always been highly personal and disciplined: from the time he assumed command of the Parti Démocratique de Guinée (PDG) well before independence (1958), his personal stamp upon Guinean political affairs was unmistakable. As R. W. Johnson puts it: "The PDG's period of political and electoral 'take-off' really dates from [Touré's] accession to power within it. . . . His position [has been] bolstered by a degree of popular and organizational support perhaps unique in West Africa."[67] Most of the rulers of Africa have been self-made men, but Touré is among the few who have been "self-taught." He never received a secondary or higher education, rising solely through his own efforts as a member of the African clerical class. Perhaps for this reason he has placed great store in the power of ideas and the possibility for ideology to serve as an instrument of social transformation and psychological decolonization. More than twenty volumes of his speeches and reflections upon Guinean and African development have been published. His faith in ideology is matched by his devotion to political organization, but he believes that ideology and organization must be entirely subordinated to the ruler. For more than two decades Touré has succeeded in maintaining autocratic and increasingly despotic power. Rulership in Guinea is the story of Touré's fanatical devotion not only to his political beliefs, but also to his personal power; it is also the story of the political conflicts and economic difficulties that have

67. R. W. Johnson, "Sékou Touré and the Guinean Revolution," *African Affairs* 69, 277 (October 1970): 350.

arisen in the attempt to impose the dogmas of a self-styled philosopher-king.

Touré saw clearly that colonialism rested, in the final analysis, not only on power, but also on an ideology of "false consciousness," and could be defeated if that consciousness could be changed. He believed it could be changed by an ideology of nationalism organized into a strong political party. Evidence for this belief was provided by his early success as a nationalist leader and by the success of the PDG, and the ultimate confirmation was Guinea's vote for West African independence in the 1958 referendum, against the neo-colonialist proposals of de Gaulle. As in Ghana and Mali, the power of ideology, of political religion, seemed enormous, contributing to the belief that it could be used to defeat capitalism and build socialism in Guinea:

> The basic aim of Sékou Touré's socialism or noncapitalist approach . . . is to alter the relationship between human beings. This is to be done by decolonizing their viewpoints and attitudes, and by creating a new man freed from a system of capitalistic exploitation and participating with all his strength in the development of the nation.[68]

After independence, the economic costs of Touré's doctrines and policies became apparent. Some were the anticipated costs of defying the French government. Following the anti–de Gaulle vote in 1958, the French government withdrew virtually all its personnel from Guinea and terminated its programs of aid and assistance. In addition, Guinea was deprived of its privileged access to French markets (which continued to be enjoyed by all the other French-speaking African countries that had voted *oui* in the referendum). It was as if the French were using the opportunity to test the claim that Touré had made in de Gaulle's presence: "We prefer poverty in liberty to riches in slavery!" The costs to Guinea were severe, and economic hardship was felt almost immediately. The seriousness of the loss of French manpower can be seen in the fact that in 1957 the Guinean educational system graduated only thirty Guineans qualified to enter the public service, while the seriousness of the loss of French markets can be seen in the fact that in that same year coffee and banana exports to France accounted for 80 percent of Guinea's foreign exchange earnings.[69]

68. Claude Rivière, *Guinea: The Mobilization of a People*, trans. Virginia Thompson and Richard Adloff (Ithaca and London: Cornell University Press, 1977), pp. 90–91; see also Ladipo Adamolekun, *Sékou Touré's Guinea: An Experiment in Nation Building* (London: Methuen & Co., 1976).

69. See Elliot J. Berg, "Socialism and Economic Development in Tropical Africa," *Quarterly Journal of Economics* 78, 4 (November 1964): 556.

Guinea was forced to seek technical assistance, capital, and markets elsewhere. Eastern bloc countries provided some aid, and a number of African and Western intellectuals and technocrats made their services available to the new regime. In 1960 a three-year plan was announced to cope with the withdrawal of French economic support. East European technical and economic advisors and Western Marxist sympathizers collaborated to produce the plan, which aimed at reorienting the economy both away from France and toward socialist-oriented management and control. Steps were taken to place a government monopoly on all trade, to establish new industries, to reorganize the agricultural sector, and generally to subject the economy to state directives and regulations.

The economic costs and hardships endured by Guinea as a consequence of Touré's defiance of de Gaulle were a measure of the economic powerlessness of Guinea as compared with France. The costs incurred in its headlong rush toward state control of the economy and socialism were quite different, however—the results not of economic powerlessness but of government plans and policies. Touré and his advisors appeared to believe that political aspirations could easily be reconciled with economic considerations; indeed they appeared to believe in a "political economics" grounded more in ideological faith and political power than in economic analysis. The consequence has been persistent economic difficulty and equally persistent attempts by the government to hold to the ruler's ideological approach while ignoring the lessons to be learned from economic and planning failures. The mistakes of "political economics" have included the following:[70] (1) The premature creation of a state trading monopoly that became "the largest trading firm in Africa" at the time.[71] Almost overnight a group of youthful and inexperienced Guinean state managers were saddled with the task of directing the innumerable activities that previously had been handled by thousands of private traders operating independently. (2) The establishment of a number of new industries (many of them utilizing Eastern bloc capital and equipment) without due consideration to market demand or suitable manpower and, in some cases, without adequate raw material inputs and processed outputs to and from the factories. Most of the industries operated far below capacity, and very few succeeded in

70. To examine the costs and difficulties in detail would require far more space than is available here. For a critical assessment from a Marxist point of view, see Rivière, esp. chs. 1, 3, and 6.

71. Berg, "Socialism and Economic Development," p. 558.

paying their own way. (3) The expansion of public works and other sectors of government activity, resulting in a dramatic growth of government employment and bureaucratic establishments. And (4) the creation of an enormous national debt to finance the extension of state management of the economy and the growth of government. Instead of helping to finance the 1960 plan, the new state trading and industrial companies increased the burden of debt by borrowing funds to remain in operation. The exasperated remarks of a sympathetic observer give some indication of the extent of economic irrationality:

> To set up a cannery without products to can, a textile factory that lacked cotton supplies, a cigarette factory without sufficient locally grown tobacco, and to develop . . . a forest region that had no roads and trucks to carry its output . . . —all these were gambles taken by utopian idealists and ignoramuses. . . .
>
> The number of haphazard activities grew in proportion to the availability of foreign aid and easy loans. . . . Public works were undertaken without regard for planning . . . [and with] each government service jealously and selfishly striving to get the largest allocation of funds. . . . Dishonesty and careless management eroded the plan's funds. . . . By the end of 1964, the state enterprises . . . had contributed no more than 2 percent to the national revenues. And in 1968 they were operating, on the average, at only one-fourth of their productive capacity. . . . As of September 1967, Guinea's foreign debt . . . was four times as great as the state's annual revenues. . . . Guinea's indebtedness increased its dependence on the outside world.[72]

The economic costs and hardships for Guinea as a whole, and ordinary Guineans in particular, have been extensive. The opportunity costs, as measured by the discrepancy between the disastrous outcome and what might have resulted had economic wisdom prevailed, have undoubtedly been even higher. A strong indication of the inappropriateness of the whole "political economics" enterprise has been the widespread attempts by producers and traders to evade the burdensome regulations imposed upon them. Black marketeering and smuggling have been pervasive in Guinean economic life since the 1960 plan. In reaction to price controls upon such agricultural commodities as coffee and rice, farmers and traders have persistently smuggled their products out of the country to be sold in neighboring Liberia or Ivory Coast at higher international market prices. The government has met such widespread practices not with the recognition that the controlled prices are unrealistic, but rather with a renewed determination to stamp out "economic sabotage," if necessary by intim-

72. Rivière, pp. 112–14, 119.

idation and coercion. Touré has saved some of his strongest political invective for assaults on such practices, and is reported to have said in 1972 that he personally would shoot any economic saboteurs that were caught.[73] When his threats have been effective, the result has been a decline not only in smuggling, but also in the production of the cash crop commodities involved. The problems created for the operations of smaller, indigenous entrepreneurs in such a political climate are not difficult to imagine; they are not unlike those experienced under conditions of tyranny. By 1971 it was reported that there was only one private Guinean firm—Fruitaguinee—that had more than ten employees, and it was closed down "after its director was put in jail."[74]

The suppression of indigenous enterprise in Guinea has been accompanied by increasing political control as the ruling PDG, and particularly the ruler, have been faced with opposition in their attempt to maintain hegemony in the state. In the beginning, disciplined political control could be seen as the ordinary monopolistic and authoritarian rule of a one-party regime imposed with considerable popular support.[75] The PDG was seen as a plebiscitarian party with a mandate. The growth of personal rule, however, has witnessed the ascendancy of the Political Bureau over the party and the ruler over the Political Bureau: a regime that Touré himself has described as a "popular dictatorship" or a "democratic dictatorship."[76] Most laws originate simply and swiftly in the decrees and edicts of the ruler. As the supreme authority in the land, not only do his opinions prevail over all others, but they "become laws as they are uttered."[77] Here indeed is the autocratic mode of rule, of which the extreme variant is despotism: "He intervenes at his own discretion in legal cases, and decides the verdict in the name of the people's will which transcends any written code."[78] He is an authority on all matters, from philosophy to agriculture, which he has pronounced upon in his numerous writings and speeches. The National Assembly meets briefly twice a year to formally sanction legislation and budgetary requests. The party, not the National Assembly, is the embodiment of the Guinean state, and the Political Bureau is the highest state council. According to Rivière, the latter

73. Peter Enahoro, "Guinea: End of Isolationism?," *Africa* 47 (July 1975): 22.

74. Rivière, p. 198.

75. See Victor D. Du Bois, "Guinea," in *Political Parties and National Integration in Tropical Africa*, ed. Coleman and Rosberg, pp. 186–215.

76. Rivière, p. 99.

77. Lansine Kaba, "Guinean Politics: A Critical Historical Overview," *Journal of Modern African Studies* 15, 1 (1977): 34.

78. Ibid., p. 35.

handles all questions involving appointments to the bureaucracy, the management of state enterprises, the delimitation of administrative regions, economic planning, international relations, and the like. It supervises the justice dispensed in the people's courts, assesses direct taxation, and controls prices as well as the commercial agencies.[79]

Such a degree of political control over society and economy has meant that all individuals and groups who seek advancement or protection in Guinea must, in some manner or other, secure the support of the party; in practice, they secure the favor of a party cadre or leader. The party can be conceived as a network of ties of patronage and dependence, favor and submission, from top to bottom. At the very top is the ruler—Touré—who can put anyone on notice at any time. In the Guinean version of party patronage, the mechanism inducing compliance is fear more than favor. The party's monopoly of social and economic life means that exclusion from it is tantamount to exclusion not only from the polity but from modern society as a whole. To make one's way in Guinean society, one must make peace with the party, one must submit; exile is virtually the only alternative. Many thousands of Guineans have chosen this alternative or have had no choice but to live in exile: estimates of the number of exiles have ranged from 250,000 to one million, living mainly in Ivory Coast and Senegal but with significant numbers in France. Some have been intellectuals unwilling to return home or unwelcome should they try; others have been former public officials who have preferred exile to living under the conditions of Touré's rule; many others have been traders and even peasants.[80]

Touré's critics have pointed to the Stalinistic mode of his regime.[81] If not less ruthless, it is probably less efficient and therefore less able to impose punishment systematically upon its enemies and critics, real and imagined. It is perhaps more like Oriental despotism in this regard: despotic and onerous, but not quite totalitarian.[82] But in character with Stalinism and totalitarianism, the ruler in Guinea has been elevated and deified. Touré is Guide et Stratège de la Révolution and Responsable Suprême de la Révolution—the Guide and Supreme Spokesman of the Revolution.[83]

79. Rivière, p. 96.
80. Ibid., pp. 96–100.
81. Kaba, "Guinean Politics," pp. 35–36.
82. See Karl A. Wittfogel, *Oriental Despotism: A Comparative Study of Total Power* (New Haven and London: Yale University Press, 1957).
83. Among his other titles are "Our Well-Beloved Secretary-General," "The Great Son of Africa," "The Liberator of Oppressed People," "The Terror of International Imperialism, Colonialism, and Neo-Colonialism," "The Doctor of Revolutionary Sciences" (*Africa Contemporary Record*, 1974–75, p. B 659).

Somewhat like Mao and other political saints, he seems to believe that political ideology is a form of knowledge that can speak to matters requiring not only political but also economic, technical, and even practical solutions.

To disobey Touré, or to be so accused, is very likely to be subjected to an arbitrary trial in a "people's court" and to be punished, often severely, by his agents. In a 1972 report the International Commission of Jurists found reason to believe that in Touré's Guinea "arbitrary arrests, detention without judgment sometimes for years, mistreatment of prisoners and torturing of detainees have become daily practices."[84] All punishment is carried out in the name of "the people," but there is little question that it is the policy of an insecure regime and ruler. Over the course of Touré's tenure it has been noted that the use of ideology has undergone a shift away from the control of groups and classes and toward the control of individuals.[85] In a climate of political apprehension, all individuals constitute a potential threat, temptation is everywhere, and nothing less than total vigilance and loyalty is required. Touré himself has remarked that

> subversion is not a material fact that one can show people. . . . Subversion is part of one and it is in all of us. . . . Subversion inhabits every heart. . . . Of course, a cadre will never say that he has become a bourgeois. But it is easy to detect it in his manner of speaking, . . . in the way he behaves himself in regard to the people. Of course, all this denounces him without his realizing.[86]

On this undoubtedly totalitarian view, morality is subordinate to politics, and political virtue is what pleases the ruler.

In such a political climate, it should not be surprising that plots, alleged or genuine, have become a feature of political life. So recurrent have reports of them been that a theory that Touré "governs by plot" has emerged. Lending credibility to this view, Touré claimed in his 1971 New Year's message that "the Guinean Revolution was born and has developed within the framework of a permanent plot."[87] Since 1960, when the government announced the discovery of a French plot to overthrow it, there have been repeated revelations: the Teachers' Plot, the Traders' Plot, the Sol-

84. Quoted in Enahoro, p. 22. The personal memoir of a Frenchman, who had opted for Guinean citizenship and was a personal friend of the President, attesting to torture on the instructions of the President is contained in Jean-Paul Alata, "In an African Prison: A Memoir," *Dissent* 24 (Fall 1977): 418–24. Amnesty International has also reported on major human rights violations by the Guinean government; see *West Africa* 3180 (26 June 1978): 1242.
85. Johnson, "Sékou Touré and the Guinean Revolution," p. 360.
86. Ibid., p. 361.
87. Quoted in Ladipo Adamolekun, *Afriscope* 5, 3 (March 1975): 45.

diers' Plot, the Plot of the *Loi Cadre*, the Mercenary Invasion, the Foulah Plot. Each has been accompanied by political and governmental purges, giving rise to the view that the desire of the ruler to purge is the proximate cause of the plots.[88]

Every new plot has claimed its victims—many of them high-ranking party, military, or governmental officials, some of them the highest ranking. Of the seventeen original political colleagues who constituted the membership of the PDG Political Bureau in 1958, only six were surviving in 1976: "The Revolution in Guinea has devoured its children at an alarming rate."[89] Undoubtedly the most serious "plot" so far was the 1970 invasion of Guinean exiles, launched from neighboring colonial Guinea-Bissau and supported by the Portuguese authorities, which had the combined goals of eliminating Guinea-Bissau's Amílcar Cabral, whose headquarters were then in Conakry, and of overthrowing Touré's regime. The invasion failed to achieve either goal, but the episode resulted in the most extensive and severe reprisals that Touré has yet meted out. In the show trials that followed, the National Assembly was declared a People's Tribunal and each Deputy was instructed by Touré to "act as a loyal interpreter of the people's demands." Acting as judge and jury, every member ended his speech with thanks to "Comrade and Brother Ahmed Sékou Touré, the Responsable Suprême de la Révolution, for trusting him and giving him the opportunity to show his allegiance to the Party and to the Enlightened and Faithful Servant of the People."[90] In compliance with the ruler's instructions, ninety-one of the accused were condemned to death, sixty-eight to life imprisonment. Those sentenced were publicly hanged in Conakry and other towns "in a kind of PDG carnival atmosphere."[91]

Probably the second most serious episode of this kind was the "Foulah Plot" of 1976—so named after the largest ethnic group in the country (the Fulani), whose leaders Touré alleged were engaged in a conspiracy against him. This "plot" is of particular interest because the ruler of Guinea has almost always demonstrated a kind of political prudence that Machiavelli would have admired by providing ethnic groups with representation in his government roughly in proportion to their political importance—a

88. There is much in the language and logic of politics to commend this view, as we have tried to show in our general discussion of "plots" in chapter 2 above. Such an explanation is rejected by some Marxist scholars, who seek a deeper explanation in an analysis of the historical-sociological forces that move political events from the subterranean depths of society. See, for example, Rivière, ch. 4.

89. *West Africa* 3089 (13 September 1976): 1315.

90. Kaba, "Guinean Politics," p. 33.

91. Ibid.; see also Rivière, p. 136.

policy that was abandoned, at least temporarily, in the Fall of 1976, when Touré dismissed the Fulani representatives from his government, accusing them (among other things) "of not being proper Guineans since they have only been in the country for four hundred years!"[92] The former secretary-general of the OAU and leading Fulani politician Diallo Telli was accused by his old comrade-in-arms Touré of instigating the conspiracy. Telli was subsequently executed for his alleged complicity. *West Africa* commented wryly:

> M. Sékou Touré's detractors have long claimed that he "governs by plot" and, indeed, the Stalinist language in which these conspiracies are described and denounced does give them uncomfortable associations. In the present instance, moreover, there are several disquieting indications that the "May 13 [Foulah] Plot" may not have been a plot at all.[93]

Like other despots, Touré has built up "a formidable police and intelligence *apparat*,"[94] which he has used to spy on his own followers, including some leading members of the PDG. However, like a political saint, Touré insists on identifying political enemies in the name of higher principles: "the revolution," "the people," "socialism." He has sought to place his theory of the permanent plot (and of political evil more generally) within the overall framework of his theory of revolution: "Every revolution creates its own counter-revolution."[95] Touré seems to understand as well as any religious or political saint ever has that the greatest power of rhetoric is its negative power to expose threats to the moral community.[96] In speeches and in his published writings, he regularly pronounces on the counter-revolutionary threat to Guinea presented by subversive forces at home and abroad. The vocabulary of "plots" and "conspiracy," of "internal enemies" and "fifth columns," is intrinsic to such a rhetoric.[97] To it Touré has added the stock-in-trade terms of the Marxist-Leninist rhetorician: the enemies of the Guinean revolution and its people are the foreign "imperialists," the "neo-colonialists," the domestic "petit-bourgeoisie" and "lumpenbourgeoisie," the "stooges of imperialism and neo-colonialism," and the pressure for "embourgeoisement" which always threatens. Not content with the evocative power of

92. *West Africa* 3090 (20 September 1976): 1361.
93. Ibid., pp. 1361–62.
94. Johnson, "Sékou Touré and the Guinean Revolution," p. 357.
95. Ibid., p. 358.
96. Rivière sees Touré as the master "African rhetorician" who uses language to evoke support for his regime (p. 90).
97. Lansine Kaba, "Rhetoric and Reality in Conakry," *Africa Report* 23, 3 (May–June 1978): 43–47.

such terms to arouse the anger and vigilance of the people in an extensively Moslem culture, Touré has drawn analogies between the Prophet Muhammad and his own rule while denouncing the "invading spectre of Satan" represented by petit-bourgeois elements. We do not know how successful such rhetoric has been in influencing public opinion in Guinea, but it seems certain that the climate of suspicion has been heightened by it.

In a famous essay, Michael Oakeshott likens politics to cooking: both are practical activities, the knowledge of which can only be gained from experience. Political education no more than a culinary education can be obtained simply by reading ideological texts or cookbooks.[98] By their actions, most of the rulers we have studied in this book would appear to agree with Oakeshott. However, the rulers we have considered in this chapter would disagree: they have placed their faith in ideology, not in experience. Touré has been perhaps the most ideological of them all. He has demonstrated his persistent unwillingness to change his view of reality in the face of practical difficulties, as unsound economic policies have only too clearly revealed. His faith in socialism, as befits any faith seriously held, has remained immune to empirical test. Even though similar socialist policies had proved unsuccessful in the past, he has promoted economic statism and collectivization through attacks on local markets and trade. But while in the sphere of economic policy he has continued to dogmatically assert his socialist convictions, in the sphere of personal power politics he has been a complete realist. To an unusual degree he has combined ideological faith and *realpolitik*. He has used political power to attack economic problems on all fronts save the rapidly expanding enclave of foreign mining investment, where his political position might be seriously endangered. He has invited massive foreign investment in Guinea's enormous bauxite deposits—containing two-thirds of the entire world's known reserves—in canny recognition of the fact that his political power can only be enhanced thereby. Johnson has commented on this point:

> It may be that Guinea can only construct a socialist society through the good offices of the multinational aluminum corporations. . . . The world commodity boom has seen the bauxite price almost treble between 1973 and 1976. As a result the normal chronic Guinean balance of payments deficit has been transformed into a growing surplus since 1974 with some 9 million tonnes of bauxite being exported each year. Current plans allow this figure to rise by 1982 to 22 million tonnes. Under such

98. Michael Oakeshott, "Political Education," in *Philosophy, Politics and Society*, 1st series, ed. Peter Laslett (Oxford: Basil Blackwell, 1956), pp. 1–21.

circumstances the country can afford even a prolonged period of disorganized socialist experiment elsewhere in the economy. And Guinea's
other mineral wealth has not begun to be tapped, providing an almost
infinite safety valve for the regime if it wishes to auction off concessions
to generate extra revenue.[99]

In the later 1970s the ruler of Guinea encountered resistance to
his domestic power from a surprising quarter. In an ill-consid-
ered—indeed arrogant—display of ideological faith, his government implemented a decree that had the effect of abolishing
traditional rural markets by requiring peasants to deliver their
crops to government stores that were run by local party cadres who
had an eye for economic as well as political profits. The remarks of
Golan in *West Africa* are apposite:

> The traditional markets have always been a major feature of life in Af-
> rica: it is here that marriages are contracted and political gossip is passed
> on. The market is the sacred domain of the woman-trader. It is in-
> comprehensible that Sékou Touré, zealous as he might be in introducing
> revolution and socialism in his country, could have dared touch the an-
> cient institution of the village market.[100]

Despite widespread political intimidation, Guinean women engaged in mass demonstrations in Conakry and other towns to protest the shortages of basic foodstuffs and other trading commodities brought about by the policy. Their protest was also
against the "economic police"—the party cadres who employed
intimidation and coercion to enforce their new political-economic
monopoly. They were confronted by armed agents of the state who
broke up the demonstrations with violence, including some killings. As reported by Golan:

> The number of women who marched in Conakry last August [1977] is
> not officially known, but they are reported to have been many thousands.
> . . . The shock was unprecedented. This time the dead were not politi-
> cians accused of being "agents of imperialism" or "mercenaries in the
> service of international capitalism." The dead were the salt of the earth,
> the root of Sékou Touré's power. The news spread like fire, and soon the
> President had to admit publicly that shooting did indeed take place. . . .
> It is reported from Conakry that the events of that day had a shattering
> effect on the emotional Sékou Touré.[101]

Evidently these events did not seriously affect the power position of Touré and his regime. While his economic policies have

99. R. W. Johnson, "Guinea," in *West African States: Failure and Promise: A
Study in Comparative Politics*, ed. John Dunn (Cambridge: Cambridge University
Press, 1978), p. 59.
100. Tamar Golan, "Returning to the Fold," *West Africa* 3172 (1 May 1978): 843–
44.
101. Ibid.

been as misguided and damaging as those of Keita and Nkrumah, Touré alone has managed to survive. This may be due in part to the windfall of foreign investment benefits, but part is due to Touré's sense and use of personal power. Guinean exiles who may be looking forward to the day when they can return to their country have not been encouraged that that day will soon arrive. If the events of the past two decades are any guide, Touré will rule for a considerable time yet. Indeed, in 1979 he was still a relatively young man (aged 57). Considering his age in comparison with such African leaders as Houphouët-Boigny and Senghor (who were a generation older when they assumed power), he has the best chance of becoming Black Africa's longest surviving founder-ruler. Touré has given no indication that he wants to prepare the way for a successor. Indeed, his despotic rule suggests that no successor will be groomed and that his passing will create a political crisis in the state.

Julius K. Nyerere, Tanzania

Julius K. Nyerere, the socialist president of Tanzania, provides one of the best contemporary African illustrations of the importance of men and ideas as factors in historical change, of history not as "destiny and necessity" but as "chance and contingency."[102] He is an example of a ruler who recognizes that considerable structural impediments and constraints stand in the way of planned, socialist-inspired change in Africa, but who believes that appropriate actions can be taken to rationally deal with these obstacles. Nyerere offers the student of African rulers and regimes an example of a leader whose personal ideals will have made a significant difference not only to personal relations of power in the state, but also to social relations in the wider society. Nyerere's presence and ideas have made Tanzania in 1980 considerably different, socially and economically, from what it was in 1961, when he first assumed power, or even in 1967, when his government embarked upon a course of agrarian socialism that entailed fundamental change in rural Tanzanian society and economy.[103] There is no question that there are still major continuities in the institu-

102. Gordon Leff, *The Tyranny of Concepts: A Critique of Marxism,* 2nd ed. (London: Merlin Press, 1969), p. 94. Nyerere thus provides an example of the "paradox" of socialist actors in history illustrating the liberal theory of history.
103. For a digest of studies on Tanzanian socialism, see Lionel Clifle and John Saul, eds., *Socialism in Tanzania: An Interdisciplinary Reader,* 2 vols. (Nairobi: East African Publishing House, 1972).

tions and organizations of Tanzanian society, and in the habits, attitudes, and beliefs of its peoples. The past still weighs heavily on the present. Tanzania is still overwhelmingly rural, economically backward, and poor, but its poverty has been rearranged, so to speak, within a deliberately designed, politically constructed framework of rural settlements in which the socialist principle of community need rather than private or familial want has been the goal in governing relationships of production. The vast majority of the rural population has been resettled from family homesteads to village settlements; however, only a few qualify to be called *ujamaa vijijini* settlements ("village socialism" or "rural socialism").[104]

What may be most important about the intervention of Nyerere in the historical evolution of Tanzania is what he has succeeded in preventing from happening. Without Nyerere and the socialist party-state apparatus he has fashioned in hopes of implementing his socialist doctrines, Tanzania may very well have gone the way of many African countries who have been more inclined to accommodate themselves to than to seek to change the economic conditions established under colonialism. Because of certain strategic and structural disadvantages, Tanzania without Nyerere would likely have been a less successful version of "free enterprise" Kenya.[105]

Nyerere has been sub-Saharan Africa's most acclaimed political Prophet and perhaps the best example of the moral agent in political history. Of the many commentators on his rule, perhaps none has captured its character, at least in the late 1960s, as well as Cranford Pratt:

> He is not just the servant of his people. He has always been a leader with strong convictions about his people's needs. Nyerere has been, above all, a teacher, a *mwalimu*. He is a teacher of a special sort. He is a teacher of morality. However, Nyerere is not just a *mwalimu*. He is a *mwalimu-in-power*—a moral teacher who is also a political leader with a great deal of authority and power.[106]

104. Dean E. McHenry, Jr., *Tanzania's Ujamaa Villages: The Implementation of a Rural Development Strategy* (Berkeley: Institute of International Studies, 1979); Clyde R. Ingle, *From Village to State in Tanzania: The Politics of Rural Development* (Ithaca and London: Cornell University Press, 1972); and Goran Hyden, *Beyond Ujamaa in Tanzania: Underdevelopment and an Uncaptured Peasantry* (Berkeley and Los Angeles: University of California Press, 1980).

105. For a comparison of the divergence, see "Back to Back: A Survey of Kenya and Tanzania," *The Economist*, March 11, 1978, pp. 3–15.

106. Cranford Pratt, *The Critical Phase in Tanzania 1945–1968: Nyerere and the Emergence of a Socialist Strategy* (Cambridge: Cambridge University Press, 1976), p. 256. See also William Edgett Smith, *Nyerere of Tanzania* (Nairobi: Transafrica Publishers, 1974).

Nyerere is a teacher of socialist morality—and of a socialism strongly infused with Christian ethics. In the eyes of many he has become the moral leader of Africa, and to some extent of the Third World as a whole.

In keeping with his moral leadership, Nyerere has often placed principles before interests, ideals before power, broader interests before narrower ones. Like Nkrumah, he has seen African independence as ultimately indivisible. Speaking at the United Nations General Assembly at the time of Tanzania's independence in 1961, he declared: "We who are free have absolutely no right to sit comfortably and counsel patience to those who do not enjoy their freedom."[107] Nyerere became a leading spokesman for the cause of African revolutionary movements in southern Africa. He came to believe that there could be no compromise whatsoever with regimes whose supremacist political doctrines were fundamentally racialist—that such doctrines and the practices to which they gave rise made force both necessary and just. In African affairs over a period of two decades he has consistently stood on his principles, even when they have been far from popular, such as his recognition of Biafra in 1968 and his early public condemnation of Idi Amin's regime in Uganda. Nyerere has been a man of moral actions as well. After independence, Dar es Salaam became a center for political refugees from southern Africa, and Tanzania a staging area for FRELIMO operations against the Portuguese across the southern border in Mozambique. Nyerere brought about the union of Tanganyika and Zanzibar in April 1964 to form the United Republic of Tanzania. When the East African Community (Kenya, Tanzania, Uganda) collapsed in 1977, only Nyerere among the three East African rulers lamented its passing. In September 1972 he defied continental African opinion by allowing Tanzania to be used as a staging area for what turned out to be an abortive invasion of Amin's Uganda. Even more dramatically, in seeking to punish Amin for his occupation and destruction of a small region of Tanzania west of Lake Victoria, Nyerere moved his army against Amin's forces in late November 1978, and ultimately brought the tyrant and his regime down in April 1979, but at a crippling cost to the Tanzanian economy of some $500 million.

It would be a profound misconception to believe that the ruler of Tanzania has had no interest in *realpolitik*, however. As Pratt and other commentators have pointed out, he has demonstrated an acute understanding of power and a willingness to use it. But his

107. Julius K. Nyerere, *Freedom and Unity/Uhuru na Umoja* (Dar es Salaam: Oxford University Press, 1966), p. 152.

conception of state power, as revealed in both his writings and his actions, is positivist: power is to be used, in the final analysis, not for domination but for political construction and societal transformation. Without doubt it is the socialist conception of the mission of the state and the actions to achieve it that have attracted such a remarkable interest in the "Tanzanian experiment."[108] For many intellectuals, statesmen, and scholars, Nyerere's socialist experiment was until at least the early 1970s a beacon of hope—for some almost the only hopeful and worthy political and social experiment to be found anywhere in the entire sub-Saharan region.

In exploring Nyerere's theory and practice of governance in Tanzania, it is first necessary to consider his overriding moral and social goals. He is a socialist, but not a Marxist. His socialism reveals a blend of Christian ethics, particularly evident in his belief in the doctrine of "needs" and in good works. It reveals also a kind of African Fabianism, in which questions of morals and even politics, once a course of action has been agreed upon, are reduced to "administration" and practical "implementation" and "efficiency." His moral-political goals are the Christian-socialist goals of distributive or social justice and the Fabian and economistic targets of social production. The two are compatible insofar as the social product is distributed in accordance with social need, not private wants or power.

For Nyerere, the choice of socialism in the contemporary historical context of African underdevelopment and powerlessness is a rational choice. We might say that it is "structurally rational," as opposed to "instrumentally rational," in that it aims to change the structural framework of underdevelopment, not merely to gain incremental material improvement. In Nyerere's view only socialism can be chosen by the rational agent who believes in the ultimate values of African freedom (from neo-colonial power and economic entanglements) and human dignity and well-being (enabling personal and social fulfillment).[109] The concern for the promotion of these ultimate values of negative collective freedom (of Africans and Tanzanians) *from* foreign domination and exploita-

108. John Lonsdale, "The Tanzanian Experiment," *African Affairs* 67, 269 (October 1968): 330–44. For a commentary of the issues and a critique of the terms employed by analysts, see P. F. Nursey-Bray, "Tanzania: The Development Debate," *African Affairs* 79, 314 (January 1968): 55–78.

109. Julius K. Nyerere: "The Rational Choice," in *Freedom and Development/ Uhuru na Maendeleo* (London, Oxford, New York: Oxford University Press, 1973), pp. 379–90, and *Ujamaa: Essays on Socialism* (Dar es Salaam: Oxford University Press, 1968).

tion and positive individual freedom *for* personal fulfillment informs all of Nyerere's public policies and actions.[110] For him they represent not only goals but also conditions for the effective realization of material equality based on human needs (equality of result) and material progress based on collective work. Nyerere's speeches and published writings reveal, in a most striking way, the moral vocabulary of human "needs" and the managerialist vocabulary of cooperative "work" and organized "production." These are his passions, and he speaks and writes of them ceaselessly.

Since independence Nyerere has undertaken to reconstruct the Tanzanian state prior to creating a new social and economic order. He has taken steps to build first the Tanganyika African National Union (TANU) and since 1977 the new ruling party, Chama Cha Mapinduzi (CCM), into an effective party with a mass base of support—that is, into the supreme agency of the Tanzanian state.[111] He has also placed much emphasis on redesigning and hopefully strengthening the state apparatus of public administration. During the early years of independence, Nyerere succeeded in bringing Tanzania through its most "critical phase" of state-building. First he laid the groundwork for a purposeful, relatively reliable and responsible party-state.[112] Tanzania was reconstituted into a "one-party democracy" in 1965, and by 1969 sovereignty had been transferred from Parliament to the party.[113] Measures were adopted to insure that the powers, privileges, and responsibilities of TANU leaders correspond with the concept of socialism; most notable was the adoption of a "Leadership Code" contained within *The Arusha Declaration and TANU's Policy on Socialism and Self-Reliance* (1967), which gave new direction and impetus to socialism in Tanzania. Public men and women were made subject to new collectivist standards of political and moral conduct.

110. For an elaboration of "negative" and "positive" freedom, see Isaiah Berlin, "Two Concepts of Liberty," in *Four Essays on Liberty* (London and New York: Oxford University Press, 1969).

111. In 1977 Nyerere achieved a long-held ambition when TANU and Zanzibar's Afro-Shirazi Party (ASP) voluntarily merged and a new ruling party—the CCM (the Revolutionary Party), which was formally constituted on February 5—replaced them. In April 1977 a new and permanent constitution for Tanzania recognized the supremacy of the CCM. See *Africa Contemporary Record*, 1977–78, pp. B 402–4.

112. Pratt, pt. 2; and Henry Bienen, *Tanzania: Party Transformation and Economic Development* (Princeton: Princeton University Press, 1967).

113. William Tordoff, *Government and Politics in Tanzania* (Nairobi: East African Publishing House, 1967); Lionel Cliffe, ed., *One Party Democracy: The 1965 Tanzania General Elections* (Nairobi: East African Publishing House, 1967); Okwudiba Nnoli, *Self-Reliance and Foreign Policy in Tanzania: The Dynamics of the Diplomacy of a New State, 1961 to 1971* (New York and Lagos: NOK Publishers, 1978).

This is a distinctive and critically important Tanzanian goal in state-building. It is Nyerere's personal goal, and it is difficult to believe that it would have been seriously pursued without him.

The political and economic analyst must accord an important role to Tanzanian public policy in the initial success of state-building. Tanzania is among those African states whose social and economic policies are "real" in the sense of having genuine substantive effects on the society and economy, intended as well as unintended. (In many of the more corrupt and patronage-ridden personal regimes, "policy" is unlikely to escape unscathed from the governmental apparatus. This is a general problem of all governments, but underdeveloped governments, and certainly many African ones, exhibit the problem in a particularly noteworthy way.) The Tanzanian regime has created the conditions for applied social and economic sciences with an interest in policy rationality and effectiveness. (In more personalized governments these sciences are largely irrelevant simply because of government incapability.)

Following the Arusha Declaration, the government embarked upon a policy to nationalize the "commanding heights" of the economy. Major financial, commercial, and manufacturing enterprises, many of them foreign owned or the property of Tanzania's Asian minority, were taken over by the state. The usual problems of finding sufficient managerial expertise ensued after the takeover, creating the related problems of organizational ineffectiveness and lack of accountability.Compromises had to be made. Owners and managers of newly nationalized firms were often asked to stay on as public managers until Africans could take over. But after a decade, major economic problems continued to plague some of these nationalized enterprises, and Nyerere was prepared to encourage private industry to increase production of essential goods.[114]

Nyerere has been consistently critical of party leaders who do not enthusiastically and fully abide by the party leadership code, as well as of public officials for their corruption and venality and of state managers and workers for their lack of dedication, effort, and care. Perhaps his most remarkable and candid comments on this subject were in the review in 1977 of the decade since the Arusha Declaration, in which he analyzed many of the problems of making state socialism work.[115] The "root" problem was identi-

114. *Africa Contemporary Record*, 1977-78, pp. B 404-5. The technical ineffectiveness of African managers has been a frequent subject of presidential criticism

115. Nyerere, *The Arusha Declaration Ten Years After*, esp. ch. 3, "Our Mistakes and Failures," pp. 27-48. The remaining quotes in this paragraph are from this document.

fied as "our failure to understand, and to apply to our own activities, the concept of 'Self-Reliance.' " "Corrupt officials" were
seen as "more dangerous than the honest man who keeps a private
shop." Ministries were criticized for their tendency to "over-
spend" in disregard of the severe budgetary constraints faced by
the government and for "opportunistically" seeking an unjustified
share of the budget. The Rural Development Bank was issuing
loans that were not being repaid, with the prospect that its capital
would soon be "exhausted." State enterprises were operating far
below capacity, sometimes at less than 50 percent of actual capacity, and "management" was condemned for its preoccupation with
privilege and lack of initiative and enterprise in seeking to develop
markets for products. "Workers" also were criticized for their
slackness, inability, and indiscipline: "[W]e have virtually eliminated the discipline of fear; it is quite hard for a manager or em-
ployer to dismiss a worker, or even suspend or fine him for
dereliction of duty." Government itself was criticized for increasing its share of the national income from 10.9 percent in 1967 to
16 percent in 1975, and for allocating the great bulk of its funds
for recurrent expenditures, mainly on salaries and wages: "This is
absurd. . . . This kind of thing must not continue." Nyerere thus
presents us with a glimpse into his own civic virtue and into the
problems that must arise in a socialist state when the ideals of
public service and sacrifice for the common good are confronted
with ordinary human failings.

A major challenge—if not the major one—has been the government's aim of reorganizing rural agricultural society and socializing what might be called the "commanding depths" of the
economy. Between 1967 and 1977 the rural population of Tanzania grew from 11 to 14 million, and during the same period the
percentage residing in rural villages (rather than scattered homesteads) increased from less than 5 to over 90 percent. An astonish-
ing 70 percent of those resettled moved between 1974 and 1976.[116]

How was this large-scale resettlement accomplished? According to Nyerere, the movement was overwhelmingly voluntary. He
admits to the occasional use of force and has called for compensation to people who had to leave better housing behind, but he has
commented that "11 million people could not have been moved by
force in Tanzania; we do not have the physical capacity for such

116. See Dean E. McHenry, Jr., "Tanzania: The Struggle for Rural Socialism,"
in *Socialism in Sub-Saharan Africa: A New Assessment*, ed. Rosberg and Callaghy,
pp. 42–43; Michael F. Lofchie, "Agrarian Socialism in the Third World: The Tanzanian Case," *Comparative Politics* 8, 3 (April 1976): 479–99; Nyerere, *The Arusha
Declaration Ten Years After*, pp. 41–42.

forced movement, any more than we have the desire for it."[117] For Nyerere, the operative motivations in the great majority of cases were a "rational hope" for improved living conditions abetted by some "persuasion and a little help from TANU and the administration."[118]

Some observers claim that while both personal incentives and values were indeed involved, during the period of the greatest movement of people there was a "concentrated use of persuasion, inducements, and compulsion" by party and state agents—police, militia, and army personnel and equipment—in order to get the job done.[119] According to Lofchie (and McHenry would seem to agree), the goal of rural resettlement was so central and critical to the overall policy of *ujamaa* socialism in Tanzania that force had to be used if voluntarism was lacking, and Nyerere had to acquiesce privately to its employment while entering a public disclaimer against its widespread use (probably sincerely believing that the Tanzanian state lacked the coercive capability to compel large-scale resettlement).[120]

It is impossible to determine with any accuracy the effectiveness of methods of persuasion, but if they had been completely effective, nothing else would have been required. Yet incentives appeared to be important; what Nyerere called the "hope" for better living conditions was, according to some observers, translated into the "promise" of such conditions upon arrival in the resettlement areas. It might be argued that since these often were "collective goods," such as clean water, to promise them was not inconsistent with the socialist principles of the program. However, these goods were very likely perceived as offered by the government to individuals, which gave them the character of "free" goods—hardly a firm foundation upon which to build a socialist economy. In addition to such incentives, coercion does appear to have been used, but the basic point to establish in considering its importance is not whether Nyerere's claim was valid that the Tanzanian government did not possess the physical capacity to apply massive compulsion to achieve the resettlement, but rather whether the *credible threat* of coercion was sufficient. McHenry has clearly shown that the credible threat of coercion was operative in the Tanzanian experiment with rural resettlement: "The direct application of force to a very large proportion of the population was unnecessary be-

117. Ibid., p. 42.
118. Ibid.
119. McHenry, "Tanzania: The Struggle for Rural Socialism," pp. 44, 45–47; Lofchie, "Agrarian Socialism," p. 496.
120. Ibid.

cause the determination of the government soon became widely known."[121] Lofchie observes that "coercion . . . is the great conundrum of Tanzanian rural policy. Most authors . . . avoid the question altogether."[122]

Instead of increasing national production, the agrarian program led to increased subsidies.[123] The villages were designed to be self-reliant and self-sufficient, but they required considerable external state funding and support services—repeating some of the experiences with a discredited program of highly capitalized village development in the early 1960s. The extension of the scheme was correlated with a marked decline in overall agricultural production, including a temporary but important decline in the production of foodstuffs. (It should be noted that a drought contributed to the decline in foodstuff production.) In 1974 "Tanzania's food crisis was so severe that its population . . . was in imminent peril of widespread famine."[124] Food had to be imported in large quantities by the government and paid for with funds and credits that otherwise might have gone into social or productive investment. Lofchie comments:

> The ujamaa program has placed the Tanzanian government in virtual receivership to its foreign donors. . . . The great historical irony of agrarian socialism in Tanzania is that a program motivated by the principle of national self-reliance and intended to help the country sever its ties of dependence with the international market economy has ended by producing greater dependence than ever before.[125]

What went wrong? Along with this question the socialist critics have also asked (repeating Lenin): What is to be done?[126] The "production socialists" (Marxists) have argued that the program not only was badly managed by the state bureaucracy and lacked a committed body of cadres dedicated to making it work, but also was undermined and perhaps even sabotaged by bureaucrats and their allies from among the old progressive farmer class—the so-called kulaks. In a more theoretical vein, one of the Marxist com-

121. McHenry, "Tanzania: The Struggle for Rural Socialism," p. 47.
122. Lofchie, "Agrarian Socialism," p. 495.
123. Michael F. Lofchie, "Agrarian Crisis and Economic Liberalisation in Tanzania," *Journal of Modern African Studies* 16, 3 (1978): 453–58. For a critical account of this article, see Philip Raikes, "Agrarian Crisis and Economic Liberalisation in Tanzania: A Comment," ibid., 17, 2 (1979): 309–16.
124. Ibid., p. 452.
125. Lofchie, "Agrarian Socialism," p. 486.
126. Jonathan S. Barker, "The Debate on Rural Socialism in Tanzania," in *Towards Socialism in Tanzania*, ed. Bismark U. Mwansasu and Cranford Pratt (Toronto and Buffalo: University of Toronto Press, 1979), pp. 95–124, and Frances Hill, "Ujamaa: African Socialist Productionism in Tanzania," in *Socialism in the Third World*, ed. Desfosses and Levesque, pp. 216–51.

mentators has warned that the "road to socialist reconstruction [is always] difficult," with numerous "obstacles" and "contradictions,"[127] which, to be overcome and resolved, require of the socialist militant the kind of understanding and dedication of which Gramsci wrote: "Pessimism of the intelligence; optimism of the will."[128] The "production liberals," on the other hand, have called for an increased emphasis on individual/family incentives and less reliance on collectivist organization and goals. They are, as Barker comments, "skeptical of the effectiveness of communal or collective production in agriculture" and "place their bets on the self-improvement motive of families and individuals."[129] Such a view was expressed as early as 1969 by the French agronomist René Dumont, who warned the Tanzanian government against relying wholly on collectivism in agriculture: "It is not possible to omit, without major inconvenience, the stage of the 'progressive farmer.' . . . Development requires that people can *become rich* to a certain extent by hard and prolonged *work* and by *economy*."[130] As both Lofchie and Barker point out, the Marxists fear that the adoption of such a strategy could reinvigorate a progressive farmer class and end by defeating the socialist experiment as a whole.

In all of this discussion on what went wrong in the experiment, Lofchie has been virtually alone in challenging Nyerere's assumption that traditional African agriculture is a form of collective farming, and that the new collectives would be congruent with indigenous farming principles and practices. Apart from land ownership, which rested on the institution of usufruct, traditional African farming is based upon the individual, peasant practices of separate families cultivating their fields and appropriating crops for their own uses. In consequence of this discrepancy between the old ways and the new, serious disruptions and uncertainties attended the massive movement of rural people from the old system into the new, with major temporary losses in production.[131]

127. J. S. Saul, "Planning for Socialism in Tanzania: The Socio-Political Context," in *Towards Socialist Planning; Tanzania Studies No. 1*, Uchumi Editorial Board (Dar es Salaam: Tanzania Publishing House, 1974), pp. 1–25. See also Issa G. Shivji, *Class Struggles in Tanzania* (New York and London: Monthly Review Press, 1976).

128. Quoted in ibid.

129. Barker, "The Debate on Rural Socialism in Tanzania," p. 96.

130. *Tanzanian Agriculture After the Arusha Declaration: A Report by Professor René Dumont* (Dar es Salaam: Tanzania Government Printer, 1969), pp. 5, 34 (original emphasis).

131. Lofchie, "Agrarian Socialism," p. 489; see also Lofchie, "Agrarian Crisis," pp. 451–75.

While Tanzania had experienced serious difficulty in attracting foreign aid for its first five-year development plan (1964–69), the post-Arusha strategy of rural socialism was supported by substantial foreign assistance, particularly from the West. Under Nyerere's leadership, Tanzania was one of the few African governments that appeared to be responsible both financially and sociopolitically: it honored its financial obligations, and it was seriously endeavoring to reduce the poverty of its rural people. Here was a sincere African experiment in rural development that could attract the support of Western creditors, particularly the World Bank under Robert McNamara, who in the early 1970s wanted to underwrite programs in the Third World that would promote rural welfare and equity with growth. Nyerere's policies corresponded well with this doctrine of international aid. Nyerere himself was attractive: a responsible African leader dedicated to ameliorating the poverty and misery of his people according to his socialist lights. While support was high before the agricultural crisis, it increased during and afterwards as international altruism replaced economics as the grounds for extending aid to Tanzania, making its government and people among the most generously supported in the entire Third World. In 1975 total net aid was some $300 million, or $20 per capita;[132] in 1977, 59 percent of the development budget was financed by foreign assistance, while in 1978 it was 55 percent, almost half of which was in outright grants. Despite the severe economic difficulties resulting from Nyerere's agrarian social theories (and to some extent even because of these difficulties), the experiment continued to receive international support. Nyerere may well have been Tanzania's most important economic asset.

Nyerere himself ended his 1977 "Review of Arusha" speech with the statement that Tanzania's "problems can be solved" because they are problems of means and of will, not of principles or goals: "In the coming decade we must build on what we have achieved. We must increase our *discipline,* our *efficiency,* and our *self-reliance.*" Tanzanians must remember that "There is a time for planting and a time for harvesting. I am afraid for us it is still a time for planting."[133] The possibility that the overall conception might be flawed is never raised: it is a matter of ideological faith, of doctrine, and doctrines are not discarded simply because of difficulties.

132. Ibid., p. 455; see also Hyden, *Beyond Ujamaa in Tanzania*, p. 99.
133. Nyerere, *The Arusha Declaration Ten Years After*, p. 51.

The enormous costs of the war to bring down the Amin regime, declining export earnings, increased oil imports, renewed drought, and serious management problems all led at the end of the 1970s to a serious economic crisis. However, there was no evidence of a major retreat from Nyerere's socialist policies despite growing criticism by Tanzania's Western aid donors.[134] Indeed, Tanzania rejected International Monetary Fund assistance in late 1979 on the grounds that it implied moving back from socialism. Nyerere stated: "People who think Tanzania will change her cherished policies of Socialism and self-reliance because of the current difficulties are wasting their time."[135]

Nyerere's doctrine can be appraised in the light of its consequences. It is especially interesting that Nyerere himself has justified the Tanzanian experiment with socialism (1967–77) not so much by what it achieved as by what it prevented from taking place. What were the evils, in Nyerere's view, that Tanzania avoided? In a word, *capitalism,* and what capitalism implies in terms of economic exploitation and control: hardship and misery for the many, privilege and luxury for the few; a widening and hardening of class formations; control by an African middle class and its foreign economic allies.

> All these evils and many others which we are now spared, would have happened in Tanzania had we not adopted the Arusha Declaration. . . . Capitalism was beginning. And it was beginning with the leadership. . . . Fortunately, these things, this "creation of an African middle class," had not gone very far. Our leaders had begun to think that individual riches were part of the perquisites of leadership; but they had not begun actually to become rich. So the Arusha Declaration came in time.[136]

How are such avoided evils, which cannot be seen because they never took place, to be explained to the ordinary Tanzanian? Here we can see Nyerere's mastery not only of a rhetoric that has appealed to intellectuals but also of a homely style that communicates with the ordinary man. He compares socialism to a vaccination:

> We are like a man who does *not* get smallpox because he has got himself vaccinated. His arm is sore and he feels sick for a while; if he has never seen what smallpox does to people he may feel very unhappy during that period, and wish that he had never agreed to the vaccination.[137]

134. *Africa Confidential* 21, 15 (July 16, 1980): 1–4.

135. Quoted in *Africa Research Bulletin: Economic, Financial and Technical Series* 16, 10 (November 30, 1979): 5302 B.

136. Nyerere, *The Arusha Declaration Ten Years After,* pp. 6–7.

137. Ibid., p. 5 (original emphasis).

Can we assume that in the late 1970s some Tanzanians felt exactly like that man?

Nyerere's claims about prevention and avoidance are not without substance. One need not accept his own normative characterization of the effects of his government's socialist policies in order to see them. From the socialist viewpoint, the significant preventive effects of socialism in Tanzania would include the following: (1) The large political-bureaucratic elite is not as privileged or burdensome as it might have been without a leadership code actively subscribed to by the ruler; members of this elite have been given less latitude to acquire wealth through politics than the elites of less puritanical regimes. (It might be noted, in passing, that the "Leadership Code" has been extended to all party members, not just leaders, but insofar as opportunities to be exploitative are probably not available to the great majority of ordinary party members, this extension must be seen as primarily symbolic.) (2) There is less class differentiation; rural socialism seems to have lessened rural class formation based on "progressive farmers" or "kulaks." (3) There has probably been less bureaucratic corruption than in many other African states, although in the latter half of the 1970s there was a sharp increase in corruption. In addition, there has been a major restructuring of rural society and economy; the policy of "villagization" has led to a significant alteration of rural social organization, at least insofar as patterns of residence are concerned, if not so much in regard to patterns of economic production and distribution.

Some of these effects can be seen as desirable from a non-socialist viewpoint. On any view—socialist, liberal, or otherwise—the creation of a more responsible and less venal political elite (even though privileged) has to be seen as a major achievement. The diminution of class divisions, however, means not only less economic exploitation by progressive farmers and entrepreneurs, but also a decrease in the material contribution that their pursuit of wealth could make to Tanzania's economy. The suppression of this entrepreneur class has probably entailed major material sacrifice for all of Tanzania's citizens insofar as they—individually and collectively—have had to bear the opportunity cost of its foregone product. An irony of the Tanzanian experiment, on this view, is that while Nyerere has complained bitterly of worker lack of discipline and managerial lack of enterprise in Tanzania's state and cooperative enterprises, he has pursued policies that have stifled these qualities in the private sector of the economy.

In summarizing the overall consequences of Nyerere's intervention in Tanzanian history, we can say that Tanzania is probably a

"more equal" society on the socialist or distributive justice definition of material equality, of equality of result, than it would have
been without his leadership: there has been some social levelling,
there is less class differentiation, and the ratio of private to public
wealth has been reduced. At the same time, there is probably less
equality on the liberal definition of equality of opportunity.
Greater controls have been placed on the acquisition and use of
property and other forms of private wealth, and the additional resources and opportunities that ambitious and industrious men
might have created had they been given the freedom have been
lost. These changes can be stated in terms of structural versus instrumental rationality: the government has promoted, with some
evident success, a policy of structural transformation, but to the
considerable neglect of considerations of instrumental rationality
and likely costs to overall productivity and prosperity.

Africa has produced fewer political saints than might have been
expected, given the extensive underdevelopment of that continent
in an age when the state has come to be looked upon as the primary, often the sole, agency of moral and material progress.
Should not the tensions between the perceived backwardness of
African countries and the desire for social progress—a progress
that has been realized elsewhere—have favored the emergence of
more prophetic leaders? Perhaps the power of the political immediate, the short run, has prevented it in all but exceptional situations. Pre-independence was one such situation, but in most
African countries post-independence elevated the political present
as the new sovereign of political conduct at the expense of the political future.

The rulers we have studied in this chapter attempted to maintain the sovereignty of the political future over their own conduct
and the activities of their governments by substituting for the goal
of political independence a greater aim: economic independence
and development with social justice. But this goal has been sovereign more in theory than in practice. Why have socialist theory
and political practice in African states been so far removed from
each other? Has it been a failure of theory or a result of the compelling pull of practice? If the political and governmental means
have been inadequate to the tasks set down by the theory, then one
must either improve the means or modify the theory. If the necessities of practice have stood in the way, then we must inquire as to
why and how this has been so.

In the cases considered in this chapter, most of the regimes have not been able to bridge the gap between practical matters of politics and administration and the socialist blueprint. Showing considerable indifference to and little aptitude for the mundane problems of government, and an inability to control the political acquisitiveness and corruption of his disciples—thereby contributing to a decline both of government effectiveness and legitimacy—Kwame Nkrumah could not maintain his grip on the state. Sékou Touré, on the other hand, has managed to survive primarily by developing despotic power and by sharing in the economic surplus produced by foreign investors, which has compensated for the losses incurred by policies that have disoriented and disrupted the indigenous economy. Julius Nyerere alone has been able to narrow the gap between the political present and the socialist future. Tanzania is the only country with the beginnings of a bridge to socialism—even though the structure is so far a makeshift and inadequate one—and millions of Tanzanians may begin to cross over it on their way from traditional agriculture to agrarian socialism. Whether the result will prove to be worth the efforts remains to be seen; experience to date has not provided much ground for optimism. But whatever the result, the point to be emphasized is that the ruler has been critically important in the effort. There is good reason to believe that without Nyerere few if any of Tanzania's current socialist undertakings would even have been attempted, let alone achieved.

6

Tyrants and
Abusive Rule

AFRICA'S states have evolved in ways unforeseen at independence, almost all becoming essentially authoritarian in character. The nature of rulership has evolved in corresponding ways. At independence a new ruler was usually one of two types: he was often a successful nationalist leader who might have possessed some charismatic or traditional legitimacy but was almost always a coalition builder. Alternatively, he was a successful revolutionary-guerrilla leader who achieved control of the state by the mobilization of force against colonial holdouts. Most of the post-independence rulers would have described themselves—and would have been described by observers—as "nationalists" and "democrats," some as "revolutionaries"—but they all claimed to represent the African people against the domination of an alien power, and most often the claims were convincing.

We have seen that the rulers of the new African states, military and civilian alike, have exhibited many of the historic preoccupations of personal rulers—especially the love of power, the desire to hold it and wield it, and to enjoy the many privileges of rule. Most often these men have been princely or autocratic rulers, sometimes they have been prophetic rulers, but in most cases they have held power with some claim to legitimacy. However, there have been a few rulers who have entered the African political stage and attempted to remain there purely by force and fraud and who have wielded power in a ruthless, cruel, and severe way. In their unconscionable and very often unspeakable actions such rulers may deservedly be called "tyrants" and their regimes "tyrannies"— ancient words that have survived in the lexicon of political life because they continue to have application. Within the orbit of general political history tyranny is a well-established, if corrupt type

234

of rule.[1] Regrettably, the Tyrant has assumed a place among Africa's contemporary rulers.

Historically, Tyrants have ruled without any pretense to legitimacy or authority, and tyranny is therefore conceived as fundamentally illegitimate and unjust government in violation of any norms or rules or understandings; it is a government whose actions conform solely to the will and power of the ruler or his agents.[2] Thus, strictly speaking, it is a mistake to consider that Tyrants enjoy "privileges" or exercise "responsibilities" or that subjects enjoy "rights" or exercise "obligations." Strauss notes that "no subject of a tyrant could have any property rights against the tyrant."[3] Such rights presume agreements and forbearances, and their absence means, *inter alia*, that a ruler and his agents are free to plunder public and private property in a state. Hence, because Tyrants possess power and the instruments of rule but not authority or legitimacy, even more than other personal rulers, the tyrannical ruler must rely upon power and fortune alone. Since he abuses his power and has many enemies, cunning and ruthlessness in the control and uses of his power are everything to him.

The key to tyranny is the relation of the Tyrant to his mercenaries, "without whom tyranny is impossible."[4] To rule oppressively and without an ideology or religion or higher value to justify the oppression—as a Tyrant does, which distinguishes tyrannical from persecutory rule—is to require an apparatus not only of oppression, but of cooperative mercenaries. The latter are particularly characteristic of tyranny because a Tyrant rules only by the combination of coercion and reward, and mercenaries cooperate for the sake of rewards. If none are forthcoming, they may desert. In addition, mercenaries may cooperate because they are implicated in the ruler's atrocities; if the ruler falls, his agents may suffer any reprisals that are meted out. Thus tyranny is a spoils system for the Tyrant's agents, who themselves are petty tyrants and abuse their power whenever the ruler's interests are not at stake.

1. The conjunction of "tyranny" and "rule" will trouble students of the history of political ideas. Traditionally "tyranny" is distinguished from "rule" insofar as rule is seen as normal and proper and tyranny as a violation of norms, a pathological departure from the normal and the accepted. Leo Strauss gave expression to the traditional view when he wrote that "tyranny is essentially a faulty political order" (*On Tyranny* [Ithaca: Cornell University Press, 1975], pp. 66–67).

2. The *Oxford English Dictionary* defines "tyranny" as "oppressive or unjustly severe government, . . . arbitrary or oppressive exercise of power, . . . harsh, severe, or unmerciful action." A "tyrant" is defined as a "ruler who exercises his power in an oppressive, unjust, or cruel manner."

3. Strauss, p. 72. 4. Ibid., p. 70.

Tyranny can be distinguished from autocracy and despotism—both ancient forms of strong personal rule—and from totalitarianism, which is quite modern. We have already observed that autocracy is characterized by the extent of personal control or mastery of the government by the ruler. Autocracy is absolute but legitimate rule. Despotism is basically the same as autocracy, but it is more oppressive. Tyranny represents the extreme of arbitrary and oppressive rule coupled with impulsiveness and cruelty on the part of the ruler and his agents. As we have noted, the Autocrat is, as it were, the proprietor of the state, and he uses the government for purposes deemed necessary and important by him. However, a notion of property involves not only proprietary rights but also duties and therefore authority. The Tyrant regards himself neither as the proprietor of the state nor its custodian. Rather, he steals the government and plunders it and society at will. Stealing is not owning or protecting. Tyrannical rule is piracy. But when the ruler is a pirate, the state in effect ceases to exist and civil society is displaced by a system akin to Hobbes's "state of nature." Under tyrannical regimes, the ruled must either befriend the ruler and his agents, purchase protection from them, or hide from them; in every case, circumspection, apprehension, and fear—most likely some combination of them—are the accompanying dispositions for survival.

Tyranny can be distinguished from totalitarianism mainly by the greater power, reach, and effectiveness of the apparatus of control available in the latter. Totalitarian government methodically exploits the technological and organizational instruments that the scientific-industrial revolution has made available to the modern state. Tyrannical government, which is pre-modern, is lacking in the technical-organizational capability of totalitarianism.[5] Totalitarian government is bureaucratic and procedure-oriented; a totalitarian state is an impressive edifice of unjust laws—for example, the contemporary government of South Africa. Nonwhites in South Africa, especially Africans, are restricted by an array of laws controlling their movements and mode of living which are totalitarian in character and structure. A large bureaucracy has been set up to administer and enforce these racially in-

5. For additional remarks on the distinction between totalitarianism and other forms of "political oppression," see Hannah Arendt, *The Origins of Totalitarianism*, 2nd ed., enlarged (New York: Meridian Books, 1972), esp. ch. 12. Totalitarian regimes sometimes have been defined as a "state within a state," which is suggestive of their organizational power (see Hans Buchheim, *Totalitarian Rule* [Middletown, Conn.: Wesleyan University Press, 1968], pp. 96–97); tyrannical regimes lack the organization and discipline to qualify for such a definition.

spired laws designed solely to maintain power in the hands of white South Africans.

Unlike totalitarianism, tyrannical government is scarcely if at all bureaucratic; rather, it operates by providing the ruler Tyrant and all the petty tyrants in his employ with a *license* to act essentially as they see fit. The lesser tyrants are constrained not by bureaucratic rules and procedures—as they are under totalitarianism—but only by their anticipation of the interest, pleasure, or displeasure of the ruler. Under tyranny the petty tyrants become as feared and hated as the ruler Tyrant—perhaps more so, since it is usually "the tyrant [who] should do the gratifying things . . . while entrusting to others the punitive actions."[6] (In practice, of course, both the Tyrant and his agents promise gratuities and threaten punishments.) Political murder is a feature of both totalitarianism and tyranny, but in the former it is typically justified by some demented ideology, whereas in the latter it is much more arbitrary and personal:

> In Amin's Uganda murder is capricious. As in Nazi Germany, people are killed for belonging to the wrong tribe, the Acholis [*sic*] and Langis [*sic*]. But a man may also "disappear" because he refused a bank loan to a soldier or drove a flashy sports car or was on a dance floor with a beautiful woman. Death is not impersonal and methodical as it was under the Third Reich: heads are smashed with sledgehammers and car axles, and other prisoners are called in to roll around in the gore and clean it up.[7]

Cabinet ministers in Idi Amin's government who attempted to question his edicts and demands found themselves brutalized, jailed, or murdered by his agents; others were fortunate enough to escape from the country.[8]

In sum, tyranny undermines the conditions of rationality, predictability, and certainty in political, social, and even economic life, contributing to the decay and threatening the destruction not only of the state but of the general social and economic welfare also. In Uganda, a once prosperous agricultural export economy (by developing country standards) was badly damaged by Amin's chaotic tyranny because the elements of trust and confidence essential to production and exchange in a market economy were seriously eroded by the unpredictable actions and oversights of the government.

6. Strauss, p. 71.

7. John Darnton, "A Tyrant Exposed," *New York Times*, November 6, 1977.

8. Samuel Decalo, *Coups and Army Rule in Africa: Studies in Military Style* (New Haven and London: Yale University Press, 1976), p. 222.

Tyranny must be distinguished from the general political fear and terror of a "revolutionary situation" as well. The rule of a Tyrant is not the same as a "reign of terror" such as occurred in Jacobin France two centuries ago, in Russia earlier in this century, or in Ethiopia following the overthrow of Emperor Haile Selassie's regime.[9] In revolutionary Ethiopia, as in revolutionary France and Russia, the political terror spawned by the revolution and the general breakdown of public authority victimized many innocent persons; in this respect a revolutionary situation is indistinguishable from tyranny. However, in theory victimization and violence in a revolutionary situation ought only to involve partisan groups and movements who are involved in a fundamental struggle over values and beliefs. Although revolutions involve power and are settled by power, they are not about power; they are about values, beliefs, theologies, and ideologies. In Ethiopia violence and killing have been widespread—perhaps more widespread than in tyrannical Uganda—but they have been accompanied by propaganda, rhetoric, and slogans that presumably represent the moral authority to justify them. The political settlement of a revolution is never portrayed as a victory of power and violence, but as a victory of right and virtue.[10] Tyrants and their agents are much less concerned with the justification of their atrocities. The governments of Francisco Macías Nguema in Equatorial Guinea and Idi Amin in Uganda seldom officially acknowledged that any political killings and torture took place; politically prominent men and women simply "disappeared" or "committed suicide." Tyrants generally tend to cover up their crimes rather than justify them. Under tyranny the possibility of causing harm to innocent parties is as great as the discretion of the Tyrant:

> Most of those killed [in Uganda] have been completely innocent of any crime. In many cases they have been picked up and summarily killed for nothing more than a whispered complaint to someone in a position of authority (who may be no more than a private or a corporal), and often for a personal grudge.[11]

Tyranny by its very nature is conducive not only to uncertainty and fear, but especially to political instability. Ultimately respon-

9. For an account of Ethiopia's revolution and pertinent references, see our discussion in chapter 3 above.

10. It should be noted that Amin at times successfully manipulated revolutionary symbols and thereby enhanced his power—for example, his notion of an "Economic War" in 1972, which included the expulsion of Asians and confiscation of their businesses.

11. *Times* (London), June 24, 1977.

sive only to the will and wile of the Tyrant and his agents, who desire to retain their power at all costs, "tyrannical government is essentially more oppressive and hence less stable than nontyrannical government."[12] The conditions of fear may become intolerable, and some men may become sufficiently desperate to take great risks, including those of plotting and attempting to assassinate the Tyrant. Even if the Tyrant reforms—which is most unlikely—he cannot erase the evil he has done or the memories of it in the minds of those who have suffered at his or his mercenaries' hands. There is a vicious circle of tyranny: the more a Tyrant persists in his rule, the more violence he must do; tyranny cannot come to an end except by the only justice inherent in it, which is the overthrow of the Tyrant and his regime—if necessary, by the killing of the Tyrant.[13]

Before we turn our attention to the tyrannical regimes that have emerged in sub-Saharan Africa since independence, it is important to reiterate that their development was unanticipated. Why have a few governments come close to tyranny and at least two true tyrannical regimes (in Equatorial Guinea and Uganda) emerged? We have neither the space nor the assembled evidence to provide a carefully researched historical answer to such a question. Rather, we want to offer a carefully considered conjectural answer that derives from our theory of personal rule.

In brief, our argument is that tyranny presents much more temptation for a personal ruler than an institutional ruler. Institutional rule, which involves the rightful and legal powers of an institutionalized and therefore a legitimate *office,* stands in the way of tyrannical actions. Personal rulers are not restrained by an institutionalized office, and they cannot be confident of the rights and privileges of office. They are dependent solely on their *personal* legitimacy and power to maintain their rule. If one is driven by the love of power and the passion to dominate, one may very well be driven to kill in order to retain power. This is tyranny. The Tyrant is not a gifted and confident ruler. He is a desperate ruler driven by an insatiable appetite for power and by a paranoid

12. Strauss, p. 77.
13. In his essay "Cowardice, Mother of Cruelty," Montaigne asked, "What makes tyrants so bloodthirsty? It is concern for their security, and the fact that their cowardly heart furnishes them with no other means of making themselves secure than by exterminating those who can injure them. . . . The first cruelties are practiced for their own sake; thence arises the fear of a just revenge, which afterwards produces a string of new cruelties, in order to stifle the first by the others" (*The Complete Essays of Montaigne,* ed. and trans. Donald M. Frame [Stanford: Stanford University Press, 1965], p. 528).

fear of the power of others; he is a man who will stop at nothing to retain power once he possesses it.[14] The Tyrant is the classical amoral ruler. In Africa (as elsewhere under regimes of personal rule) all that stands in the way of tyranny are the forbearances of the ruler and his agents and the power of others. To the extent that regimes of personal rule have arisen in sub-Saharan Africa, the temptation of tyranny has arisen also and has proved irresistible to rulers or other powerseekers lacking in the peaceful political arts.

Perhaps better than any other type of rule, tyranny illustrates a relationship appreciated in traditional political thought but sometimes lost upon the student of the modern constitutional-democratic state—namely, the maintenance of a civil society is ultimately dependent upon the conduct of government, particularly the ruler and his agents. Thus as we have argued in chapter 2, the emergence of tyranny is not primarily a matter of predisposing historical or social conditions—however important these might be—but of rulers and their cohorts. In both Equatorial Guinea and Uganda—as we shall see below—the civil condition became more and more uncertain and deteriorated as the ruler and his agents committed more and more atrocities and as the awareness of them spread. The actions and omissions of the Tyrant and his agents may appropriately be regarded as the immediate cause of first political and then social and economic deterioration in a country.

The possibility of tyranny exists in states where there is personal rule, but it is also possible that particular social characteristics can affect its emergence, making some countries less vulnerable than others. In more economically developed and complex countries the emergence of tyranny may be hindered in two related ways. First, a modern economy is dependent upon the certainty and stability of currency and market transactions and upon the institutions that make such transactions possible (a police force to protect property, a legal system for enforcing agreements and contracts, a workable system of public administration and regulation, and so on) and cannot tolerate purely arbitrary government. Second, modern interest groups such as trade unions, businessmen, cash crop farmers, or civil servants, who stand in need of stable, predictable, and consistent government, might take action against a ruler who refuses to make and keep political policy bargains. On this reasoning, tyranny would be far less damaging to

14. Our characterization of a Tyrant as an individual who has a passion for power is influenced by Albert O. Hirschman's insightful *The Passions and the Interests: Political Arguments for Capitalism Before Its Triumph* (Princeton: Princeton University Press, 1977), pt. 1.

less developed, subsistence economies, where impersonal social exchange is not critical to production and where there is little in the way of abstract capital and technical expertise (including foreign investment and assistance) to harm or frighten away. We cannot say, however, that a more developed economy will prevent tyranny: it did not in Uganda. We can only say that if a ruler is at all amenable to rational arguments, he will recognize the economic as well as the political costs of purely arbitrary rule. It is specifically rationality, and the sophistication and enlightenment that stand behind it, that did not seem to be in the possession of either Francisco Macías or Idi Amin, whose arbitrary actions largely destroyed the confidence and predictability of commercial and political life in Equatorial Guinea and Uganda respectively. As a result, there was (among other things) a marked deterioration in the productivity of the modern sectors of both economies.

A few post-independence authoritarian African governments have engaged from time to time in political practices that could be regarded as tyrannical. Perhaps the earliest intimation of tyranny was the rule of Sheikh Abeid Karume that developed on Tanzania's offshore islands of Zanzibar and Pemba following a revolution in 1964; among other things, the regime forced selected Asian and Arab women into marriages with African men—most notably Karume and members of his Revolutionary Council. Karume's rule, often in defiance of the mainland-based government, was ended in 1972 by his assassination. Elements of tyranny have been present in Burundi in the rule of Michel Micombero— especially in atrocities perpetrated in 1972. But the dominant cause of political terror was ethnic persecution, in which the government, representing one ethnic community, carried out a policy of selective genocide against members (especially leaders) of another.[15] Elements of tyranny were evident in Chad under Tombalbaye in his desperate bid to cling to power in the later years of his rule in what was becoming an ungovernable state replete with civil warfare and intense factionalism. The reign of terror in post-imperial Ethiopia in 1976–77 involved elements of tyranny—as we noted above—but the overall situation in Ethiopia better qualifies for the designation "revolutionary" because political violence and killing were justified in the name of a higher moral authority—in this case, the "Ethiopian people."

15. See René Lemarchand and David Martin, *Selective Genocide in Burundi* (London: Minority Rights Group, 1974, Report No. 20); Warren Weinstein, "Conflict and Confrontation in Central Africa: The Revolt in Burundi, 1972," *Africa Today* 19, 4 (Fall 1972): 17–37.

A highly personal and increasingly abusive regime that exhibited marked features of tyranny was Central African Republic under Jean-Bédel Bokassa, a soldier who seized power in 1966. In a world region that has exhibited more than an ordinary preoccupation of rulers with pomp and ceremony, the contrived search for grandeur by Bokassa was without rival. Perhaps more than any other contemporary African ruler, Bokassa exhibited characteristics of megalomania. His hero was Napoleon; if Bokassa could not emulate Napoleon's military feats, he could at least recreate his imperial grandeur in an African context. By personal fiat in 1976 he renamed the country the Central African Empire and installed himself in a lavish and much publicized "coronation" in 1977 as Emperor Bokassa I. In retrospect, the coronation—an extravaganza costing some twenty million dollars—may be viewed as the beginning of the end for Bokassa, for it was an event that hastened the loss of external resources and support from Western countries that heretofore had bolstered his power and position. In late 1977 the United States announced the ending of its aid in response to Bokassa's violation of human rights. Eventually the French began to withdraw their support of Bokassa—but not their *realpolitik*—not only by withholding critically important aid but also evidently by contemplating possible actions to have him removed from power (see below).[16] The coronation itself was almost universally condemned as fraudulent, ludicrous, and unconscionably expensive. In a continent that still proclaimed—albeit faintly in the 1970s—its faith in "democracy" and still more in "socialism," the "Emperor" was not only an object of derision, but a distinct embarrassment.[17] While Bokassa's coronation created a new political context in which the ruler's base of power and support was being narrowed, making his rule increasingly uncertain and capricious, other political actions of the "Emperor" were the immediate causes of his downfall.

Bokassa originally assumed power after a military coup against his cousin, President David Dacko, who had taken over the government on the eve of independence in 1959, when the country's acknowledged paramount nationalist leader, the charismatic Barthélémy Boganda, was killed in an aircraft accident. (Boganda was an uncle of both Dacko and Bokassa.) Over a decade Bokassa built up and consolidated his personal rule in what was one of Africa's more backward hinterland countries. He was by no

16. Ian Mather, "Bokassa Takes French Leave," *The Observer*, 23 September 1979.
17. See "Folie de grandeur?" *West Africa* 3153 (12 December 1977): 2499–2501.

means an unastute or ineffective practitioner of personal politics; in several respects he was a more able personal politician than Dacko. Although he had a penchant for theatrical politics, it would be misleading to view Bokassa only or even primarily as a sensation-seeking buffoon.

After the loss of support that followed Bokassa's coronation—especially a withdrawal of the aid programs and financial support of Western governments—Bokassa began to behave in a manner in character with tyranny. He became frustrated and despondent, acted erratically, impulsively, and brutally in his personal dealings with clients as well as enemies, and grew bad tempered and abusive. In 1977 Amnesty International learned that a lycée teacher and four students had been arrested for referring to the country by its former name. The teacher and three of the students were charged with crimes against the internal security of the state and with offending Emperor Bokassa; they were sentenced to ten years' imprisonment.[18] Other reports circulated, and were later confirmed, that an English journalist was arrested on the Emperor's order and personally assaulted by him.[19] In defending himself against accusations of having personally participated in human rights violations, Bokassa remarked, "I am not cruel, but sometimes a leader must exercise discipline."[20] The clearest case of tyrannical rule in Central African Empire occurred in April 1979, when schoolchildren demonstrated against Bokassa's edicts while shouting "Death to the Emperor!" Amnesty International reported that more than one hundred children were rounded up and brutally murdered for their "political offenses";[21] some witnesses claimed that Bokassa had personally participated in the massacre.[22] An additional forty people may have been executed for having provided information to an international commission of inquiry investigating atrocities.[23] The various reports underline the impulsiveness and uncontrollable anger in the actions of Bokassa, lapses of personal control, and violent explosions in his relations with individuals perceived as standing in his way. As indicated, there have been reliable accounts of Bokassa personally physically

18. "A Voice for Those in Prison," *West Africa* 3212 (5 February 1979): 199.
19. Ibid.
20. *Africa Contemporary Record: Annual Survey and Documents*; 1968–70, ed. Colin Legum and John Drysdale (London: Africa Research, 1969–70); 1970–72, ed. Colin Legum (London: Rex Collings, 1971; London: Rex Collings, and New York: Africana Publications, 1972); 1972–79, ed. Colin Legum (New York: Africana Publications, 1973–79); on Bokassa, see 1977–78, p. B 532.
21. *Africa News* 13, 13 (September 28, 1979): 8–9.
22. *San Francisco Examiner and Chronicle*, September 30, 1979.
23. *The Observer*, 23 September 1979.

abusing reporters and emissaries from powerful states—for example, "beating up" an American journalist with his gold-handled cane and attempting to strike a personal representative of President Giscard d'Estaing of France.[24] After investigating the reports of atrocities and abuses of political power in Central African Empire, a journalist for *Le Monde* wrote of Bokassa: "Seized by real fits of madness, he pitches in personally."[25]

According to reports, a few African countries had begun to demand the withdrawal of French support, which had been a major prop upholding Bokassa's rule. The French government not only withdrew support, but also planned Bokassa's overthrow with Dacko and friendly African nations during July and August 1979.[26] In September Dacko claimed the government was overthrown by coup, and France backed up the claim by swiftly moving troops into the country. However, the "Emperor" had the last laugh. After the coup he commanded his jet to fly to France, where he claimed to enjoy French citizenship and apparently still collected a pension as a former sergeant in the French Army.[27] He created considerable embarrassment in Paris and a minor diplomatic incident which was not resolved until Ivory Coast gave him political asylum as an act of "Christian charity." The final word on Bokassa was pronounced by President Houphouët-Boigny, who said, "It is not for us to judge the acts of our unfortunate guest. God will take care of that."[28]

Two unequivocal cases of tyranny emerged in sub-Saharan Africa since independence—in Equatorial Guinea and Uganda. In both, tyranny grew out of despotic situations in which power was used to persecute heretofore privileged political minorities, but deteriorated quickly into general oppressions in which seemingly no individual or group could feel completely safe. In both, eventually everyone became a candidate for victimization—even collaborators or relatives of the ruler; for everyone—not least the ruler and his agents—survival became a contingency of life governed solely by power, influence, or fortune.

24. In abusing emissaries the Emperor was violating a principle of the inviolability of envoys that has been central to the civilized conduct of international relations at least since the sixteenth century (see Hedley Bull, *The Anarchical Society: A Study of Order in World Politics* [London: Macmillan, 1977], p. 32).

25. Jean de la Guerivière, "Paris-Bangui: A Reprehensible Cooperation," *Le Monde/The Guardian*, June 17, 1979.

26. *New York Times*, September 23, 1979.

27. Ibid.

28. Ibid., September 25, 1979.

Francisco Macías Nguema Biyogo, Equatorial Guinea

Tyranny in Equatorial Guinea developed out of a Spanish colonial system of racial-ethnic stratification based on a largely plantation economy.[29] Spanish Guinea comprised the island of Fernando Póo, several smaller islands, and the coastal enclave of Rio Muni.[30] The combined population of the islands—about 15,000 Bubis, 4,000 Fernandinos (descendants of former slaves liberated by the Royal Navy), 5,000 Fangs from Rio Muni, and a large contract labor force of Nigerian plantation workers (mainly Ibos)—was much less than that of Rio Muni—composed of approximately 185,000 Fangs—but under Spanish rule Fernando Póo was favored and had relatively prosperous cocoa and coffee plantations, while the mainland enclave of peasants and fishermen was poor and neglected. The per capita income of the islands at independence was about $250 annually—more than six times that of Rio Muni.[31]

A constitutional transfer of power, begun in the early 1960s and completed at independence in 1968, unleashed strong political pressures for restratification, placing predominant voting power in the hands of the numerous but impoverished Fang of Rio Muni and relegating the comparatively rich Bubi and the other communities of Fernando Póo to the status of political minorities. A unitary form of government under a president elected by universal suffrage was proposed and approved by Spain. However, before approving the unitary constitution of the new African state, eighty deputies of the Spanish Cortes (Parliament) expressed fears that the minority populations of Fernando Póo would be dominated and therefore exploited by the mainland Fang majority—despite constitutional provisions favoring Fernando Póo. Not only would Spanish commercial interests suffer, but also civil and religious institutions might be harmed. Indeed, the stage was set for serious tensions between the privileged minorities and the poor and less educated Fang, who were suddenly promoted to a position of political predominance.

Events since 1968 have proved the fears to be more than justified. In the first elections under the independence constitution, held in September 1968, Francisco Macías Nguema, a Fang and

29. Suzanne Cronje, *Equatorial Guinea—The Forgotten Dictatorship: Forced Labor and Political Murder in Central Africa* (London: Anti-Slavery Society, 1976).
30. During Macías's regime, Fernando Póo was called Macías Nguema Biyogo.
31. *Africa Contemporary Record*, 1968–69, p. 479.

former civil servant, was elected President. It was reported that upon assuming power, the Macías government installed 7,000 of its Fang supporters in government positions in the capital of Malabo (on Fernando Póo). Clearly the new government was not to be a Guinean government so much as a Fang government. Leaders of the opposition prepared to protect their interests—if necessary by unconstitutional means. For some, control of the government seemed necessary; for others, political separation from the Fang-dominated regime. In March 1969 a coup was attempted. The government was temporarily seized, but forces loyal to Macías and members of his paramilitary "Guinean Youth" (Juventud en Marcha con Macías—JMCM),[32] which was armed, were successful in recapturing it. The coup set in motion a wave of political repressions in which leading politicians were either killed or jailed. In addition to the plotters, numerous persons alleged to be conspirators, sympathizers, or in other ways associated with the coup conspiracy were subjected not only to arbitrary arrest, but also to torture or killing. Macías suspended the constitution and proceeded to rule by decree.[33]

The crucial event in Equatorial Guinea which set in motion what we have called the vicious circle of tyranny was the violent overreaction of Macías and his followers to the 1969 coup attempt. Had Macías been a confident and responsible ruler, he would have arrested and punished the plotters—as many other African rulers have done—without resorting to widespread killing and terror. The events suggest that the Guinean ruler was not only unsure of his power, but also fearful and deeply suspicious and distrustful of all other leaders, for he embarked upon a round of arbitrary beatings, arrests, brutality, torture, and killing that extended well beyond the plotters, which led to heightened fear and apprehension, to which Macías responded by additional killing and brutality.[34]

During his regime in Equatorial Guinea (1968–79) Macías's political actions became increasingly arbitrary and severe, with ever-widening circles of Guineans affected by his inhumanity. It was estimated that more than one-third of the entire population (i.e., over 100,000 out of a population of approximately 300,000)

32. Ibid., 1969–70, p. 457.
33. See ibid.
34. When Macías was finally overthrown, survivors cast new light upon his paranoia. A former minister of industry was quoted as saying: "He seemed to think everyone was plotting against him" ("Equatorial Guinea Rises from Terror," *Washington Post*, August 19, 1979).

had fled and were living as refugees in neighboring countries.[35] Macías has been described as a "paranoic, cruel, and megalomaniac" personality who imposed "a reign of arbitrary terror" in which no individual or group was safe[36]—not even the tyrant's own community, the Fang.[37] The political executive decreased from a cabinet of ten ministers in 1968 to a known three in 1976 (Macías, who was also Minister of Defense and Chairman of the ruling United National Workers Party, a Vice-President who was also Minister of National Security, and a Minister of Foreign Affairs).[38] The government appeared to consist of the ruler and his agents of oppression: a Presidential Militia, an armed National Guard, and the JMCM. The regime had all the earmarks of tyranny—arbitary arrest and imprisonment, brutal execution or torture for alleged political crimes, various atrocities, and the expansion of prisons and detention camps around the tiny country. In consequence there was a widespread breakdown in general social and economic norms.[39] The economy in particular deteriorated badly. Fernando Póo, where the greatest amount of plundering and killing took place, was referred to in the African press as "Devil Island."[40] To prevent the escape of Guineans, fishing by locals was prohibited, and the Russian fishing fleet was granted exclusive fishing rights in exchange for a share of the catch.[41]

Between 1969 and 1979 Equatorial Guinea was the scene of virtually a continuous political purge—initially of politicians and political leaders, but subsequently of anyone suspected, with or without reason, of opposing Macías and his regime. As we have noted, a first round of purges followed the attempted coup in 1969. Subsequent purges followed. By the mid-1970s the small class of modern and educated persons associated with the independence movement and the African government in Equatorial Guinea was

35. "Of the 100,000 plus refugees outside the country, 60,000 appear to be in Gabon; 30,000 in Cameroon; 5,000 in Nigeria, and 6,000 (or more) in Spain" (*Africa Contemporary Record*, 1976–77, p. B 504).

36. Ibid., p. B 501.

37. Ibid., 1975–76, p. B 484, and 1976–77, p. B 501.

38. Ibid., 1968–69, p. B 483, and 1976–77, p. B 504.

39. During the period Macías ruled by dictatorial powers a strict policy of press censorship was enforced, preventing accurate firsthand accounts of his tyrannical rule. Many reports were provided either by refugees or by the few Western officials or businessmen who had access to the country. Until 1976 the Spanish government maintained its own press censorship on Guinean news, justifying it as necessary to protect the small number of Spanish nationals still resident in the country (see ibid., pp. B 501–2).

40. "Life on 'Devil Island,' " *Africa* 34 (June 1974): 21–22.

41. Ibid., p. 21; *Africa Confidential* 20, 21 (October 17, 1979): 3.

all but destroyed, most of its members either killed, imprisoned, forced into exile, or cowed into servile submission to the regime. Toward the end of 1974 it was reported that as many as two-thirds of the independence leaders had "disappeared."[42] An Amnesty International investigation found it plausible that there had been 319 political executions of prominent individuals since the suspension of the constitution in 1969.[43] Former colleagues of the tyrant were not exempt from punishment. *West Africa* reported in 1976 that "President Macías' purge of the Bubis, . . . has entailed the 'disappearance,' 'suicide,' or death of nearly all former ministers and senior civil servants."[44] According to another report, "At least seven of Mr. Macías' former government ministers are known to have been executed."[45] Provincial governors, police and army officials, diplomats, bankers, doctors, teachers, and priests also "disappeared." By 1976, the number of named victims of the regime had exceeded 500.[46] Amnesty International and the Anti-Slavery Society described the Macías regime as "among the most brutal and unpredictable in the world."[47]

In 1976, following an abortive coup against his regime, Macías was reported to have retired to his mainland birthplace of Mongomo (a remote village close to the Gabonese border), leaving his nephew, the chief of the National Guard, Lt. Col. Teodoro Obiango Nguema Mbasogo, in charge of the day-to-day problems of keeping order in the country. (Though Macías avoided Malabo and may have felt safer in his home area, he did officially travel outside the country.) The Macías tyranny was brought to an end by a coup on August 3, 1979, led by Mbasogo. For a few days following the coup Macías tried to hold out in Mongomo with the aid of his personal bodyguard, but most of his aides deserted him and he was captured and arrested. In September 1979 he was brought to a trial that was attended not only by Guineans, but also by representatives of the few remaining embassies in the country and an observer from the International Commission of Jurists in Geneva.[48] The deposed ruler was charged with genocide, murder,

42. *Africa Contemporary Record*, 1976–77, pp. B 501–2.
43. Ibid., 1975–76, p. B 483; also *West Africa* 3017 (21 April 1975): 462.
44. Ibid., 3099 (22 November 1976): 1744. Macías is reported to have said: "These so-called intellectuals are the greatest problem facing Africa today. They are polluting our climate with foreign culture" (quoted in Cronje, p. 23).
45. *New York Herald-Tribune*, January 27, 1978.
46. *Africa Contemporary Record*, 1976–77, pp. B 501–3.
47. *New York Herald-Tribune*, January 27, 1978.
48. The embassies included those of the Soviet Union, Cuba, China, and France. Spain had broken off diplomatic relations but reestablished them immediately following the August 1979 coup.

the violation of human rights, treason, and the misappropriation of public funds. During the trial Macías protested his innocence and declared: "I have not killed anybody. . . . I don't think I have committed any offense. I regard all Guineans as my sons."[49] After a four-day trial he was found guilty and was executed along with six former aides. The observer from the International Commission of Jurists reported that the trial had been conducted properly and fairly and had brought to light abundant evidence of Macías' crimes, which included not only his participation in numerous murders, but also his virtual theft of the national treasury—the tribunal mentioned payments to Macías of nearly $5 million during a two-month period in 1978.

The overthrow of Macías in Equatorial Guinea has disquieting elements, however. Some Guinean sources believe the motivation behind Mbasogo's coup was revenge for the murder of his brother by Macías in an earlier purge. Others claim that Mbasogo was implicated in his uncle's crimes.[50] An exile group of Guineans in Spain has charged that Mbasogo had been Macías' executioner and had perpetuated the tyranny before ending it. When asked about a return of democracy in Equatorial Guinea, Mbasogo replied: "We intend to begin a gradual process to reestablish democracy. . . . We can add that we are not in a hurry."[51]

The tyranny in Equatorial Guinea affected virtually all segments of society—perhaps as much as half the population directly (by killing, detention, torture, and exile) and the remaining population indirectly (forcing it to live under a regime of terror). The purges were accelerated by a mechanism of social representation peculiar to elites in African societies—that is, a clientelist view of responsibility and morality by which elites unofficially "represent" their families, villages, communal groups, and organizations within the government and its agencies and by which clients are viewed as implicated in their patrons' acts. On this view a purge of patrons must necessarily involve the purge of their clients, regardless of the latter's guilt or innocence. Thus Macías punished not only political leaders, but also their families, friends, supporters, villages, and so forth. By this mechanism the oppression became proportionately as wide as the purges.

As we have noted, during Macías' regime there was a marked

49. Quoted in "Equatorial Guinea's Ex-Dictator Sentenced to Die," *New York Times*, September 30, 1979.

50. *Africa Confidential* 20, 21 (October 17, 1979): 1.

51. Quoted in Leon Dash, "Equatorial Guinea Rises from Terror," *Washington Post*, August 19, 1979.

deterioration of general social norms—particularly evident in regard to the Christian churches, the provision of social and technical services, and the poor productivity of the cash crop economy. As one might expect of a former Spanish colony, Equatorial Guinea was one of the most Christianized countries of Africa. After 1969 the churches, the clergy, and parishioners were subjected to not only widespread interference and harassment, but persecution and repression also. Some reports claimed that the regime proscribed religious charities and pastoral travel and censored sermons; a United Nations Development Program report claimed that all religious activities were banned and that the ruler's agents were instructed to report any "subversive" activities of the clergy, particularly missionaries. Officers of the churches—in particular some members of the Catholic Church hierarchy—as well as priests and nuns were subjected to arbitrary arrest and in some instances detention, torture, and execution.[52] In consequence, not only religious rites but also social services ordinarily provided by religious agencies were badly disrupted.

The indigenous elite of professionals, never large, were a particular target of Macías' regime, with seriously disruptive consequences for the provision of social and technical services—particularly in medicine and education. By the mid-1970s the technical personnel required to operate and maintain the telephone service, the radio broadcasting facilities, and the nation's television station were not available in sufficient numbers to prevent uncertainty of operation, and there were reports of infrastructural breakdowns due to an absence of qualified personnel, neglect, and a lack of spare parts.[53] It was reported that civil servants were in general not regularly paid—unlike the tyrant's agents, who were handsomely rewarded for their services.[54]

Perhaps the most manifest deterioration of norms in Equatorial Guinea occurred in the modern economic sector—particularly in a marked decline of cocoa and coffee production. Historically, Spanish and Fernandino planters operated the plantation economy in mercantilist fashion, with the cooperation of colonial authorities, by means of indentured labor.[55] The mercantilist system of indentured labor was later replaced by the capitalist method of recruitment through cash incentives and labor contracts. The plantation

52. *Africa Contemporary Record*, 1975–76, p. B 484, and 1976–77, p. B 504. Dash reported that in 1979 all churches and mosques were closed.
53. *Africa Contemporary Record*, 1976–77, p. B 505.
54. *Africa* 34 (June 1974): 21.
55. René Pélissier, "Equatorial Guinea: Recent History," in *Africa: South of the Sahara, 1976–77* (London: Europa Publications, 1976), p. 286.

economy on Fernando Póo came to depend on large numbers of Nigerian contract workers to cultivate and harvest cocoa. An early effect of tyrannical rule was to render the supply of Nigerian labor much more uncertain—in large part because laborers were doubtful that wages would be paid or contracts honored. Cocoa production declined "from a level of nearly 50,000 tons in 1970 to only 22,000 tons in 1972 . . . to about 12,000 tons or less [in 1976]."[56] In 1976 harassment of and brutality toward the Nigerian workers on Fernando Póo, as well as reports of Guinean violations of contractual agreements, resulted in a massive repatriation of an estimated 20,000 workers to Nigeria (with the assistance of the Nigerian government)—not without some violence and killing. Similar problems beset the coffee economy in Rio Muni, resulting in a mass exodus of Guinean workers across the border into Cameroon. In response to an impending crisis, the regime in March 1976 decreed that agricultural work would henceforth be compulsory, and proceeded to press Rio Munians into working on the Fernando Póo cocoa plantations. The enforcement of the decree was sufficiently severe to move the Anti-Slavery Society of London to investigate the labor conditions; it was convinced that the Macías regime had reinstated measures of forced labor reminiscent of the worst features of Spanish colonial mercantilism.[57]

Following the 1979 coup Western journalists were able to visit Equatorial Guinea and report on conditions. They found a dispirited people and a seriously dislocated society, most of whose institutions were badly damaged and barely functioning; the country had ceased to possess an "economy" or government "administration" in the ordinary meaning of these words. A French reporter noted not only that fishing by locals was forbidden, but also that fishing boats had been destroyed by the regime to prevent attempts at escape from Fernando Póo; as a result there were severe food shortages. Many of the island's shops were closed, and civil servants had gone unpaid for months. The reporter was told by the new rulers that everything would have to be "started from scratch, rebuilt."[58]

56. *West Africa* 3099 (22 November 1976): 1744; also *Africa Contemporary Record*, 1976–77, p. B 505. In 1979 cocoa production was reported to be less than 5,000 tons (Dash).

57. *Africa Contemporary Record*, 1976–77, p. B 504; also *Africa Confidential* 17, 14 (June 9, 1976): 7.

58. Quoted in "Equatorial Guinea: Is the Change Real?" *Africa News* 13, 7 (August 17, 1979): 4. An article by a leading authority came to our attention after the above had been written, arguing that Macías was insane; see René Pélissier, "Equatorial Guinea: Autopsy of a Miracle," *Africa Report* 25, 3 (May–June 1980): 10–14.

Idi Amin Dada, Uganda

Tyranny in Uganda (1971–79) arose in an historical context of government coercion and political violence, on the one hand,[59] and inequity among groups—especially in their access to government-controlled privileges and opportunities—on the other. The government of Milton Obote, which had come to power at independence in 1962, at times resorted to force to maintain the authority of the state. Obote was typical of the majority of Africa's personal rulers: he operated an authoritarian government which deprived political opponents of political liberties; he jailed some; he was not loath to use other measures of political force. But he did not kill or terrorize his opponents—let alone the general population; he curbed his appetite and will for power. While Obote created political enemies, disaffection, and discontent, he never created the apprehension and fear pervasive in tyrannies.

Among East African countries Uganda had exhibited an unusual degree of social violence, and the incidence of armed robbery—*kondoism*—had increased since independence. Unauthorized but unpunished violence by Ugandan soldiers could be traced to an army mutiny in 1964 over issues of pay and promotion. However, the deliberate use of the military by the Obote government for basically political purposes in 1966—when the Ugandan army was used to suppress the traditional government of Buganda—had the appearance of authorizing (or at least encouraging) military indiscipline and brutality. Force and violence were used against ethnic and socioeconomic dissidents and opponents of the Obote regime, many of them members of the relatively wealthy Ganda people from the southern part of the country in and around Kampala. Obote's regime was seen to favor the Langi and Acholi communities, who were an important base of support and who in return were favored with privileged access to government, although not entirely at the expense of other groups.[60]

59. See Lutakome A. Kayiira and Edward Kannyo, "Politics and Violence in Uganda," *Africa Report* 23, 1 (January–February 1978): 39. For the Obote period, see Ali A. Mazrui, "Leadership in Africa: Obote of Uganda," *International Journal* 25, 3 (Summer 1970): 538–64; James H. Mittelman, *Ideology and Politics in Uganda: From Obote to Amin* (Ithaca and London: Cornell University Press, 1975); Akiiki B. Mujaju, "The Role of the UPC as a Party of Government in Uganda," *Canadian Journal of African Studies* 10, 3 (1976): 443–67; T. V. Sathyamurthy, "The Social Base of the Uganda Peoples' Congress, 1958–70," *African Affairs* 74, 297 (October 1975): 442–60; and Peter Willetts, "The Politics of Uganda as a One-Party State, 1969–1970," ibid., 74, 292 (July 1975): 278–99.

60. See Nelson Kasfir, "Cultural Sub-Nationalism in Uganda," in *The Politics of Cultural Sub-Nationalism in Africa*, ed. Victor A. Olorunsola (Garden City, N.Y.: Anchor Books, 1972), pp. 123–26.

Idi Amin Dada was born in West Nile District in about 1928 of northern Ugandan parentage, but as an infant was brought by his mother to southern Uganda after his parents separated. In what has historically been a Christian country whose center of gravity was in the south, Amin was a minority Nubian of the Kakwa group from the north and a Moslem.[61] Like many Nubians before him, Amin was recruited by the King's African Rifles in 1946; he became a cook and proved himself to be an accomplished boxer. Like other African recruits, he had little formal education. His unusual size and height, Nubian origins, and lack of education made him an ideal recruit for the British, who believed that the Nubians were fighters and obedient if without education.

Amin rose quickly in the ranks, and his rise was greatly accelerated by his good fortune to be an officer with demonstrated qualities of leadership at the time of independence.[62] Furthermore, as one of the first African officers, he was in some ways privileged and protected. Amin's military record, however, is far from responsible. Reports of his sadism and brutal approach to his duties are well documented.[63] As early as 1962, in command of a company of troops deployed to stop Turkana-Karamajong clashes that were occurring in northwest Kenya, he is reported to have used excessive force (including beatings, torture, and killings). Obote (who was then Prime Minister) was informed of Amin's misconduct by the departing British authorities, who had wanted to bring him to trial but were concerned about the political repercussions of such an action just prior to independence and therefore advised that he be given only a "severe reprimand." By 1966 Amin had been made Commander of the Ugandan army by Obote, who had by then suspended the constitution and become President.

61. "It is very difficult to define who exactly is a Nubian, as the term is often used loosely as synonymous with all black Sudanese. In the present Uganda army the Nubians are the descendants of the black Moslem Sudanese who settled all over East Africa after service in the armies of the colonial period" (Garth Glentworth and Ian Hancock, "Obote and Amin: Change and Continuity In Modern Uganda Politics," *African Affairs* 72, 288 [July 1973]: 251). The presence in Uganda of the Nubians, or Nubi, who are Moslems, is one of several historical ironies connected to the emergence of Amin, for they were originally recruited in the Sudan by British colonial agents and explorers during the era of European colonization and brought south into Uganda as mercenaries. David Martin writes that "long before the 1971 *coup* . . . they enjoyed an unenviable reputation of having one of the world's highest homicide rates. The Nubians were renowned for their sadistic brutality, lack of formal education, for poisoning enemies and for their refusal to integrate, even in the urban centres" (*General Amin* [London: Faber and Faber, 1974], p. 14). See also Aidan Southall, "General Amin and the Coup: Great Man or Historical Inevitability?" *Journal of Modern African Studies* 13, 1 (1975): 85–105.

62. See the account in Martin, *General Amin*, pp. 17–26.

63. Ibid., pp. 17–20.

Ironically, it was Amin who carried out Obote's orders to use force against political dissidents and opponents of the Obote regime in 1966.

Following a December 1969 assassination attempt upon him, Obote began to be suspicious of Amin. It was widely rumored that Amin was implicated in the murder of his second in command, Brigadier Pierino Okoya, who had emerged as Amin's rival and possibly Obote's favorite. (Okoya's wife was also murdered.) According to Martin, Obote doubted Amin's involvement; in any case, no trial ever took place. It was also rumored that Amin was implicated in the disappearance of £2,500,000 of army funds and weapons found in the possession of *kondos* (armed thieves). In January 1971, Obote demanded an accounting from Amin and others upon his return from a Commonwealth conference in Singapore. Obote had by this time removed Amin as Commander and made him Chief of the Defense Staff, hoping to neutralize Amin while not antagonizing his many army supporters. "Then Obote flew out to Singapore. He had loaded the gun and pointed it directly at his own head. To survive, Amin had no other choice but to pull the trigger."[64] In late January 1971 he staged a coup.

Idi Amin's coup toppled the government of Obote. His new military government was initially welcomed by disaffected opponents of the Obote regime, as well as by foreign investors and Western countries (including Britain), who saw it as putting an end to Obote's experiments with socialism, which had been threatening to foreign investors who had sizable holdings in Uganda.[65] It was received with relief by important domestic and foreign groups that had a stake in Ugandan political and economic affairs. Lonsdale writes:

> [Amin] had initially won support among many of the people, his flamboyant personality and good will tours throughout the country being well received. The powerful Baganda tribe was delighted at his decision to allow the former Kabaka to be buried in the ancestral tomb at Kasubi, though disappointed that his son was not made heir.[66]

Undoubtedly, Amin's most well-received political stroke after the coup was his ordered expulsion of the nearly 50,000-member

64. Ibid., p. 26.

65. See Ruth First, "Uganda: The Latest *Coup d'Etat* in Africa," *The World Today* 27, 3 (March 1971): 131–38; James H. Mittelman: "The Anatomy of a Coup: Uganda, 1971," *Africa Quarterly* 11, 3 (October–December 1971): 184–202, and *Ideology and Politics in Uganda*; Michael Twaddle, "The Amin Coup," *Journal of Commonwealth Political Studies* 10, 2 (July 1972): 99–112.

66. John Lonsdale, "Recent History Until 1971," in *Africa: South of the Sahara, 1976–77* (London: Europa Publications, 1976), p. 932.

Asian community in August 1972—an action for which he was rewarded with a wide measure of apparent popularity. (Few who favored the action, including Amin himself, envisaged the socioeconomic costs that would be incurred by such an abrupt withdrawal of a key supply of professional, technical, administrative, and business skills from the country.)[67] In sum, in the beginning Amin appeared to be just another African military ruler who had successfully perpetrated a coup.

Even while Amin's government was being viewed in a favorable light, a darker view began to emerge which would create an ambivalent attitude toward him. Disquieting signs of lawlessness among some of his military agents began to appear virtually from the beginning of his rule. It is now clear that Amin and his army supporters—from the Nubian groups (including especially his own Kakwa people), which he had recruited and promoted while a senior officer—were sufficiently fearful of Obote's chief ethnic supporters to undertake violent purges of the Langi and Acholi in the army and police.[68] "Where Obote had imprisoned opponents, Amin had them physically eliminated; instead of harassing ethnic groups he distrusted, Amin simply massacred them."[69] According to a report of the International Commission of Jurists, which investigated the Amin regime:

> In the first few months of the new government, a pattern of random and continued violence began to emerge. One of the first groups to be affected were the police. By one account, at the end of February, barely one month after the coup, there were nine police killed, five injured, four missing, eight in detention and thirteen had run away.[70]

The purge within the army was much more extensive and violent than within the police. The same International Commission of Jurists report refers to a "series of mass killings in the armed forces, aimed primarily at the soldiers of the Acholi and Langi tribes."[71] Decalo writes that "Extermination squads . . . purged the various army camps of suspected Obote loyalist officers and soldiers. Langi and Acholi officers were sequestered and individually mur-

---

67. See D. A. Low, "Uganda Unhinged," *International Affairs* 49, 2 (April 1973): 219–28; Justin O'Brien, "General Amin and the Uganda Asians: Doing the Unthinkable," *The Round Table* 249 (January 1973): 91–104.

68. Southall, p. 89.

69. Kayiira and Kannyo, p. 42.

70. "From Racism to Genocide: Extracts from the Report of The International Commission of Jurists," *Transition* 49 (July–September 1975): 12; Michael H. Posner, "Violations of Human Rights in Uganda, 1971–1978" (New York: The Lawyers Committee for International Human Rights, 1978; mimeo).

71. "From Racism to Genocide," p. 12.

dered both before and after the attempted 1972 pro-Obote invasion from Tanzania."[72] The scale of killings was soon quite extensive, and relatives and friends began to make inquiries to authorities about missing persons. As awareness of the "disappearances" spread and as harassment, intimidation, and abuse of civilians increased, public apprehension began to grow. The International Commission of Jurists reported growing fear among the police and noted that a letter was sent by senior police officers to their minister seeking instruction for handling the growing apprehension, as well as the increased inquiries "for missing relatives who could not be traced at any known place of destination. . . . Many of those responsible for this letter were subsequently dismissed, killed, or disappeared. . . . The killing began to spread to every segment of the society."[73]

While an undercurrent of lawless violence and fear was developing and some of the atrocities began to be known, Amin began to issue decrees abolishing not only constitutional rights but also common legal protections and safeguards. In March 1971 the Armed Forces (Power of Arrest) Decree essentially gave the army a license to search persons and premises and seize property at will. In effect the police were being displaced by military agents of the regime. The Detention (Prescription of Time Limit) Decree, also of March 1971, granted agents discretionary powers to detain persons indefinitely without trial, and the Robbery Suspects' Decree gave them authority to shoot *kondos* on sight.[74] Perhaps the most telling portent of the full tyranny that would develop under Amin was Retroactive Decree No. 8, which granted immunity to the government and its agents from civil or criminal proceedings in the courts in respect of their actions or omissions. Comments of the editors of *Transition* in 1975 were apposite:

72. Decalo, *Coups and Army Rule in Africa*, p. 212. Seven of the eight Brigade and Battalion Commanders in the army, as well as one of the two Air Force Squadron Leaders—all of whom were Acholi or Langi—were killed either in Amin's coup or in a massacre of Acholi and Langi officers in March 1971. One of the eight—Colonel Tito Okello—escaped to Tanzania and led the September 1972 invasion of Uganda and with Lt. Col. Oyite Ojok led the military operation of the Uganda National Liberation Front, which took part with the Tanzanian army in the overthrow of the Amin regime in 1979. (See F. J. Ravenhill, "The Military and Politics in Uganda," *Africa Quarterly* 19, 2 [July–September 1979]: 10).

73. "From Racism to Genocide," p. 12.

74. Lonsdale, "Recent History Until 1971," p. 931. For a systematic listing of the decrees of the Amin regime, see F. J. Ravenhill, "Military Rule in Uganda: The Politics of Survival," *African Studies Review* 17, 1 (April 1974): 252–60. Lutakome Kayiira, the former head of the Uganda Prisons' Research Bureau, commented: "It is not difficult to see that Amin had legally authorized soldiers, police, and prison officers to kill robbery 'suspects' or anybody so described" (Kayiira and Kannyo, p. 41).

The effect of this Decree . . . is to eliminate all legal means of controlling the actions of the armed forces. It absolves them from any legal responsibility for the arrests, murders, ill-treatment, and despoliation. The armed forces are placed outside the law. In the most literal sense, the rule of law has been abandoned.[75]

In 1975 Amin was "promoted" to Field Marshal, and in June 1976 his appointed Defense Council named him President for Life.

In retrospect, in the years immediately following the coup Amin merely carried forward the same practices that had brought him to power—now with all the resources of the government at his disposal. A military leader of considerable prowess, as well as physical and personal charisma, in an army staffed with a large segment of his co-religious, co-ethnic, and equally uneducated persons, Amin had attracted a sizable personal following and clientele.[76] The army was divided on ethnic, religious, and educational lines and did not have the organization and discipline we associate with modern military formations;[77] Decalo has noted that the Ugandan army was a law unto itself in garrison towns and "moved as though in feudal domains."[78] It is not surprising, therefore, that personally led factional-ethnic formations had arisen. Following the purges of the Acholi and Langi elements within the army in 1971 and 1972, Amin transformed what had been his factional-ethnic clique into virtually an army within an army—a kind of mercenary army of rule comprising loyal Nubians and Kakwa. The size of this inner-core army by 1977 was estimated at 5,000 men.[79] It very likely was built up not so much according to a master plan as with Amin's acute political instinct to move into positions of power persons who would protect him from rival power-seekers.

The Nubian army-within-an-army was the general protector of the Ugandan tyrant and his overall agent of oppression, but the

75. Quoted in "From Racism to Genocide," p. 11.

76. A former company commander of Amin's in the King's African Rifles has remarked: "He was the most natural born leader that I've ever met. But he was also limited by his African education, and the two formed a fairly explosive combination" (quoted in *Chicago Tribune*, June 12, 1974).

77. At independence there were no officers who had been trained overseas, a situation which fostered fundamental cleavages in the post-independence army. As non-commissioned officers (largely northerners and poorly educated), such as Amin, became officers, a division appeared between them and the better educated, academy-trained officers (primarily Ganda, Acholi, and Langi). Minorities and political leaders attempted actions to exploit these cleavages to their advantage.

78. Decalo, *Coups and Army Rule in Africa*, p. 207.

79. *Africa Contemporary Record*, 1976–77, p. B 374.

specialized instruments of terror specific to the tyranny were the "killer squads"—the Public Safety Unit, State Research Department, Military Police, and Presidential Bodyguard (which was staffed by members of the other three and employed Palestinian advisers). These—especially the Public Safety Unit—were the perpetrators of most of the atrocities that took place in Uganda under Amin. The killers were either Kakwa or other Nubians/ Sudanese who shared their leader's parochial prejudices in despising educated people.[80] Undoubtedly, the factors that made Amin's tyranny possible were a fortuitous combination of ethnic fears and prejudices, the presence in the army of a large number of Amin's supporters who were capable of grossly inhuman actions, and the availability of booty to make it profitable for mercenaries. Ultimately—as in all tyrannies—there was a shared interest in the perpetuation of the tyranny between the ruler and his clients.

In Uganda under Amin the conduct of regime agents was scarcely distinguishable from that of ordinary criminals, revealing the essential banditry of tyranny. Property—cars, homes, land, and so forth—was seized with impunity by those who possessed on-the-spot power.[81] There were reports that attractive women were kidnapped, their husbands or escorts simply disregarded; if the men resisted or complained, they were beaten or even murdered. It is claimed that Amin himself committed or authorized murder to possess the women of other men.[82] According to one report, in 1976 Amin warned ministers and high-ranking security and government officers not "to acquire land by force and to stop such practices immediately," stating that he had reports that they had "used bulldozers and tractors to pull down houses and destroy crops when they went to establish farms or ranches."[83] However, large amounts of property were seized by the regime and redistributed to leading supporters. The most prominent example was the seizure of the property of the expelled Asian community— plantations, farms, houses, businesses, and other property. A former cabinet minister claimed that Amin's "ethnic kith and kin, as every Ugandan knows, have done extremely well out of the allocations of the businesses, and other assets left behind by the expel-

80. Ibid., p. B 375. For descriptive accounts of the atrocities, see Martin, *General Amin*.

81. Here we see "property" clearly for what it is: an institution of authorized ownership, not a power-derived possession. In effect, property ceased to exist in Uganda under Amin.

82. Kayiira and Kannyo, p. 42.

83. *Africa Contemporary Record*, 1976–77, p. B 376.

lees," and that Amin himself had "freely shared in the booty."[84] In addition, members of Amin's retinue were awarded lucrative importing and exporting licenses. Perhaps the most striking illustration of the plundering of wealth by Amin's regime was the use of increasingly scarce foreign exchange (some of it held originally in private bank accounts by Ugandan Asians) not only to purchase weapons for enforcing the tyranny, but also to reward the privileged (especially the military hierarchy) with expensive imported goods. For example, a Boeing 707 or C-130 transport aircraft arrived nearly weekly at Stanstead Airport in England to be loaded not only with essentials in short supply in Uganda, but also with luxury goods (whiskey, clothes, furniture) for Amin's and his agents' personal use. The result of this massive misappropriation of private and national property was the creation of a comparatively privileged military elite, "[who live] in the best houses in the capital's most salubrious suburbs . . . [and] drive Peugeots and Fiats. . . .[85] It is worth pointing out that privileges were at their highest during the period the Ugandan economy was deteriorating badly. While the economy was in near ruins in 1976–78, the elite structure was saved from collapse by the unusually high world price of coffee. However, for some 85 percent of the population, survival meant a return to subsistence agriculture.

Between 1971 and 1979 Uganda was subjected to one of the most capricious, terror-ridden, and inhumane governments yet to emerge in sub-Saharan Africa—perhaps one of the most tyrannical regimes to emerge anywhere in the underdeveloped world since the end of World War II. In June 1976, following one of several assassination attempts on Amin, his co-ethnic accomplice and Vice-President, General Mustapha Adrisi, warned that any other attempt at assassinating the President would "be an invitation to the soldiers to teach the country a lesson they will never forget because they would have started the fire by themselves."[86] In December 1976 repressive searches for plotters and weapons—involving much intimidation, beating, and cruelty—carried out principally among the Acholi and Langi groups, were sufficiently severe to be denounced by the Christian clergy—most notably Anglican Archbishop Janani Luwum and his fellow Bishops. It was estimated that between 50,000 and 300,000 persons had been

84. Wanume Kibedi, "Open Letter to Amin," *Transition* 49 (July–September 1975): 26.
85. *Africa Contemporary Record*, 1976–77, p. B 374.
86. Ibid., pp. 376–77.

killed by 1977.[87] The worst series of mass atrocities occurred in the early months of 1977 during a period of intense insecurity for the regime and widespread rumors of plots by Acholi and Langi dissidents or by Christians. In late January 1977, the military ruling clique launched a massive attack against Acholi and Langi villages and towns in the north and other towns elsewhere by killer units and trusted soldiers.[88] Obote's native village of five hundred houses was destroyed, and all villagers who did not escape were killed. Thousands were killed and additional thousands fled. Many of the educated African elites who remained were further intimidated, some were killed, and others escaped into exile. Reportedly only the Nubian groups and the Moslems were left entirely alone.[89] Archbishop Luwum and two ministers suspected of "plotting" were murdered in the craze to eliminate all would-be opposition

We can offer only a conjecture as to why Amin did not possess the self-restraint to prevent tyranny. As we have noted—and the point is important—rulers (and their agents) are responsible for tyrannies, and the prevention of tyranny will depend on the moral sense of the rulers. Most African rulers have had such a moral sense. Excluding insanity, amorality—contempt for the rights, property, and persons of powerless individuals and a pure power hunger—is the only explanation that can begin to make sense of the unspeakable actions of a Tyrant. No decency, concern, responsibility, compassion, or conscience[90] is present in the amoral personal ruler to curb his drive for power.[91] It is abundantly clear from the evidence and reports that have become available that Amin was essentially an amoral man.

Amin appeared to lack an understanding of the complexities of a modern civil order, as well as a sense of civility, reasoning, and restraint required to operate peacefully and effectively in such an order. He was without question an ignorant, uneducated, and unsophisticated man, although he was not stupid. However, his intelligence appeared not in the slightest degree to be tempered by either compassion or responsibility; it appeared rather to focus on

87. Ibid., p. 373.
88. Ibid., pp. 378–79.
89. Ibid.
90. In Hobbes's "state of nature," "conscience" is the only source of morality (see M. M. Goldsmith, *Hobbes's Science of Politics* [New York: Columbia University Press, 1966], p. 129).
91. For an account of Amin's amorality by a highly placed member of his regime, see Henry Kyemba, *A State of Blood: The Inside Story of Idi Amin* (New York: Ace Books, 1977).

acquiring and holding pure personal sway and on surviving in a world full of "dangers," such as the cunning of others. Amin once boasted about his treatment of persons alleged to have plotted against him: "I ate them before they ate me."[92] Here surely was Hobbes's man in the state of nature: a man totally preoccupied with a fear of death and a lesser fear of being dominated by others, and so a man who uses all of his intelligence, strength, and power to allay his fears.[93]

Like Equatorial Guinea, Amin's Uganda offers a striking example of the destructive impact of tyrannical rule on the basic but often implicit norms and understandings that make a society possible. As in Equatorial Guinea, there was a major deterioration of political, social, and economic norms—especially in law and legal institutions, civic morals, government policy and administration, and the modern sectors of the economy.

The decrees that licensed the tyrant's agents to operate entirely outside legal controls, and the numerous and completely arbitrary actions unleashed thereby, contributed to what the International Commission of Jurists (among others) described as "a total breakdown of the rule of law."[94] In Uganda all aspects of the judicial process were undermined. The independence of the judiciary was terminated, and judges and magistrates, as well as other legal professionals, were reduced to cowed and fearful functionaries of the regime almost from the beginning—especially following the "disappearance" of the Chief Justice of the High Court, Benedicto Kiwanuka, in 1972. Amin's incomprehension of a "court" as an independent institution was revealed in a statement to judges and magistrates in 1976, when he noted that although he "respects and attaches great importance to the rule of law," he was disposed to transfer cases to military tribunals "who do their work quicker."[95] Legal professionals were killed, imprisoned, tortured, forced into exile, and otherwise harassed and intimidated to the point of no longer being able to function properly and responsibly. Under such conditions of political fear and coercion no magistrate could make a legal ruling against the government or its agents, quite apart from the legal immunities decreed. The International Commission of Jurists reported the direct testimony of one Ugandan:

92. Quoted in *Africa Contemporary Record*, 1977–78, p. B 436.

93. *The Leviathan*, ed. Michael Oakeshott (New York: Collier Books, 1962), ch. 13.

94. "Violations of Human Rights and the Rule of Law in Uganda"; Conclusions of a Study by the International Commission of Jurists (May 1974); reprinted in *Africa Contemporary Record*, 1974–75, pp. C 90–91.

95. Ibid., 1976–77, pp. B 392–93.

"A defence counsel could be in serious trouble, notably with the Public Safety Unit . . . if he successfully defended an alleged criminal."[96]

Inevitably and inextricably associated with the decline of law was the degradation of civic morals—that is, the moral rules which normally operate at a social level beyond the family, clique, or clan, or ethnic, religious, or other ascriptive groups. As we have noted, property was taken by soldiers (as well as by other robbers) who did not hesitate to kill for it.[97] The word *magendo* (whose meaning covers various nefarious activities from bribery to black marketeering) was prominent in the everyday vocabulary. There developed a psychology of insecurity and a corresponding social calculus whereby connections, influence, bribes, and the like were used to protect oneself, one's family, and one's property against the regime or its agents. Were it not for such a possibility of self-defense, it is probable that the effects of the tyranny would have been even worse.

The managerial and administrative capability of the Ugandan government was of course adversely affected by the tyranny. As in Equatorial Guinea, "government" in the ordinary sense of the term was probably rendered largely nonexistent. The government apparatus was affected directly by the loss of many of the ablest policymakers, administrators, and technocrats, and indirectly by the terribly uncertain conditions imposed by the tyranny; in many ways government could not operate with much effect—or at all. Those who remained carried out the wishes of the tyrant in order to survive. For instance, in the spheres of financial policymaking and currency management the government lost much of its ability to function. The Central Bank of Uganda was greatly restricted in its ability to provide foreign exchange to pay for imports—owing in large part to the theft and diversion of funds by the regime to purchase the foreign goods that the tyrant's mercenaries had come to expect as payment for their services. In 1977 the Uganda currency was reported to have lost about 80 percent of its former value in relation to the currency of neighboring Kenya. Furthermore, the financial and currency crisis had the effect of depriving the business economy and system of trade in Uganda of the goods (especially imported goods) they needed to sell.

Clearly, rules and agreements that permit a modern cash ex-

96. "From Racism to Genocide," p. 11.
97. "The Tragedy of Amin's Unspeakable Rule in Uganda," *Times* (London), June 24, 1977.

change economy to operate were seriously eroded in Amin's Uganda. Legal markets were replaced in many places by black markets; smuggling increased—especially of coffee, which was transported illegally across the border into Kenya and sold at a high price in a valuable currency. (The punishment for smuggling was great, but it was probably possible to bribe the soldiers who policed illicit activities.) So extensive was the illicit trade in necessities unavailable in Uganda, and so openly was it conducted (suggesting a widespread complicity of the tyrant's agents), that in 1977 Amin made smuggling a capital offense and warned that it would be applied to anyone— "Ministers, Army and Government officials, and even to his own relatives."[98] The most serious overall effect on the modern cash exchange economy in Uganda was a marked decline in the production of the country's chief cash crops and its one mineral export—copper. In a remarkable 1976 budget speech the Finance Minister disclosed that cotton was at its lowest level since 1948, and that from the previous year tea was down 18 percent, cotton sales were down 11.6 percent, the industrial sector had declined by 10 percent, and the volume of trade by 11 percent. Copper production had become insignificant. Even more remarkable, in 1977 the Minister of Planning and Economic Development revealed that there had been a negative rate of growth since 1972.[99] Much that had been built up since independence was in serious economic jeopardy, and much else was lost. The *Times* of London commented that "Uganda has largely returned to a peasant subsistence economy."[100]

Over the eight years of Amin's tyranny some dozen attempts were made on his life—most of them by military officers—but he survived them all without ever being seriously wounded. In fact, such attempts played into a game at which he was the acknowledged master: it was futile to outfox or outbox Amin. His downfall came at the hands of the unlikely person of President Nyerere of Tanzania. After Amin's forces had invaded and pillaged a large area of Tanzania west of Lake Victoria late in 1978, Nyerere threw the support of his army behind a group of exiled Ugandan forces in an invasion of Uganda. At first Nyerere was determined to punish the despoilers, but later he became committed to bringing down a regime that had dishonored Africa. Over a period of about six months the forces succeeded in capturing Kampala, the

98. *Africa Contemporary Record*, 1976–77, p. B 391.
99. Ibid., pp. B 396–97.
100. *Times* (London), June 24, 1977.

capital, and effectively deposing Amin, who managed to escape with his family and closest supporters. The ability of Nyerere's forces to readily defeat those of Amin is a demonstration not so much of the strength of Tanzania's army as of the deceptive power of a Tyrant's troops. When confronted, Amin's forces acted more like rabble than an army. Of the greatest political significance was Nyerere's decision to disregard an OAU taboo concerning the sanctity and inviolability of African state boundaries—for some doubtlessly a disquieting move in the international history of African states made by a ruler otherwise regarded as one of Africa's political saints.

Prior to the final collapse of the Amin regime, steps were taken under the auspices of Nyerere to bring together exiled Ugandan leaders and organizations to plan the restoration of orderly and lawful government. By agreement among the exile leaders, the former Principal and Vice-Chancellor of Makerere University, Usuf K. Lule, was made interim President until elections could be held (in about two years). However, in scarcely more than two months factional maneuvers among the new leadership resulted in the replacement of Lule by Godfrey Binaisa, a lawyer and cabinet minister in the Obote regime. It began to be apparent that serious political, economic, and social uncertainty had not been reduced. The economy was in a shambles, and the organs of government needed to be rebuilt to prevent the country from sliding into anarchy. But instead of national reconciliation in the months immediately after Amin, Uganda suffered persistent and widespread criminal lawlessness which seriously undermined personal security and delayed reconstruction. In addition, factional conflicts and rivalries grounded not only in personal differences among leaders, but also in underlying ideological and ethnic divisions exacerbated attempts to reestablish effective and orderly government. It was becoming clear that the costs of tyranny might have to be borne by the peoples of Uganda for some considerable time.

Equatorial Guinea under Macías has been described as "suffocating" and a country "living on the margin of international society."[101] Uganda under Amin has been called a "slaughterhouse";[102] President Kaunda of Zambia has stated that "Amin's name has come to be associated with the defiance of the worth and

101. *New York Herald-Tribune*, January 27, 1978; quoted in *Africa Contemporary Record*, 1974–75, p. B 584.
102. Richard H. Ullman, "Human Rights and Economic Power: The United States versus Idi Amin," *Foreign Affairs* 56, 3 (April 1978): 529.

sanctity of the human person."[103] Such descriptions are among the most ominous yet to be applied to any independent African government and evoke the worst political horrors of twentieth-century barbarism. Both tyrannical regimes have been toppled, but they nevertheless provide yet other examples of the essential vulnerability of the civil condition. It is regrettable that the lesson of Thomas Hobbes has had to be learned anew down through the centuries.

103. Quoted in *Africa Research Bulletin: Political, Social and Cultural Series* 16, 4 (April 1–30, 1979): 5224A.

7

Prospects for
Institutional Government

IN most African countries there is little sign that the drama
of personal rule will soon give way to more settled institutional
forms of conducting the affairs of states. Military coups and other
personal-political struggles and conflicts continue to be marked
features of political life. For the time being the inquiring student
of African politics may be better advised to read Machiavelli or
Hobbes than the "constitutions," official plans, or party programs
of most African governments if he wishes to understand their central characteristics and dynamics.[1]

Yet, while personal rule should be expected to continue, some of
its features are likely to change. It seems reasonable to assume
that, with the passage of time, more stabilized and durable regimes of personal rule are likely to emerge in a growing number of
countries as some strongman or faction succeeds in overcoming opposition, taking control of the state, and becoming entrenched in
power. It is rather like a game of chance: sooner or later an effective ruler or ruling group capable of changing the course of history
is bound to turn up. Among the better illustrations of this general
tendency in systems of personal rule are Zaire, Sudan, and Benin.
Zaire experienced six changes of political leadership between
1960 and 1965 before the current ruler (Mobutu) assumed control
of the government; Sudan had eight changes in leadership before
Numeiri intervened in 1969; and Benin—perhaps the best illustration of this tendency—had experienced ten changes of ruler
between 1960 and 1972, when the present ruler (Kerekou) assumed power. Of course there is always the possibility that the
failure, misfortune, or death of a central actor in a previously sta-

1. When asked to comment on the political situation in Congo-Brazzaville, a government official suggested some explanation could be found by reading *Macbeth*
(*Africa Confidential* 20, 5 [February 28, 1979]: 8).

ble regime of personal rule will throw the state into uncertainty, even turmoil, as Ethiopia following the decline and displacement of Haile Selassie so vividly illustrates.

And it is possible, if as yet uncommon in contemporary Africa, for the political structures associated with strong individual rulers or ruling oligarchies to develop an independent authority and survive the men who founded them. It is probably in connection with presidential offices that a process of institutionalization is most likely to occur—that is, a distinction between offices and their temporary incumbents. Succession is a case in point. If successors find it politically advantageous to accept an office and maintain it intact, they inadvertently endow it with impersonal legitimacy. A similar legitimation takes place with the acceptance of succession and other constitutional rules by a ruling class; for in accepting these rules for the sake of their class interests, the oligarchy endows the rules with value and effectiveness extending beyond those interests. There is some evidence, albeit ambiguous, of such political developments in a few African countries.

The two most clearly discernible dimensions of state-building during the last two decades of African independence have been the bureaucratization of the instruments of state power and the legalization of the discretionary powers of personal rulers: a trend toward state organization rather than institutionalization. This is a general feature of early modern state-building: it marks political development not only in Africa but also in other parts of the Third World, as well as historically in Europe. Also, it is a feature of pre-constitutional government. In the evolution of most Western states the issues of the constitutionalization and later the democratization of the state arose only after an absolutist and centralized bureaucratic state had been built up. In most African countries the concentration of state power has yet to stimulate serious demands for liberalization. Opposition has been concerned with claiming power—not with establishing rules with which all powerholders must comply. A small but increasing number of rulers—soldiers and civilians alike—have acquired more solidly based power by the legalization and bureaucratization of their instruments of rule. The building up of state power remains the central political development task of Africa's personal rulers.

In its structure and *modus operandi,* the state bequeathed to most Africans at independence was, by and large, a centralized-bureaucratic organ little altered by belated colonial attempts to constitutionalize it. However—as we noted earlier—this colonial bureaucratic legacy has been undermined by the widespread and quite rapid moves taken by African governments to Africanize the civil service, the military, and other state and parastatal organizations. During the first decade of independence—and sometimes over an even longer period—there was a rather marked deterioration in the reliability and capability of state organizations as less competent, often less dutiful, and certainly less experienced officials replaced their European predecessors. The organizational deterioration consisted both in a decline of administrative effectiveness (owing to lower levels of staff competence) and a decline of administrative responsibility (owing to the penetration of state organizations by African sociocultural norms, which have inhibited objective choices by African officials).

A number of rulers in Africa are trying to resolve the problems of administrative incompetence and disobedience. One mechanism of control which some rulers appear to have exploited with success is for the ruler to identify particular state policies as crucial to his interests, and to make a conspicuous display of his concern for them; in consequence, those officials who are responsible for carrying out these policies will think long and hard before sabotaging them. Strong government and effective policies depend upon the obedience and cooperation of state officials, and successful state-oriented rulers are those, like Houphouët-Boigny, Banda, and Nyerere, who capture the attention and direct the anticipations of subordinates. Such cooperation, if it is not inspired by the goals themselves or the ruler's charisma, can be grounded in apprehension and a desire not to displease those in command—what Carl Friedrich calls the "psychology of discouragement."[2] The effective command of an organization, therefore, is not only a matter of formal orders and instructions but also of the informal rules by which subordinates remain alert to the wishes and desires of those in command.[3] The areas of policy and administration in which such a mechanism of command is most likely to develop are those crucial to the power interests of rulers: areas of political control. But it need not be confined to such domains if the ruler can demonstrate his concern for other policy goals—for example, Houphouët-Boigny has promoted capitalist development in Ivory Coast, Bongo has advanced economic nationalism in Gabon, and Nyerere has pursued socialism in Tanzania. Thus strong government can

2. Carl J. Friedrich, *Constitutional Government and Democracy*, rev. ed. (Boston: Ginn & Co., 1950), p. 398

3. In this respect, Friedrich has referred to the "rule of anticipated reaction" (ibid., p. 49).

arise not only from a ruler's preoccupation with political control but also from his desire to achieve non-political, economic goals. In a world that judges governments as much by their economic performance as by anything else, one might expect those African rulers who are seeking great power and international stature to take a keen interest in promoting economic development in their countries.

The second dimension of state-building in contemporary Africa, the legitimation of the discretionary powers of personal rulers, is perhaps of greater significance than bureaucratization. Africa's personal rulers, whether civilians or soldiers, have sought to clothe themselves in the garb of legality and legitimacy.[4] During the period since independence there has been an almost universal trend toward the establishment of exalted and legally unencumbered presidential offices. Frequently, state constitutions have been fundamentally revised or abolished and replaced by others personally tailored to the political needs of the ruler. Rather than distinguishing the office from the incumbent, Africa's presidential "constitutions" have made it difficult to make such distinctions. Some of Africa's rulers have been declared "life presidents" (Nkrumah, Banda, Amin, Macías); some have been in a position to secure such lifetime title to their offices but have refused to seek it (Kaunda, Kenyatta); and some others have been de facto in positions of permanent political tenure. (As we noted in chapter 6, Bokassa even installed himself as "emperor" with the aim, we presume, of establishing a dynasty.) Of course, as the Nkrumah, Amin, and Macías examples indicate, legally defined tenure by itself provides no ultimate political security. Legality of this kind is only effective to the extent that it dictates political conduct.

If Africa's personal rulers have pursued legality in the establishment of unrestricted presidential offices, they have sought legitimacy through the holding of plebiscites and uncontested elections to authorize their incumbency. The search for legitimacy is inherent in all rulership: certainly the desire for a popular mandate, usually but not always sought by means of elections, is a marked historical characteristic of modernizing rulers. In most African countries the typical method of confirming a president in office has been to hold a national election in the form of a plebiscite (sometimes with provision for a "yes" vote only). Such elections are rarely contested, and it is not unusual for the ruler/candidate to receive an overwhelming majority of the votes cast—99 percent

4. See Bereket H. Selassie, *The Executive in African Governments* (London: Heinemann, 1974).

or more. The use of presidential plebiscites has not been confined to civilian rulers: soldiers who seized power initially through coups have often resorted to such legitimizing devices afterwards. Indeed, the search for electoral legitimacy has been, if anything, more compelling for soldiers who have initially acquired ruling power by coercion. Military no less than civilian rulers have directed the writing of new constitutions aimed at legitimizing their rule, and both have sought to demonstrate the popularity of their rule through the organization of personal parties.

The creation of personally tailored offices and the pursuit of legitimacy through the use of controlled plebiscites and the formation of personal parties ought not to be regarded as signs of institutionalization, but rather as evidence of political authoritarianism. For an authoritarian president to become an institutional ruler he would, as a minimum, be required to accept his office as the final arbiter in his conduct rather than his own or his party's interests. This would require that he specify the situations, occasions, and spheres of action in which authority was limited or circumscribed—areas of jurisdiction, rights and powers, tenure in office, and so on. Institutionalization would require not only his own acceptance of these rules, but also their acceptance by others to whom they applied. In other words, institutionalization of African presidencies and other high state offices would require acts of forbearance by leaders demonstrating respect for the offices they occupy and the rules that define them.

We have been arguing that regimes of personal rule may become more organizationally and legally authoritarian as the ruler and his collaborators search for political security, but that such a process of state-building in itself is not sufficient to institutionalize a state. Personal rule can be expected to continue as a central characteristic of African states, probably with a trend toward greater organizational and legal authoritarianism. How might the institutionalization of such states conceivably begin to take place, and is there any evidence of this happening?

There appear to be two ways that political institutionalization could begin to occur under the present conditions of personal-authoritarian rule in Black Africa. One is by fundamental attempts to constitute or reconstitute the state, as in the largely peaceful transfers of authority from Europeans to Africans in British and French colonies, and more recently in the efforts to transfer governments from soldiers to civilian rulers. The other is by an incremental process of institutionalization at the apex of state power—

that is, in the office of the ruler himself and in other leading offices and arenas of power that he and his colleagues or successors see fit to subject to institutional rules. The first—a rationalist and constructivist *method* of state institutionalization—is relatively easy to comprehend and promote but very difficult to achieve. A new constitution can be drawn up and put in place without effectively channeling governmental and political behavior. The second—a *process* of state institutionalization—is more difficult to observe but more likely to succeed insofar as it consists of specific responses, based on practical experience and expedience, to the political demands of situations and to the political needs of a ruler or a ruling class. Each approach can be identified with a distinctive tradition in modern constitutional history: the first with the "radical" or rationalist tradition best exemplified in the American and French constitutional experiences and, in our own time, in the widespread practice of designing brand-new constitutions to launch the independence of new states; the second with the "conservative" or incremental-evolutionary tradition best exemplified in the British constitutional experience. Incremental constitutional adaptation can be seen as the normal process of constitutional change once a viable constitution has been established, however it was originally arrived at—as in the United States since the late eighteenth century.

Attempts to constitute or reconstitute a state by deliberate efforts at constitution-making are among the most fundamental political acts that penetrate to the central questions and issues of political life. For this reason such attempts are "radical," and their chances of success are highly problematical, to say the least. Of the many constitutions designed for modern states, only a few have succeeded in gaining acceptance and becoming institutionalized.[5] This has certainly been the case in Africa. Of the numerous governments that began their independent existence with new constitutions, very few have retained them and continued to abide by their principles.

While acts of constitution-making are usually associated with fundamental political changes, such as revolutions, breakdowns of regimes, or conquests, they can also accompany peaceful transfers of authority from one ruling class to another. Contemporary Af-

5. Karl Loewenstein commented in 1951—well before the full impact of decolonization had been felt—that "the epidemic of constitution-making in the wake of World War II has no parallel in history." The epidemic has spread much further since then. (See his "Reflections on the Value of Constitutions in Our Revolutionary Age," in *Comparative Politics: A Reader*, ed. Harry Eckstein and David E. Apter [New York: Free Press, 1963], p. 149.)

rican experiments with constitution-making have been associated more with peaceful transfers of ruling authority than with fundamental political changes. Situations of fundamental change sometimes existed—for example, the collapse of the Abboud regime in Sudan (1964) and the Amin tyranny in Uganda (1979)[6]—but transfers of authority associated either with decolonization or with the withdrawal of soldiers from ruling positions have been the usual circumstances of constitution-making.[7] The transfers during decolonization very rarely resulted in the establishment of constitutional government; it remains to be seen whether the more recent transfers will be any more successful.

Questions of constitutionalism are basically about "limited government": about the legitimate powers of government and the appropriate spheres for their exercise.[8] Historically, the demands for limits on government have been made by political oppositions, not by rulers in control, and actions to establish or restore constitutionalism have been taken most often when the capacity or desire of rulers to continue to exercise power has come into question. This was the case with British colonial terminal rule. It has been the case also with those soldier-rulers who have not sought to entrench themselves in power by civilianizing their regimes. Graceful exit from state power by such soldier-rulers seems to require renewed efforts at constitution-making because the deposed former regime is discredited by definition, and its "constitution" cannot therefore be restored.

Constitutional issues are bound to arise once soldiers accept the principle of restoring civilian government, for such a restoration raises questions of who shall rule and how this may be fairly determined. The principle is difficult for soldiers to ignore so long as their rule is viewed as exceptional, as the temporary rule of military intruders (however necessary or acceptable their initial intervention may have been). Those soldier-rulers who succeed in evading the principle and retaining governmental power usually achieve this by "civilianizing" and "politicizing" their own rule—for example, by founding political parties and other organizations and often by seeking popular mandates through the holding of un-

6. The post-1964 attempt at reconstitution in Sudan failed to overcome the intense factionalism of civilian politics and was followed by Numeiri's coup in 1969. The Uganda attempt was only beginning at the time of writing.

7. We exclude "constitutions" drawn up by soldier-rulers who seek only to legitimate their own personal rule.

8. See Carl J. Friedrich, *Limited Government: A Comparison* (Englewood Cliffs, N.J.: Prentice-Hall, 1974); for an account pertinent to Africa, see B. O. Nwabueze, *Constitutionalism in the Emergent States* (London: C. Hurst & Co., 1973).

contested presidential elections. This has been the case with Numeiri in Sudan, Mobutu in Zaire, Eyadéma in Togo, Siad Barre in Somalia, Kerekou in Benin, Habyalimana in Rwanda, Jean-Baptiste Bagaza in Burundi, and Traoré in Mali. But soldiers who have ruled as soldiers and without serious pretensions to "political" legitimacy—for example, General Gowon in Nigeria and General Acheampong in Ghana—have found themselves in increasingly anomalous governing situations. With the passage of time from their initial intervention and with the likely growth of factionalism within the military itself, not to mention the growing opposition from without, what legitimacy soldier-rulers possess may fade once the old regime is no longer a threat. If important elites and organized groups stand to gain from a restoration of open government, then political pressures will likely be pushing in that direction. And if the soldiers have made public promises to withdraw, these can be used against them the longer they remain in power *qua* soldiers—a problem that confronted the military rulers of Ghana, Nigeria, and Upper Volta.

In some African countries, the military has willingly taken action to restore the government to civilians; in other countries it has been compelled to do so. In the case of Ghana's first government of soldiers after the overthrow of President Nkrumah in 1966, a promise was made almost immediately to restore constitutional government after suitable planning and preparation had taken place; the promise was kept and a second republic was inaugurated in 1969.[9] Following a second military coup in 1972 the new ruler—the late General Acheampong—seemed determined to retain power indefinitely in the conviction that party politics had been the root cause of Ghana's considerable political and economic difficulties. This time the soldiers relinquished their hold on government only reluctantly after several years of growing pressure from diverse, mainly urban and middle-class groups—particularly students, lawyers, and other professionals—and in the face of persistent corruption and increasingly serious economic problems after 1974.[10] Struggling with declining legitimacy and power, the Acheampong government initiated steps to draw up a new constitution. The government was overthrown in 1978 by Lt. Gen. Frederick Akuffo, who in turn was ousted by Flight Lt. Jerry Rawlings barely a year later (June 4, 1979), and a civilian govern-

9. Robert Pinkney, *Ghana Under Military Rule, 1966–1969* (London: Methuen & Co., 1972).

10. Jon Kraus, "The Decline of Ghana's Military Government" *Current History* 73, 432 (December 1977): 214–17, 227–29.

ment was installed in September 1979 after being elected according to constitutional provisions.[11]

In Nigeria both obligation and compulsion worked in favor of reconstitution. As early as 1967 General Gowon had acknowledged the goal of constitutional restoration and set forth conditions for its realization. The Nigerian civil war intervened, but the war ended in January 1970. In October 1970 Gowon renewed his commitment and specified the basic tasks of state rebuilding that had to be accomplished in order to restore constitutional government by 1976. By 1974 Gowon's rule was beginning to falter, and he postponed indefinitely the planned restoration.[12] These difficulties preceded his overthrow by army officers in late July 1975; three months later, on October 1, his successor, Brig. Gen. Murtala Muhammed, promised a return to constitutional government and announced a program for its achievement by October 1979.[13] Muhammed was assassinated only a few months after this announcement, but his successor—General Olusegun Obasanjo— carried out the promise, and a civilian government under a new federal constitution was elected to office in July and August 1979.

In Upper Volta, constitutional government was restored in 1978 after twelve years of military rule that was interrupted, between 1970 and 1974, by a period of mixed military-civilian government. Intense personal rivalry and factional-party conflict had led President Sangoulé Lamizana to end the mixed government experiment in 1974. Under pressure from trade unionists, who had been instrumental in bringing the military to power in 1966, the military rulers initiated actions which led to the restoration of constitutional government in 1978.[14] It remains to be seen whether these recent attempts at reconstitution will be any more successful than earlier ones in regulating the exercise of power in the state.

The practical steps of reconstituting a state prior to transferring government from military to civilian politicians usually include

11. Following the Rawlings coup, the Armed Forces Revolutionary Council executed three former soldier-rulers—Generals Acheampong and Akuffo and Lt. Gen. Akwasi Afrifa—as well as some other leaders, after they had been summarily tried and found guilty of "corruption."

12. See Ian Campbell, "Military Withdrawal Debate in Nigeria: The Prelude to 1975 Coup," *West African Journal of Sociology and Political Science* 1, 3 (January 1978): 335.

13. Jon Kraus, "From Military to Civilian Regimes in Ghana and Nigeria," *Current History* 76, 445 (March 1979): 122–26, 134–36, 138.

14. Richard Vengraff, "Africa's New Hope for Democracy," *African Report* 23, 4 (July–August 1978): 59–64; *West Africa* 3147 (31 October 1977): 2193, 2195; ibid., 3174 (15 May 1978): 920; ibid., 3181 (3 July 1978): 1273–75.

several stages of constitution-making. A typical initial stage is the appointment by the military of a commission or committee to draft a new constitution which will take into account the country's distinctive characteristics and problems. Almost inevitably the draft proposal will also reflect the constitutional theories and precepts then most in favor.[15] In addition, the commissioners will be alert to the interests, values, and perhaps instructions or guidelines of the incumbent soldier-rulers who appointed them. The commissions may be selected with an eye to representativeness, but this may be diminished by the need for legal expertise and a likelihood that professional, middle-class groups will be overrepresented. In the first return to constitutional government in Ghana, the selection of commission members from among Nkrumah's old "bourgeois" opponents and defectors from his government was undoubtedly an important factor in the drafting of a very "liberal" constitution reflecting middle-class biases and interests. The Nigerian constitutional committee comprised forty-nine members; there were two from each state plus several others. The membership included lawyers, businessmen, economists, university lecturers and administrators, and one army officer (a chaplain). Of course no constitutional commission could be entirely free of bias or perfectly representative.

Ordinarily such commissions initiate proceedings which result in a draft written constitution. During the course of the deliberations, and often continuing after the presentation of draft proposals, a constitutional debate is likely to take place—especially in countries, such as Nigeria and Ghana, where sophisticated and articulate political interest groups are present—over the general principles and specific provisions of the proposed constitution.

A later stage of constitution-making is the submission of the draft constitution to a higher authority for ratification—usually either to the people in a referendum or to a constituent assembly. In the first procedure, followed in Upper Volta, there is no provision for further amendment; in the second, followed in Ghana (twice) and in Nigeria, further discussion and amendment are possible prior to final ratification, but changes are likely to be con-

15. For Nigeria, see Keith Panter-Brick, "The Constitution Drafting Committee," in *Soldiers and Oil: The Political Transformation of Nigeria*, ed. Keith Panter-Brick (London and Totowa, N.J.: Frank Cass & Co., 1978), pp. 291–350; for Ghana, see Robin Luckham, "The Constitutional Commission 1966–69," in *Politicians and Soldiers in Ghana: 1966–1972*, ed. Dennis Austin and Robin Luckham (London and Portland, Ore.: Frank Cass & Co., 1975), pp. 62–88.

fined largely to details without affecting the overall structure of the commission's design.[16] At least in theory, such changes ought to bring the constitution more into line with the practical requirements and political tendencies of the country. Then the newly ratified constitution must be implemented by the military government-in-power, who needs to set up the necessary machinery, such as electoral commissions, to administer and enforce the rules by which a new government is elected and installed in office. The final stage completes the transfer of power and the reconstitution of the state in a formal-legal sense.

In addition to transferring governmental power from soldiers to civilians, acts of reconstitution in contemporary Africa can be seen as attempts to resolve basic political problems that have plagued states in the past, in the hope of preventing them from recurring in the future. In this regard, modern constitution-making is a rationalist exercise that can be best understood by referring to the problems the constitutional designers are grappling with and the goals they are trying to achieve. If, as in Nigeria, powerful regionalism is perceived as a threat to undermine—if not to immobilize—the federal government, then constitutional measures must be contrived to counter this threat.[17] Or if, as in Ghana during the first attempted reconstitution, a perception of the fear of "tyranny" dominates the constitutional exercise, then provisions for preventing it are likely to be key elements in the final design.[18] We can increase our understanding of the reconstitutions of various African states by examining the problems being addressed and goals being aimed at in each case.

The problem that has been dominant in most reconstitution exercises in Africa has been internal disunity and disorder; thus the uppermost concern of constitutional engineers in Nigeria, Ghana (during the second reconstitution), and Upper Volta has been to avert the disorders and disruptive conflicts threatened by intense party-factional rivalries operating within societies having deep-rooted ethnic-regional divisions and antagonisms. The basic question being asked by African constitution-makers is the following: What set of offices, rules, and procedures can prevent such party-factional disorders and conflicts from arising within the state?

16. See Robin Luckham and Stephen Nkrumah, "The Constituent Assembly—A Social and Political Portrait," in *Politicians and Soldiers in Ghana*, ed. Austin and Luckham, pp. 117–18.

17. Ali D. Yahaya, "The Creation of States," in *Soldiers and Oil*, ed. Panter-Brick, pp. 201–3; see, for another key issue, S. Egite Oyovbaire, "The Politics of Revenue Allocation," in ibid., pp. 224–49.

18. F. K. Drah, "Political Tradition and the Search for Constitutional Democracy in Ghana: A Prolegomenon," *Ghana Journal of Sociology* 6, 1 (February 1970): 1.

The answers that typically have been provided derive from the dual principles that (1) regional and local entities should have specified powers and rights in the state and (2) such powers should be limited to prevent their abuse for the sake of narrow and divisive sectional interests possibly threatening the state. A good illustration of the implementation of the first principle is in Nigeria, where the number of states in the federal structure was increased from twelve to nineteen in 1976 in response to the demands of the regional minorities, with each state having the right to at least one minister in the federal cabinet. The 1979 Nigerian constitution makes it extremely difficult to create new states: to change the boundaries of states requires a two-thirds majority in both houses of the federal legislature and approval of two-thirds of the state assemblies. Thus in these and other ways the new Nigerian constitution provides regional entities with specified rights and powers in a reconstituted state.

But perhaps the most important—certainly the most original—African constitutional measures are rules that regulate party systems.[19] In such rules we see the attempts of African constitutionalists to grapple with the problems that party-competitive democracy poses for ethnically divided societies—that is, the undermining of national unity and central authority by the organization of parties and the mobilization of party support on an ethnic-regional basis. In Ghana's second reconstitution, the initial proposal by the military for a system of "union government" in which parties would be constitutionally proscribed was one attempt to address this problem.[20] Although it was supported by important rural and traditional sectors of public opinion, as well as by the urban poor, this proposal was vigorously rejected by modern groups and informed legal opinion, and finally was dropped in late 1978. The difficulties such a proposal presented to constitutional government based upon the principles of political freedom—including the freedom to form and join parties—are clear. But the proposal was also unrealistic in that informal political parties almost certainly would have emerged as individual politicians would seek out and aid one another. Moreover, the social divisions that had given rise to parties in the past would still be present to make claims upon politicians and governments.

It is in Upper Volta and Nigeria that the most detailed attempts

19. The West German Constitution also regulates political parties by regarding them as constitutional organs rather than voluntary associations—the usual case in constitutional democracies. See F. F. Ridley, *The Study of Government* (London: George Allen & Unwin, 1975), pp. 83–84.

20. See Maxwell Owusu, "Politics Without Parties: Reflections on the Union Government Proposals in Ghana," *African Studies Review* 22, 1 (April 1979): 89–108.

to regulate parties constitutionally are to be found. Article 112 of the Voltaic Constitution (1977) restricts the number of post-election parties to three—that is, only the three most successful parties in an election are allowed to remain in existence. (The reasons for allowing three—rather than, say, two or four—were not provided.) Others must either dissolve or merge with one of the winning parties.[21] Without such restrictions, it was feared that a stable party system could not emerge. The constitution also requires that the president be elected in a separate national election and that he not be a leader of any political party. The constitutional ideal is the monarchical one that the president represent all of the people and be above partisanship.

Perhaps the most elaborate attempt yet made to regulate a party system by constitutional means in contemporary Africa, employing rules that are quite novel to constitutional government, is Nigeria's second independence constitution (which otherwise bears many similarities to the United States Constitution). An important section of the draft constitution (Chapter VI, Part IX) strictly defines the regulations governing the organization and operation of political parties.[22] Responsibilities for administering and enforcing the regulations are given to a new constitutional body—the Nigerian Electoral Commission—which is specifically empowered to register and review political parties in accordance with the constitution's provisions. Among these provisions are the following: (1) party membership must be open to all Nigerians; (2) each party's constitution must be registered with the electoral commission; (3) a party's "name, emblem, or motto" must have "no ethnic or religious connotation" and must not "give the appearance that the association's activities are confined to a part only of the geographical area of Nigeria"; and (4) memberships of party executives must "reflect the federal character of Nigeria."[23] The constitution provides for the punishment of party officials who contravene these requirements. The revival of former parties or the conversion of existing organizations into political parties is expressly forbidden, party programs must be national in character, and parties must canvass for support by making national ap-

21. *Africa Contemporary Record: Annual Survey and Documents*; 1968–70, ed. Colin Legum and John Drysdale (London: Africa Research, 1969–70); 1970–72, ed. Colin Legum (London: Rex Collings, 1971; London: Rex Collings, and New York: Africana Publications, 1972); 1972–79, ed. Colin Legum (New York: Africana Publications, 1973–79); see 1977–78, p. B 798.

22. The draft constitution is reprinted in *Africa Contemporary Record*, 1976–77, pp. C 64–114.

23. Ibid., p. C 105.

peals. For the 1979 elections five parties qualified for registration by the electoral commission.

There is no question that new constitutions can be designed and adopted; whether they can be implemented and effective is another question altogether. No serious student of African politics can be sanguine about the prospects for the success of constructivist constitution-making in the future when it has failed so often in the past. Such experiments severely test the confidence, security, and self-restraint of powerful men and groups who are being asked to accept not only new constitutional rules but also their administration and interpretation by newly authorized agencies. These rules may have adverse effects upon the interests of various individuals and groups while failing to have the desired effects on the political system as a whole. Such failures of the new rules—for example, their failure to achieve the nationalization of politics, to prevent the politicization of regionalism, or to prevent biases in their application—may promote narrow, self-interested actions to evade or alter them. Those who cannot win within the rules may try to achieve their goals outside of them. The losers may not accept defeat, and the winners may not want to run the risk of losing next time around.

There was evidence of difficulties with the new Nigerian constitution following its first test in the July and August 1979 elections.[24] That the elections were held at all, and were conducted without violence and bloodshed and apparently with a minimum of irregularities and manipulation, is of course a significant achievement. But the outcome of the elections and the steps taken to deal with the results have revealed continuing problems. The goal of preventing underlying ethnic-regional cleavages from being reflected in the party system and in representation in the National Assembly was not achieved. Of the five parties contesting for National Assembly seats, only one—the National Party of Nigeria (NPN), led by Alhaji Shehu Shagari—began to achieve anything like "national," transregional support. In the presidential election the largest share of the vote (33.8 percent) was won by Shagari, whose nearest rivals, the old political war horses Chief Obafemi Awolowo and Dr. Nnamdi Azikiwe, gained 29.2 percent and 16.7 percent respectively. The constitution provides that in order to win without a run-off election a presidential candidate must receive at least 25 percent of the votes in two-thirds of

24. See *Africa Confidential* 20, 23 (November 14, 1979): 1–4, and *Africa Research Bulletin: Political, Social, and Cultural Series* 16, 8 (September 15, 1979): B 5367–C 5370.

Nigeria's nineteen states. Shagari won at least 25 percent in twelve states and 20 percent in the state of Kano. The electoral commission declared that this met the requirement of the constitution and that Shagari was elected. Three of the losing candidates appealed the decision and called upon the Supreme Military Council to "annul" the commission's ruling on the grounds that twelve is less than two-thirds of nineteen. They were unsuccessful in their appeal.

Under any new constitutional arrangement of power and authority in a state there must be a period of adjustment when ambiguities and defects in the rules and procedures are clarified and remedied. But during such a period—which may extend for a considerable length of time until the rules begin to acquire familiarity and legitimacy—the decisions of the duly constituted authorities who preside over the constitution must be accepted as final. Acceptance of properly constituted rules and authorities is the litmus test of constitutionalism. It remains to be seen whether all of Nigeria's politicians will accept the rulings that will have to be made. Here we encounter perhaps the central obstacle confronting the constructivist constitutionalization of a new state, like Nigeria, that lacks a viable constitutional tradition: the requirements of a spirit of constitutional acceptance and good will by politicians and other powerholders who are in a position to prevent the constitution from working. The fact that the losers in the presidential election made an appeal to the military, which is not empowered to effect constitutional changes, is an initial source of doubt that constitutionalism will take hold in Nigeria this time.

It is therefore difficult to be optimistic about the chances for the success of constitutional engineering in Africa. Yet it is entirely understandable that African countries should turn their attention to questions of reconstituting the state whenever the opportunity arises. Perhaps this is the most noteworthy feature of modern constructivist constitutionalism: however often it may fail in practice, it remains the theory of the state that is most in line with the modern world's emphasis on rationalism and planning—an emphasis that is pronounced in African political thought.[25] Even when a constitution fails, the constitution-making exercise still remains an important opportunity for a country's political and intellectual leaders to assess their political resources and problems and attempt to deal with them in an impersonal, non-authoritarian way. The reconstitutional exercise provides both participants and ob-

25. See Gideon-Cyrus M. Mutiso and S. W. Rohio, eds., *Readings in African Political Thought* (London: Heinemann, 1975).

servers with important insights into the political problems and
possibilities of a country. It provides, in other words, the opportunity for a political education.

The alternative to state reconstitution by comprehensive design
is a piecemeal process of incremental institutionalization and
evolving political practice that serves more limited political purposes and consists in specific and concrete responses to particular
political experiences. Unlike wholesale constitutional engineering, such a process is more difficult to study because it is harder
to discern. It is less deliberate, momentous, and public; more un-
planned, fortuitous, and expedient. It is made up of specific responses to immediate problems: an institutional coup rather than
a revolution; a hesitant step or two, not a great leap forward. It is
often ambiguous and obscure because it is not usually clear, in a
given instance, that impersonal rules have superseded considerations of power as the arbiters of political behavior. With these
caveats in mind, we have discerned two ways in which a process of
piecemeal institutionalization at the center of an African state can
take place. One way is something like *partial* constitutional engineering, as illustrated by the cautious and somewhat restricted
liberalization of the party system in Senegal. The second way is
more specific, limited, and evolutionary, as illustrated by the constitutional transfer of presidential offices in connection with the
issues of ruler succession and resignation in Liberia until 1980,
Kenya, and Tanzania.

The opening up of the Senegalese polity in the later 1970s by
allowing four parties to compete for electoral support—although
on a less than completely open basis because of restrictions placed
on the identities of the new parties[26]—is clearly an attempt to introduce rules as arbiters in the political struggle for state power. It
is an attempt to move toward a kind of semi-competitive, multiparty democracy. But some facets of this attempt are more clearly
defined than others. It is clear that even in a semi-competitive democracy where the dominant party enjoys a competitive advantage
that is upheld in part by a bias in the electoral rules, the system is
nevertheless rule-governed or institutional to the extent that all
parties freely consent to the rules. It is not so clear to what degree
the acceptance of the electoral rules by the parties of Senegal has
depended upon the continuing presence of President Senghor. Is it
his personal authority that has upheld the rules in the last analy-

26. See chapter 3 above.

sis? To the extent that we are uncertain about the authority that Senghor has given to the rules, we are also uncertain about their degree of institutionalization. If the rules do not survive Senghor, that would be fairly clear evidence that they depended on his authority for their acceptance.[27] If they are maintained and enable rivals of the ruling party to gain ground politically, it will be important to see whether the latter attempts to change them to insure against electoral defeat. By the same token, if the present rules enable the dominant party to hold power at little or no risk, it will be interesting to see whether the rival parties will continue to accept them. In this regard, there may have to be at least a minimal degree of perceived "fairness" in constitutional or electoral rules if they are to be respected by all parties concerned.[28] One indication of the absence of institutionalization in the Senegalese party system is the exclusion of significant parties (most notably Diop's "progressive" RND) for refusing to accept the assignment of official ideological labels. In addition, there is a likelihood of continued clandestine politics in Senegal by excluded parties and factions, which is an indication not of institutional but of personal-authoritarian rule. All of this suggests that the Senegalese experiment with qualified democracy is at best a mixed and somewhat contradictory example of political institutionalization.

Another approach to the piecemeal process of political institutionalization in personal-authoritarian regimes is the acceptance of strategic political offices as arbiters of power, by the separation of the authority of the offices from that of the incumbents. It may develop in the succession of presidential offices from one ruler to another. Both democratic election and constitutional succession are institutional attempts to resolve the crucial question "Who shall govern?" In terms of constitutional logic, the two institutional mechanisms are somewhat at odds: if elections are crucial in a polity, then rules of succession are likely to be less important. (Rules of succession are crucial to monarchy, whereas elections are central to democracy.) In authoritarian regimes, as in monarchies, the tendency for the highest officeholder to enjoy life tenure increases the importance of succession as the principal way that

27. Here we are touching on a central point in Weber's sociology of authority: the possibility of institutions initially gaining their authority from the personal legitimacy of rulers. See Max Weber, *Economy and Society: An Outline of Interpretive Sociology*, ed. Guenther A. Roth and Clause Wittich (New York: Bedminster Press, 1968), vol. 1, ch. 3, and vol. 3, ch. 14.

28. We take this to be one of the central themes of John Rawls, *A Theory of Justice* (Cambridge, Mass.: Harvard University Press, Belknap Press, 1971), esp. pp. 108–14.

ruling office changes hands. If the political process in Senegal in the immediate future turns primarily on the question of succession, this will be a sign that the critical political struggle is a factional one within the ruling party and not an electoral one among the several rival parties. It will be an indication that the new party system is not becoming institutionalized because it is not crucial in determinations of power.

The manner in which succession has taken place in Liberia and Kenya is consistent with the process of piecemeal institutionalization. The succession of Tolbert to the Liberian presidency was an instance of a constitutional transfer of power. To the extent that the constitution of Liberia existed primarily to uphold Americo-Liberian supremacy, conformity to its provisions by Americo-Liberians was a weak test of institutionalization because little forbearance was involved. But to the extent that narrower factional or personal power interests *within* the aristocracy—such as the desire to control the presidency—were being curbed, it was a stronger test. Clearly, constitutionalism can be aristocratic as well as democratic, although in Liberia with the seizure of power in April 1980 by soldiers the issues of succession and institutionalization are no longer relevant.

From all outward appearance, the succession of Moi to the Kenyan presidency was an instance of a constitutional transfer of ruling power. However, the bias in the Kenyan rules of succession made it relatively easy for Moi's faction to succeed, and such an alignment of constitutional rules with power interests reduces the significance of the Kenyan succession as a test of institutionalization. It may have been a greater test for the opposing faction, who was not favored by the rules and who attempted without success to change them beforehand to increase its chances of inheriting Kenyatta's mantle of rule. The strength of Moi's position also reduced the significance of the succession as a test of institutional rules, because the opposition's weak position meant that its acceptance of the procedures was very likely an act of prudence. We do not know for certain why no challenge to Moi was made during the succession, but the logic of the political situation strongly suggests that the various uncommitted politicians and their factions were betting on the favorite. Perhaps all that can be said in the Kenya case is that the constitutional rules, whatever their particular bias—and no rules are entirely without some bias[29]—were upheld

29. The Kenyan biases appear no greater than those of other constitutions. Perfectly fair rules are a constitutional ideal more than a practical achievement in most institutionalized states.

by all powerful groups whose interests were affected by them. Not only the ruling oligarchy as a collectivity, but also the broader citizenry benefitted from this peaceful transition in not being subjected to the instability and uncertainty or greater political evils that almost certainly would have been caused by struggle over the succession.

Piecemeal political institutionalization can be witnessed in the uncoerced resignation, in conformity with the terms of his office, of an incumbent president and the constitutional transfer of the office to another person. The separation of the continuing office from its temporary incumbents is a sign of institutionalization. There is a possibility of such transfers of high offices in Tanzania. President Nyerere has expressed his desire to make way for another incumbent. It is clear that Nyerere wants to begin the process of transferring to a new generation the control of the Tanzanian state that he and his colleagues have built. (In speaking of this transfer, he has borrowed the ceremonial term *kung'atuka* from his own ethnic language [Zanaki], which is employed when the old generation of warriors lays down its spears and admonishes the new generation to pick them up and use them honorably.)[30] Less clear will be his personal role in determining the success of the transfer. The fact that he desires and advocates such change suggests that his personal authority will stand behind it, and the fact that he will very likely remain active in the ruling party after he has vacated the presidency suggests that he will continue to support the change. It is less clear, therefore, whether the movement of a new generation into the highest government and party offices will reflect the institutionalization of these offices or Nyerere's continuing personal authority. It is clear that a peaceful and procedural transfer of ruling power in Tanzania will go against the grain of contemporary African political history, in which power has usually been transferred by means of violence or threats of violence, but we must await the verdict of history to see if it is a significant instance of institutionalization.

The process of political institutionalization is difficult to analyze concurrently with the events, not only because it is ambiguous, but also because the final test of institutionalization is an historical one. Time is necessarily involved—time for a series of situations and actions to recur that can be judged against the timeless rules prescribing and proscribing conduct in respect of them.

30. *Africa Contemporary Record*, 1977–78, p. B 403.

The realization of an abstract institution (to return to Rawls's terminology) is not one act but a series of consistent acts that recur over an extended period of time. Ultimately, it is the emergence of a pattern of conduct that conforms with the rules. We agree with Huntington that the degree of institutionalization is indicated roughly by the age of institutional rules and procedures: "Political institutions are thus not created overnight."[31] Nor are they adequately tested by one political storm, although the survival of such a test may stimulate the confidence required for an institution to become effective and to survive future tests. Like other modes of authority, including personal authority, political institutions are only effective to the extent that people have confidence in them. Such confidence grows out of a recognition of their usefulness and value in concrete situations. The ultimate confidence is to take them entirely for granted, to regard them as natural phenomena and not as the political artifacts that they are.

In conclusion, it may be appropriate to provide some theoretical reflections on the process of political institutionalization at the center of a typical African state. What seems to be required for such a process to occur? The most important requirement is well-established, strong, and stable government. All of our examples of incremental institutionalization are from well-established, relatively long-standing systems of personal rule. A recognizable and determinate government must exist before it can become institutionalized. For this reason only a few of Africa's states are as yet in a position to become institutionalized. The historical experience in Western states of constitutionalism following upon a period of absolutism seems consistent with this proposition. For the same reason, constitutional engineering may be an unpromising method of political institutionalization in new states, for it is all too often called upon not only to constitutionalize the government but to establish it in the first place.

For a well-established government to become "institutionalized" in fact as well as in name, rules must be followed in actual political conduct. Even the most powerful actors—including the ruler—must be subject to these rules; otherwise the interests of the state cannot be separated from their own personal-political interests. The acceptance of some rules by all save the ruler is an uncertain indication of institutionalization because it is possible that such rules are followed solely out of consideration for his personal authority or power.

31. Samuel P. Huntington, *Political Order in Changing Societies* (New Haven and London: Yale University Press, 1968), p. 14.

Why should strong regimes of personal rule subject themselves to the restraints of non-instrumental rules? From our analysis it has been possible to derive the following explanation. Such rules appear to arise more out of a recognition of their political advantages and uses than of their intrinsic virtues as ideal standards of conduct. They seem to arise in concrete situations where their practical advantages can be readily perceived by those involved. (The need for practical solutions to problems in concrete situations may explain why piecemeal rule-making is more apt to bear institutional fruit than the more abstract and general activity of constructivist constitution-making.) In contemporary Black Africa one situation has been the necessity to transfer a presidential office from one ruler to another. Rules providing for such a transfer of office may be accepted by all interested leaders and factions because the alternatives appear wholly unacceptable. Another situation has been the need for political accommodation among the conflicting interests of rival leaders or factions of oligarchies when a personal authority is not able to perform such a function. Rules and procedures may be defined and accepted in preference to stalemate and the risk that a conflict will deteriorate into a violent confrontation. In a similar way, rules may become accepted as the least objectionable basis for personal and factional competition for positions within oligarchical governments—the case with one-party elections in Kenya.

In these situations rules appear to be accepted not to achieve something better so much as to prevent something worse; they are accepted for negative reasons rather than positive ones. The political mechanism of institutionalization behind such acceptances might be conceived of as an "invisible hand" bringing the actions of powerful men into line with rules of conduct in situations where everyone has become apprehensive about the consequences of not accepting them. The attraction of such an explanation is its realism. It does not require material incentives or virtuous men to operate so much as it requires an awareness of the uncertainty and disorder—the public evils—that might result if the rules are not followed.

Appendix

BLACK AFRICAN COUNTRIES AND RULERS AS OF SEPTEMBER 1980

Country	Date of Independence	Current Ruler; Title; Effective Date of Rule	Prior Rulers Since Independence
Angola	November 11, 1975	José Eduardo dos Santos President 1979	Founding President Antônio Agostinho Neto dies September 10, 1979. Central Committee of Movimento Popular de Libertação de Angola (MPLA) on September 20, 1979, determines that successor be dos Santos (aged 37), who had been First Deputy Prime Minister, Planning Minister, and head of National Planning Commission.
Benin (formerly Dahomey, 1960–75)	August 1, 1960	Lt. Col. Mathieu Kerekou President 1972	1. May 22, 1959: Herbert Maga elected Prime Minister of self-governing (French) Dahomey; becomes President December 31, 1960. 2. October 28, 1963: military coup. Col. (later Gen.) Christophe Soglo becomes President. 3. January 1964: civilian government restored; national elections held. Sourou Migan Apithy becomes President and Justin Ahomadegbe, Vice-President. 4. November 29, 1965: Apithy and Ahomadegbe forced by Soglo to resign; succeeded by Tahirou Congacou, President of National Assembly, as provided by constitution. 5. December 22, 1965: military coup. Soglo, now Army Chief of Staff, assumes presidency. 6. December 16, 1967: military counter-coup led by Maj. (later Lt. Col.) Kerekou and Col. Maurice Kouandété; Army Chief of Staff Lt. Col. Alphonse Alley made President and Kouandété, Prime Minister.

288

7. Alley and Kouandété unable to rule in tandem and army cannot agree on third military candidate, so civilian Émile-Derin Zinsou is chosen President and confirmed by popular referendum July 1968.

8. December 10, 1969: Kouandété leads military coup ousting Zinsou. Kouandété's following not sufficient to assure him top post. "Political moderate" Lt. Col. Paul Émile de Souza made President of three-man ruling military directorate.

9. May 1970: civilian rule restored; Maga chosen President and head of presidential troika including Apithy and Ahomadegbe. Presidency rotates every two years among them.

10. May 1972: Ahomadegbe becomes President and second head of troika.

11. October 26, 1972: military coup. Kerekou assumes presidency.

Botswana   September 30, 1966   Quett Masire President 1980

Founding President Sir Seretse Khama dies July 13, 1980; constitutionally succeeded by Vice-President Masire, new leader of ruling Botswana Democratic Party.

Burundi   July 1, 1962   Col. Jean-Baptiste Bagaza President 1976

1. Mwami (King) Mwambutsa II, 1915–66. Prime Ministers under Mwambutsa:
   André Muhirwa, 1962–63
   Pierre Ngendandumwe, 1963
   Albin Nyamoya, 1964–65
   Pierre Ngendandumwe, 1965 (assassinated January 1965)
   Joseph Bamina, 1965
   Leopold Biha, 1965

BLACK AFRICAN COUNTRIES AND RULERS AS OF SEPTEMBER 1980 (Continued)

Country	Date of Independence	Current Ruler; Title; Effective Date of Rule	Prior Rulers Since Independence
Burundi (cont.)			2. July 8, 1966: Mwambutsa II's son, Prince Charles Ndizeye, deposes father and becomes Mwami Ntare IV; Capt. (later Col.) Michel Micombero appointed Prime Minister. 3. November 29, 1966: Ntare IV overthrown by military coup led by Micombero, who declares Burundi a republic and himself President. 4. November 1, 1976: military counter-coup by Lt. Col. (later Col.) Bagaza.
Cameroon (1960–61: Republic of East Cameroon; October 1961–72: Federal Republic of Cameroon—composed of the East [former French Trust Territory] and West [part of former British Trust Territory]; 1972: United Cameroon Republic)	January 1, 1960	Ahmadou Ahidjo President 1960	Ahidjo becomes Prime Minister of French Trust Territory of East Cameroon in January 1958. Elected President May 5, 1960.

Country	Date	Events
Central African Republic (1976–79: Central African Empire)	August 13, 1966	1. April 1959: Dacko becomes Prime Minister following legislative elections, succeeding Barthélémy Boganda, first Prime Minister of self-governing (French) Central African Republic (formerly Oubangi-Chari). Dacko becomes President November 17, 1960. 2. December 31, 1965: military coup by Army Chief of Staff, Col. (later Field Marshal) Jean-Bédel Bokassa. 3. March 2, 1972: Bokassa proclaimed "President for Life." 4. December 4, 1977: Bokassa crowned emperor. 5. September 20, 1979: Bokassa deposed in coup; replaced by Dacko.
David Dacko President 1979		
Chad	August 11, 1960	1. March 1959: Ngarta (formerly François) Tombalbaye elected Prime Minister by legislative assembly under (French) internal autonomy regime; becomes head of state at independence; formally "elected" President April 22, 1962. 2. April 13, 1975: Tombalbaye killed in military coup. Gen. Félix Malloum, detained since 1973, released and becomes President. 3. August 31, 1978: Hissène Habré, warring factional leader, appointed Prime Minister to foster policy of national reconciliation. 4. March 23, 1979: Malloum and Habré resign following first Kano Conference, calling for transitional government of national union. 5. March 24, 1979: Weddeye named Chairman of Provisional Council.
Goukouni Weddeye President November 11, 1979		

BLACK AFRICAN COUNTRIES AND RULERS AS OF SEPTEMBER 1980 (Continued)

Country	Date of Independence	Current Ruler; Title; Effective Date of Rule	Prior Rulers Since Independence
Chad (cont.)			6. April 29, 1979: following second Kano Conference, Lal Mohamat Choua becomes head of interim Government of National Union. 7. August 22, 1979: following first Lagos Conference on Chad Reconciliation (August 14–21), Weddeye, a northern Moslem leader and long-time opponent of southern, Sara-dominated government, is named President and Col. Abdelkader Kamougué, a southerner, Vice-President. 8. November 11, 1979: Weddeye becomes President of National Union Government composed of all major factions and personalities.
Congo-Brazzaville	August 15, 1960	Col. Denis Sassou-Nguesso President 1979	1. November 21, 1959: Fulbert Youlou elected President under pre-independence constitution. 2. Military coup following general strike August 13–15, 1963; Alphonse Massamba-Débat formally elected President December 19, 1963. 3. August 2, 1968: Military coup by supporters of Capt. Marien Ngouabi, then in prison. Massamba-Débat recalled to presidency August 4, 1968, but resigns September 4, 1968. Governing National Revolutionary Council formed August 5, 1968, chaired by Ngouabi; Ngouabi shares power with Maj. Alfred Raoul, Prime Minister and temporary head of state, September 5, 1968.

4. December 31, 1968: Ngouabi assumes presidency.
5. March 18, 1977: Ngouabi assassinated; March 25, 1977: Massamba-Débat executed as chief figure in assassination. Col. (later Brig. Gen.) Joachim Yhombi-Opango nominated President by Military Committee of Parti Congolais du Travail (PCT).
6. February 5, 1979: Yhombi-Opango forced to resign by Military Committee of PCT for ideological and factional reasons.
7. February 9, 1979: Maj. Sassou-Nguesso, First Vice-President and PCT's number two man, named President by the Central Committee of PCT. Yhombi-Opango demoted to private and placed under arrest for "high treason" October 20, 1979.

Djibouti — June 27, 1977 — Hassan Gouled Aptidon President 1977

1. June 24, 1977: Hassan Gouled elected first President by acclamation by Chamber of Deputies.
2. July 12, 1977: Ahmed Dini Ahmed named first Prime Minister.
3. December 16, 1977: Ahmed resigns; new government formed February 6, 1978; Abdullah Mohamed Kamil appointed Prime Minister.
4. September 21, 1978: Gouled dismisses cabinet; September 30, 1978: names Senator Barkad Gourad Hamadou Prime Minister.

Equatorial Guinea — October 12, 1968 — Lt. Col. Teodoro Obiango Nguema Mbasogo President 1979

1. September 29, 1968: Francisco Macías Nguema elected President; proclaimed Life President July 14, 1972.
2. August 3, 1979: military coup led by Mbasogo. Macías tried and executed September 1979.
3. October 12, 1980: Mbasogo becomes President.

BLACK AFRICAN COUNTRIES AND RULERS AS OF SEPTEMBER 1980 (Continued)

Country	Date of Independence	Current Ruler; Title; Effective Date of Rule	Prior Rulers Since Independence
Ethiopia	Historic	Lt. Col. Mengistu Haile Mariam Chairman of Provisional Military Administrative Council (PMAC) 1977	1. Succession of emperors until Haile Selassie, crowned in 1930. 2. September 12, 1974: Haile Selassie deposed by military and dies under mysterious circumstances eleven months later. 3. Lt. Gen. Aman Andom is Chairman of PMAC (Dergue) until November 1974, when he is killed while resisting arrest by the military. 4. Brig. Gen. Teferi Banti succeeds Andom as Chairman of PMAC; however, power actually held by Vice-Chairman Maj. (later Lt. Col.) Mengistu and Lt. Col. Atnafu Abate. 5. February 3, 1977: Banti killed in purge which leads to ascendance of Mengistu as Chairman of PMAC.
Gabon	August 17, 1960	Omar Bongo President 1967	1. February 27, 1959: Leon M'Ba elected Prime Minister under (French) internal autonomy regime; becomes head of state at independence; formally "elected" President February 12, 1961. 2. November 28, 1967: M'Ba dies in office; succeeded by Vice-President (then Albert-Bernard) Bongo.
The Gambia	February 18, 1965	Alhaji Sir Dauda K. Jawara President 1965	1. 1965–70: The Gambia a constitutional monarchy with Dauda Jawara as elected Prime Minister. 2. April 1970: The Gambia becomes a republic and Jawara first President April 24; reelected in 1972 and 1977.

Ghana

March 6, 1957

Dr. Hilla Limann
President
1979

1. 1957–60: Ghana is constitutional monarchy; Kwame Nkrumah elected Prime Minister; becomes republic in 1960; Nkrumah "elected" President.

2. February 24, 1966: Nkrumah overthrown by military coup; Lt. Gen. Joseph Ankrah made Chairman of National Liberation Council; forced to resign in 1969; replaced by Brig. Gen. Akwasi Afrifa.

3. September 1969–January 1972: competitive electoral politics restored by military; Kofi Busia elected Prime Minister.

4. January 13, 1972: military coup; Lt. Col. (later Gen.) Ignatius Kutu Acheampong becomes Chairman of National Redemption Council, which is replaced in 1975 by Supreme Military Council.

5. July 5, 1978: military counter-coup; Lt. Gen. Frederick Akuffo, Acheampong's deputy and Chief of Staff, takes power.

6. June 4, 1979: Flight Lt. Jerry Rawlings seizes power. Military court finds Acheampong, Akuffo, and Afrifa guilty of corruption; they are executed June 1979. Rawlings becomes Chairman of Armed Forces Revolutionary Council.

7. July 1979: Limann elected President; September 24, 1979: Rawlings hands over power to Limann.

Country	Date of Independence	Current Ruler; Title; Effective Date of Rule	Prior Rulers Since Independence
Guinea	October 2, 1958	Ahmed Sékou Touré President 1958	
Guinea-Bissau	September 10, 1974	Luiz De Almeida Cabral President 1974	
Ivory Coast	August 7, 1960	Félix Houphouët-Boigny President 1960	May 1, 1959: Houphouët-Boigny invested Prime Minister; "elected" first President November 27, 1960.
Kenya	December 12, 1963	Daniel Toiritich arap Moi President 1978	1. 1963-64: Kenya is constitutional monarchy; Jomo Kenyatta is Prime Minister. 2. 1964: Kenyatta becomes President; dies in office August 22, 1978 (about 86 years old). Constitutionally succeeded by Vice-President Moi.
Lesotho	October 4, 1966	Chief J. Leabua Jonathan Prime Minister 1966	Constitutional monarchy under King Motlotlehi Moshoeshoe II. Competitive constitutional rule until January 1970, when Chief Jonathan in civilian coup seizes power and suspends constitution following his apparent defeat at the polls.
Liberia	1847	Master Sgt. Samuel K. Doe Chairman of People's Redemption Council 1980	1. Until 1944, 18 presidents. 2. 1944: William V. S. Tubman becomes President; dies in office in 1971 (age 75); constitutionally succeeded by Vice-President William R. Tolbert. 3. April 12, 1980: Tolbert killed during military coup led by Doe.

Malawi	July 6, 1964	Ngwazi Dr. Hastings Kamazu Banda President 1964	1964–66: Malawi is a constitutional monarchy; Banda is Prime Minister; becomes President when Malawi becomes republic. Self-appointed President for Life, July 6, 1971.
Mali (April 4, 1959–August 20, 1960: Mali Federation)	September 22, 1960 (June 20, 1960: independence of Mali Federation)	Moussa Traoré President 1968	1. April 4, 1959–August 20, 1960: Modibo Keita is President of Mali Federation; becomes President of Soudan Government April 15, 1959; President of Mali, 1960–68. 2. November 19, 1968: military coup led by Lt. (later Brig. Gen.) Traoré, who is Chairman of Military Committee of National Liberation until June 1979. 3. June 19, 1979: Traoré "elected" President in a one-party national electoral structure.
Mauritania	November 28, 1960	Lt. Col. Mohamed Khouna Ould Haidalla Chairman of Comité Militaire de Salut National (CMSN) 1980	1. June 26, 1959: Moktar Ould Daddah becomes Prime Minister of pre-independence Mauritania; elected President August 20, 1961. 2. July 10, 1978: military coup by Armed Forces Chief of Staff, Lt. Col. Mustapha Ould Mohamed Salek, who becomes President of Comité Militaire de Redressement National (CMRN). 3. April 6, 1979: "palace revolution" leads to replacement of CMRN by CMSN; Lt. Col. Ahmed Ould Bouceif becomes Prime Minister. 4. May 27, 1979: Bouceif dies in aircraft accident.

297

Country	Date of Independence	Current Ruler; Title; Effective Date of Rule	Prior Rulers Since Independence
Mauritania (cont.)			5. May 31, 1979: Haidalla appointed Prime Minister by Salek.
			6. CMSN forces Salek to resign and appoints Lt. Col. Mohamed Mahmoud Ould Louly President.
			7. January 4, 1980: Haidalla ousts Louly and succeeds him as head of state and Chairman of CMSN.
			8. January 9, 1980: new constitutional charter states that head of government and head of state is Chairman of CMSN.
Mozambique	June 25, 1975	Samora Moisés Machel President 1975	
Niger	August 8, 1960	Col. Segni Kountché President of Supreme Military Council 1974	1. Hamani Diori is Prime Minister during period of autonomous rule prior to independence; "elected" President November 9, 1960.
			2. April 15, 1974: military coup led by Lt. Col. and Chief of Staff Kountché.
Nigeria	October 1, 1960	Alhaji Shehu Shagari President 1979	1. Sir Abubakar Tafawa Balewa, Prime Minister, 1960–66; Nnamdi Azikiwe is Governor-General, 1960–63, and President, 1963–66.
			2. January 15, 1966: military coup led by junior officers who assassinate Balewa. Maj. Gen. Johnson Aguiyi-Ironsi becomes head of Federal Military Government.

3. July 29, 1966: military coup by northern officers who kill Aguiyi-Ironsi. Lt. Col. (later Gen.) Yakubu Gowon made head of Federal Military Government.
4. July 29, 1975: military coup; Brig. (later Gen.) Murtala Ramat Muhammed becomes Chief of Supreme Military Council and head of state.
5. February 13, 1976: Muhammed assassinated in abortive coup. Lt. Gen. Olusegun Obasanjo succeeds Muhammed.
6. July–August 1979: Shagari elected President in competitive party election.
7. October 1, 1979: Shagari installed in office and civilian rule restored.

Country	Date	President	Events
Rwanda	July 1, 1962	Maj. Gen. Juvénal Habyalimana President 1973	1. October 26, 1961: Grégoire Kayibanda becomes President. 2. July 5, 1973: military coup led by Habyalimana.
Senegal (April 14, 1959– August 20, 1960: Mali Federation)	August 20, 1960 (June 20, 1960: independence of Mali Federation)	Léopold Sédar Senghor President 1960	

BLACK AFRICAN COUNTRIES AND RULERS AS OF SEPTEMBER 1980 (Continued)

Country	Date of Independence	Current Ruler; Title; Effective Date of Rule	Prior Rulers Since Independence
Sierra Leone	April 27, 1961	Siaka Probyn Stevens President 1968	1. Sir Milton Margai, Prime Minister, 1961–64, under Sierra Leone's constitutional monarchy (died in office—aged 69). 2. Sir Albert Margai, Prime Minister, 1964–67. 3. March 1967: general competitive party elections won by Stevens' All People's Congress, but military seizes power in a coup. Lt. Col. Andrew Juxon-Smith becomes Chairman of National Reformation Council. 4. April 1968: military counter-coup puts Stevens in power as Prime Minister. 5. April 1971: Sierra Leone becomes republic and Stevens becomes President.
Somalia	July 1, 1960	Maj. Gen. Mohamed Siad Barre President 1969	1. Aden Abdulla Osman, President, 1960–67; Abdirashid Ali Shermarke, Prime Minister, 1960–64; Abdirazak Hassein, Prime Minister, 1964–67. 2. Shermarke elected President, 1967–69, and Mohammed Ibrahim Egal, Prime Minister. 3. October 1969: Shermarke assassinated; military coup.
Sudan	January 1, 1956	Field Marshal Gaafar Mohamed Numeiri President 1969	1. Ismail al-Azhari, Prime Minister, 1956. 2. Abdulla Khalil, Prime Minister, 1956–58. 3. November 17, 1958: military coup; Lt. Gen. Ibrahim Abboud, Prime Minister, 1958–64. 4. October 20–30, 1964: revolt; military abdicates; Sir el-Khalim el-Khalifah, Prime Minister, 1964–65.

			5. Muhammad Ahmad Mahgoub, Prime Minister, 1965–66. 6. Sayed Siddik El Mahdi, Prime Minister, 1966–67. 7. Mahgoub, Prime Minister, 1967–69. 8. Abubakr Awadallah, Prime Minister, 1969. 9. May 25, 1969: military coup by Col. (later Gen.) Numeiri.
Swaziland (Hereditary monarchy)	September 9, 1968	King Sobhuza II 1922	1. Prince Makhosini Dlamini, Prime Minister, 1968–76. 2. Col. (later Maj. Gen.) Maphevu Dlamini, Prime Minister, 1976–79 (dies in office). 3. Prince Mandabala Fred Dlamini, Prime Minister as of October 1979.
Tanzania (As Tanganyika joined with Zanzibar to form United Republic of Tanzania in April 1964)	December 9, 1961	Julius K. Nyerere President 1961	1. Nyerere is Prime Minister from independence until January 1962. 2. Nyerere resigns January 23, 1962; Rashidi M. Kawawa is Prime Minister until December 1962. 3. Tanzania becomes a republic in December 1962; Nyerere elected President. (Zanzibar has had autonomous government while part of Tanzania. 1964–72: head of government is Sheikh Abeid Karume, assassinated in April 1972; current head of government: Aboud Jumbe, Chairman of Zanzibar Revolutionary Council and Vice-President of Tanzania.)

BLACK AFRICAN COUNTRIES AND RULERS AS OF SEPTEMBER 1980 (Continued)

Country	Date of Independence	Current Ruler; Title; Effective Date of Rule	Prior Rulers Since Independence
Togo	April 12, 1960	Gen. Gnassingbé Eyadéma President 1967	1. May 16, 1958: Sylvanus Olympio becomes Prime Minister of self-governing (French) Trust Territory; "elected" President April 9, 1961. 2. January 13, 1963: Olympio assassinated in military coup. 3. January 16, 1963: temporary civilian government installed under Nicholas Grunitzky, a former Prime Minister. 4. May 5, 1963: Grunitzky elected President and head of four-party coalition government. 5. January 13, 1967: Col. (then Étienne) Eyadéma demands Grunitzky resignation in de facto coup; Col. Kléber Dadjo becomes Chairman of eight-man civilian Comité de Réconciliation Nationale (CRN). 6. April 14, 1967: Eyadéma directly assumes power, dissolves CRN, and declares himself President.
Uganda	October 9, 1962	Paulo Mwanga Chairman, Military Commission of Ugandan National Liberation Front (UNLF) 1980	1. 1962–66: Apollo Milton Obote is Prime Minister, and Sir Edward Mutesa is President. 2. February 22, 1966: Obote deposes Mutesa and in April introduces a constitution with himself as President. 3. January 25, 1971: military coup led by Maj. Gen. Idi Amin. In 1975 Amin "promoted" to Field Marshal and in June 1976 named President for Life.

4. November 1978: Tanzanian troops and UNLF counterattack Amin's forces.

5. April 11, 1979: Kampala falls to Tanzanian forces and UNLF.

6. Yusuf Lule becomes President of Provisional Government.

7. June 20, 1979: National Consultation Council (Uganda's acting Parliament) elects Godfrey Lukonga Binaisa Chairman of UNLF Executive Council and thereby President.

8. May 11, 1980: military coup; Mwanga made Chairman of Military Commission.

Upper Volta   August 5, 1960   Gen. Sangoulé Lamizana
                                             President
                                             1966

1. April 19, 1959: Maurice Yaméogo becomes Prime Minister in self-governing pre-independence government; "elected" President December 8, 1960.

2. January 3, 1966: military coup; Lt. Col. (later Gen.) Lamizana becomes President.

3. May 1978: competitive party election; Lamizana elected President for five-year term.

4. July 7, 1978: Joseph Issoufou Conombo elected Prime Minister.

BLACK AFRICAN COUNTRIES AND RULERS AS OF SEPTEMBER 1980 (Continued)

Country	Date of Independence	Current Ruler; Title; Effective Date of Rule	Prior Rulers Since Independence
Zaire (formerly Congo-Kinshasa)	June 30, 1960	Gen. Mobutu Sese Seko Ngendu Wa Zabanda President 1965	1. Patrice Lumumba, Prime Minister, June–September 5, 1960; Joseph Kasavubu is President until 1965. 2. September 14, 1960: military coup led by Col. (then Joseph) Mobutu; state authority placed in hands of College of Commissioners, which rules until February 9, 1961. 3. Joseph Ileo, Prime Minister, February–August 1961. 4. Cyril Adoula, Prime Minister, August 1961–July 1964. 5. Moise Tshombe, Prime Minister, July 1964–October 1965. 6. Evariste Kimba, Prime Minister, October–November 1965. 7. November 24, 1965: military coup by Mobutu.
Zambia	October 24, 1964	Kenneth David Kaunda President 1964	
Zimbabwe	April 18, 1980	Robert Mugabe Prime Minister 1980	February 27–29, 1980: Mugabe elected Prime Minister in competitive party election. Rev. Cannan Banana, only candidate for President and backed by Mugabe, declared President-elect April 11, 1980.

Index

reconstitution, 269; restraints upon, 19, 25, 27; soldier-rulers as, 32–38; and statecraft, 139, 175–177, 181, 187; stratagems of, 25–26; types of, 20–21; and tyrannical rule, 239, 240; vulnerabilities of, 19, 26–27, 28–31, 66. *See also* Personal rule
Plebiscitarianism, 161, 170, 177, 269–270, 273
Plots: in Congo-Brazzaville, 192–193; and factionalism, 48, 49; and foreign aid, 29; in Guinea, 214–216; as integral to personal rule, 6, 18, 58–63; in Malawi, 164, 167; in Senegal, 97; and succession, 69, 71; under tyranny, 239. *See also* Conspiratorial politics; Coups
Pluralism. *See* Ethnicity
Police state in Cameroon, 154–155
Political actors, 7, 76–77
"Political economics" in Guinea, 210, 211
Political exiles, 213, 215, 263–264. *See also* Detentions, political; Political prisoners; Political refugees
Political fights. *See* Personal rule, as political "fight"
Political freedom, 24, 95, 103–104, 149, 154, 252, 277
Political games. *See* Personal rule, as political game
Political goods, 3, 3n, 6, 19
Political insecurity. *See* Uncertainty, political
Political institutions, 1, 3, 5, 9–10. *See also* Institutionalization; Institutionalized systems; Political traditions
Political intrigue. *See* Conspiratorial politics; Coups; Plots
"Political machine" party model, 52
Political minorities, 245. *See also* Asian people
Political monopoly. *See* Monopoly, political
Political participation. *See* Authoritarianism; Depoliticization; Monopoly, political
Political prisoners, 155, 159, 164, 167. *See also* Detentions, political; Political exiles; Political refugees
Political protest, 118, 129–130, 171, 179, 218. *See also* Opposition groups
Political refugees, 198, 221, 246–247,

249, 251. *See also* Detentions, political; Political exiles; Political prisoners
Political religion: in Ghana, 149, 183–184, 200–201; in Guinea, 208–209, 217; in Tanzania, 183–184, 185, 220–221
Political rhetoric, 116, 173, 192–193, 198, 216–217, 230
Political traditions, 5, 21–22, 74–75, 121, 126–127. *See also* Military, African, lack of traditions in; Political institutions
"Politician politics," 77–79, 90, 92, 141, 144, 180–181
Portugal, 21, 165, 186, 215
Post, Ken, 24
Potholm, Christian P., 72
Power: under authoritarianism, 23; in autocratic rule, 78, 170–171; discretionary, 25; and factionalism, 48–49; and incremental institutionalization, 284; in politics, 12, 14–15; in princely rule, 122–123, 140; in prophetic rule, 79, 182, 222; restraints on, in personal rule, 65; in tyrannical rule, 80, 141, 234–235, 239–240
Praetorianism, 40
Pratt, Cranford, 220, 221
Preservation of Public Security Act (Kenya), 104
Price, Robert M., 207
Primogeniture, 70, 72, 144
Prince, The: and political accommodation, 141–142, 180; definition of, 77–79; and political spoils, 202–203; sub-types of, 83–89. *See also* Princely rule; Royalism
Princely rule, 20–21, 77, 81, 83, 84. *See also* Prince, The; Royalism
Production liberals in Tanzania, 228
Production socialists in Tanzania, 227
Progressive Alliance of Liberia (PAL), 118
Progressive People's Party (PPP) (Liberia), 118–119
Prophet, The, 77, 83, 141, 182–188, 202–203, 232–233. *See also* Prophetic rule
Prophetic rule, 21, 73, 79–80. *See also* Prophet, The
Protests. *See* Political protests
"Providence Societies" in Senegal, 92